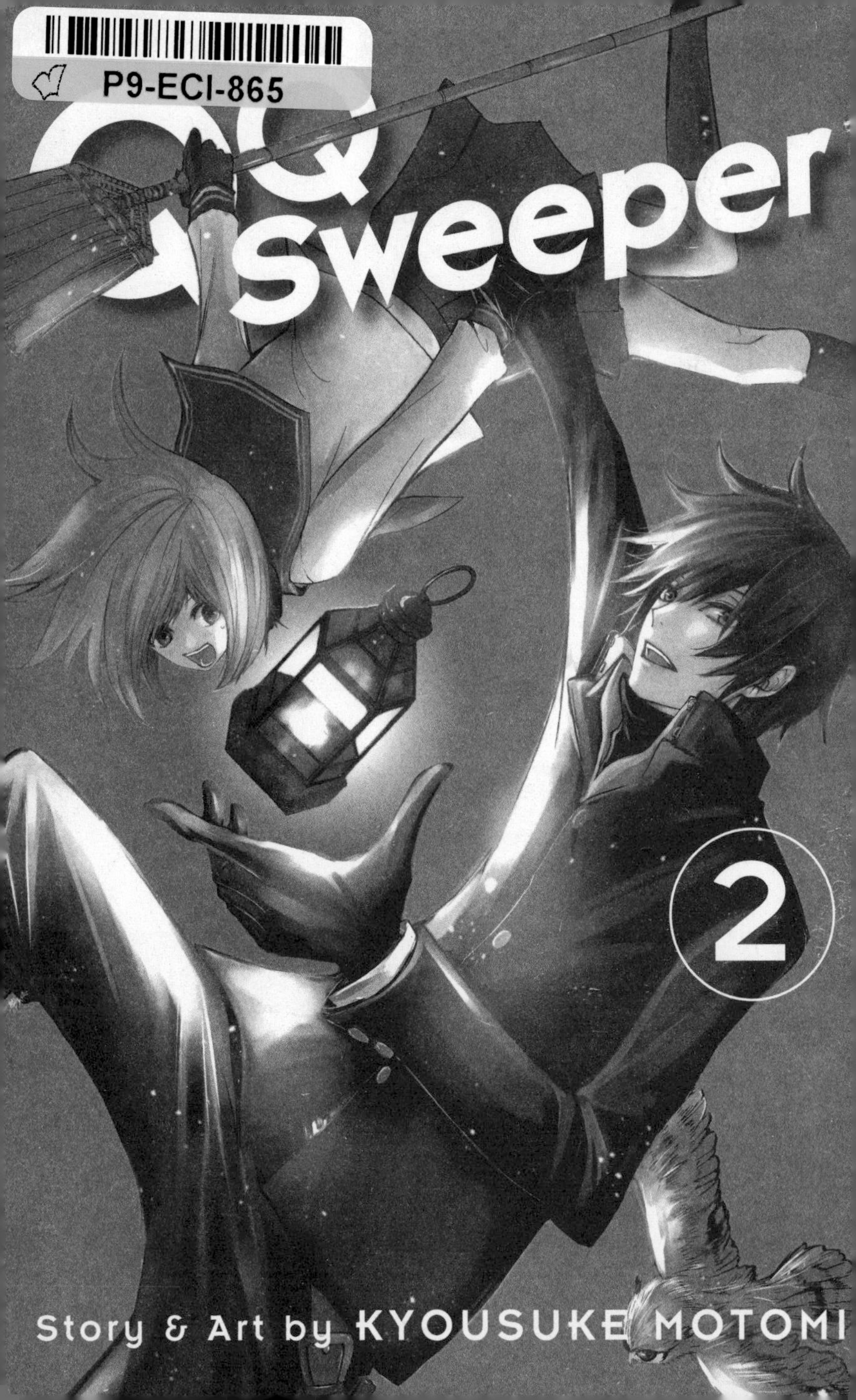
QQ Sweeper
2
Story & Art by KYOUSUKE MOTOMI

QQ Sweeper

2

Sweep 6 — 3

Sweep 7 — 39

Sweep 8 — 77

Sweep 9 — 113

Sweep 10 — 149

SWEEP 6

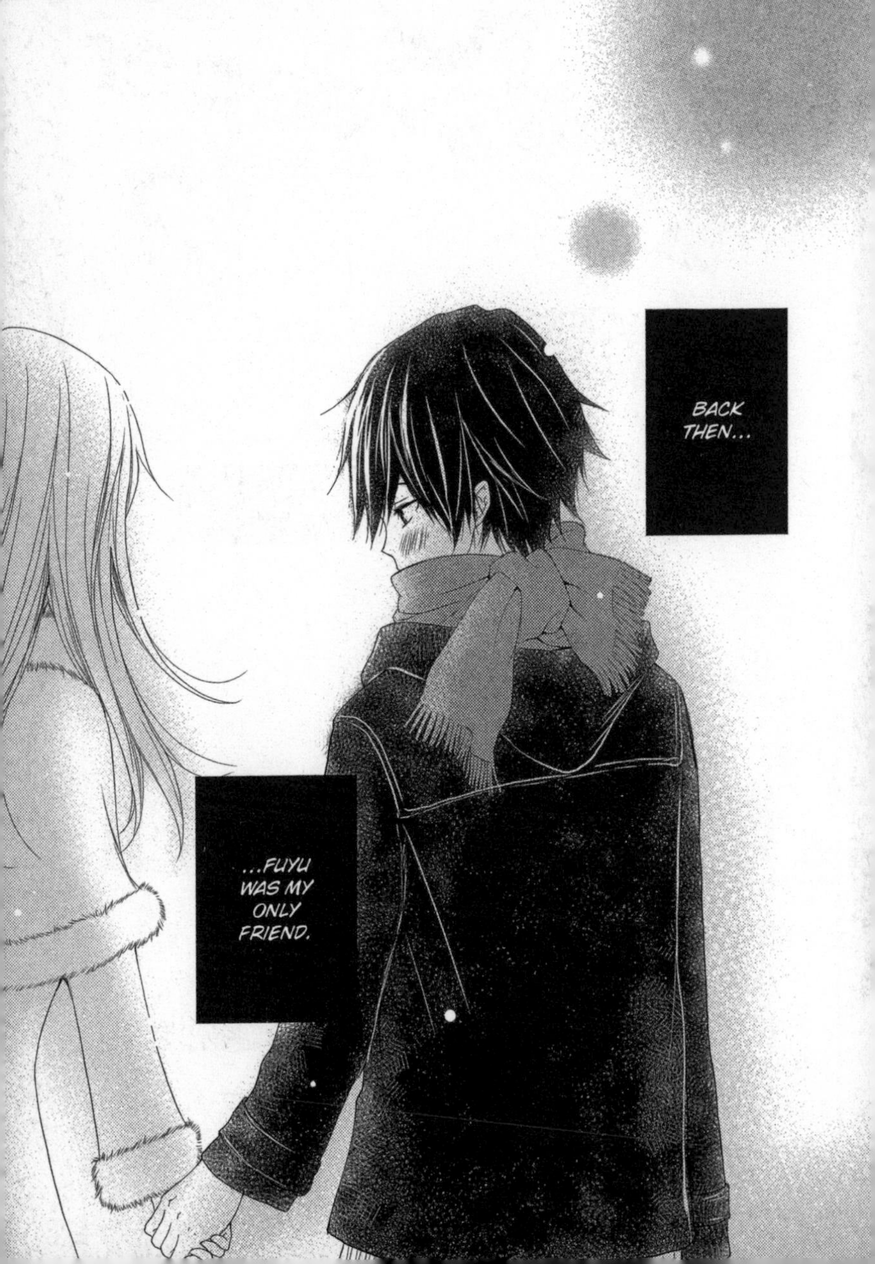
BACK THEN...
...FUYU WAS MY ONLY FRIEND.

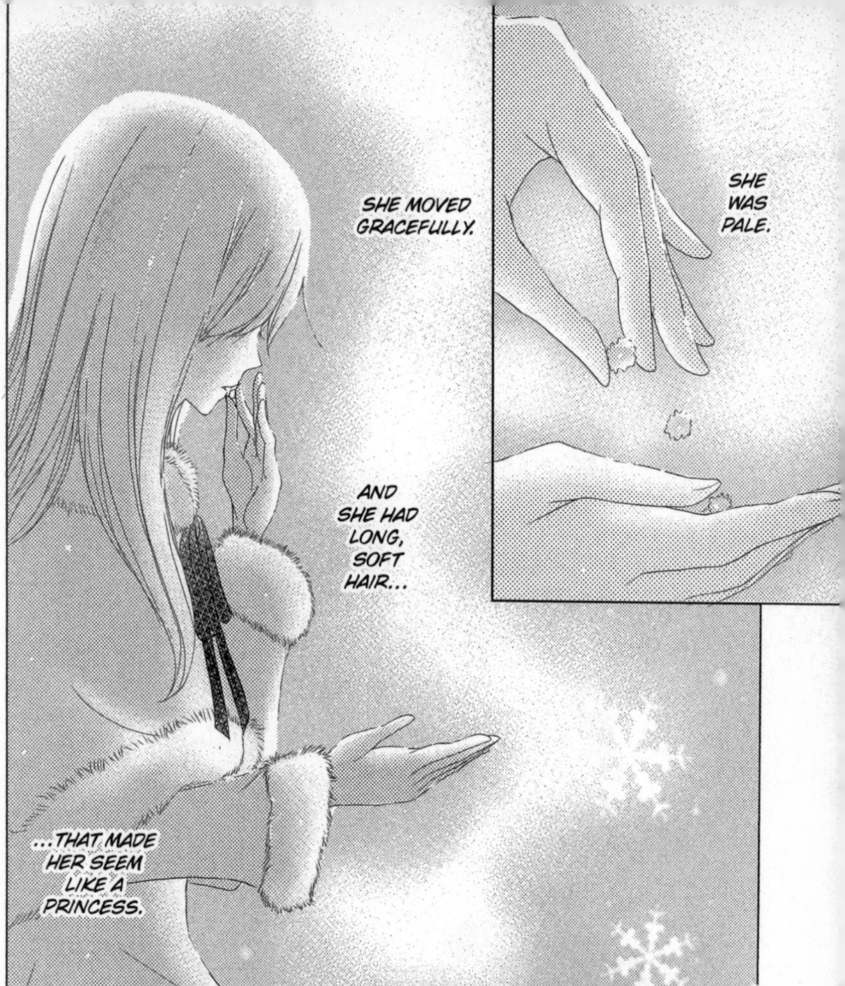
SHE WAS PALE.
SHE MOVED GRACEFULLY.
AND SHE HAD LONG, SOFT HAIR...
...THAT MADE HER SEEM LIKE A PRINCESS.

Hello, everyone! I'm Kyousuke Motomi. Thanks to all of you, I've been able to keep working on QQ Sweeper, and here we are on volume 2! I hope you enjoy it. Thank you!!

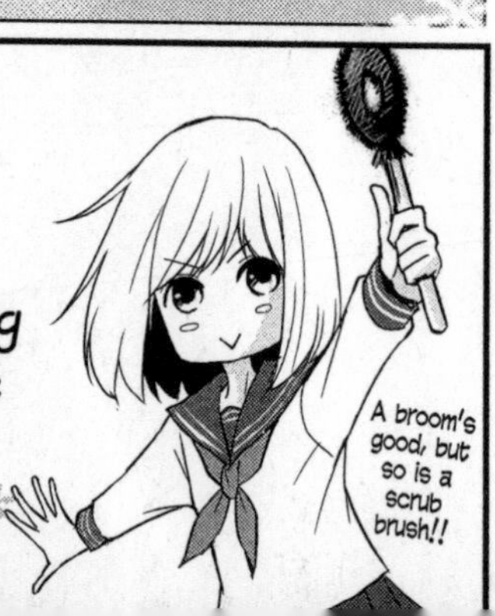
A broom's good, but so is a scrub brush!!

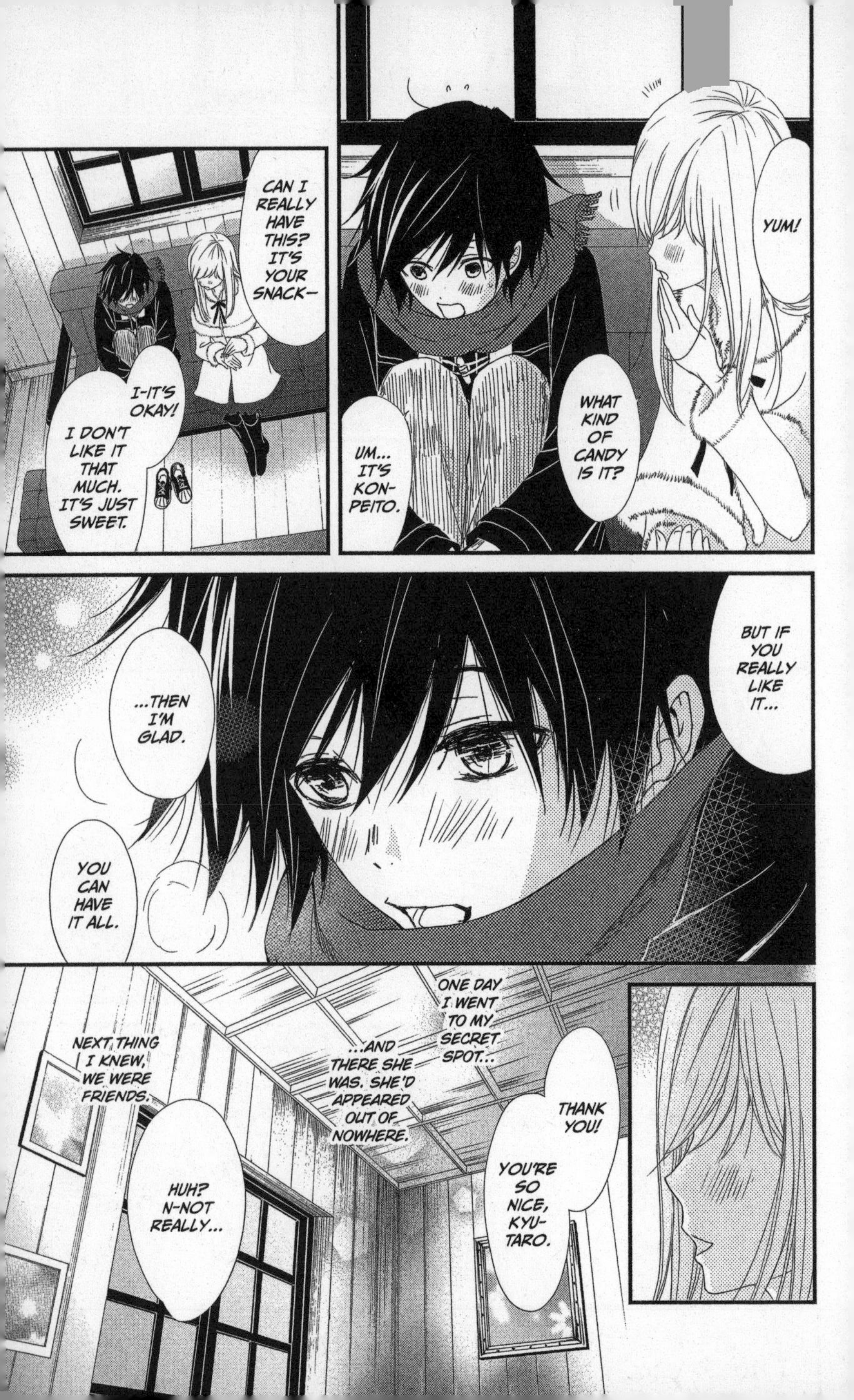
YUM!
WHAT KIND OF CANDY IS IT?
UM... IT'S KON-PEITO.
CAN I REALLY HAVE THIS? IT'S YOUR SNACK—
I-IT'S OKAY! I DON'T LIKE IT THAT MUCH. IT'S JUST SWEET.
BUT IF YOU REALLY LIKE IT...
...THEN I'M GLAD.
YOU CAN HAVE IT ALL.
ONE DAY I WENT TO MY SECRET SPOT...
THANK YOU!
YOU'RE SO NICE, KYU-TARO.
...AND THERE SHE WAS. SHE'D APPEARED OUT OF NOWHERE.
NEXT THING I KNEW, WE WERE FRIENDS.
HUH? N-NOT REALLY...

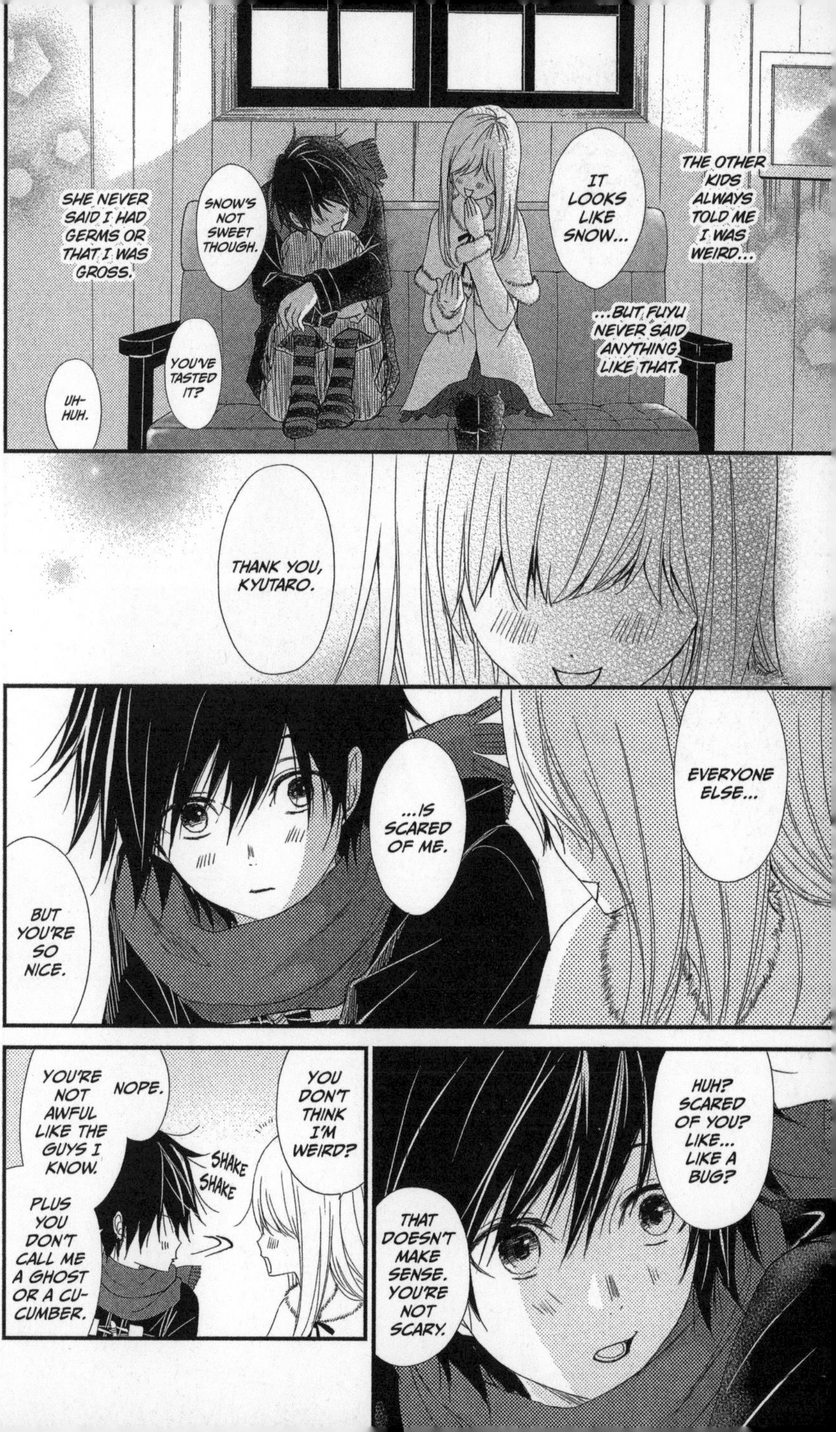
THE OTHER KIDS ALWAYS TOLD ME I WAS WEIRD...
IT LOOKS LIKE SNOW...
...BUT FUYU NEVER SAID ANYTHING LIKE THAT.
SNOW'S NOT SWEET THOUGH.
SHE NEVER SAID I HAD GERMS OR THAT I WAS GROSS.
YOU'VE TASTED IT?
UH-HUH.
THANK YOU, KYUTARO.
EVERYONE ELSE...
...IS SCARED OF ME.
BUT YOU'RE SO NICE.
HUH? SCARED OF YOU? LIKE... LIKE A BUG?
THAT DOESN'T MAKE SENSE. YOU'RE NOT SCARY.
YOU DON'T THINK I'M WEIRD?
SHAKE SHAKE
NOPE.
YOU'RE NOT AWFUL LIKE THE GUYS I KNOW.
PLUS YOU DON'T CALL ME A GHOST OR A CU-CUMBER.

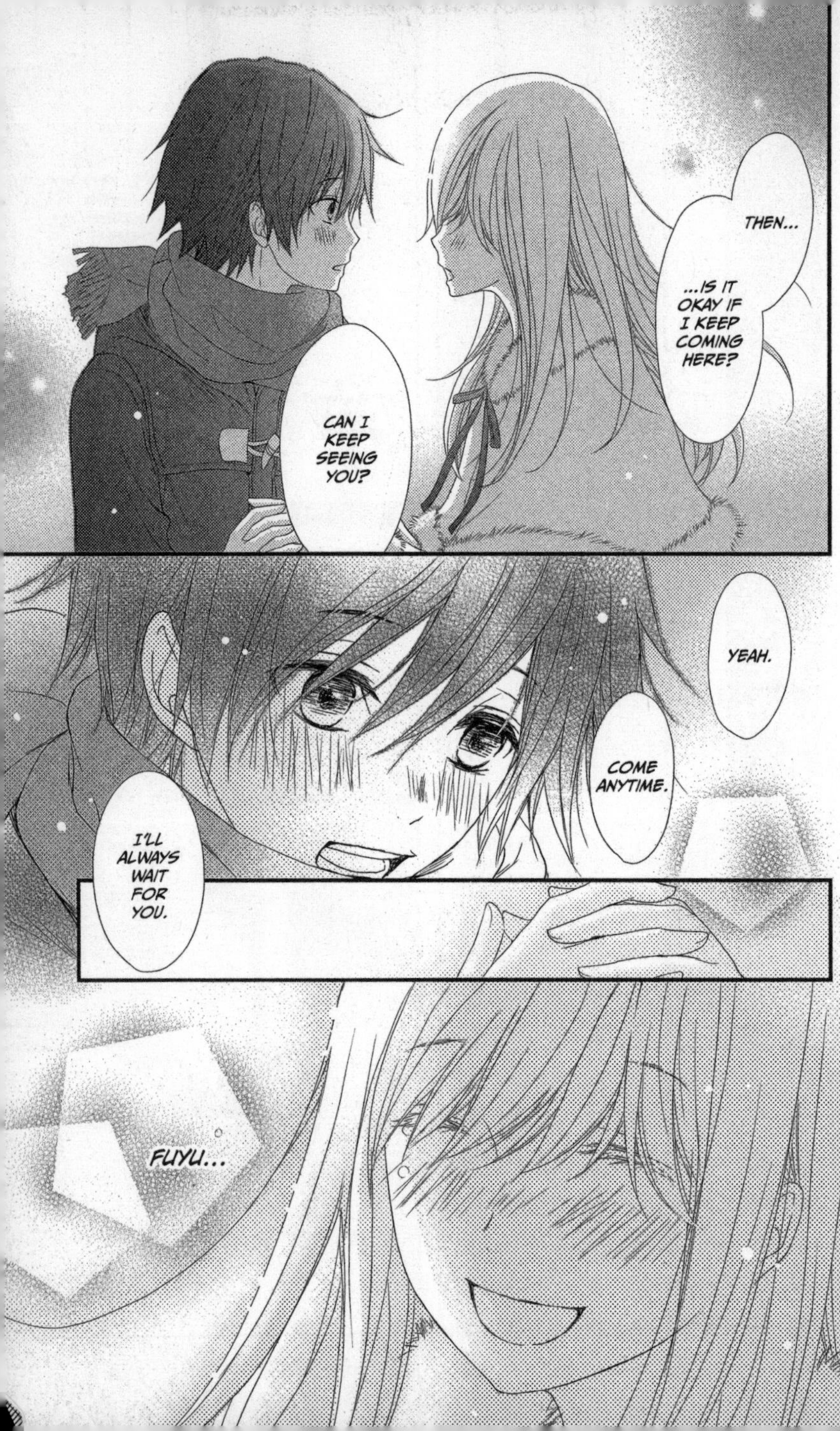
THEN...
...IS IT OKAY IF I KEEP COMING HERE?
CAN I KEEP SEEING YOU?
YEAH.
COME ANYTIME.
I'LL ALWAYS WAIT FOR YOU.
FUYU...

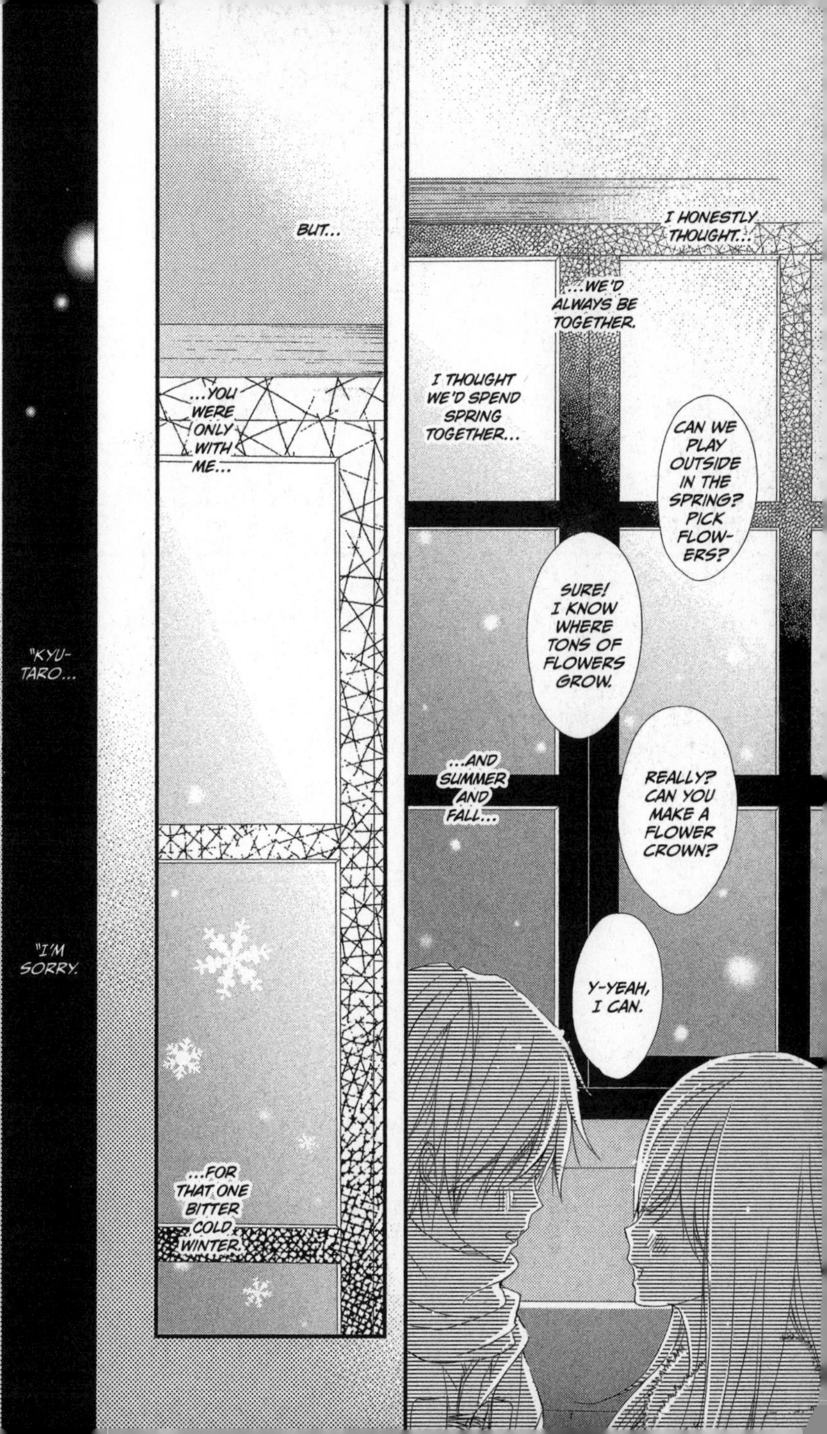
I HONESTLY THOUGHT...
...WE'D ALWAYS BE TOGETHER.
I THOUGHT WE'D SPEND SPRING TOGETHER...
CAN WE PLAY OUTSIDE IN THE SPRING? PICK FLOW-ERS?
SURE! I KNOW WHERE TONS OF FLOWERS GROW.
...AND SUMMER AND FALL...
REALLY? CAN YOU MAKE A FLOWER CROWN?
Y-YEAH, I CAN.
BUT...
...YOU WERE ONLY WITH ME...
...FOR THAT ONE BITTER COLD WINTER.
"KYU-TARO...
"I'M SORRY.

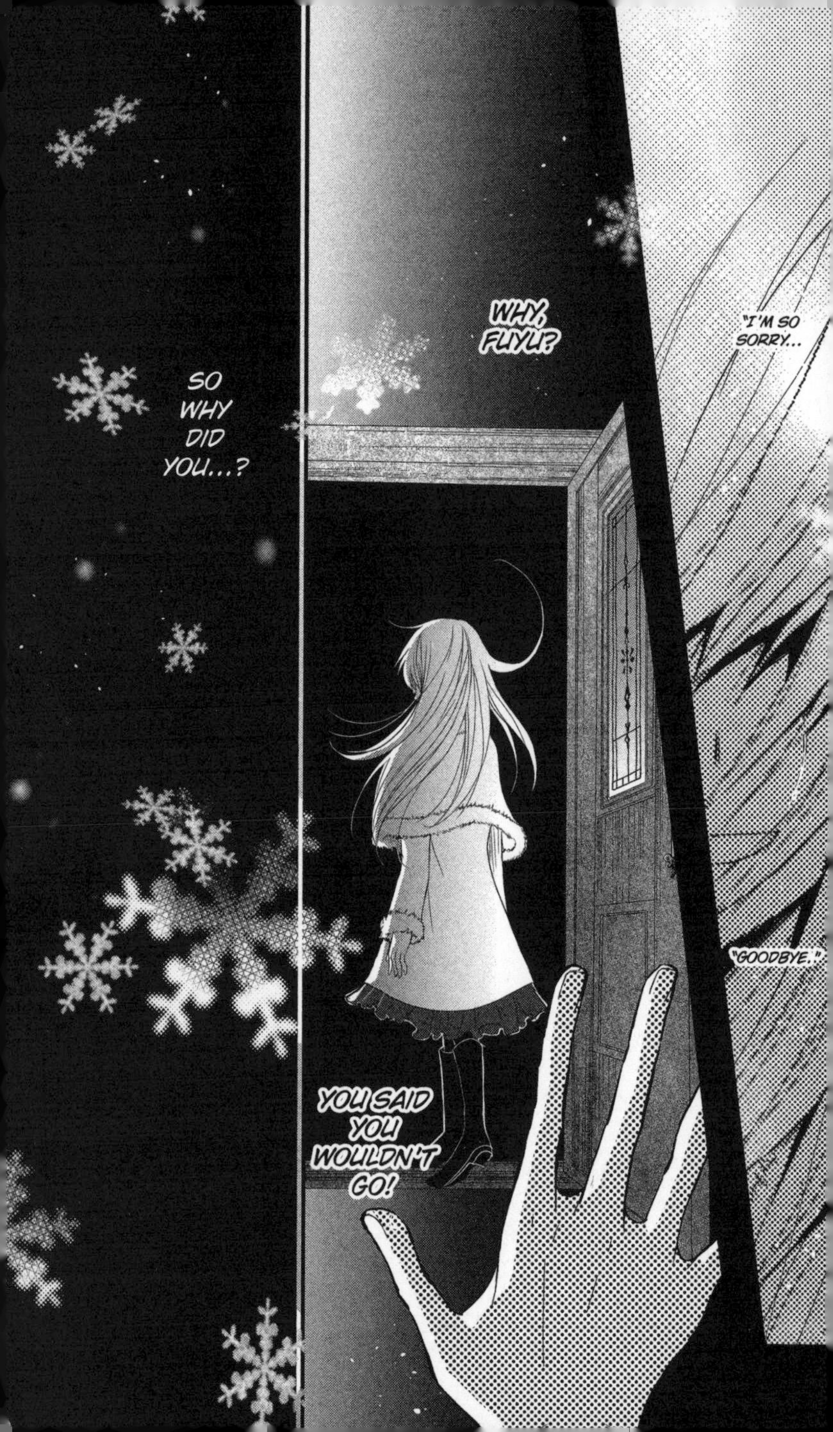
"I'M SO SORRY...
WHY, FUYU?
"GOODBYE."
YOU SAID YOU WOULDN'T GO!
SO WHY DID YOU...?

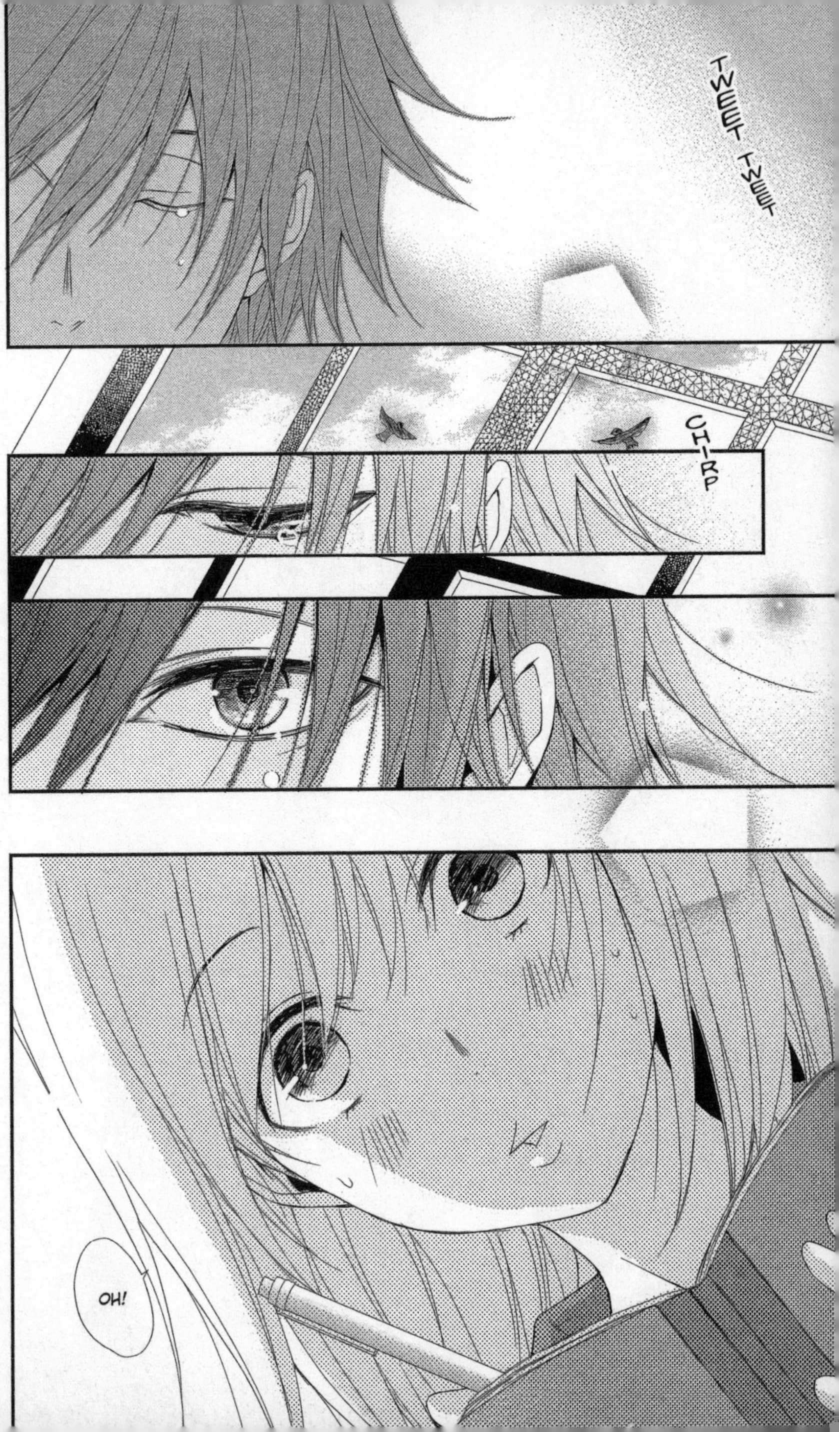
TWEET TWEET
CHIRP
OH!

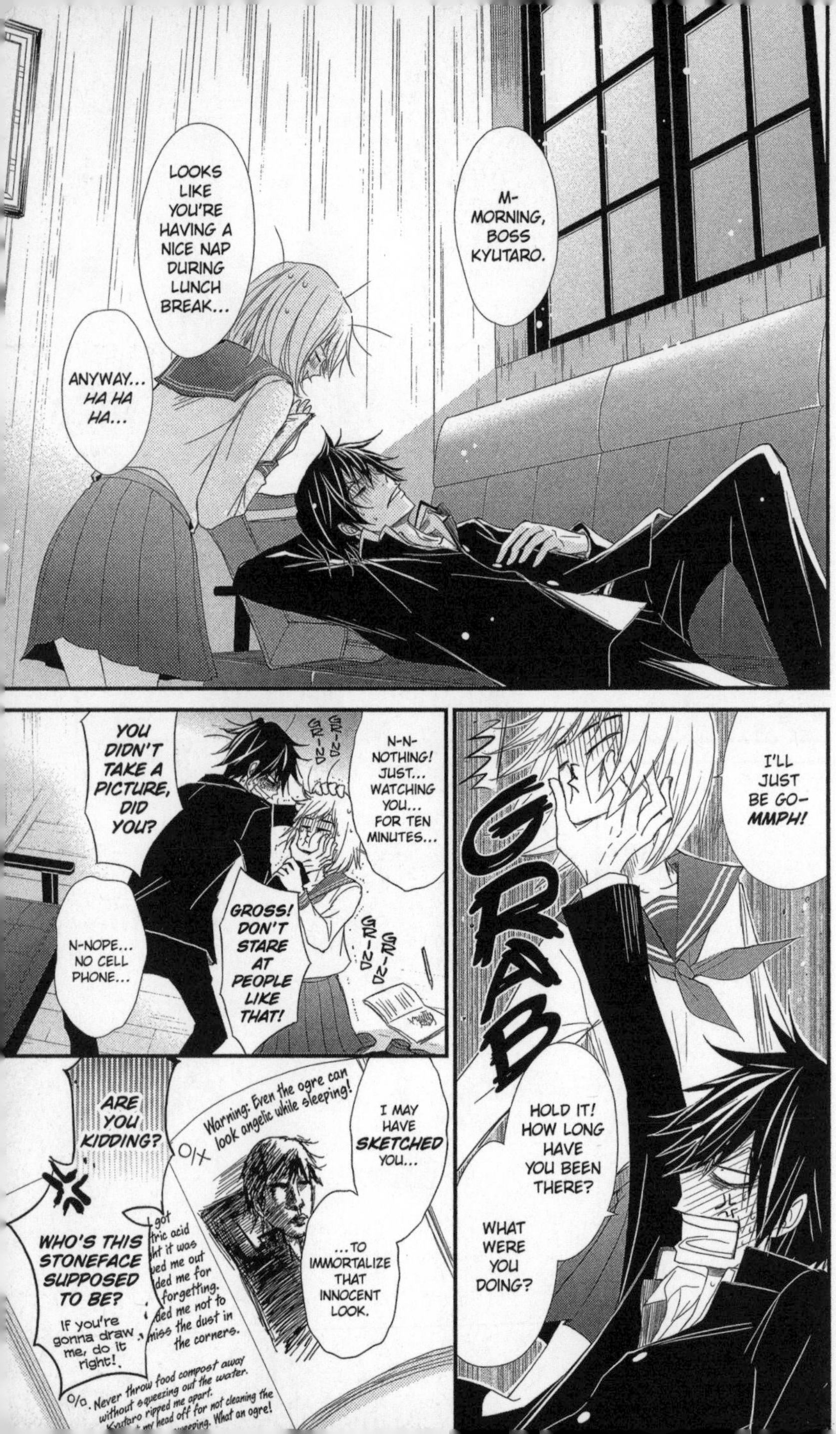

M-MORNING, BOSS KYUTARO.
LOOKS LIKE YOU'RE HAVING A NICE NAP DURING LUNCH BREAK...
ANYWAY... HA HA HA...
I'LL JUST BE GO-MMPH!
GRAB
HOLD IT! HOW LONG HAVE YOU BEEN THERE?
WHAT WERE YOU DOING?
N-N-NOTHING! JUST... WATCHING YOU... FOR TEN MINUTES...
GRIND GRIND
YOU DIDN'T TAKE A PICTURE, DID YOU?
GROSS! DON'T STARE AT PEOPLE LIKE THAT!
GRIND GRIND
N-NOPE... NO CELL PHONE...
I MAY HAVE SKETCHED YOU...
...TO IMMORTALIZE THAT INNOCENT LOOK.
Warning: Even the ogre can look angelic while sleeping!
ARE YOU KIDDING?
WHO'S THIS STONEFACE SUPPOSED TO BE?
If you're gonna draw me, do it right!
Never throw food compost away without squeezing out the water.

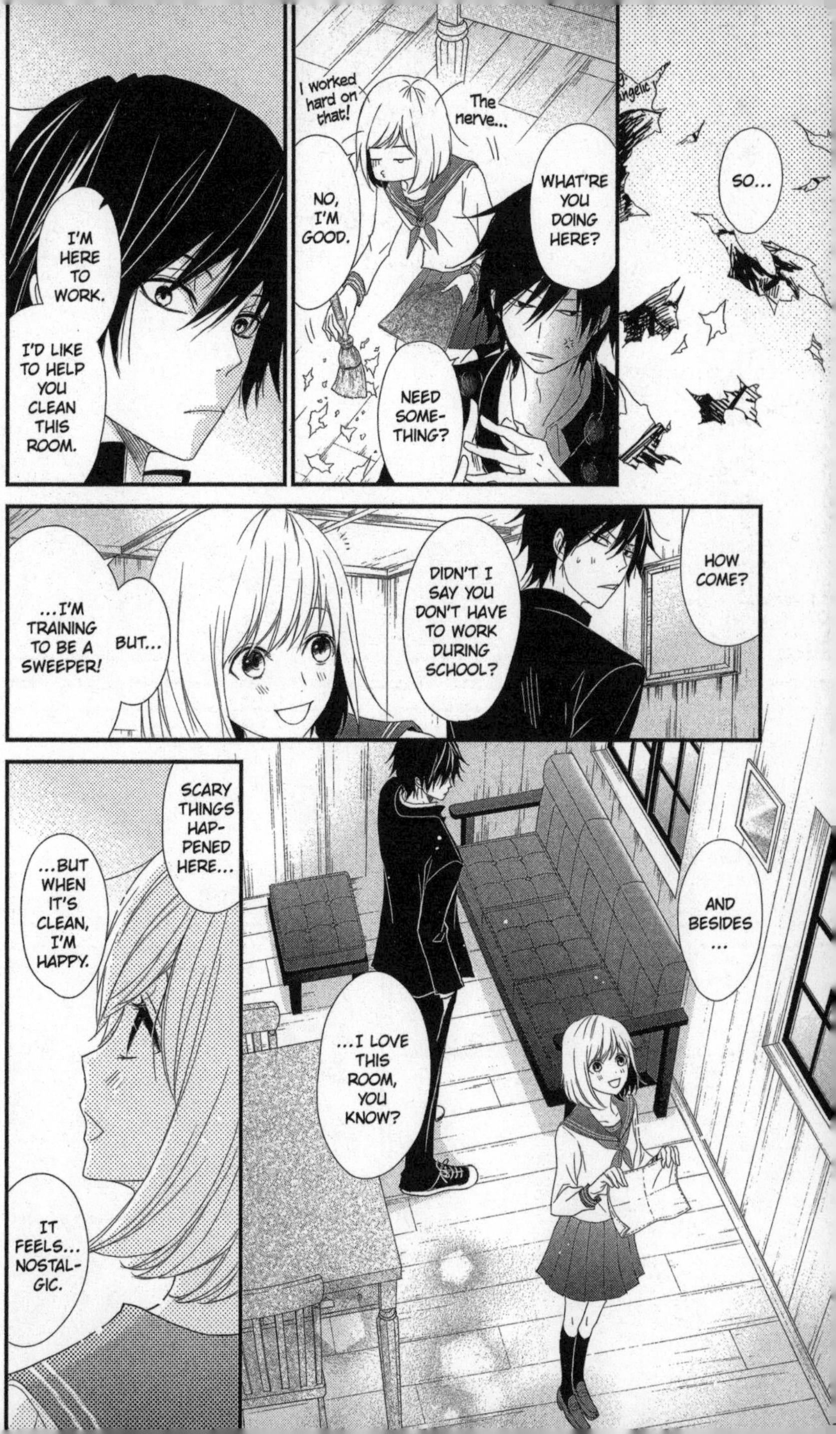
SO...
WHAT'RE YOU DOING HERE?
NEED SOME-THING?
The nerve...
NO, I'M GOOD.
I worked hard on that!
I'M HERE TO WORK.
I'D LIKE TO HELP YOU CLEAN THIS ROOM.
HOW COME?
DIDN'T I SAY YOU DON'T HAVE TO WORK DURING SCHOOL?
BUT...
...I'M TRAINING TO BE A SWEEPER!
AND BESIDES...
...I LOVE THIS ROOM, YOU KNOW?
SCARY THINGS HAP-PENED HERE...
...BUT WHEN IT'S CLEAN, I'M HAPPY.
IT FEELS... NOSTAL-GIC.

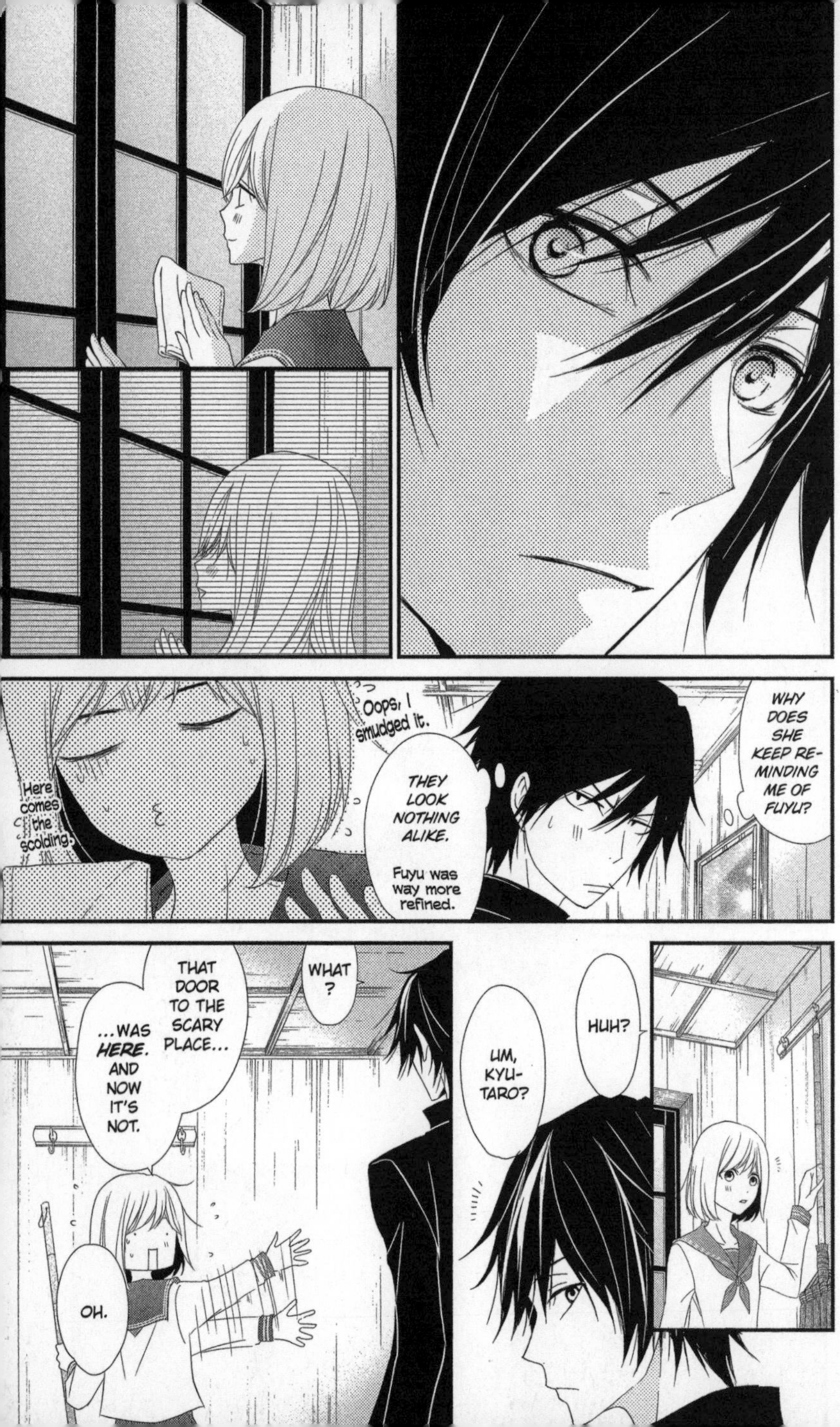
WHY DOES SHE KEEP RE-MINDING ME OF FUYU?
THEY LOOK NOTHING ALIKE.
Fuyu was way more refined.
Oops, I smudged it.
Here comes the scolding.
HUH?
UM, KYU-TARO?
WHAT?
THAT DOOR TO THE SCARY PLACE...
...WAS *HERE*. AND NOW IT'S NOT.
OH.

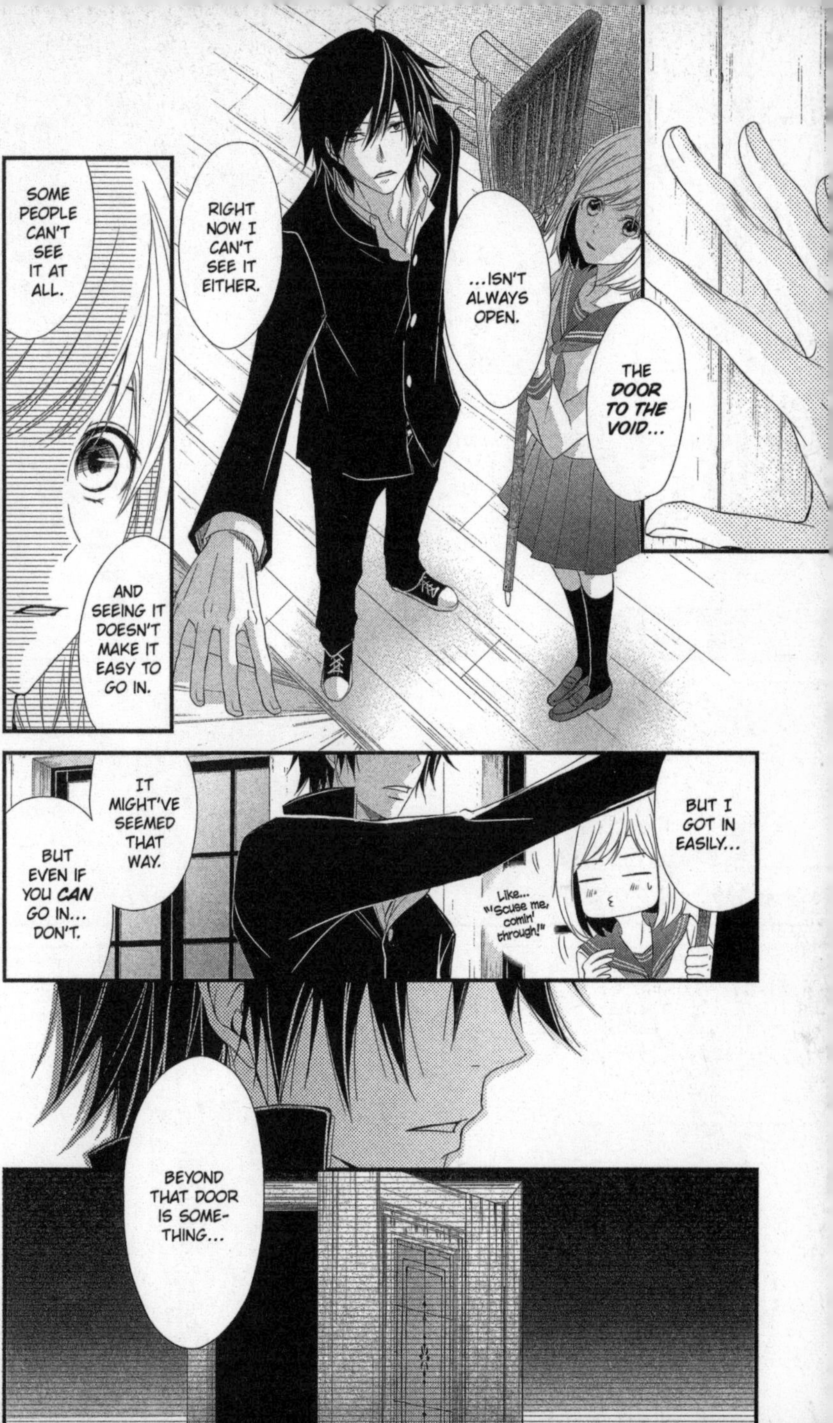
THE DOOR TO THE VOID...
...ISN'T ALWAYS OPEN.
RIGHT NOW I CAN'T SEE IT EITHER.
SOME PEOPLE CAN'T SEE IT AT ALL.
AND SEEING IT DOESN'T MAKE IT EASY TO GO IN.
BUT I GOT IN EASILY...
Like... "'Scuse me, comin' through!"
IT MIGHT'VE SEEMED THAT WAY.
BUT EVEN IF YOU CAN GO IN... DON'T.
BEYOND THAT DOOR IS SOME-THING...

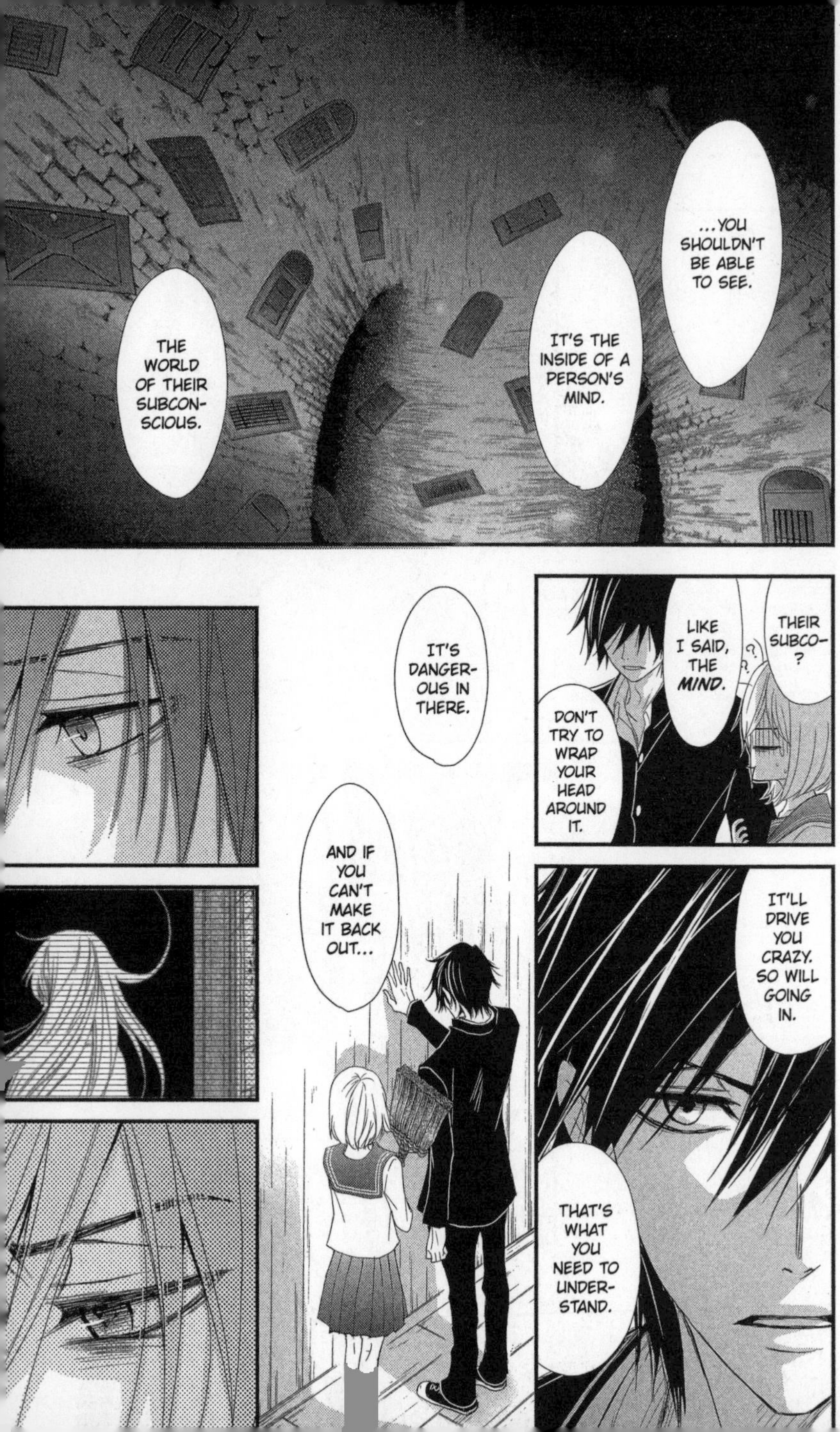
...YOU SHOULDN'T BE ABLE TO SEE.
IT'S THE INSIDE OF A PERSON'S MIND.
THE WORLD OF THEIR SUBCONSCIOUS.
THEIR SUBCO-?
LIKE I SAID, THE *MIND*.
DON'T TRY TO WRAP YOUR HEAD AROUND IT.
IT'S DANGEROUS IN THERE.
AND IF YOU CAN'T MAKE IT BACK OUT...
IT'LL DRIVE YOU CRAZY. SO WILL GOING IN.
THAT'S WHAT YOU NEED TO UNDERSTAND.

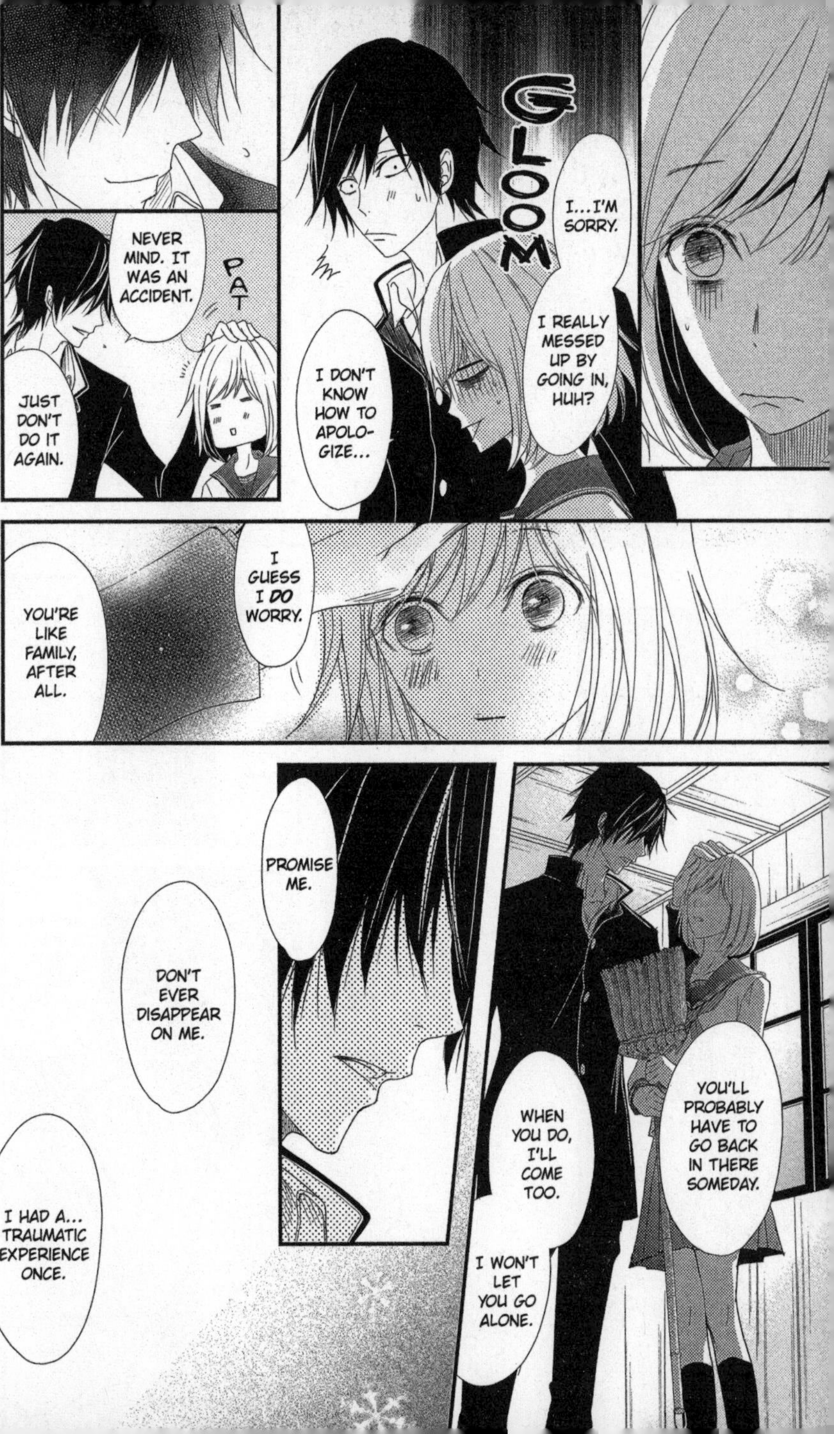
GLOOM
I...I'M SORRY.
I REALLY MESSED UP BY GOING IN, HUH?
I DON'T KNOW HOW TO APOLOGIZE...
NEVER MIND. IT WAS AN ACCIDENT.
PAT
JUST DON'T DO IT AGAIN.
I GUESS I *DO* WORRY.
YOU'RE LIKE FAMILY, AFTER ALL.
YOU'LL PROBABLY HAVE TO GO BACK IN THERE SOMEDAY.
WHEN YOU DO, I'LL COME TOO.
I WON'T LET YOU GO ALONE.
PROMISE ME.
DON'T EVER DISAPPEAR ON ME.
I HAD A... TRAUMATIC EXPERIENCE ONCE.

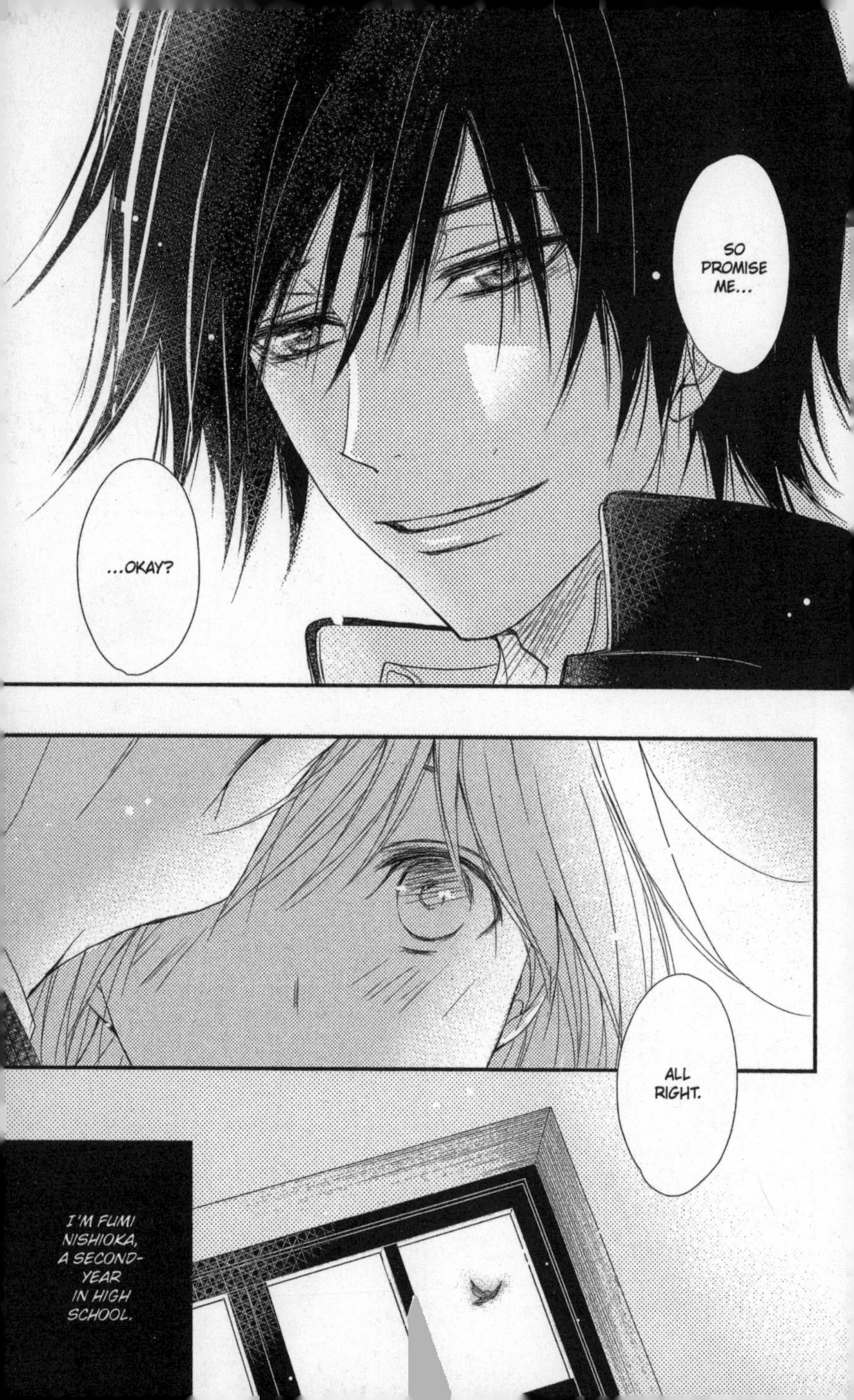
SO PROMISE ME...
...OKAY?
ALL RIGHT.
I'M FUMI NISHIOKA, A SECOND-YEAR IN HIGH SCHOOL.

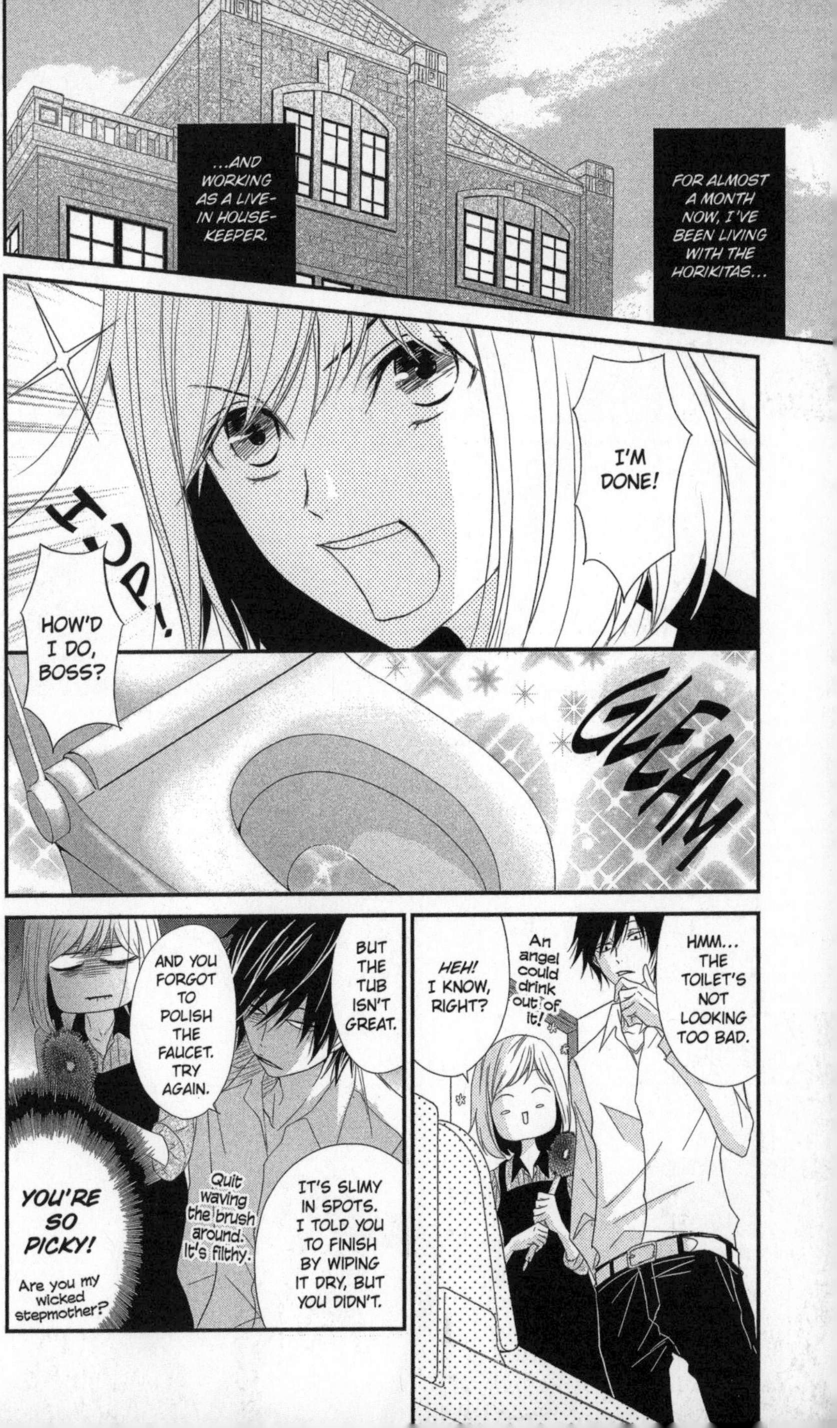
FOR ALMOST A MONTH NOW, I'VE BEEN LIVING WITH THE HORIKITAS...
...AND WORKING AS A LIVE-IN HOUSEKEEPER.
I'M DONE!
HOP!
HOW'D I DO, BOSS?
GLEAM
HMM... THE TOILET'S NOT LOOKING TOO BAD.
HEH! I KNOW, RIGHT?
An angel could drink out of it!
BUT THE TUB ISN'T GREAT.
AND YOU FORGOT TO POLISH THE FAUCET. TRY AGAIN.
IT'S SLIMY IN SPOTS. I TOLD YOU TO FINISH BY WIPING IT DRY, BUT YOU DIDN'T.
Quit waving the brush around. It's filthy.
YOU'RE SO PICKY!
Are you my wicked stepmother?

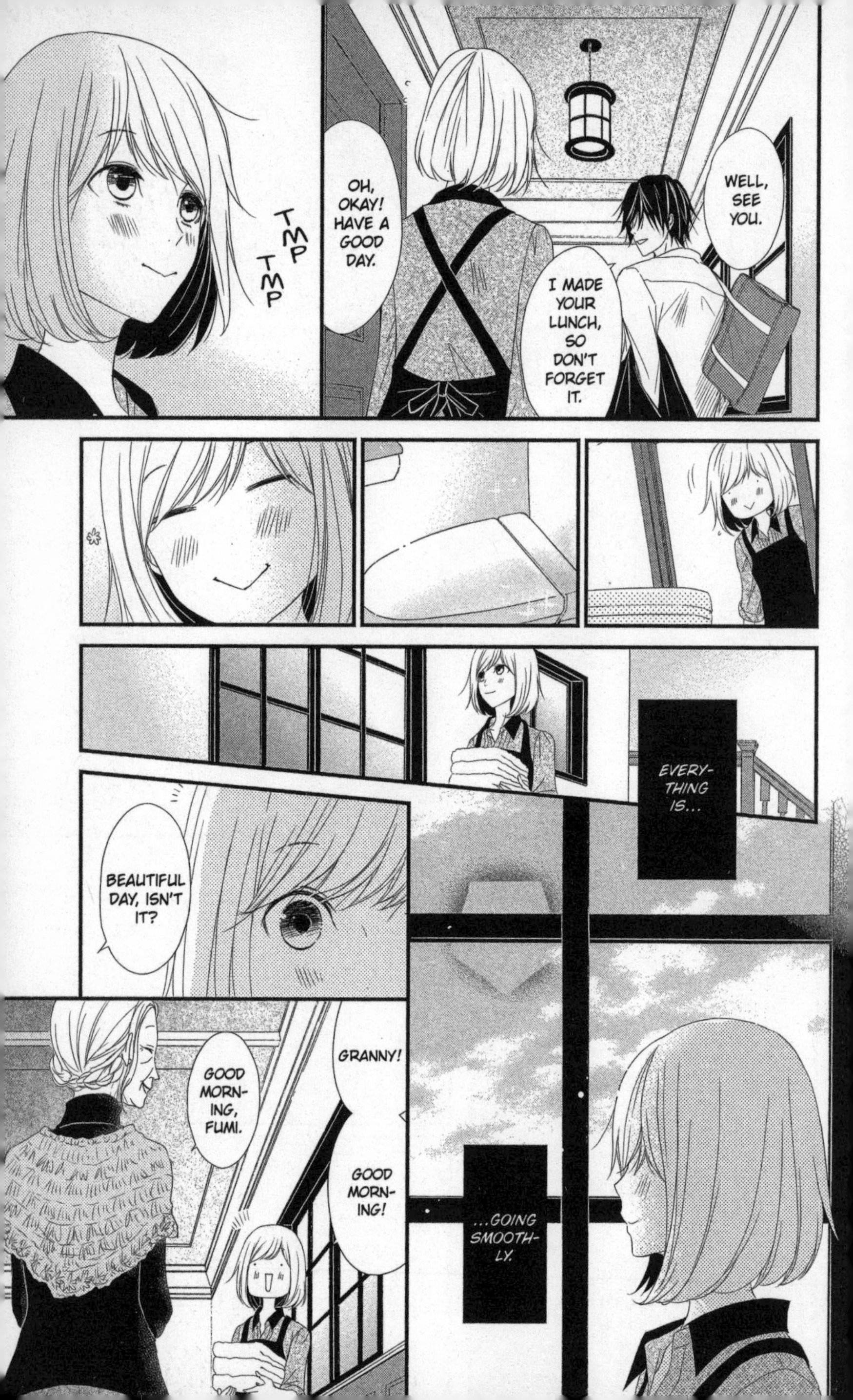
WELL, SEE YOU.
I MADE YOUR LUNCH, SO DON'T FORGET IT.
OH, OKAY! HAVE A GOOD DAY.
TMP TMP
EVERY-THING IS...
...GOING SMOOTH-LY.
BEAUTIFUL DAY, ISN'T IT?
GRANNY!
GOOD MORN-ING, FUMI.
GOOD MORN-ING!

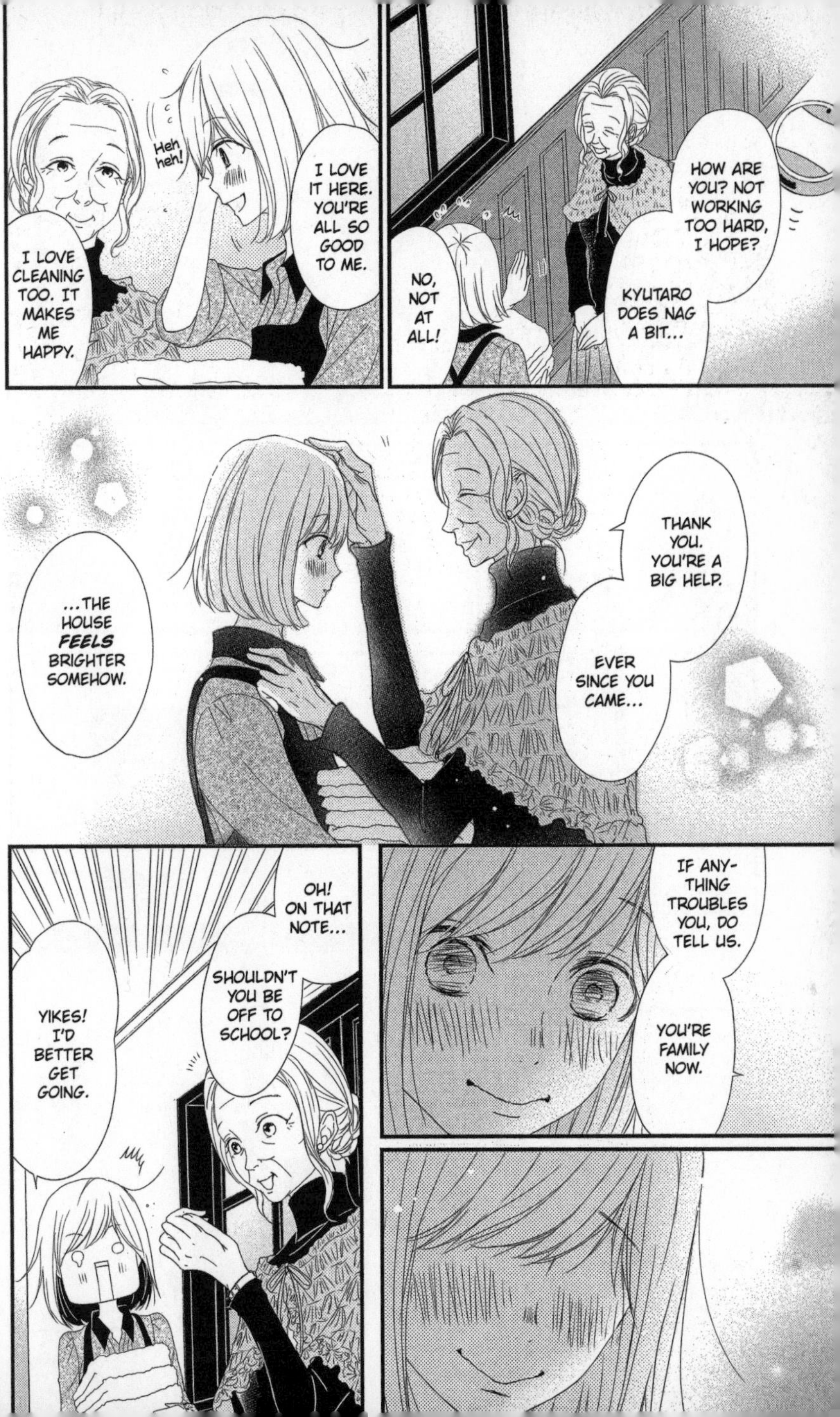
HOW ARE YOU? NOT WORKING TOO HARD, I HOPE?
KYUTARO DOES NAG A BIT...
NO, NOT AT ALL!
I LOVE IT HERE. YOU'RE ALL SO GOOD TO ME.
Heh heh!
I LOVE CLEANING TOO. IT MAKES ME HAPPY.
THANK YOU. YOU'RE A BIG HELP.
EVER SINCE YOU CAME...
...THE HOUSE FEELS BRIGHTER SOMEHOW.
IF ANYTHING TROUBLES YOU, DO TELL US.
YOU'RE FAMILY NOW.
OH! ON THAT NOTE...
SHOULDN'T YOU BE OFF TO SCHOOL?
YIKES! I'D BETTER GET GOING.

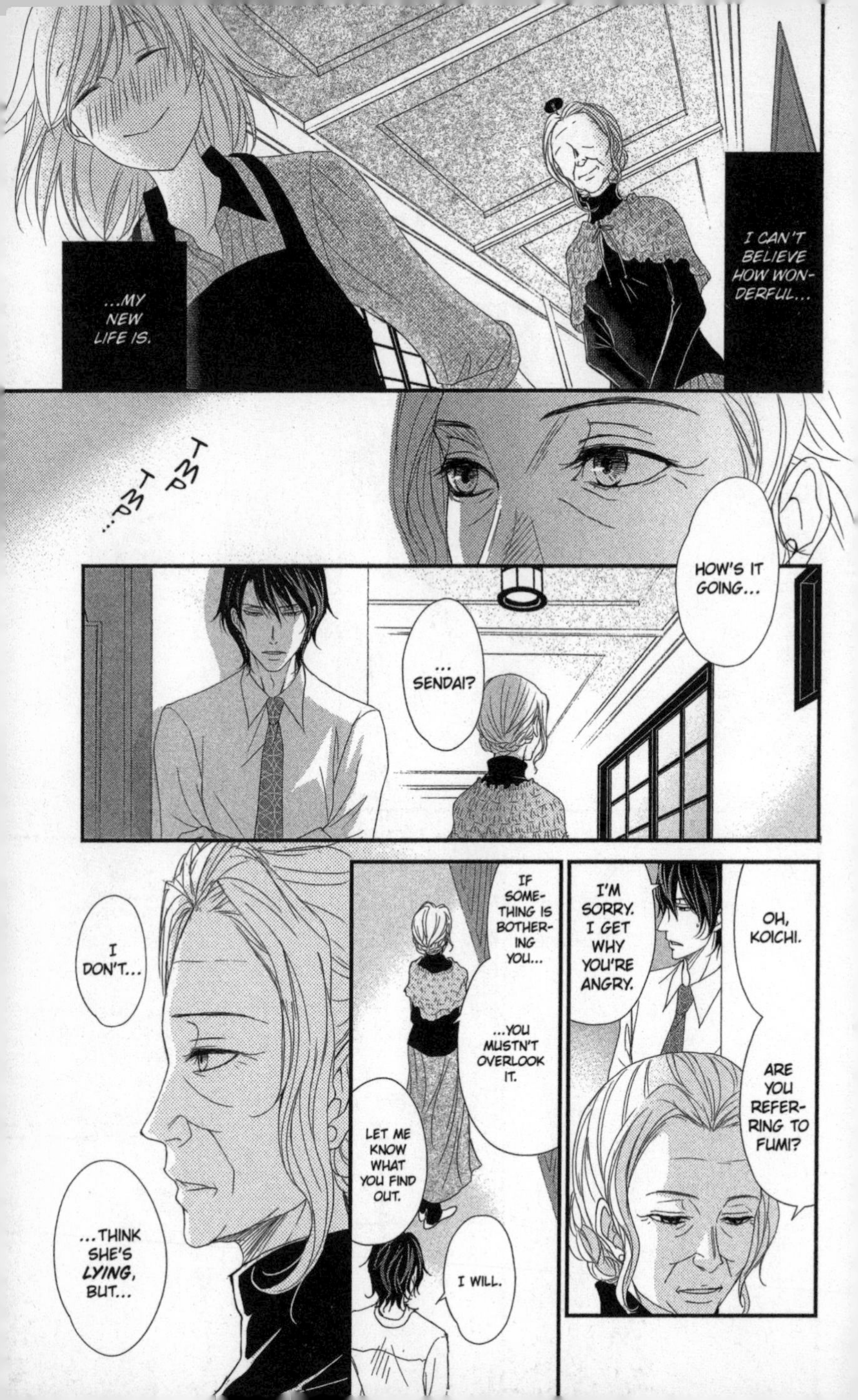
I CAN'T BELIEVE HOW WON-DERFUL...
...MY NEW LIFE IS.
TMP TMP...
HOW'S IT GOING...
...SENDAI?
OH, KOICHI.
I'M SORRY. I GET WHY YOU'RE ANGRY.
ARE YOU REFER-RING TO FUMI?
IF SOME-THING IS BOTHER-ING YOU...
...YOU MUSTN'T OVERLOOK IT.
LET ME KNOW WHAT YOU FIND OUT.
I WILL.
I DON'T...
...THINK SHE'S *LYING*, BUT...

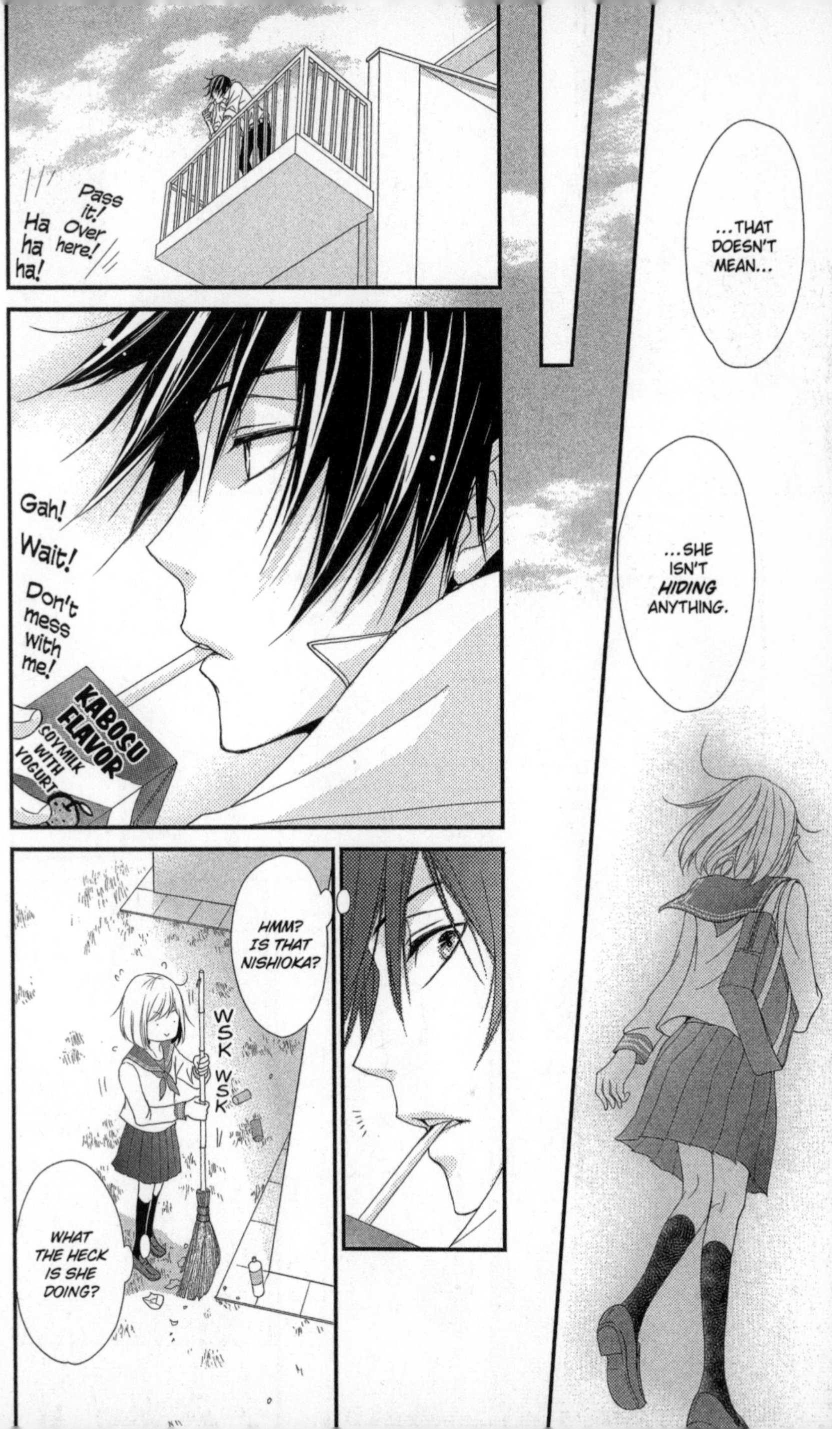
...THAT DOESN'T MEAN...
...SHE ISN'T HIDING ANYTHING.
Pass it! Over here!
Ha ha ha!
Gah!
Wait!
Don't mess with me!
KABOSU FLAVOR
SOYMILK WITH YOGURT
HMM? IS THAT NISHIOKA?
WSK WSK
WHAT THE HECK IS SHE DOING?

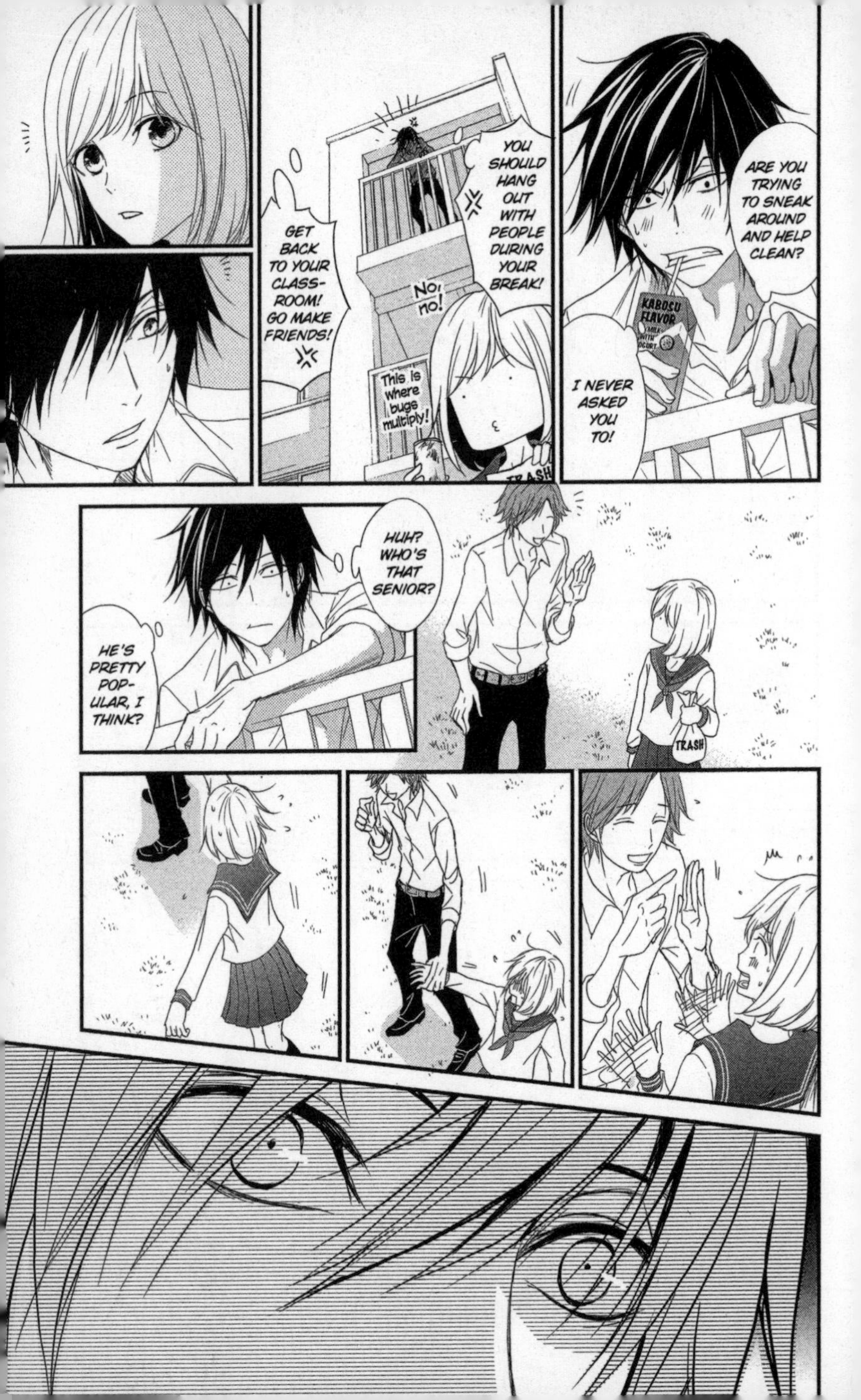
ARE YOU TRYING TO SNEAK AROUND AND HELP CLEAN?
KABOSU FLAVOR
I NEVER ASKED YOU TO!
YOU SHOULD HANG OUT WITH PEOPLE DURING YOUR BREAK!
GET BACK TO YOUR CLASSROOM! GO MAKE FRIENDS!
No, no!
This is where bugs multiply!
TRASH
HUH? WHO'S THAT SENIOR?
HE'S PRETTY POPULAR, I THINK?
TRASH

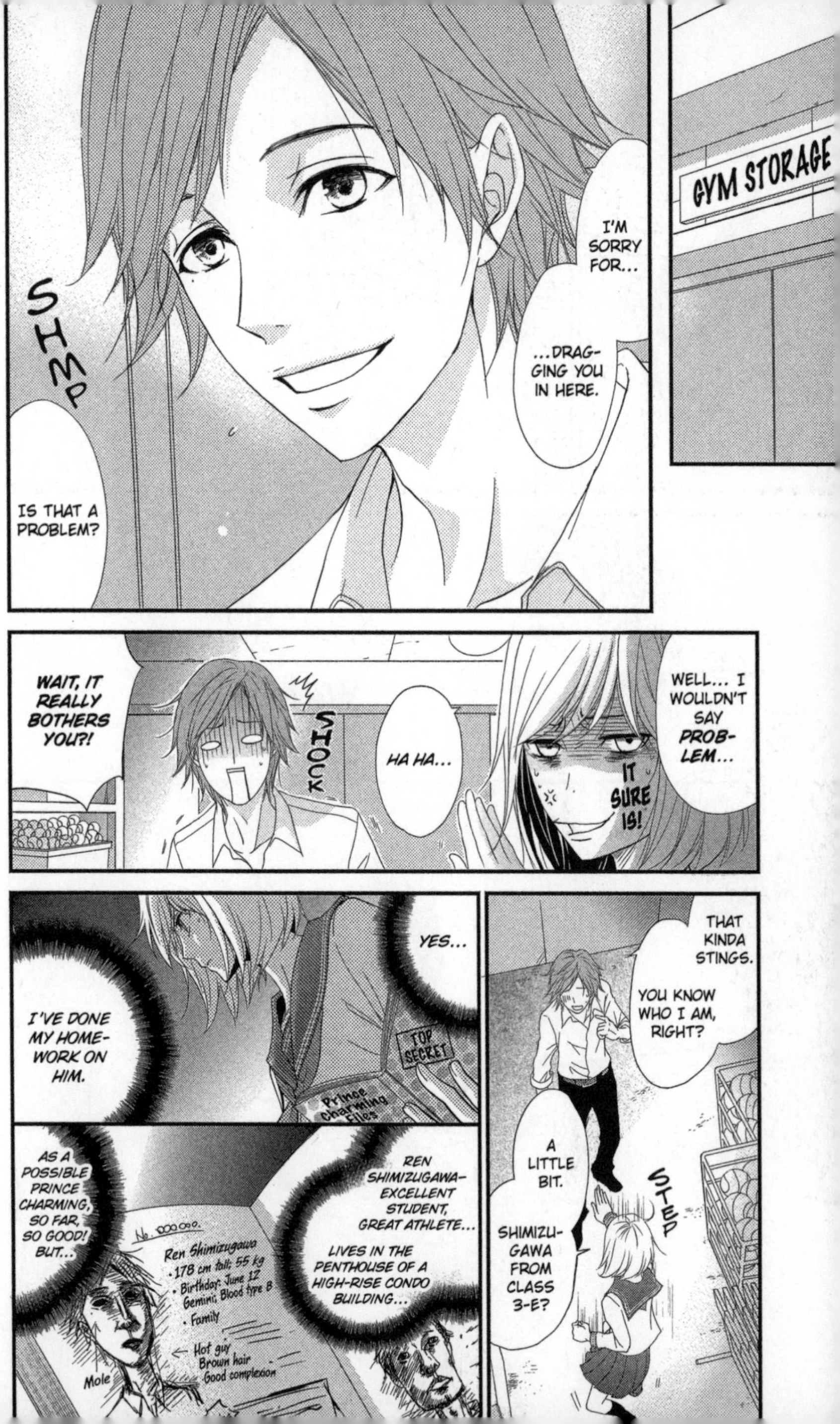
GYM STORAGE
I'M SORRY FOR...
...DRAG-GING YOU IN HERE.
SHMP
IS THAT A PROBLEM?
WELL... I WOULDN'T SAY PROB-LEM...
IT SURE IS!
HA HA...
SHOCK
WAIT, IT REALLY BOTHERS YOU?!
THAT KINDA STINGS.
YOU KNOW WHO I AM, RIGHT?
STEP
A LITTLE BIT.
SHIMIZU-GAWA FROM CLASS 3-E?
YES...
I'VE DONE MY HOME-WORK ON HIM.
TOP SECRET
Prince Charming Files
REN SHIMIZUGAWA—EXCELLENT STUDENT, GREAT ATHLETE...
LIVES IN THE PENTHOUSE OF A HIGH-RISE CONDO BUILDING...
AS A POSSIBLE PRINCE CHARMING, SO FAR, SO GOOD! BUT...
No. 000000.
Ren Shimizugawa
• 178 cm tall; 55 kg
• Birthday: June 12 Gemini; Blood type B
• Family
Hot guy
Brown hair
Good complexion
Mole

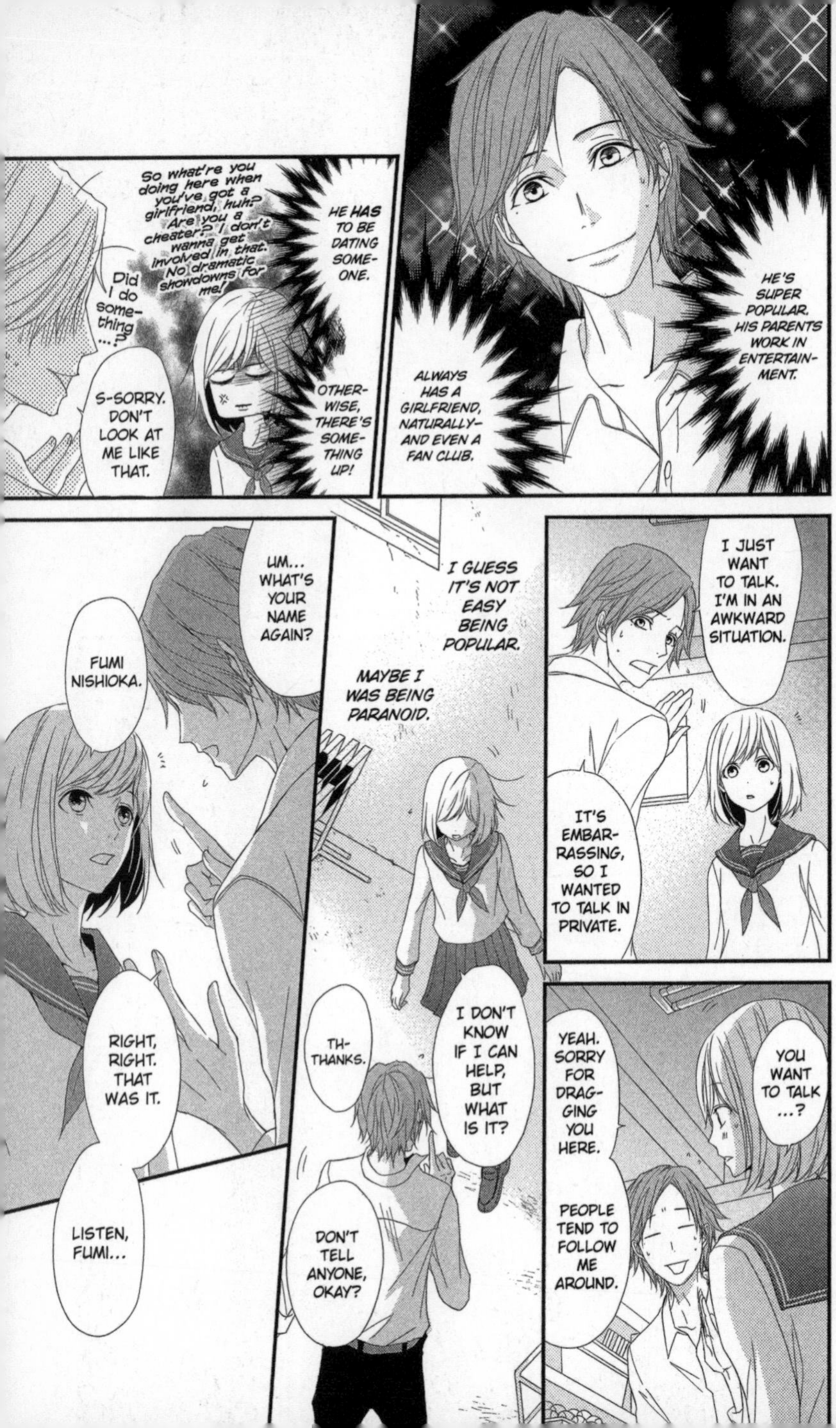
HE'S SUPER POPULAR. HIS PARENTS WORK IN ENTERTAINMENT.
ALWAYS HAS A GIRLFRIEND, NATURALLY—AND EVEN A FAN CLUB.
HE HAS TO BE DATING SOMEONE.
OTHERWISE, THERE'S SOMETHING UP!
So what're you doing here when you've got a girlfriend, huh? Are you a cheater? I don't wanna get involved in that. No dramatic showdowns for me!
Did I do something...?
S-SORRY. DON'T LOOK AT ME LIKE THAT.
I JUST WANT TO TALK. I'M IN AN AWKWARD SITUATION.
IT'S EMBARRASSING, SO I WANTED TO TALK IN PRIVATE.
YOU WANT TO TALK...?
YEAH. SORRY FOR DRAGGING YOU HERE.
PEOPLE TEND TO FOLLOW ME AROUND.
I GUESS IT'S NOT EASY BEING POPULAR.
MAYBE I WAS BEING PARANOID.
I DON'T KNOW IF I CAN HELP, BUT WHAT IS IT?
TH-THANKS.
DON'T TELL ANYONE, OKAY?
UM... WHAT'S YOUR NAME AGAIN?
FUMI NISHIOKA.
RIGHT, RIGHT. THAT WAS IT.
LISTEN, FUMI...

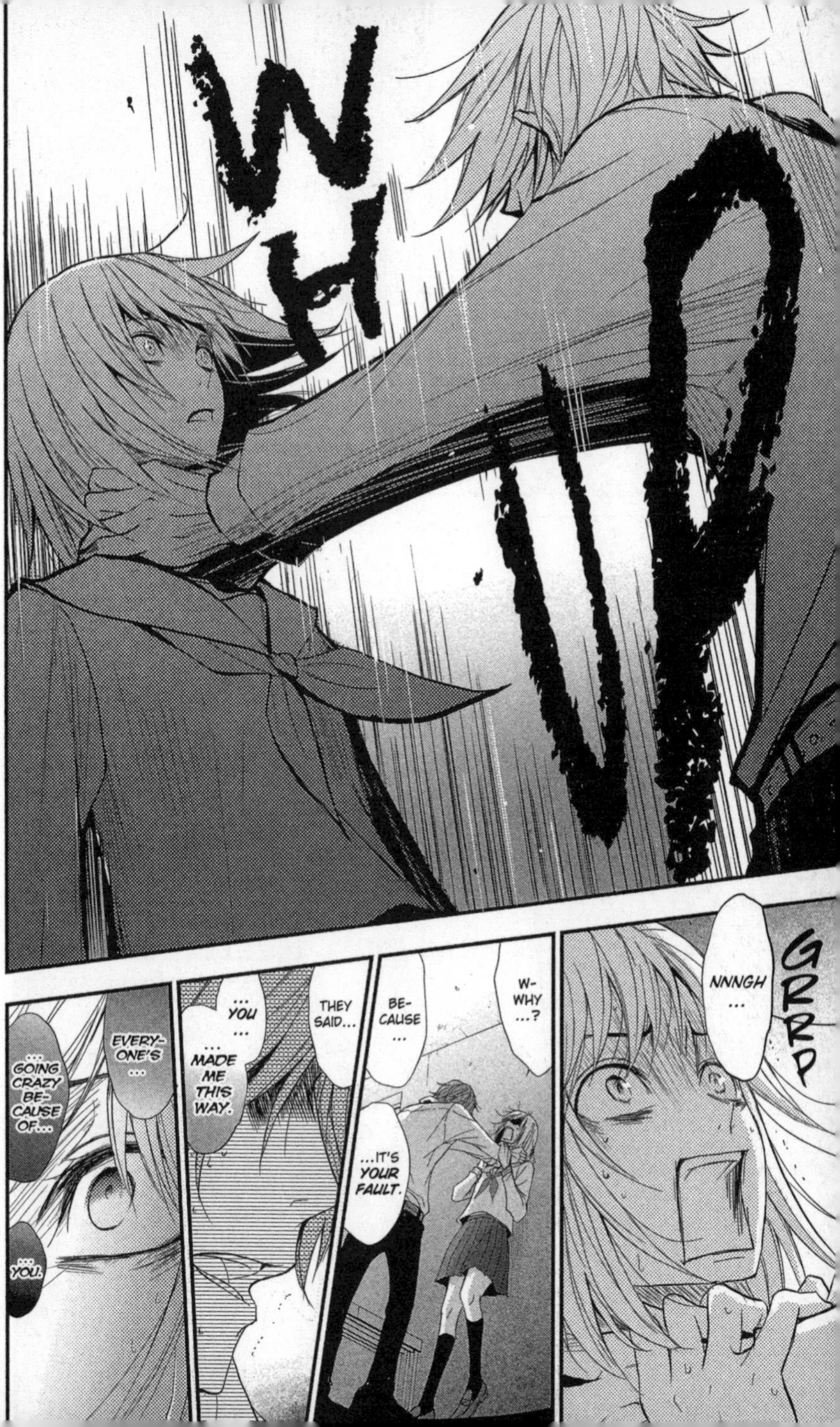
WHUP
NNNGH...
GRRP
W-WHY...?
BE-CAUSE...
THEY SAID...
...IT'S YOUR FAULT.
...YOU...
...MADE ME THIS WAY.
EVERY-ONE'S...
...GOING CRAZY BE-CAUSE OF...
...YOU.

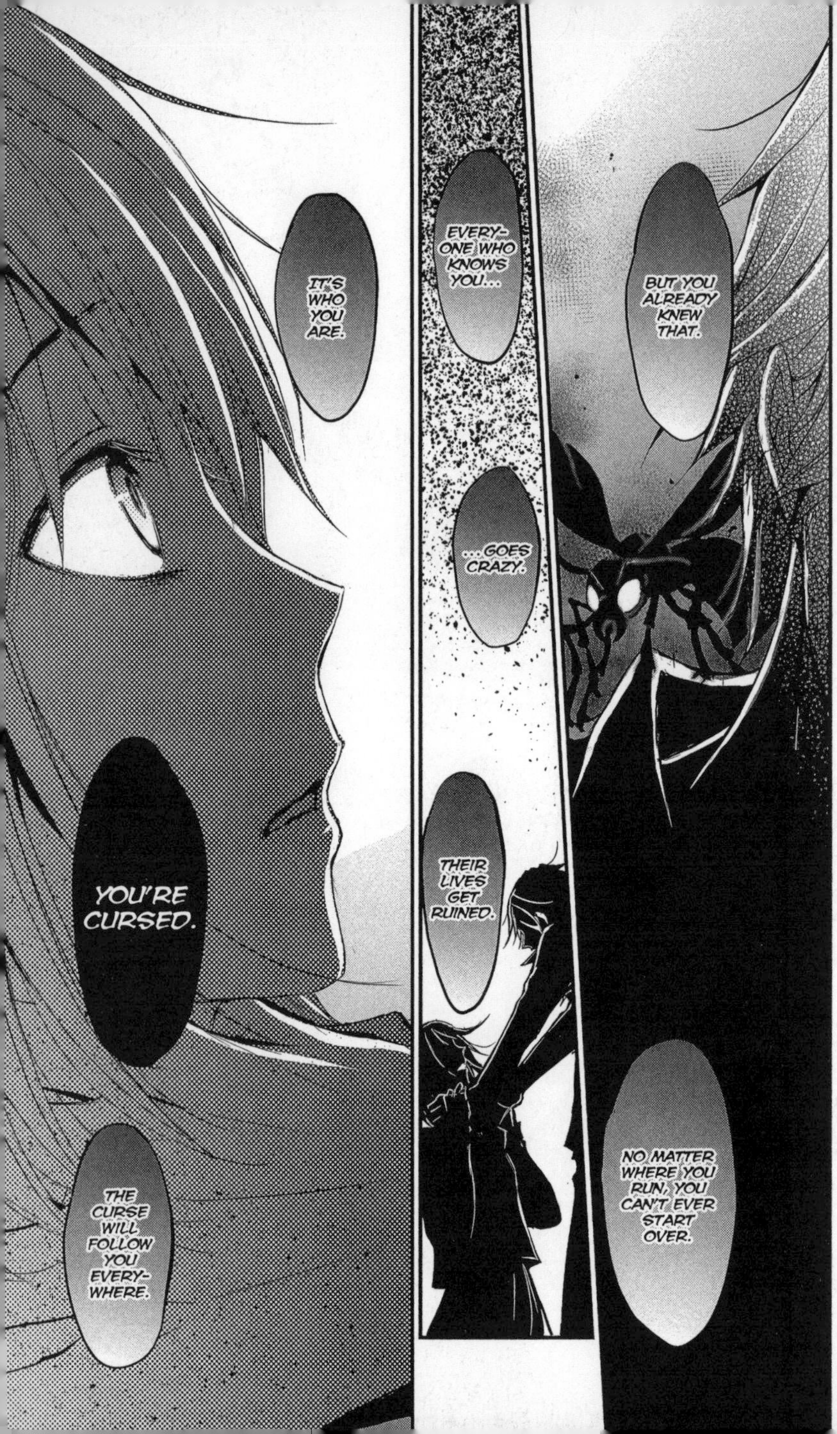
BUT YOU ALREADY KNEW THAT.
EVERY-ONE WHO KNOWS YOU...
...GOES CRAZY.
THEIR LIVES GET RUINED.
NO MATTER WHERE YOU RUN, YOU CAN'T EVER START OVER.
IT'S WHO YOU ARE.
YOU'RE CURSED.
THE CURSE WILL FOLLOW YOU EVERY-WHERE.

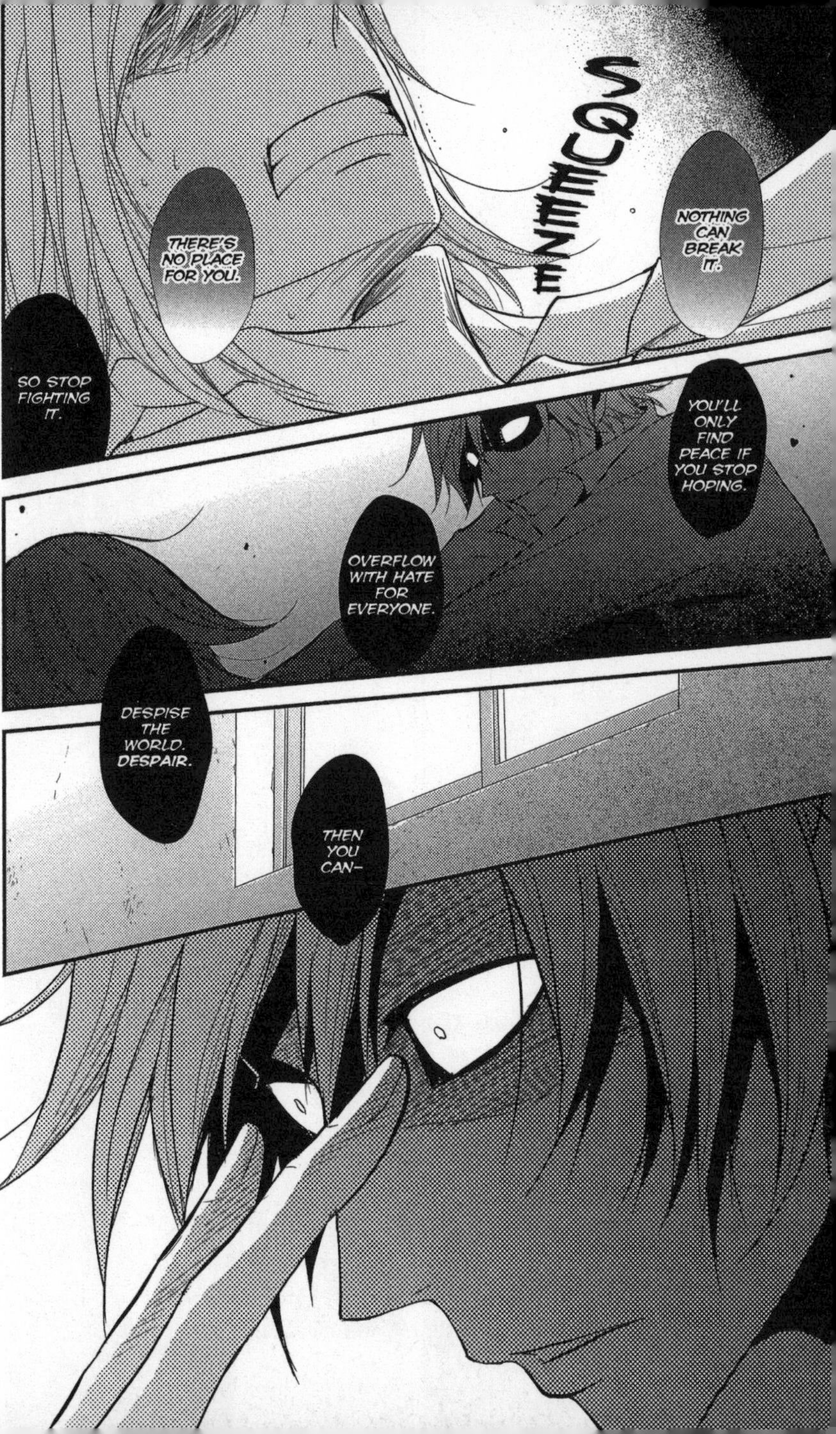
SQUEEZE
NOTHING CAN BREAK IT.
THERE'S NO PLACE FOR YOU.
SO STOP FIGHTING IT.
YOU'LL ONLY FIND PEACE IF YOU STOP HOPING.
OVERFLOW WITH HATE FOR EVERYONE.
DESPISE THE WORLD. DESPAIR.
THEN YOU CAN-

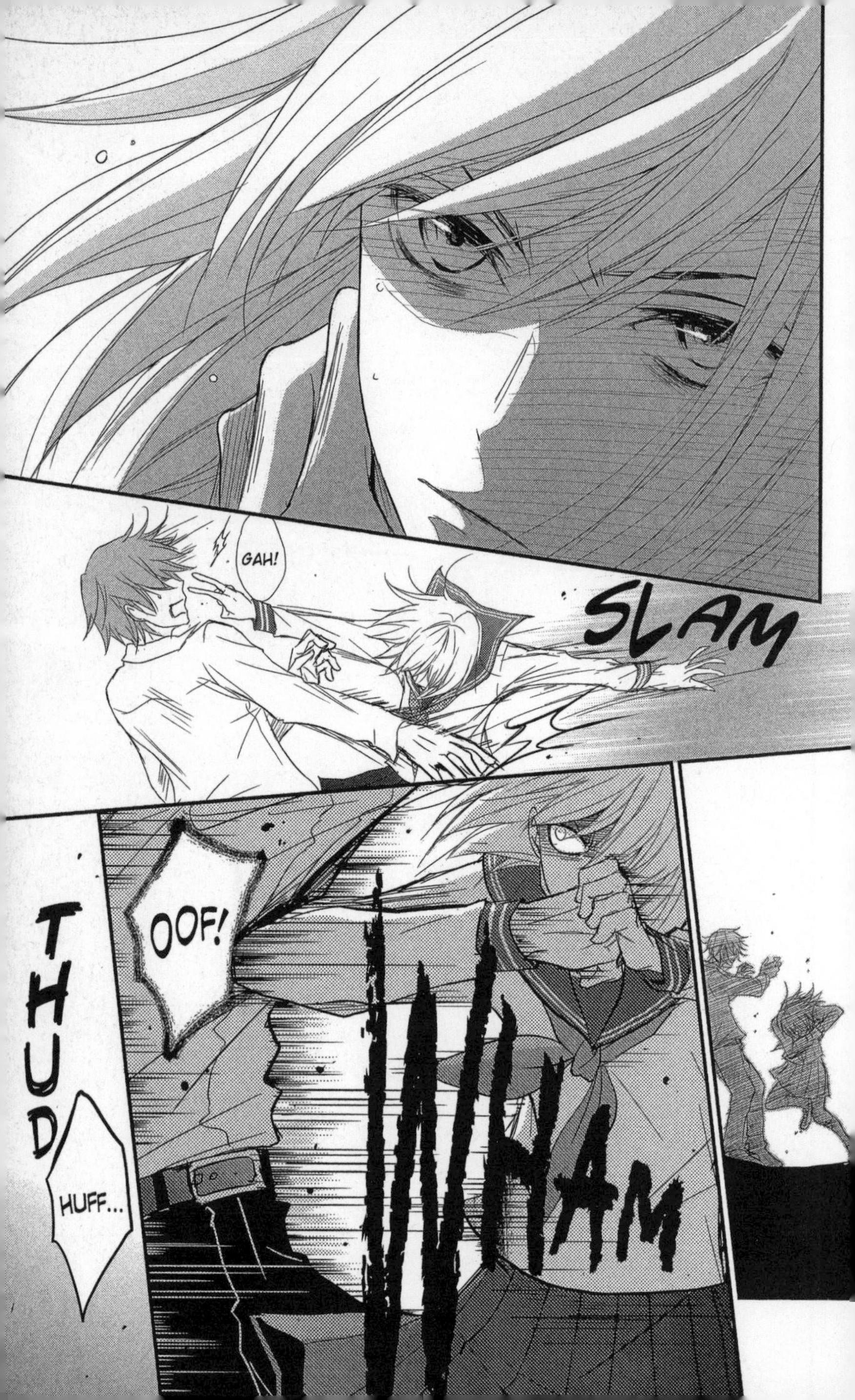
SLAM
GAH!
OOF!
WHAM
THUD
HUFF...

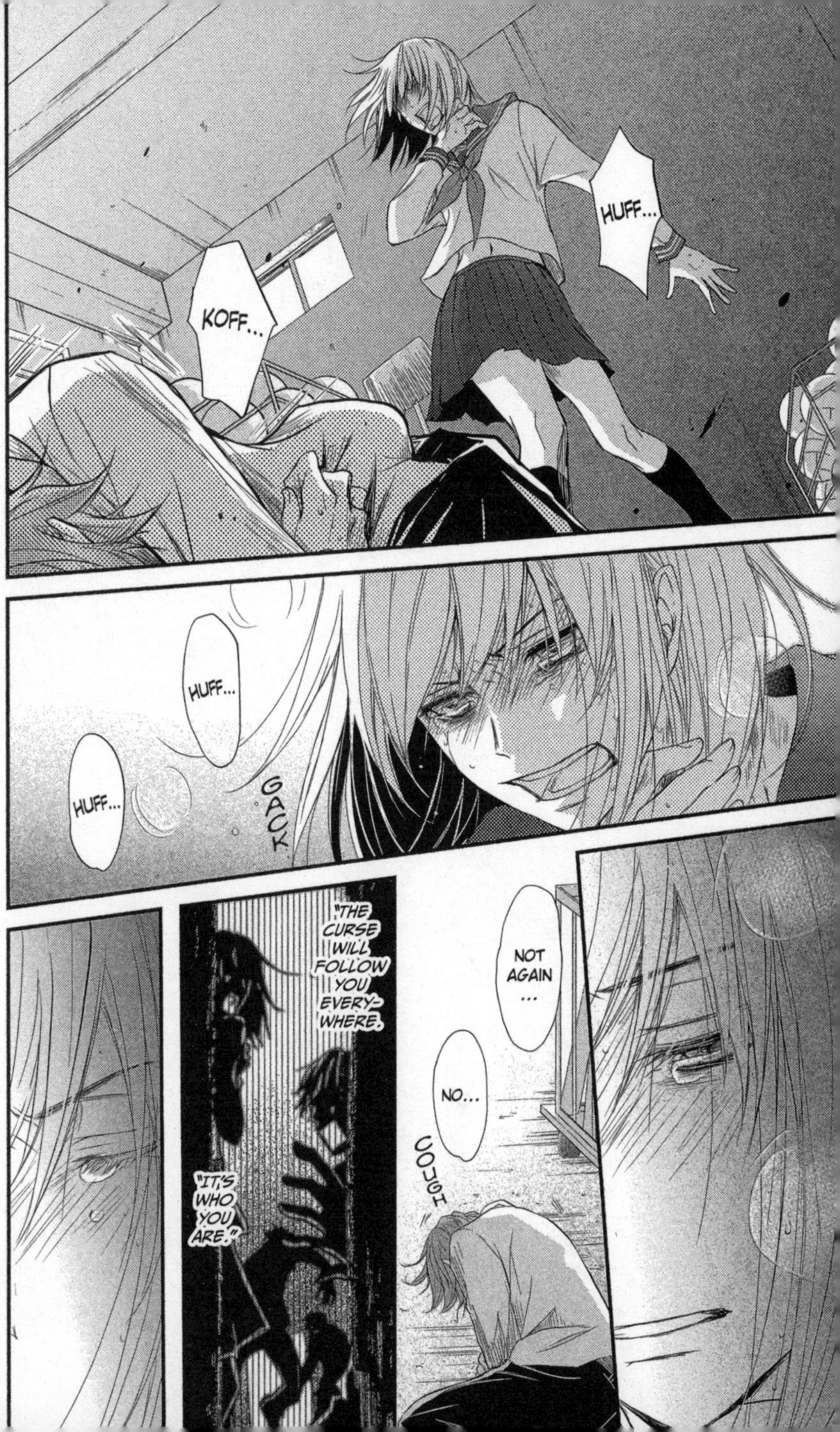
HUFF...
KOFF...
HUFF...
GACK
HUFF...
NOT AGAIN...
NO...
COUGH
"THE CURSE WILL FOLLOW YOU EVERY-WHERE.
"IT'S WHO YOU ARE."

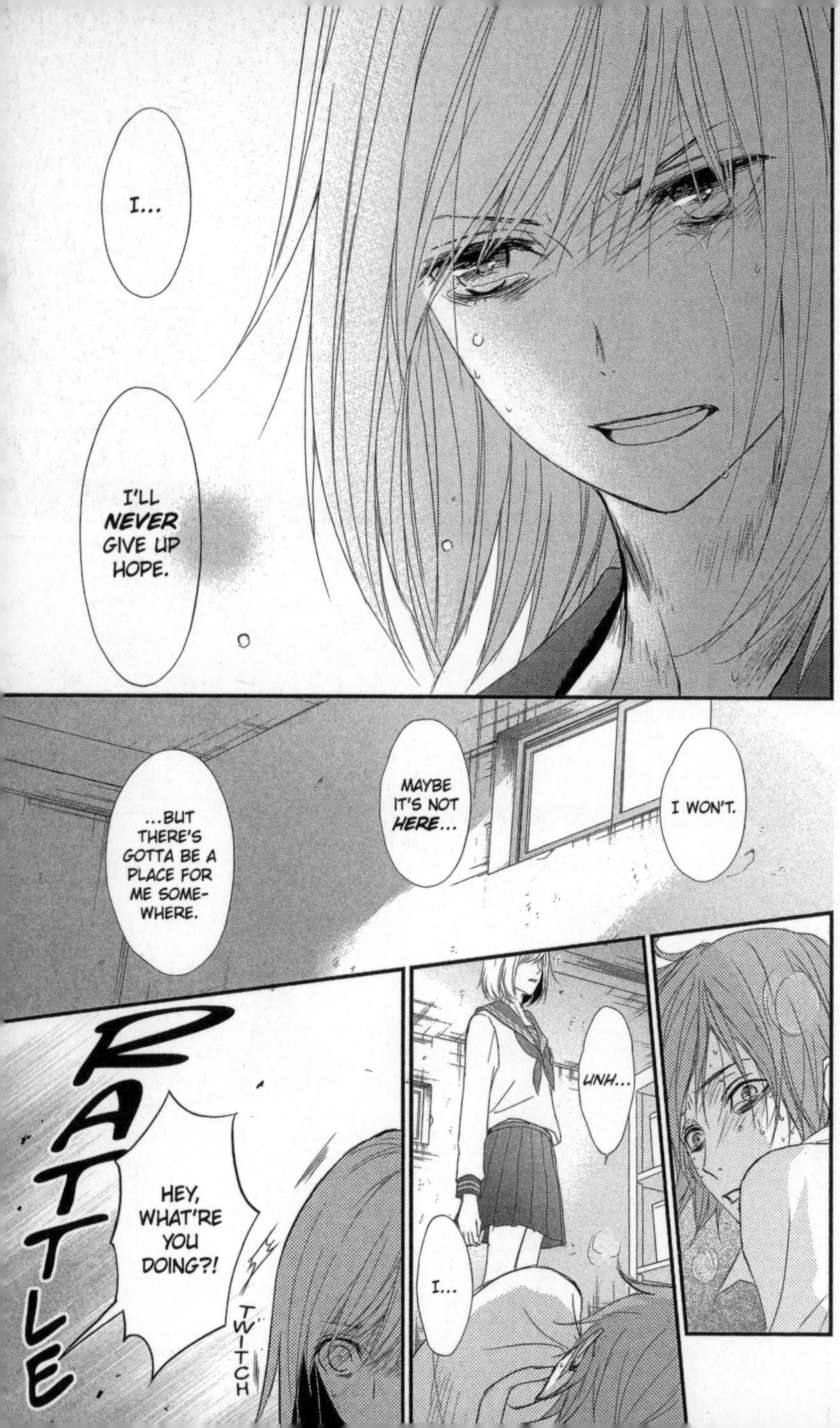
I...
I'LL NEVER GIVE UP HOPE.
I WON'T.
MAYBE IT'S NOT HERE...
...BUT THERE'S GOTTA BE A PLACE FOR ME SOME-WHERE.
UNH...
I...
RATTLE
HEY, WHAT'RE YOU DOING?!
TWITCH

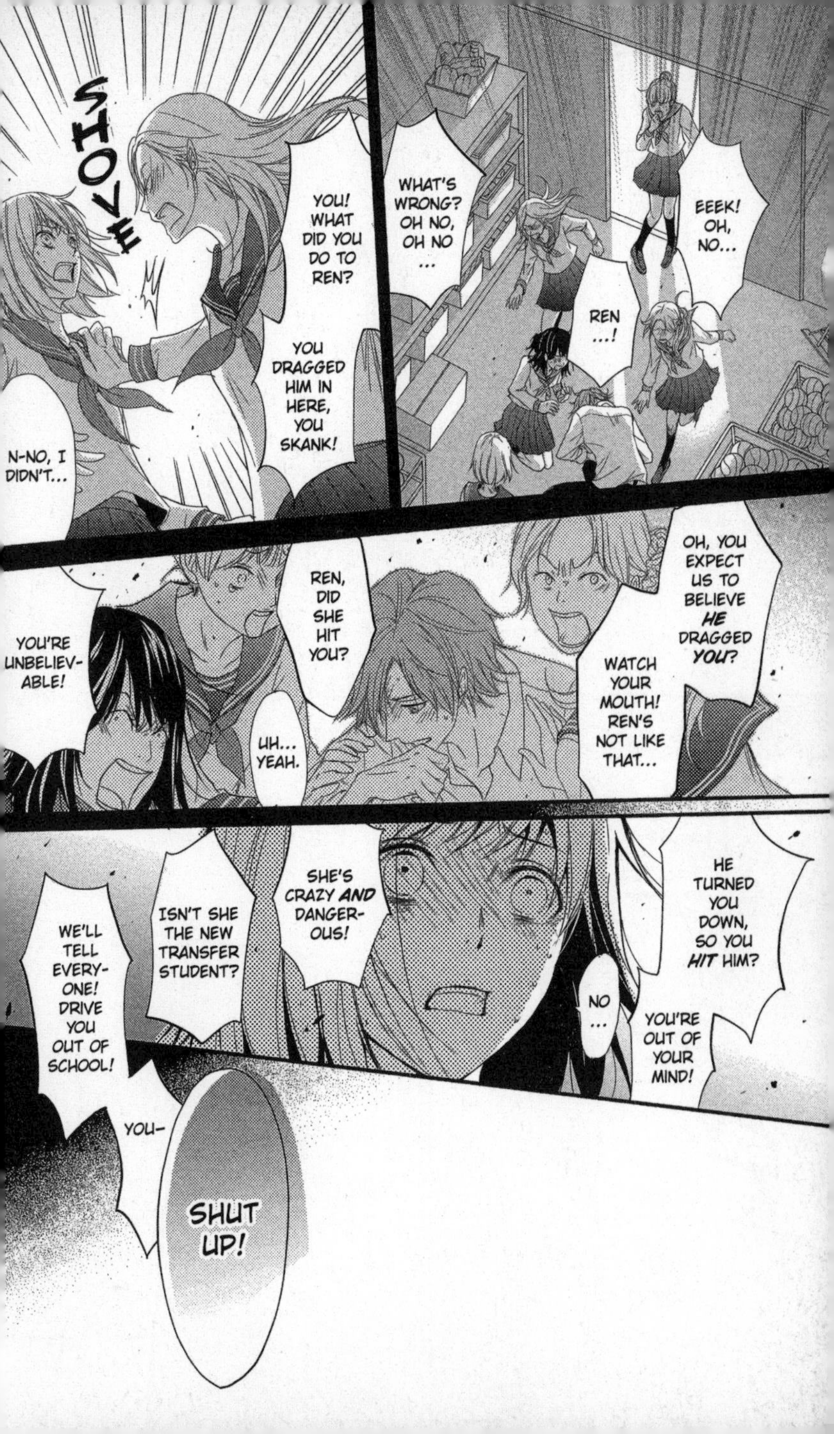
EEEK! OH, NO...
WHAT'S WRONG? OH NO, OH NO ...
REN ...!
SHOVE
YOU! WHAT DID YOU DO TO REN?
YOU DRAGGED HIM IN HERE, YOU SKANK!
N-NO, I DIDN'T...
OH, YOU EXPECT US TO BELIEVE *HE* DRAGGED *YOU*?
WATCH YOUR MOUTH! REN'S NOT LIKE THAT...
REN, DID SHE HIT YOU?
UH... YEAH.
YOU'RE UNBELIEV-ABLE!
HE TURNED YOU DOWN, SO YOU *HIT* HIM?
YOU'RE OUT OF YOUR MIND!
NO ...
SHE'S CRAZY *AND* DANGER-OUS!
ISN'T SHE THE NEW TRANSFER STUDENT?
WE'LL TELL EVERY-ONE! DRIVE YOU OUT OF SCHOOL!
YOU-
SHUT UP!

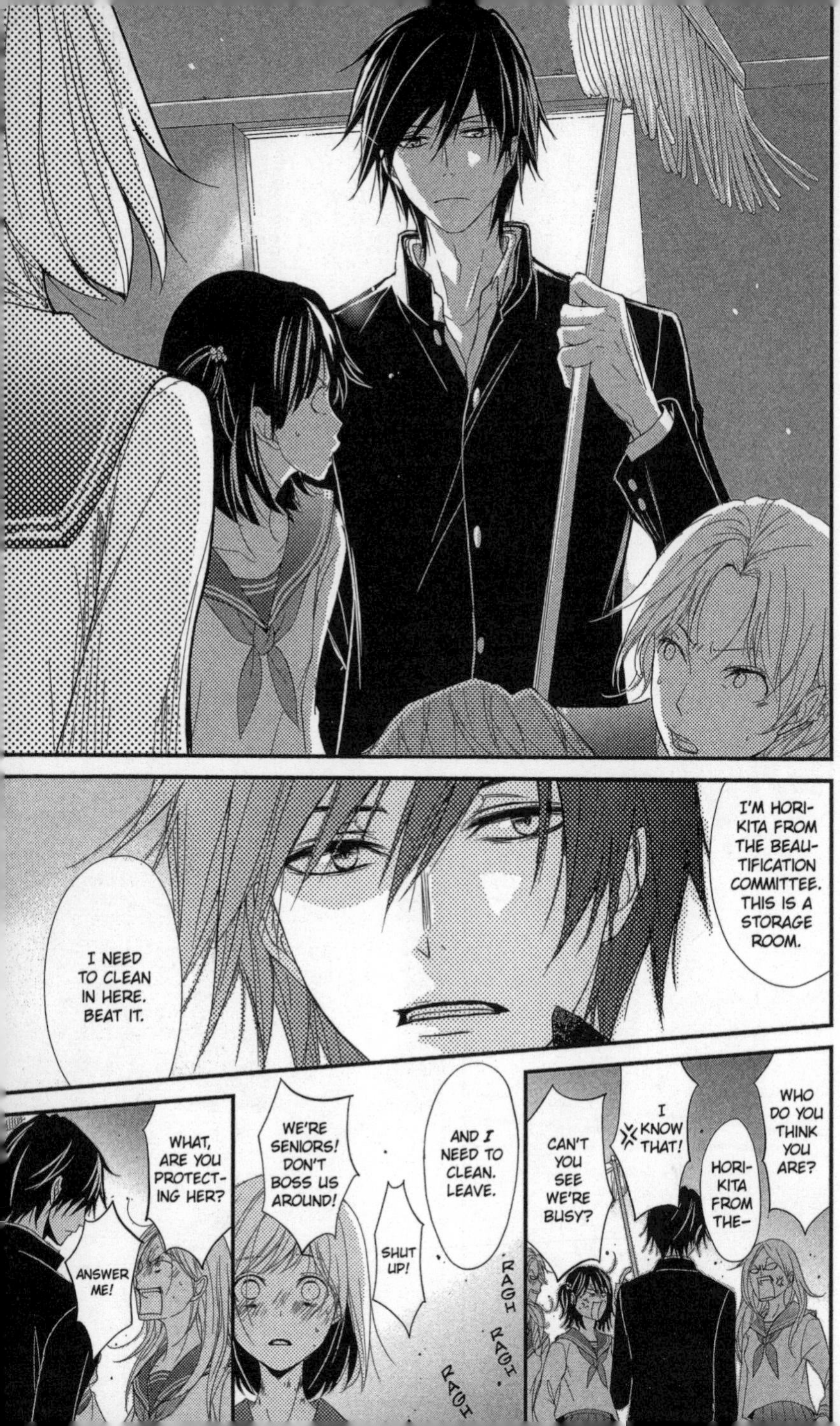
I'M HORI-KITA FROM THE BEAU-TIFICATION COMMITTEE. THIS IS A STORAGE ROOM.
I NEED TO CLEAN IN HERE. BEAT IT.
WHO DO YOU THINK YOU ARE?
HORI-KITA FROM THE–
I KNOW THAT!
CAN'T YOU SEE WE'RE BUSY?
AND I NEED TO CLEAN. LEAVE.
RAGH
RAGI
RAGI
SHUT UP!
WE'RE SENIORS! DON'T BOSS US AROUND!
WHAT, ARE YOU PROTECTING HER?
ANSWER ME!

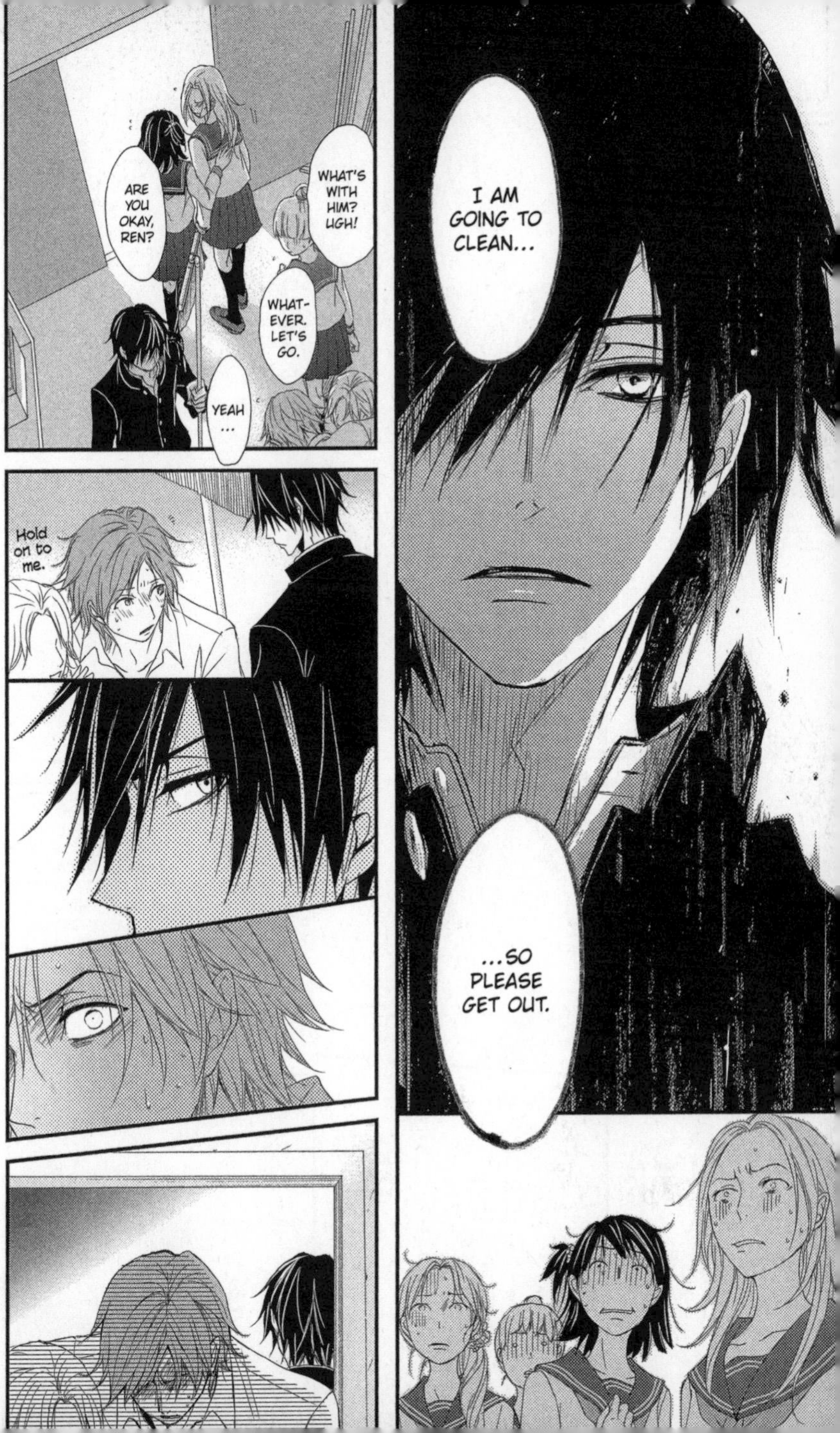
I AM GOING TO CLEAN...
...SO PLEASE GET OUT.
WHAT'S WITH HIM? UGH!
ARE YOU OKAY, REN?
WHAT-EVER. LET'S GO.
YEAH...
Hold on to me.

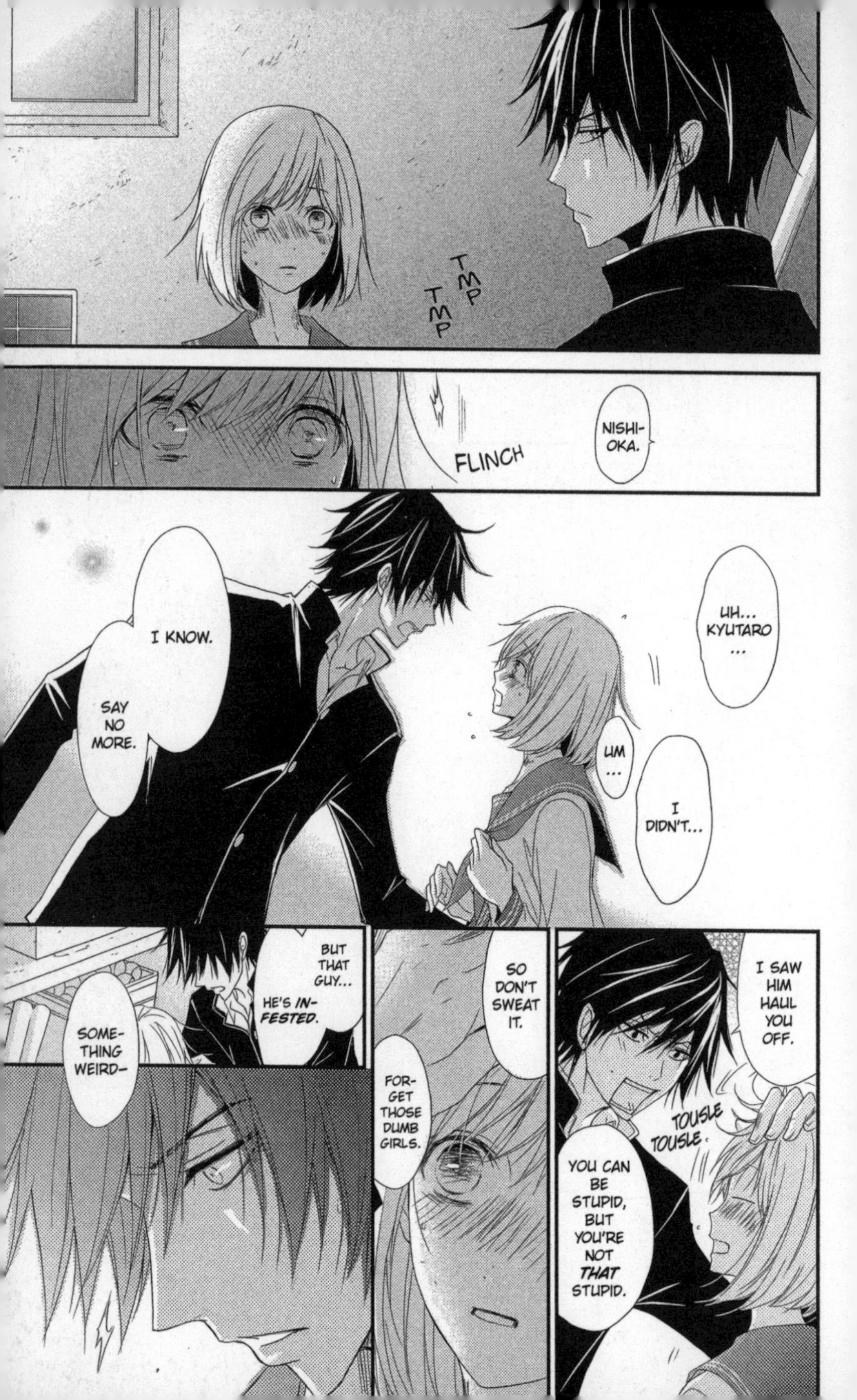
TMP TMP
NISHIOKA.
FLINCH
UH... KYUTARO...
I DIDN'T...
UM...
I KNOW.
SAY NO MORE.
I SAW HIM HAUL YOU OFF.
TOUSLE TOUSLE
YOU CAN BE STUPID, BUT YOU'RE NOT *THAT* STUPID.
SO DON'T SWEAT IT.
FORGET THOSE DUMB GIRLS.
BUT THAT GUY...
HE'S *INFESTED*.
SOMETHING WEIRD-

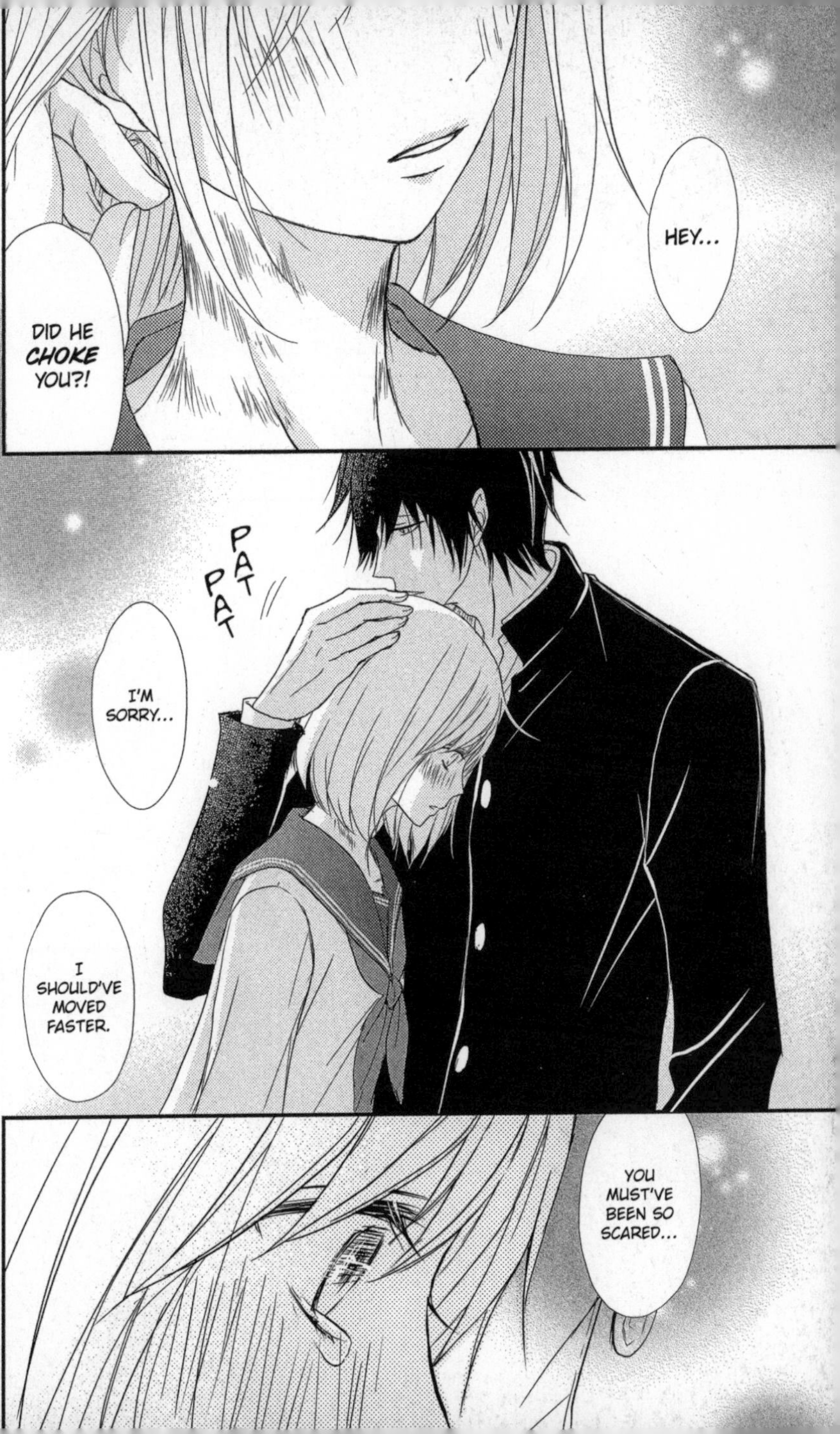
HEY...
DID HE CHOKE YOU?!
PAT PAT
I'M SORRY...
I SHOULD'VE MOVED FASTER.
YOU MUST'VE BEEN SO SCARED...

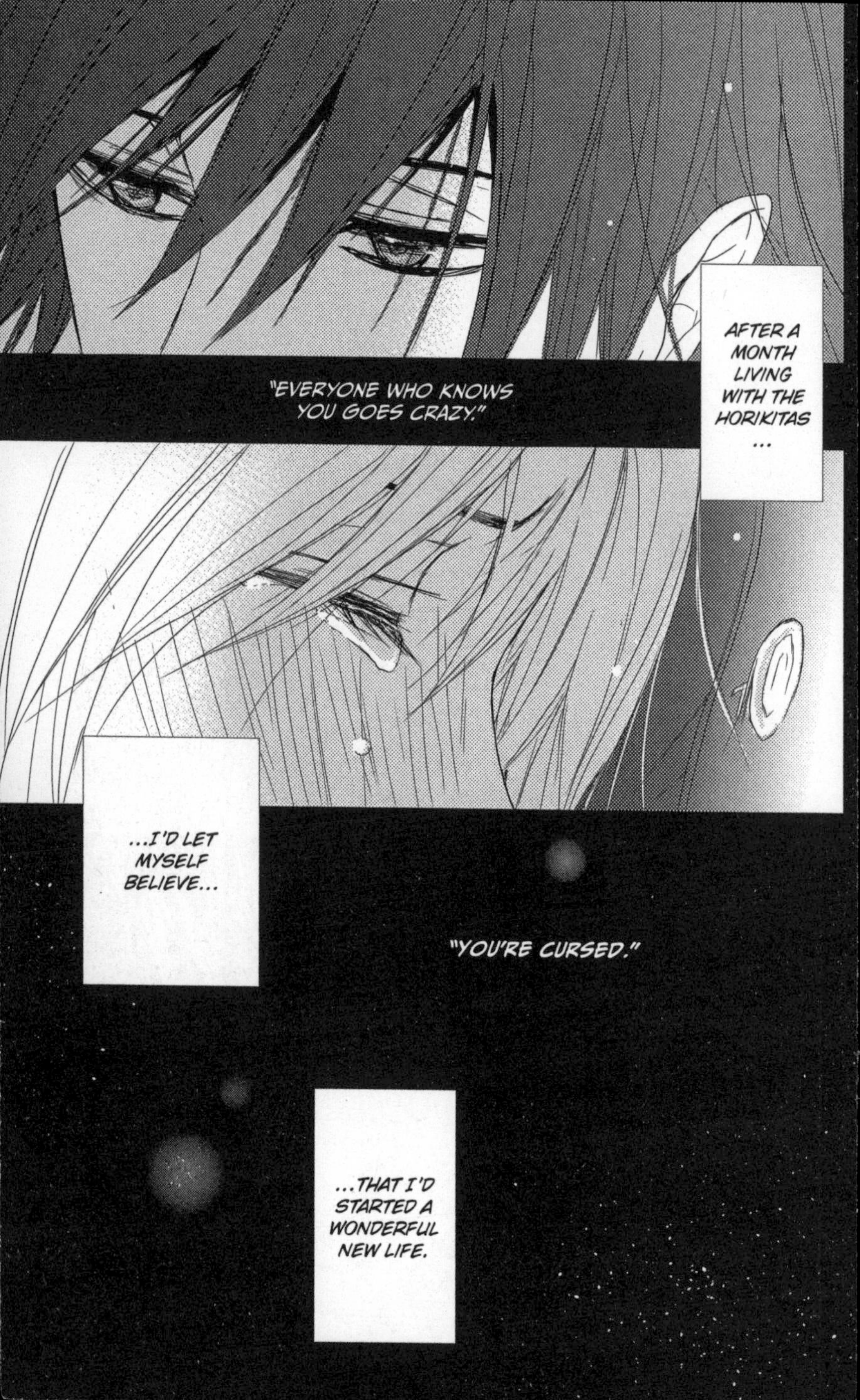
AFTER A MONTH LIVING WITH THE HORIKITAS ...
"EVERYONE WHO KNOWS YOU GOES CRAZY."
...I'D LET MYSELF BELIEVE...
"YOU'RE CURSED."
...THAT I'D STARTED A WONDERFUL NEW LIFE.

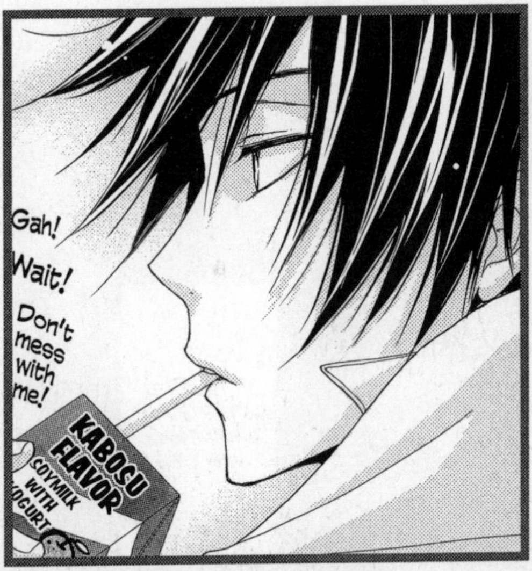
Gah!
Wait!
Don't mess with me!
KABOSU FLAVOR
SOYMILK WITH YOGURT

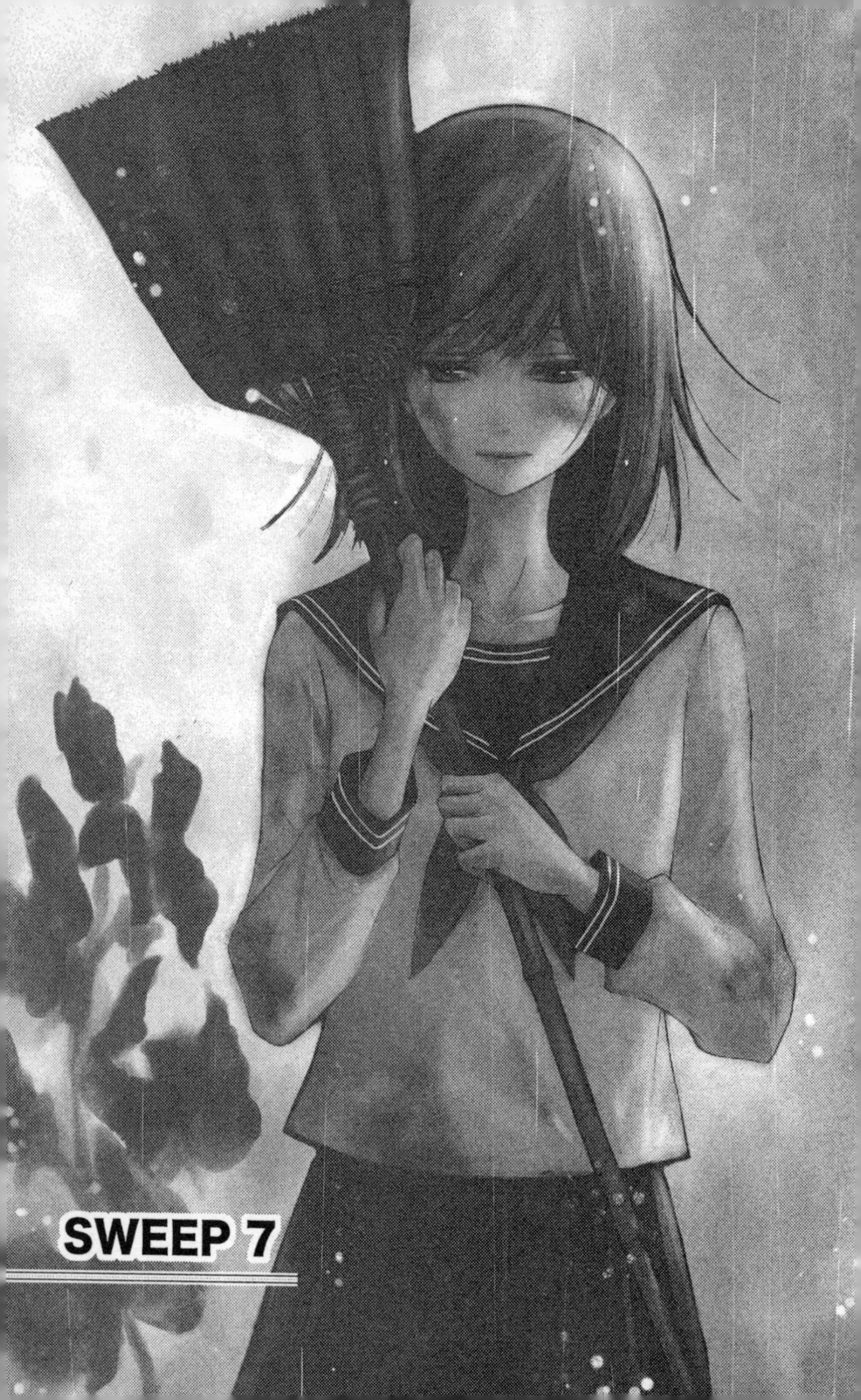
SWEEP 7

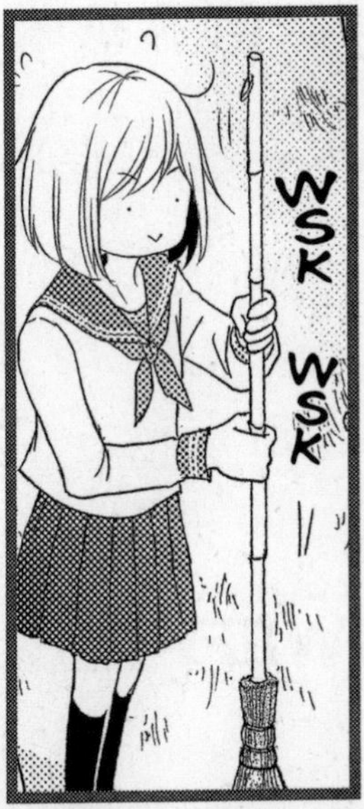
WSK
WSK

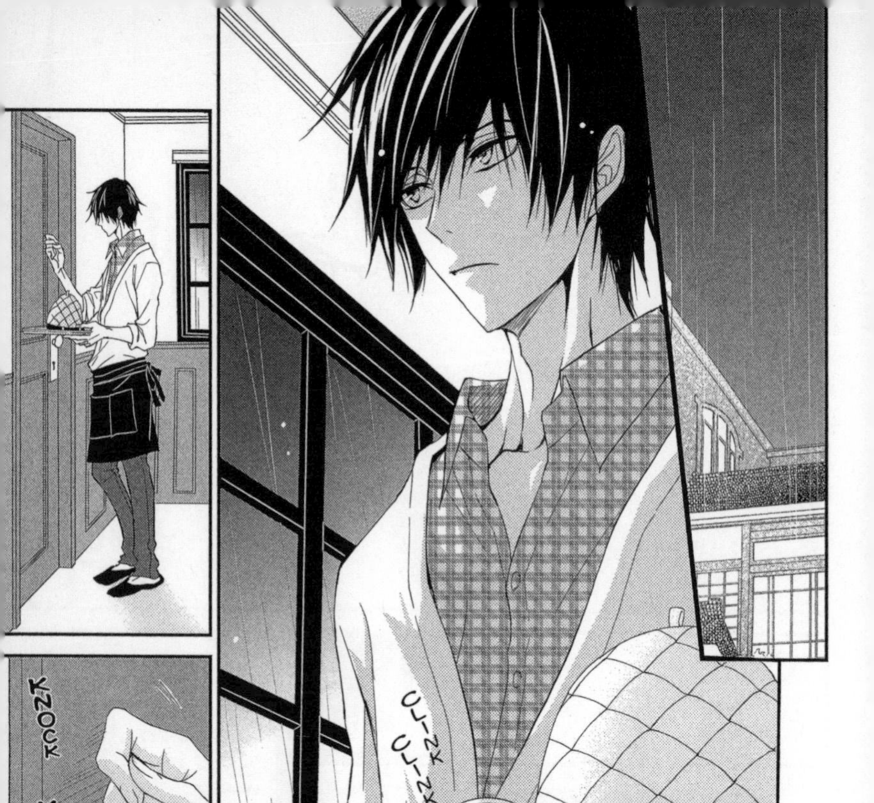
CLINK
CLINK
KNOCK
KNOCK
COME IN.

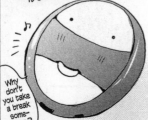

My cleaning robot is made by S company. I picked that particular one because it talks. It's a useless feature, honestly, but it's fun. The robot butts in on my assistants' conversations! It's annoying but cute.

There's a panel in Sweep 6 where you may have noticed a cleaning robot. You might be surprised to see professional cleaners using a robot, but I think pros would be more likely to use robots—they'd know how convenient robots are! Personally, I saved up and bought one for myself, and it works so hard! My room gleams! It probably works a thousand times harder than this author...

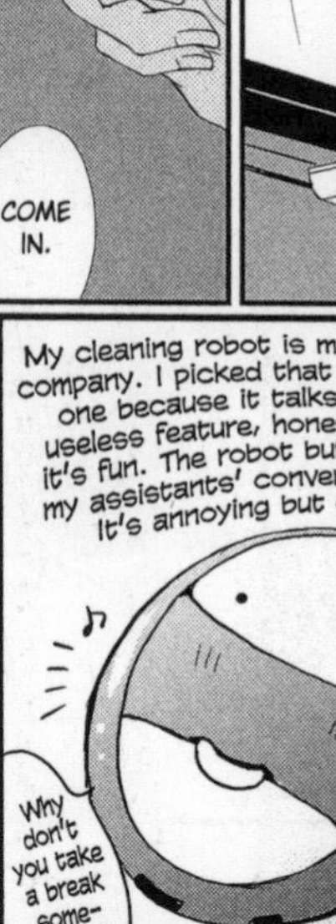
Why don't you take a break sometimes?

← It's irritating when it says this and I have a deadline.

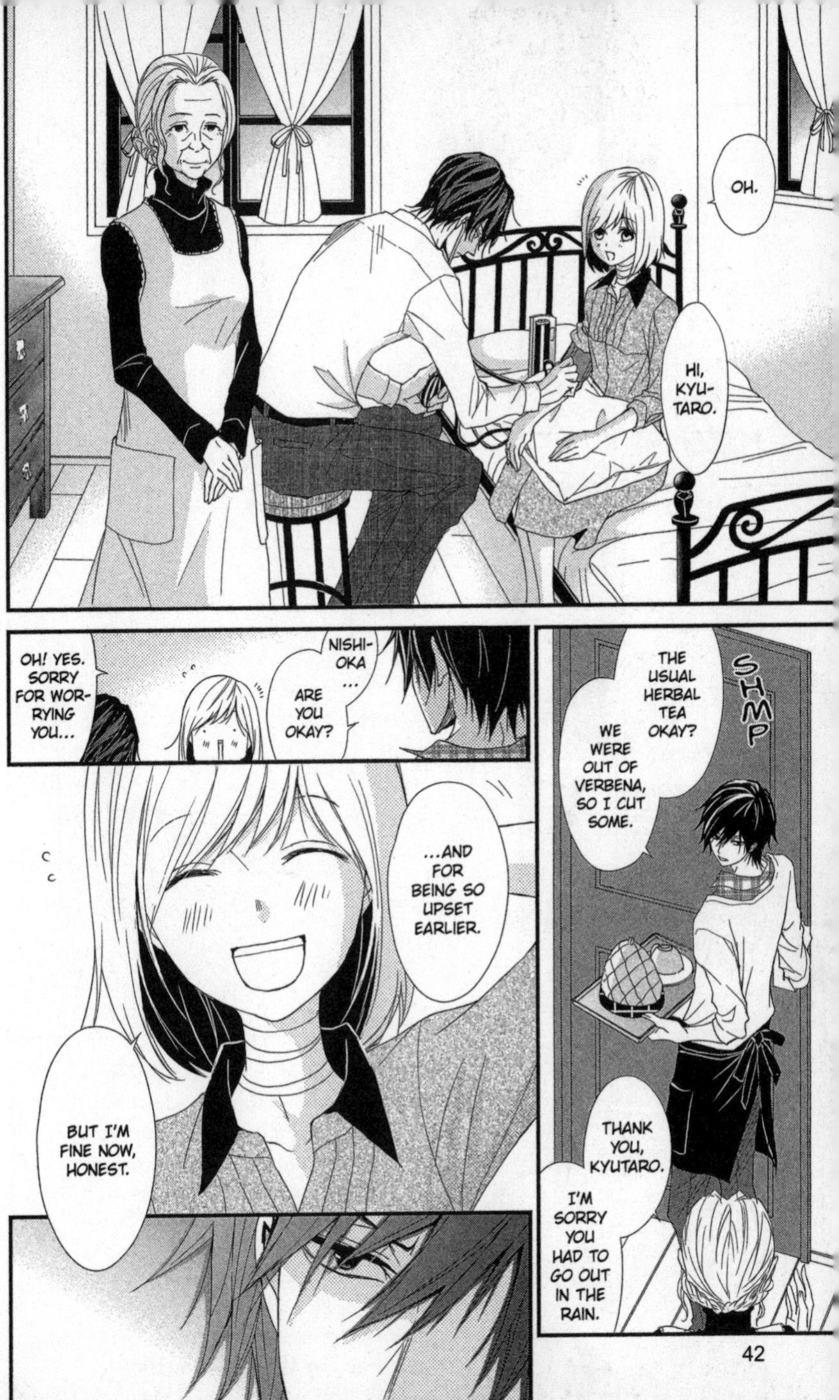
OH.
HI, KYU-TARO.
SHMP
THE USUAL HERBAL TEA OKAY?
WE WERE OUT OF VERBENA, SO I CUT SOME.
THANK YOU, KYUTARO.
I'M SORRY YOU HAD TO GO OUT IN THE RAIN.
NISHI-OKA ...
ARE YOU OKAY?
OH! YES. SORRY FOR WOR-RYING YOU...
...AND FOR BEING SO UPSET EARLIER.
BUT I'M FINE NOW, HONEST.

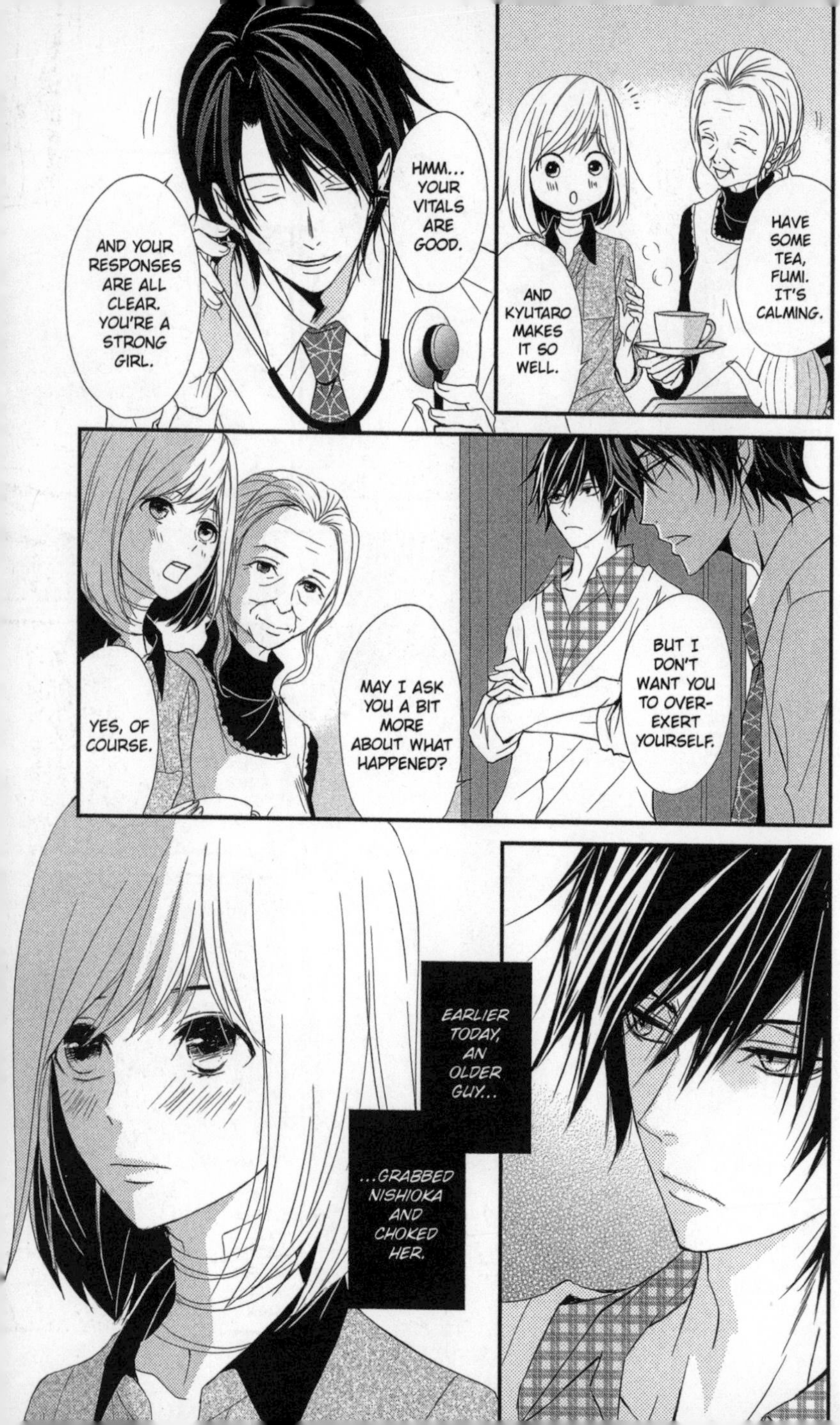
HAVE SOME TEA, FUMI. IT'S CALMING.
AND KYUTARO MAKES IT SO WELL.
HMM... YOUR VITALS ARE GOOD.
AND YOUR RESPONSES ARE ALL CLEAR. YOU'RE A STRONG GIRL.
BUT I DON'T WANT YOU TO OVER-EXERT YOURSELF.
MAY I ASK YOU A BIT MORE ABOUT WHAT HAPPENED?
YES, OF COURSE.
EARLIER TODAY, AN OLDER GUY...
...GRABBED NISHIOKA AND CHOKED HER.

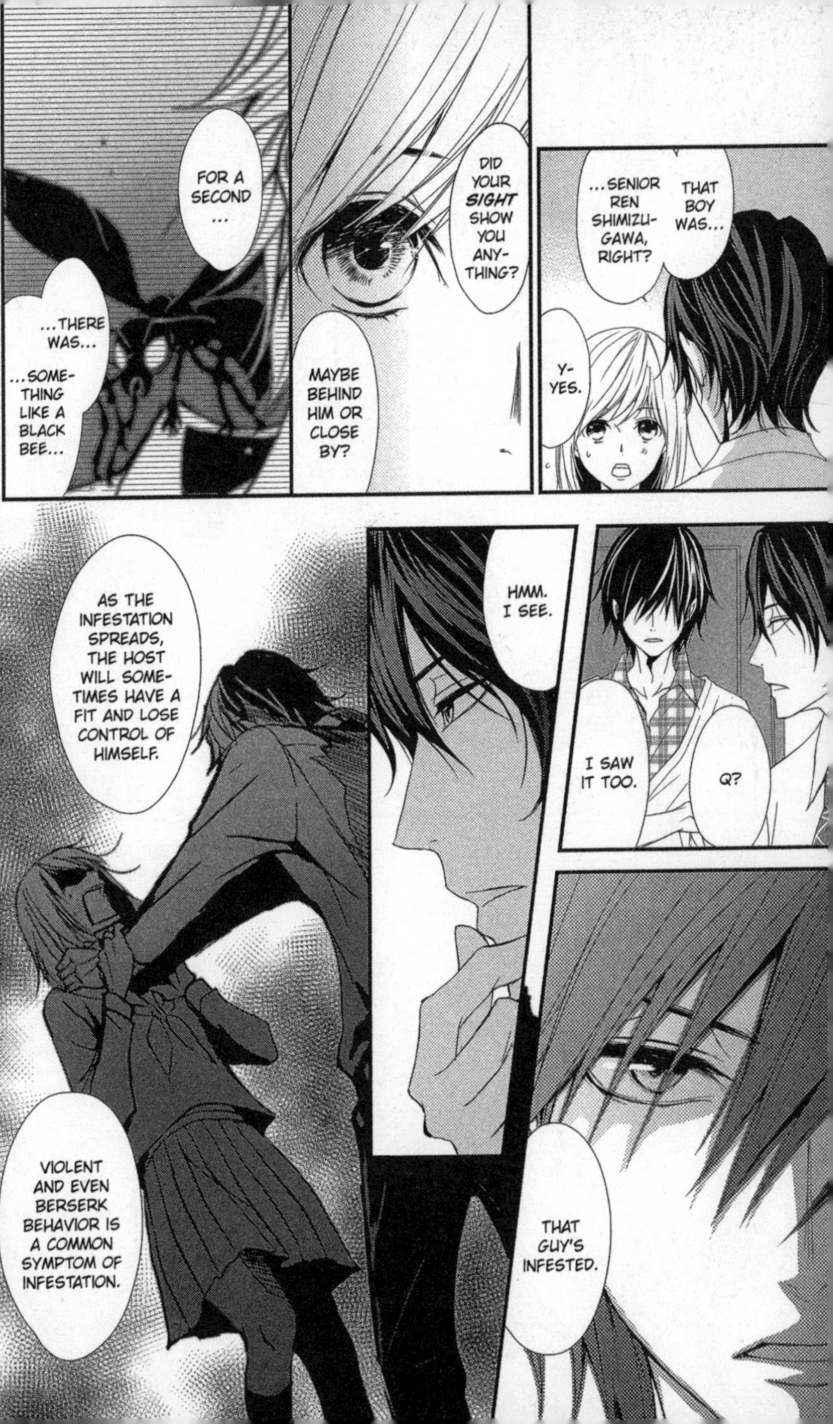
THAT BOY WAS...
...SENIOR REN SHIMIZU-GAWA, RIGHT?
Y-YES.
DID YOUR SIGHT SHOW YOU ANY-THING?
MAYBE BEHIND HIM OR CLOSE BY?
FOR A SECOND...
...THERE WAS...
...SOME-THING LIKE A BLACK BEE...
Q?
I SAW IT TOO.
THAT GUY'S INFESTED.
HMM. I SEE.
AS THE INFESTATION SPREADS, THE HOST WILL SOME-TIMES HAVE A FIT AND LOSE CONTROL OF HIMSELF.
VIOLENT AND EVEN BERSERK BEHAVIOR IS A COMMON SYMPTOM OF INFESTATION.

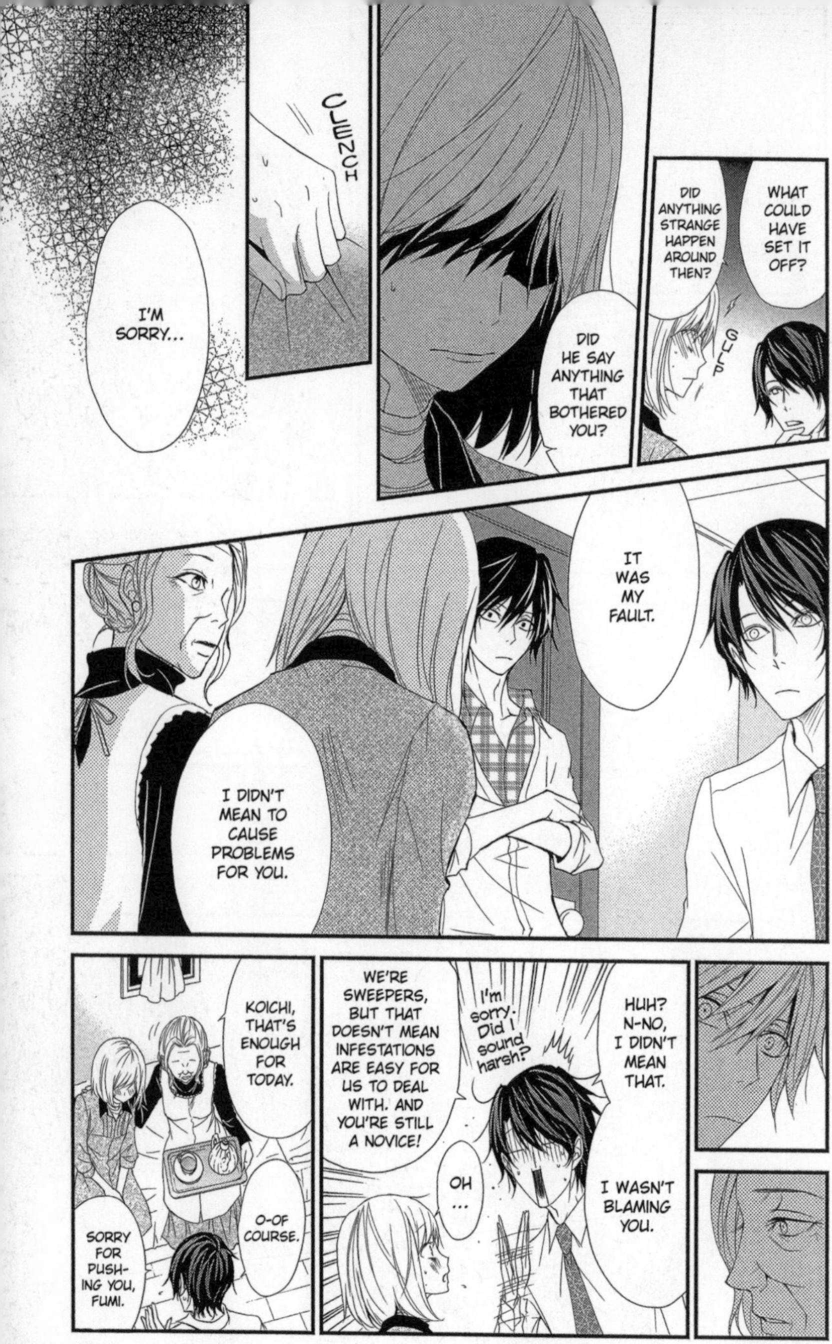
WHAT COULD HAVE SET IT OFF?
DID ANYTHING STRANGE HAPPEN AROUND THEN?
GULP
DID HE SAY ANYTHING THAT BOTHERED YOU?
CLENCH
I'M SORRY...
IT WAS MY FAULT.
I DIDN'T MEAN TO CAUSE PROBLEMS FOR YOU.
HUH? N-NO, I DIDN'T MEAN THAT.
I'm sorry. Did I sound harsh?
WE'RE SWEEPERS, BUT THAT DOESN'T MEAN INFESTATIONS ARE EASY FOR US TO DEAL WITH. AND YOU'RE STILL A NOVICE!
I WASN'T BLAMING YOU.
OH ...
KOICHI, THAT'S ENOUGH FOR TODAY.
O-OF COURSE.
SORRY FOR PUSHING YOU, FUMI.

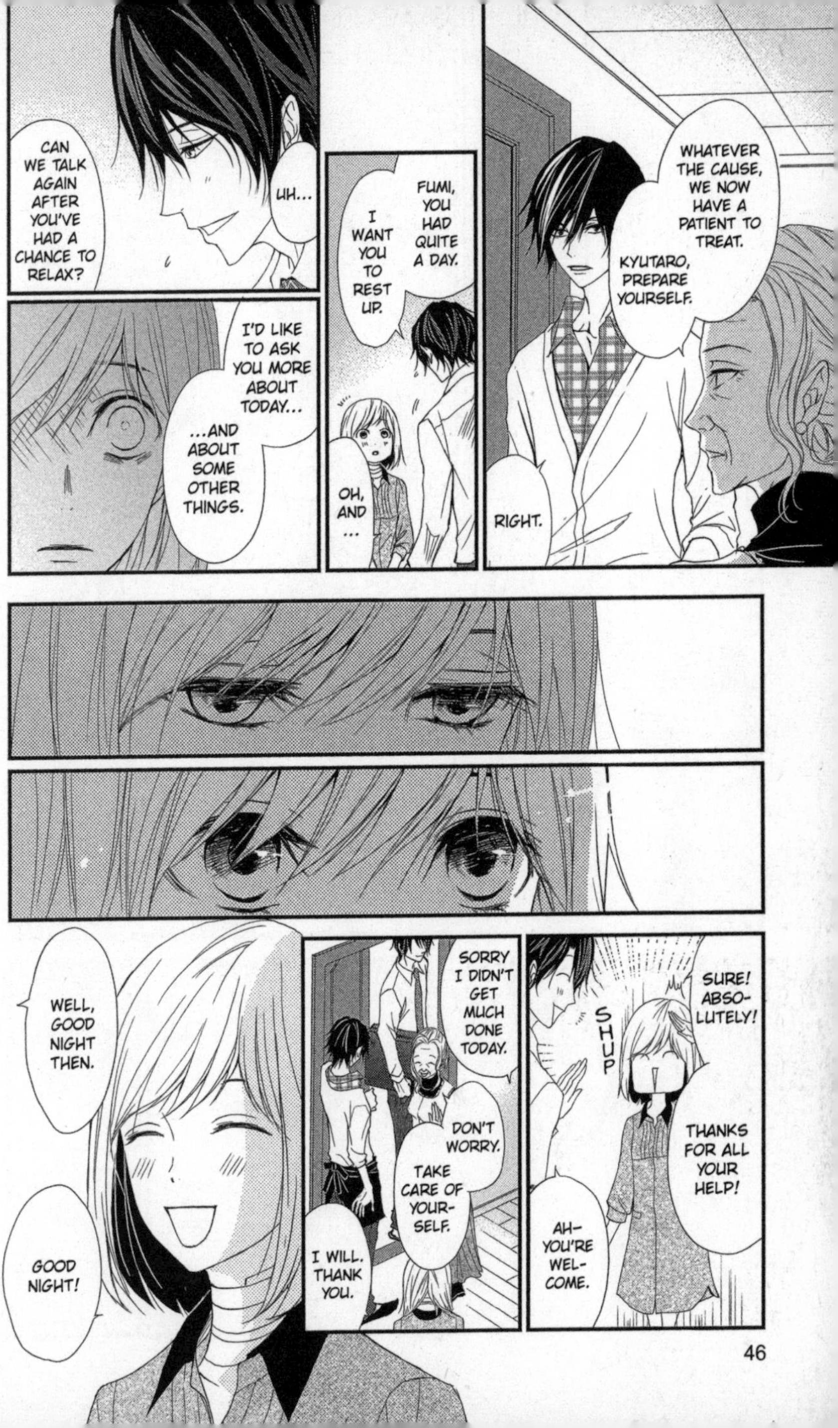
WHATEVER THE CAUSE, WE NOW HAVE A PATIENT TO TREAT.
KYUTARO, PREPARE YOURSELF.
RIGHT.
FUMI, YOU HAD QUITE A DAY.
I WANT YOU TO REST UP.
OH, AND ...
CAN WE TALK AGAIN AFTER YOU'VE HAD A CHANCE TO RELAX?
UH...
I'D LIKE TO ASK YOU MORE ABOUT TODAY...
...AND ABOUT SOME OTHER THINGS.
SURE! ABSO-LUTELY!
SHUP
THANKS FOR ALL YOUR HELP!
AH— YOU'RE WEL-COME.
SORRY I DIDN'T GET MUCH DONE TODAY.
DON'T WORRY.
TAKE CARE OF YOUR-SELF.
I WILL. THANK YOU.
WELL, GOOD NIGHT THEN.
GOOD NIGHT!

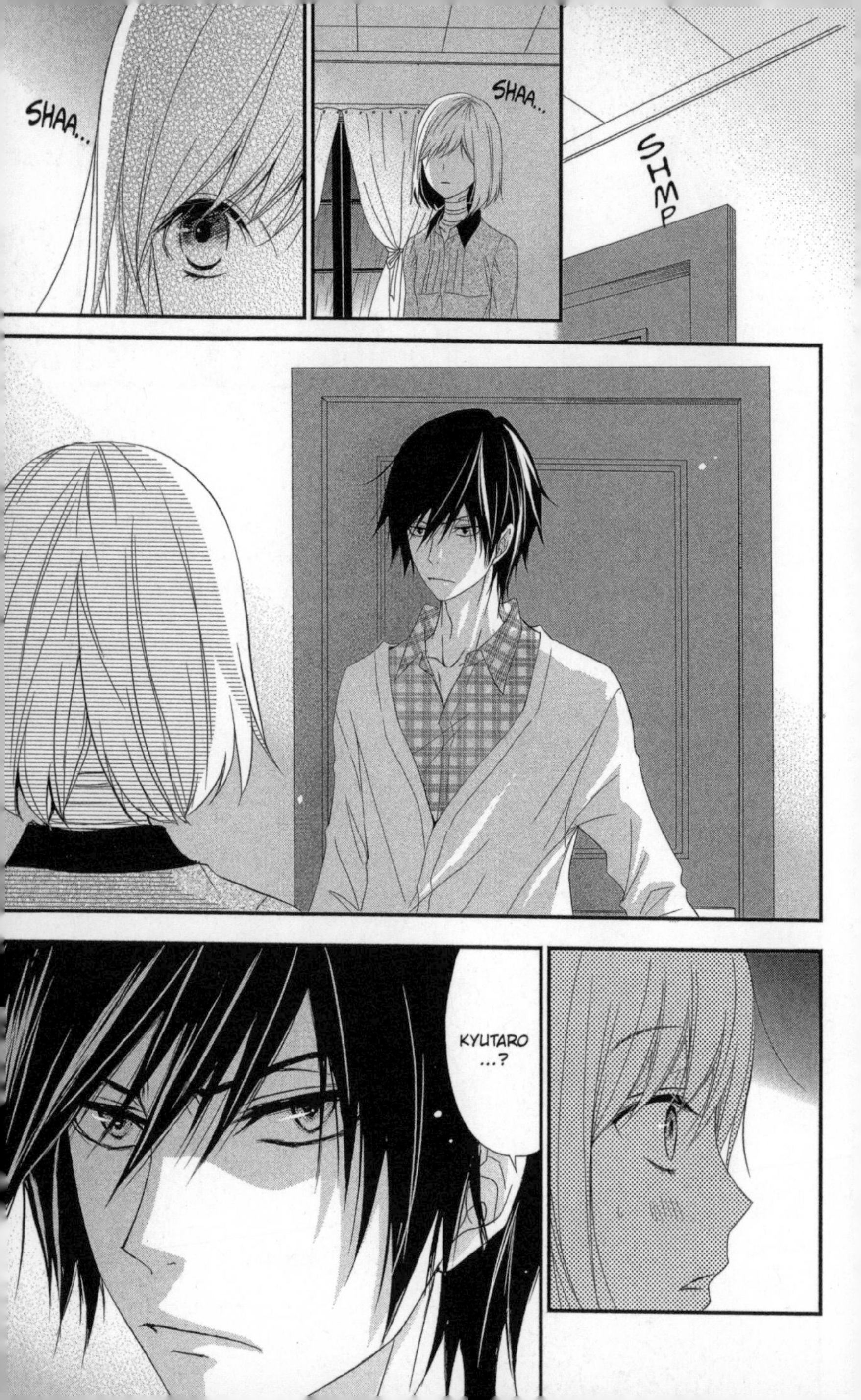
SHMP
SHAA...
SHAA...
KYUTARO ...?

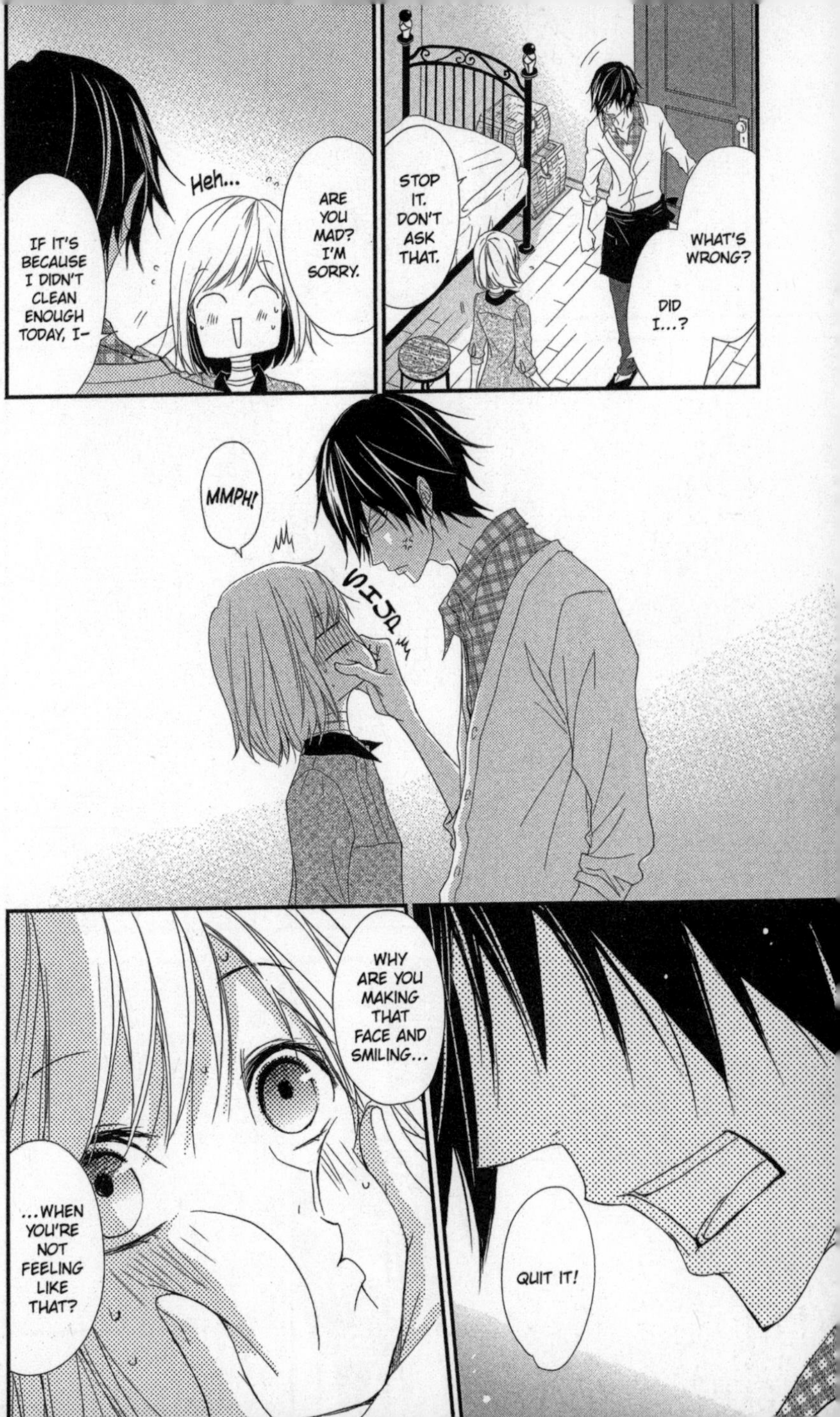
WHAT'S WRONG?
DID I...?
STOP IT. DON'T ASK THAT.
ARE YOU MAD? I'M SORRY.
Heh...
IF IT'S BECAUSE I DIDN'T CLEAN ENOUGH TODAY, I-
MMPH!
WHY ARE YOU MAKING THAT FACE AND SMILING...
...WHEN YOU'RE NOT FEELING LIKE THAT?
QUIT IT!

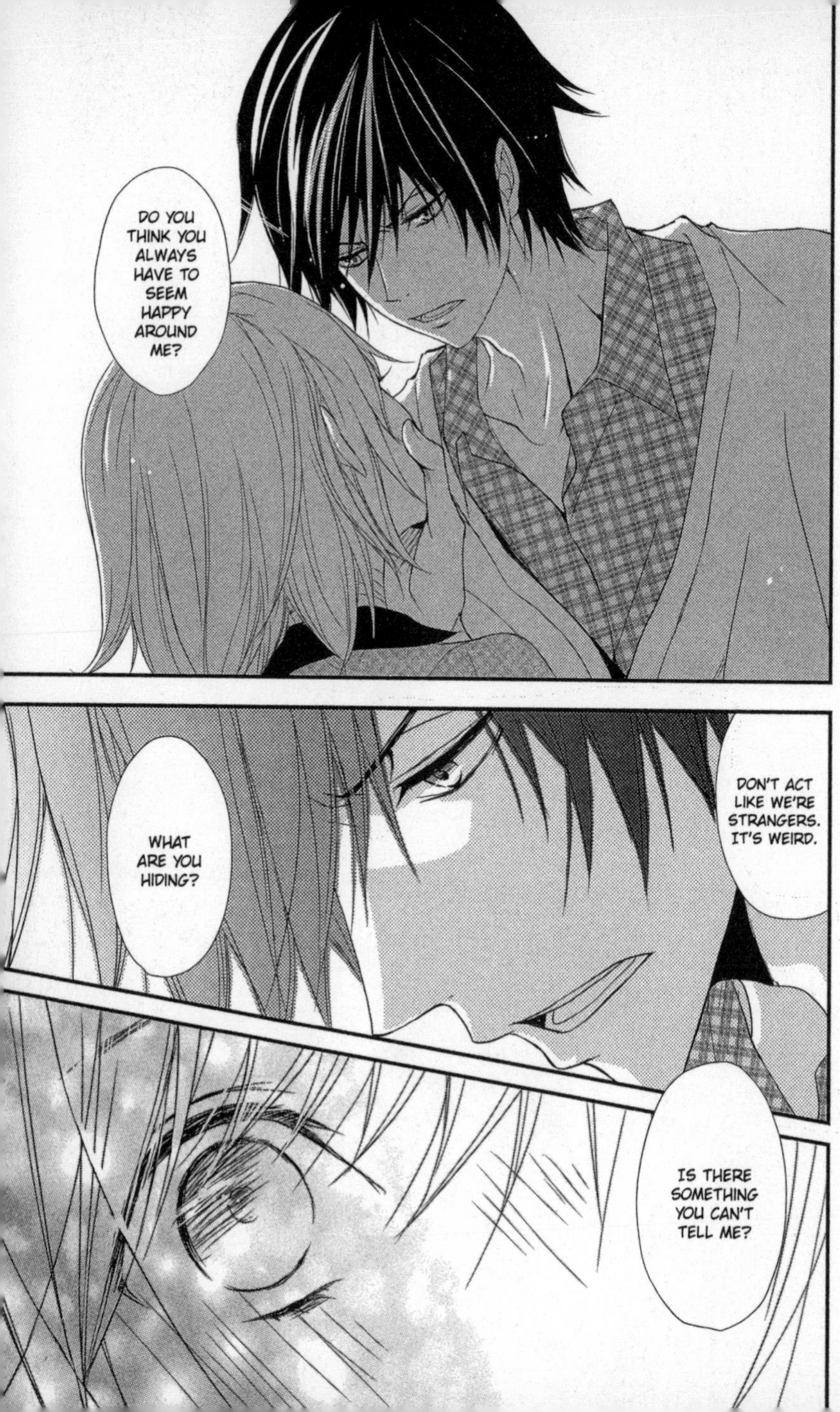
DO YOU THINK YOU ALWAYS HAVE TO SEEM HAPPY AROUND ME?
DON'T ACT LIKE WE'RE STRANGERS. IT'S WEIRD.
WHAT ARE YOU HIDING?
IS THERE SOMETHING YOU CAN'T TELL ME?

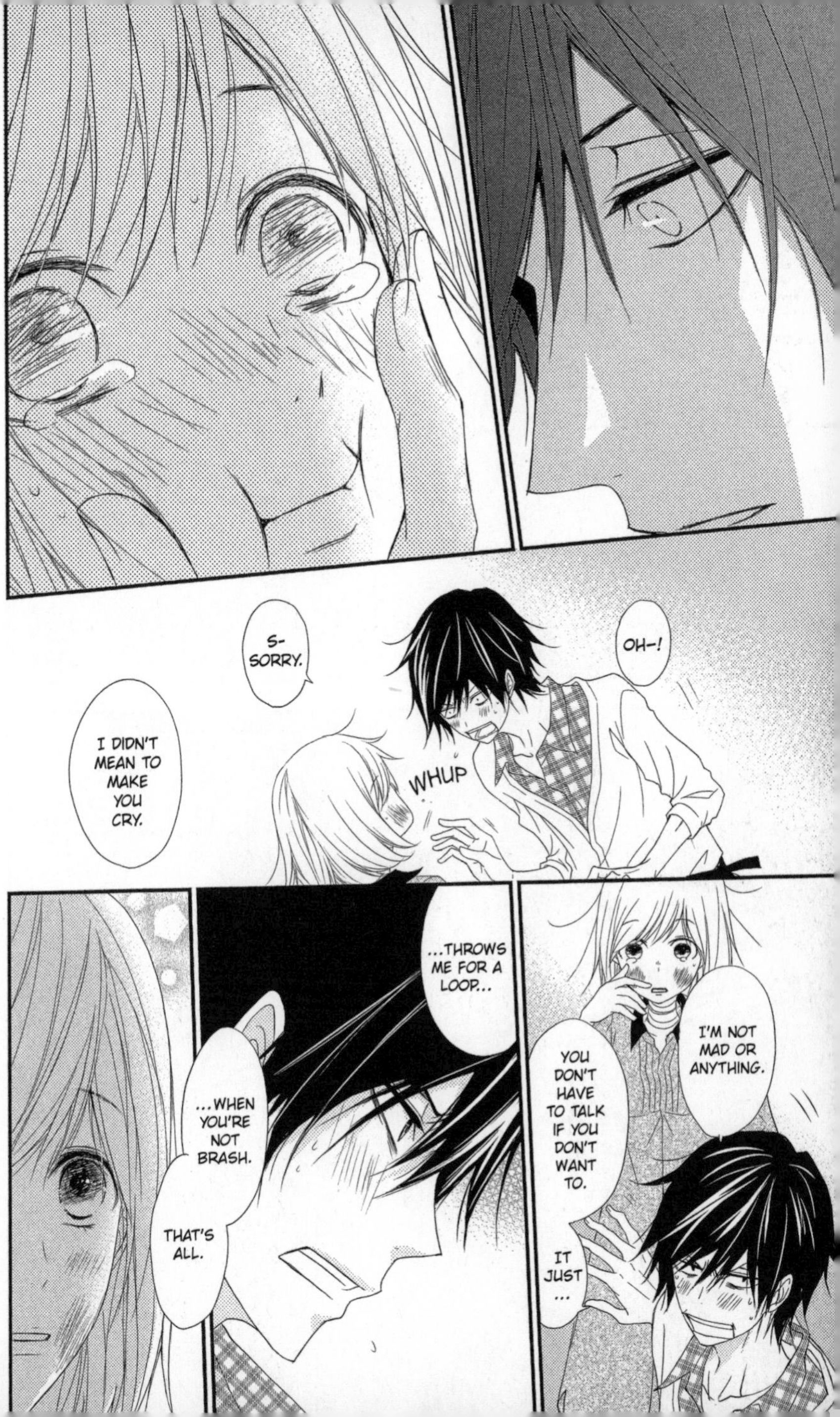
OH–!
WHUP
S-SORRY.
I DIDN'T MEAN TO MAKE YOU CRY.
I'M NOT MAD OR ANYTHING.
YOU DON'T HAVE TO TALK IF YOU DON'T WANT TO.
IT JUST ...
...THROWS ME FOR A LOOP...
...WHEN YOU'RE NOT BRASH.
THAT'S ALL.

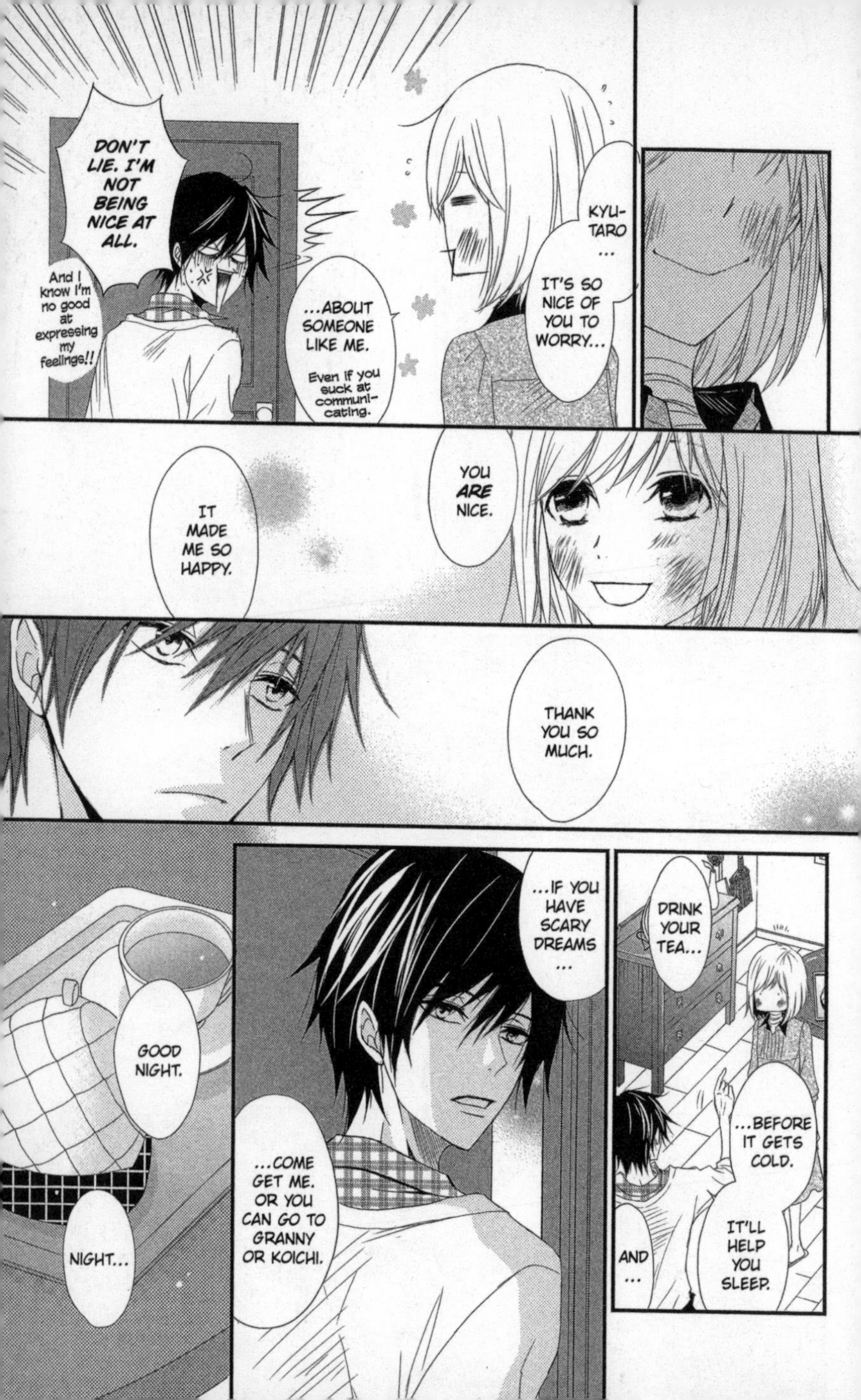
KYU-TARO...
IT'S SO NICE OF YOU TO WORRY...
...ABOUT SOMEONE LIKE ME.
Even if you suck at communicating.
DON'T LIE. I'M NOT BEING NICE AT ALL.
And I know I'm no good at expressing my feelings!!
YOU *ARE* NICE.
IT MADE ME SO HAPPY.
THANK YOU SO MUCH.
DRINK YOUR TEA...
...BEFORE IT GETS COLD.
IT'LL HELP YOU SLEEP.
AND...
...IF YOU HAVE SCARY DREAMS...
...COME GET ME. OR YOU CAN GO TO GRANNY OR KOICHI.
GOOD NIGHT.
NIGHT...

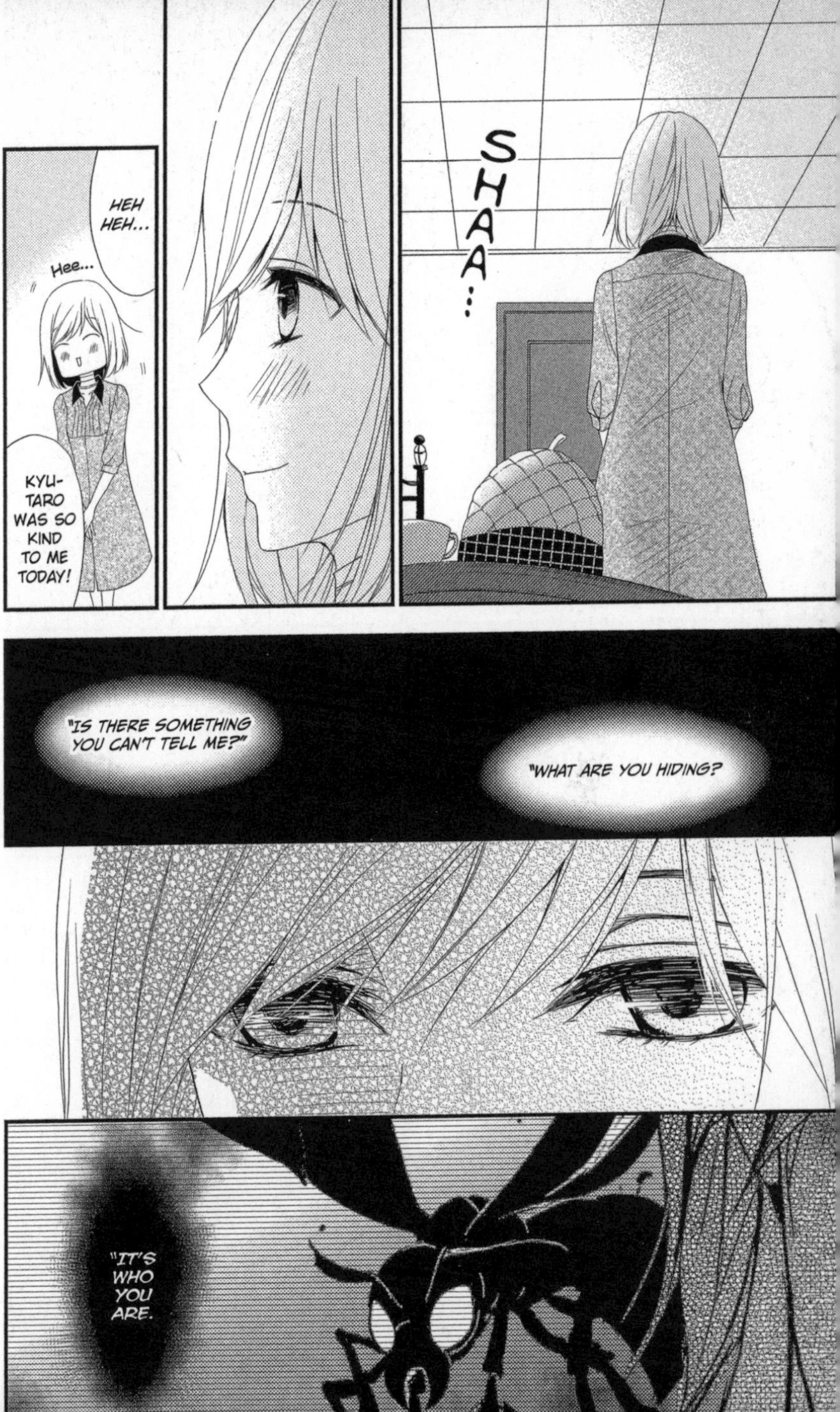
SHAA...
HEH HEH...
Hee...
KYU-TARO WAS SO KIND TO ME TODAY!
"WHAT ARE YOU HIDING?
"IS THERE SOMETHING YOU CAN'T TELL ME?"
"IT'S WHO YOU ARE.

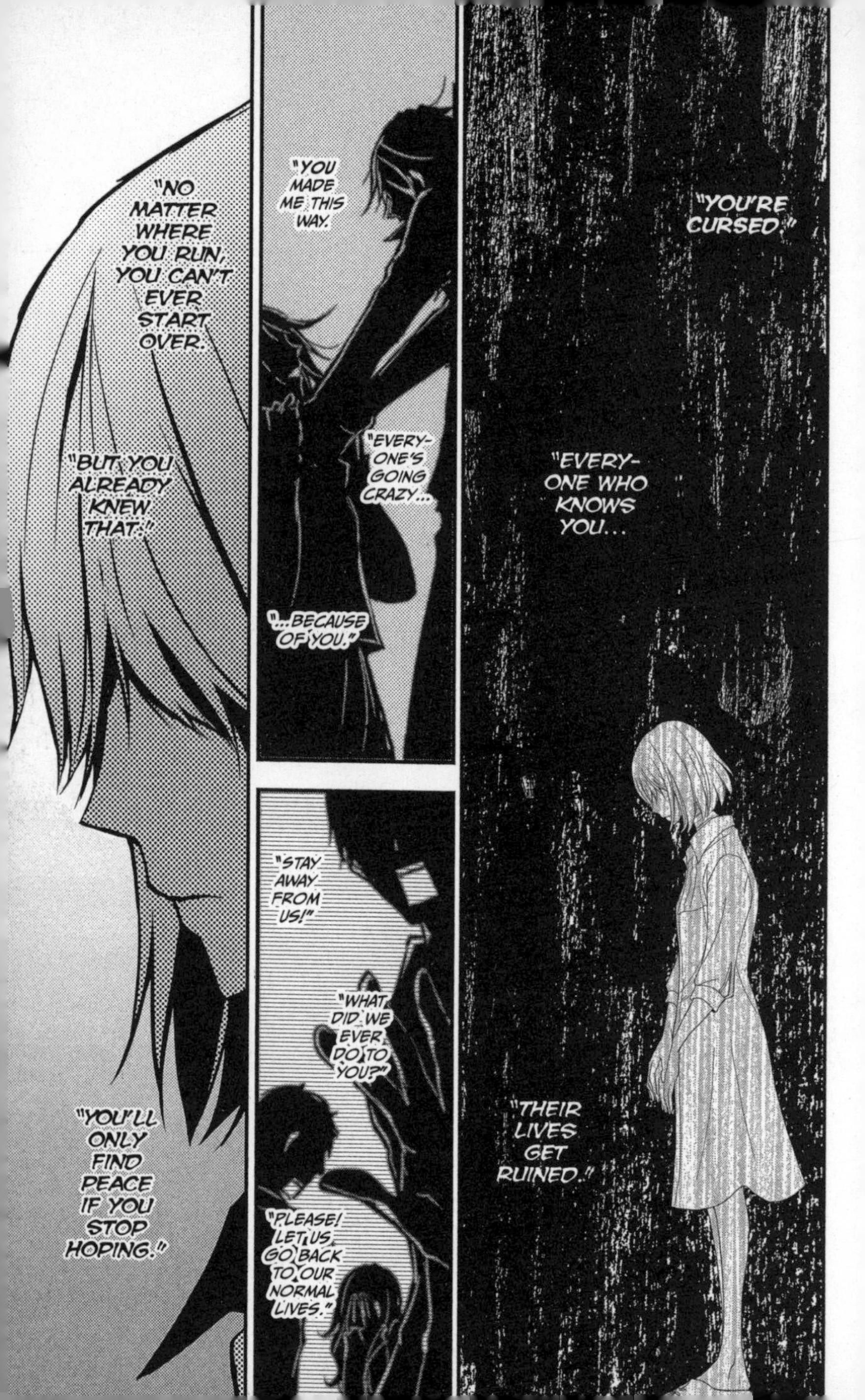
"YOU'RE CURSED."
"EVERY-ONE WHO KNOWS YOU...
"THEIR LIVES GET RUINED."
"YOU MADE ME THIS WAY.
"EVERY-ONE'S GOING CRAZY...
"...BECAUSE OF YOU."
"STAY AWAY FROM US!"
"WHAT DID WE EVER DO TO YOU?"
"PLEASE! LET US GO BACK TO OUR NORMAL LIVES."
"NO MATTER WHERE YOU RUN, YOU CAN'T EVER START OVER.
"BUT YOU ALREADY KNEW THAT."
"YOU'LL ONLY FIND PEACE IF YOU STOP HOPING."

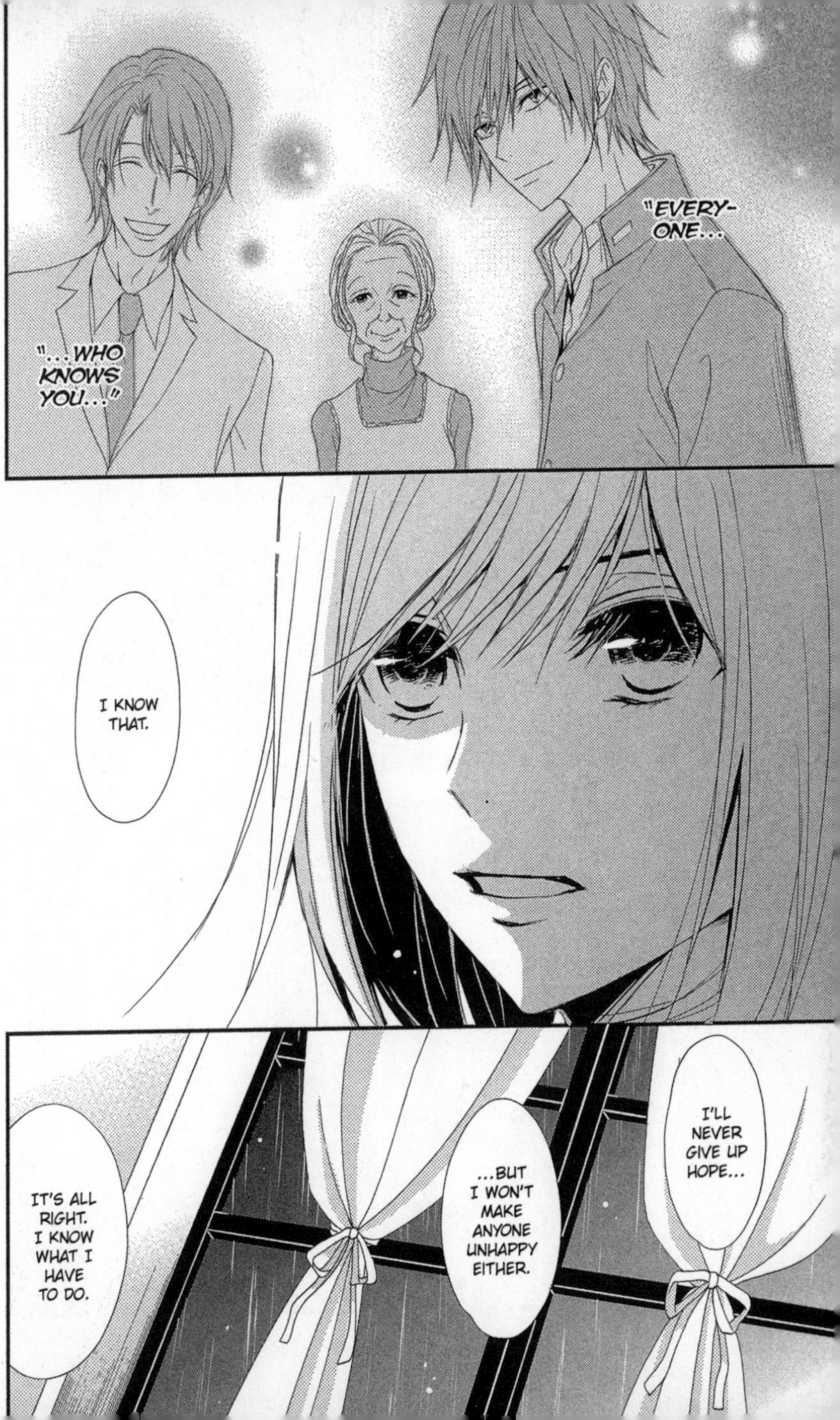
"EVERY-ONE...
"...WHO KNOWS YOU..."
I KNOW THAT.
I'LL NEVER GIVE UP HOPE...
...BUT I WON'T MAKE ANYONE UNHAPPY EITHER.
IT'S ALL RIGHT. I KNOW WHAT I HAVE TO DO.

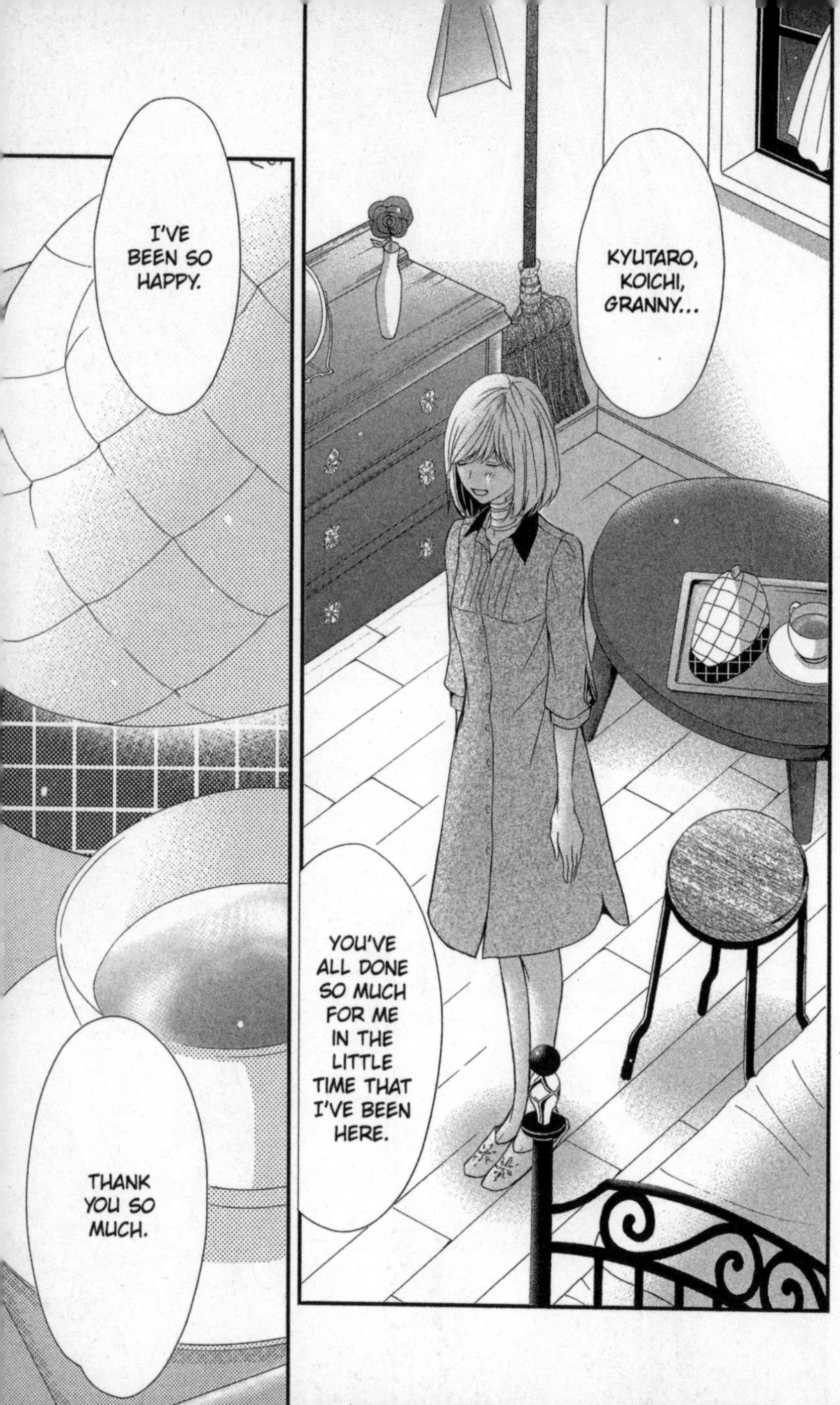
KYUTARO, KOICHI, GRANNY...
YOU'VE ALL DONE SO MUCH FOR ME IN THE LITTLE TIME THAT I'VE BEEN HERE.
I'VE BEEN SO HAPPY.
THANK YOU SO MUCH.

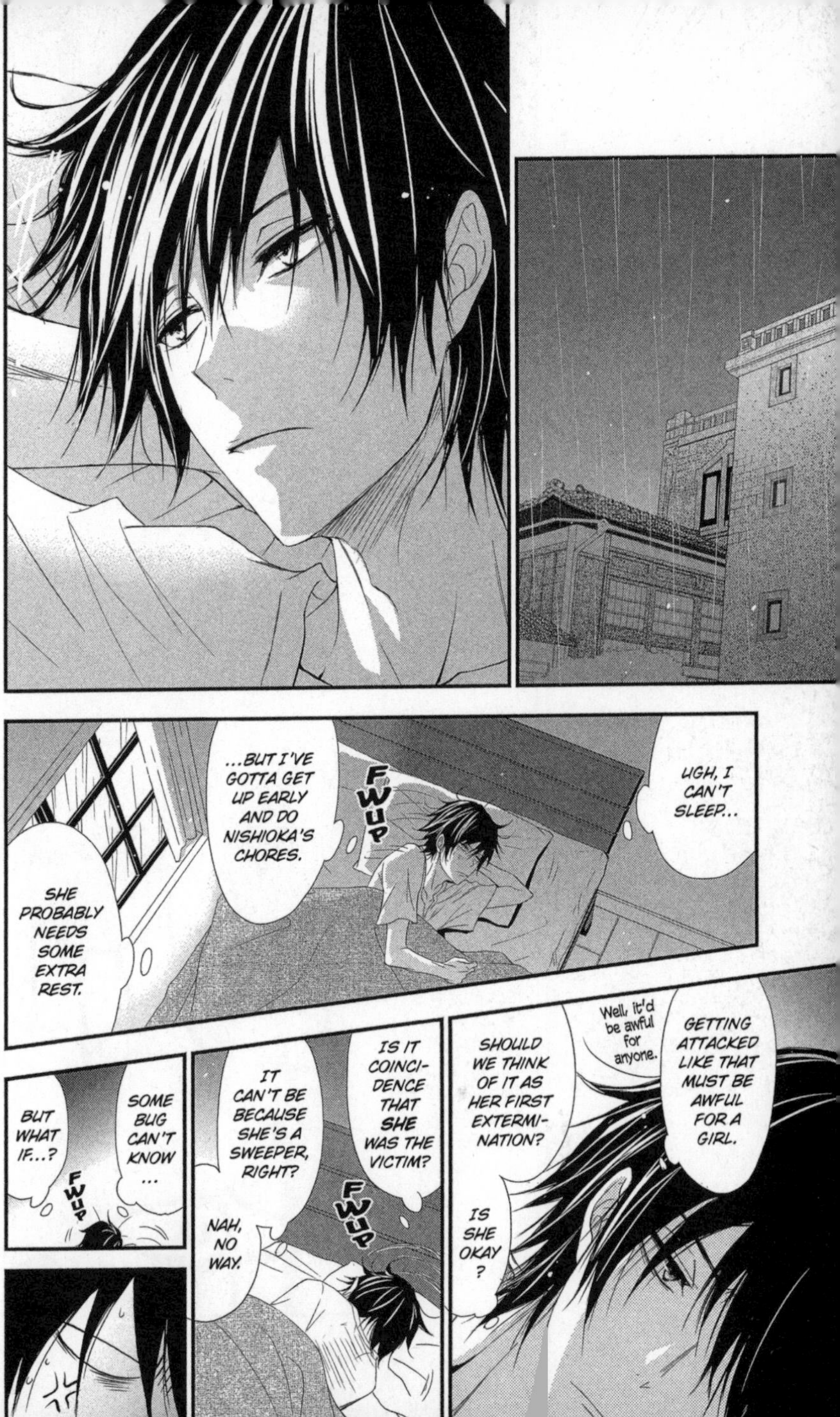
UGH, I CAN'T SLEEP...
...BUT I'VE GOTTA GET UP EARLY AND DO NISHIOKA'S CHORES.
FWUP
SHE PROBABLY NEEDS SOME EXTRA REST.
GETTING ATTACKED LIKE THAT MUST BE AWFUL FOR A GIRL.
Well, it'd be awful for anyone.
SHOULD WE THINK OF IT AS HER FIRST EXTERMINATION?
IS SHE OKAY?
IS IT COINCIDENCE THAT SHE WAS THE VICTIM?
IT CAN'T BE BECAUSE SHE'S A SWEEPER, RIGHT?
FWUP
NAH, NO WAY.
SOME BUG CAN'T KNOW...
BUT WHAT IF...?
FWUP

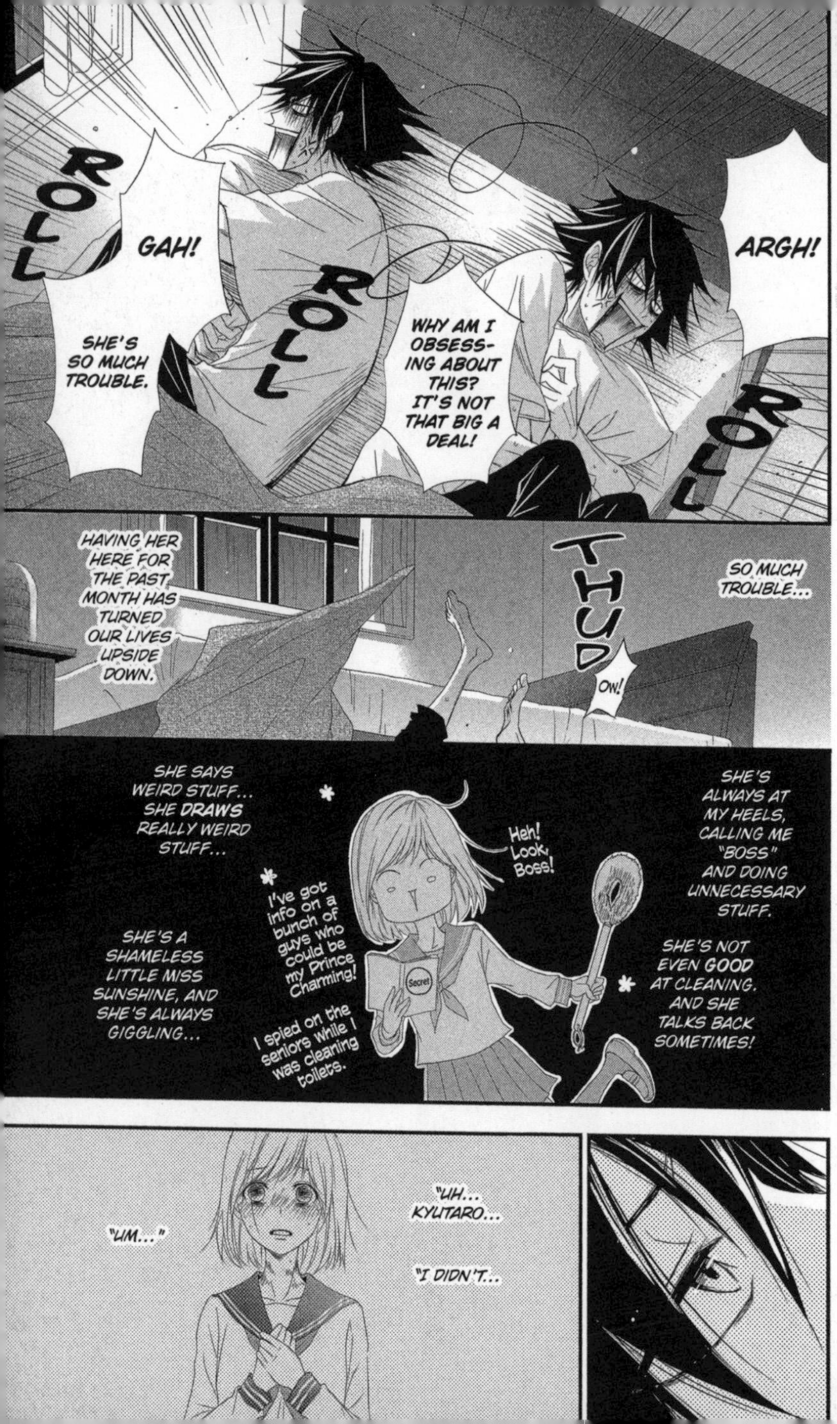
ARGH!
ROLL
WHY AM I OBSESS-ING ABOUT THIS? IT'S NOT THAT BIG A DEAL!
ROLL
GAH!
ROLL
SHE'S SO MUCH TROUBLE.
SO MUCH TROUBLE...
THUD
OW!
HAVING HER HERE FOR THE PAST MONTH HAS TURNED OUR LIVES UPSIDE DOWN.
SHE'S ALWAYS AT MY HEELS, CALLING ME "BOSS" AND DOING UNNECESSARY STUFF.
SHE'S NOT EVEN GOOD AT CLEANING. AND SHE TALKS BACK SOMETIMES!
Heh! Look, Boss!
I've got info on a bunch of guys who could be my Prince Charming!
Secret
I spied on the seniors while I was cleaning toilets.
SHE SAYS WEIRD STUFF... SHE DRAWS REALLY WEIRD STUFF...
SHE'S A SHAMELESS LITTLE MISS SUNSHINE, AND SHE'S ALWAYS GIGGLING...
"UH... KYUTARO...
"I DIDN'T...
"UM..."

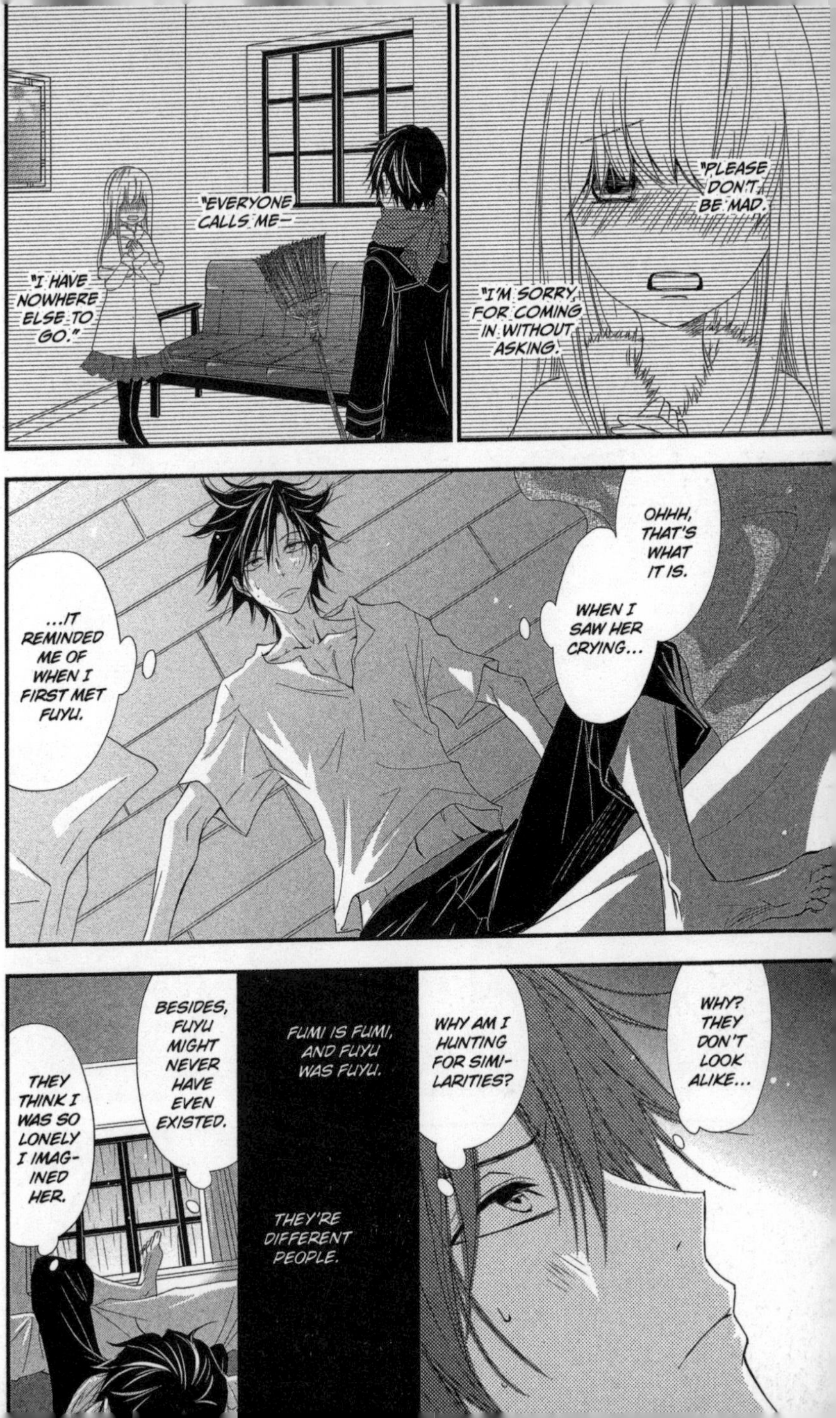
"PLEASE DON'T BE MAD.
"I'M SORRY FOR COMING IN WITHOUT ASKING.
"EVERYONE CALLS ME—
"I HAVE NOWHERE ELSE TO GO."
OHHH, THAT'S WHAT IT IS.
WHEN I SAW HER CRYING...
...IT REMINDED ME OF WHEN I FIRST MET FUYU.
WHY? THEY DON'T LOOK ALIKE...
WHY AM I HUNTING FOR SIMI-LARITIES?
FUMI IS FUMI, AND FUYU WAS FUYU.
THEY'RE DIFFERENT PEOPLE.
BESIDES, FUYU MIGHT NEVER HAVE EVEN EXISTED.
THEY THINK I WAS SO LONELY I IMAGINED HER.

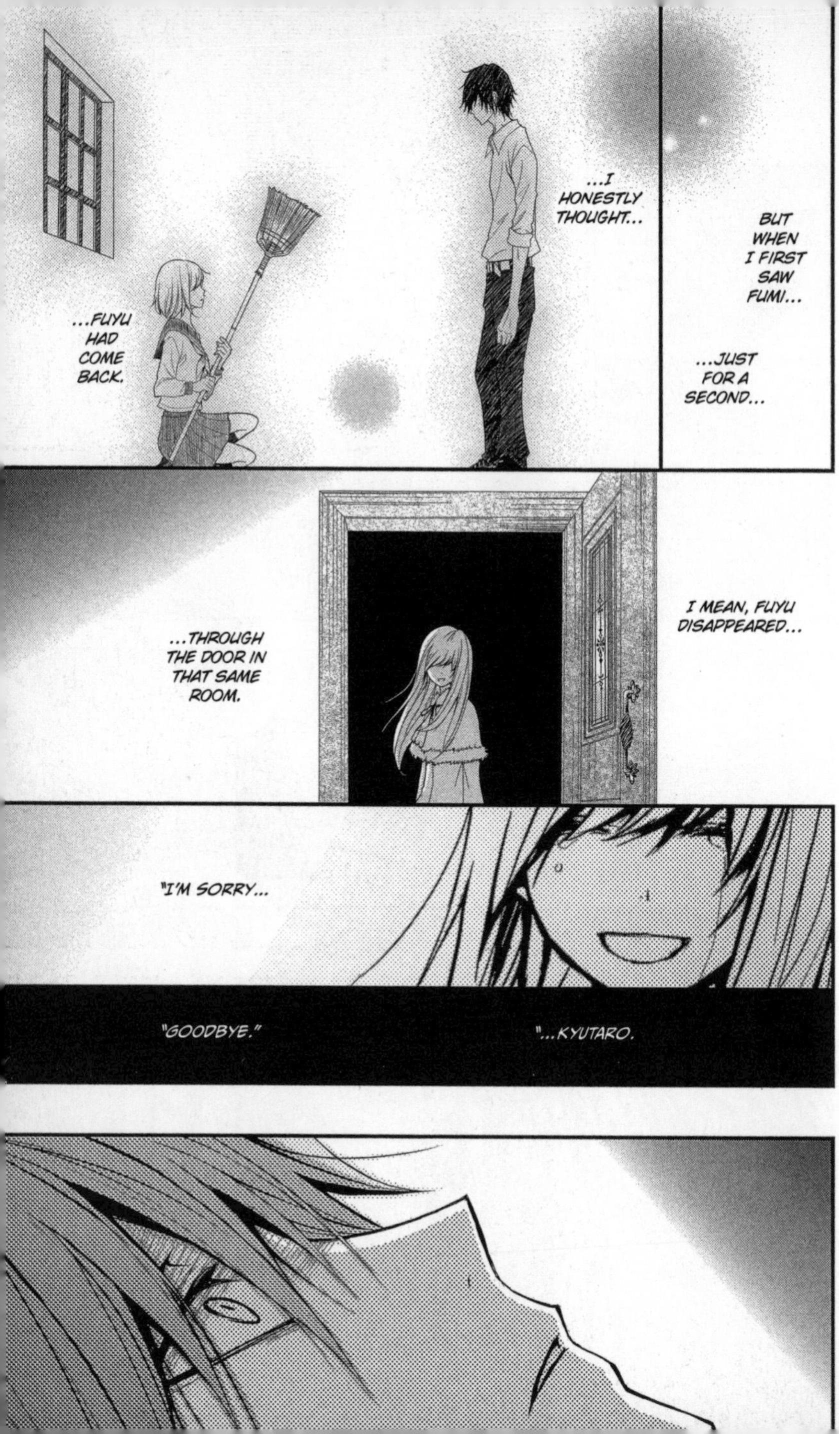
BUT WHEN I FIRST SAW FUMI...
...JUST FOR A SECOND...
...I HONESTLY THOUGHT...
...FUYU HAD COME BACK.
I MEAN, FUYU DISAPPEARED...
...THROUGH THE DOOR IN THAT SAME ROOM.
"I'M SORRY...
"...KYUTARO.
"GOODBYE."

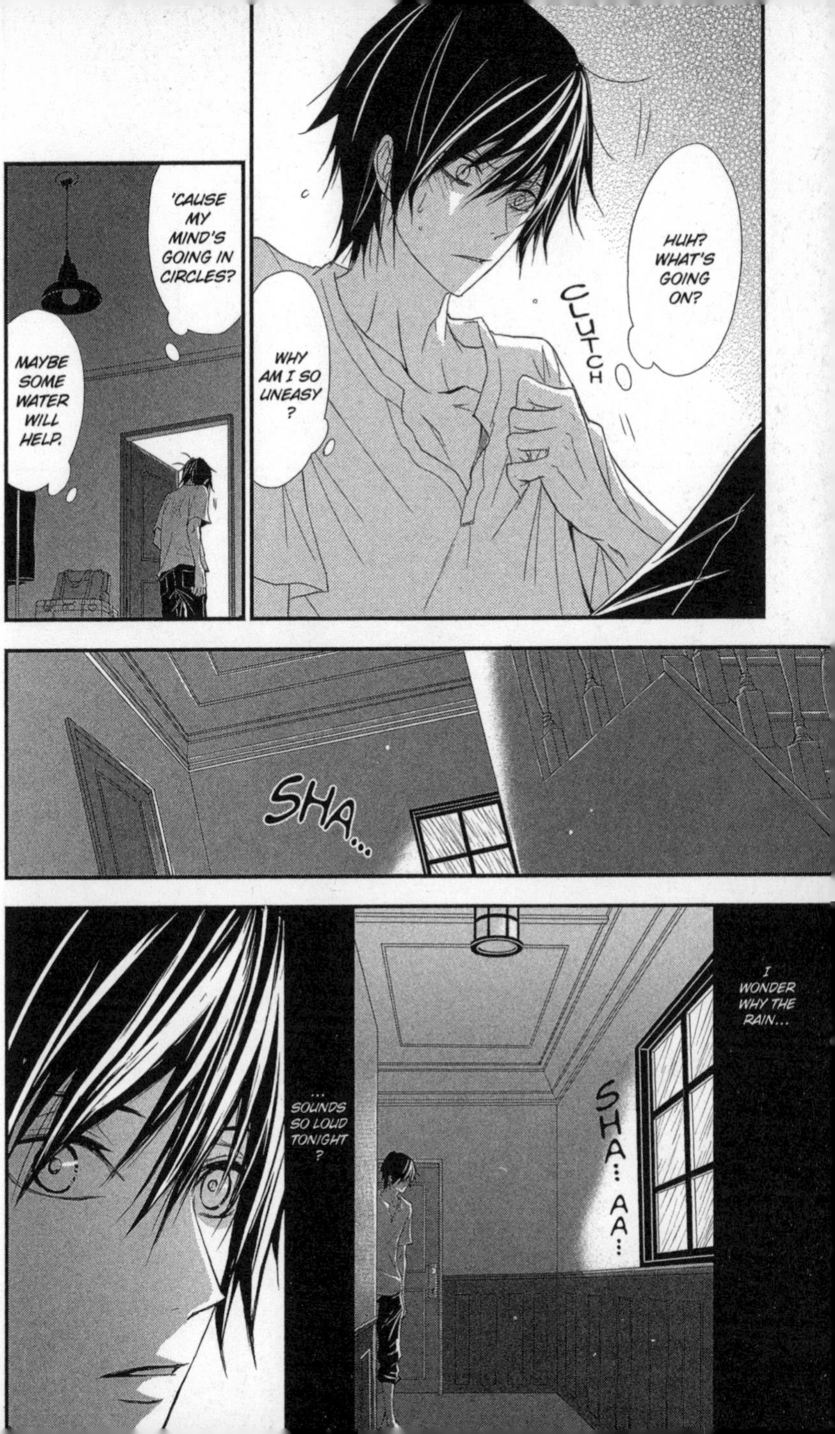
HUH? WHAT'S GOING ON?
CLUTCH
WHY AM I SO UNEASY?
'CAUSE MY MIND'S GOING IN CIRCLES?
MAYBE SOME WATER WILL HELP.
SHA...
I WONDER WHY THE RAIN...
SHA... AA...
...SOUNDS SO LOUD TONIGHT?

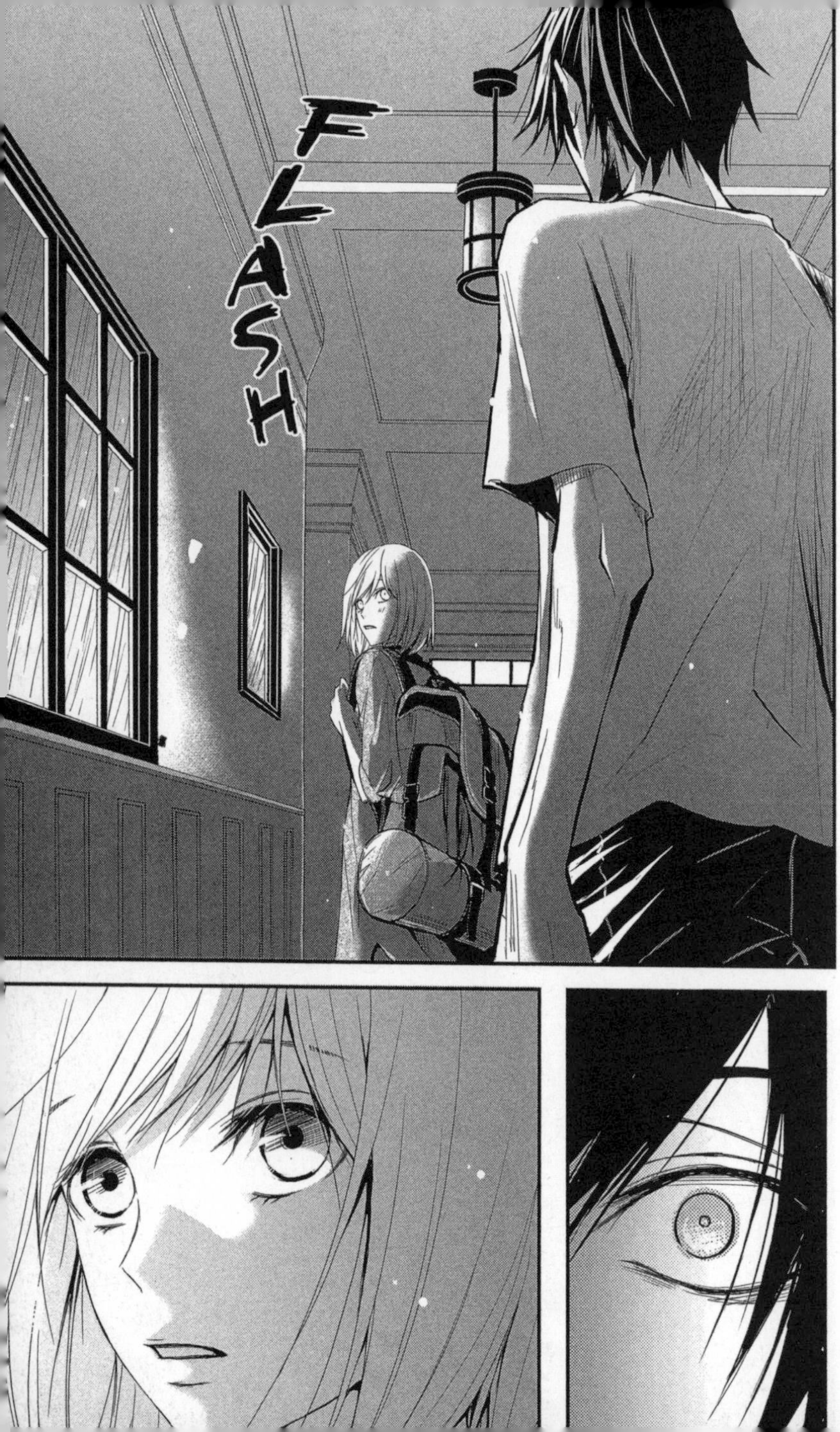
FLASH

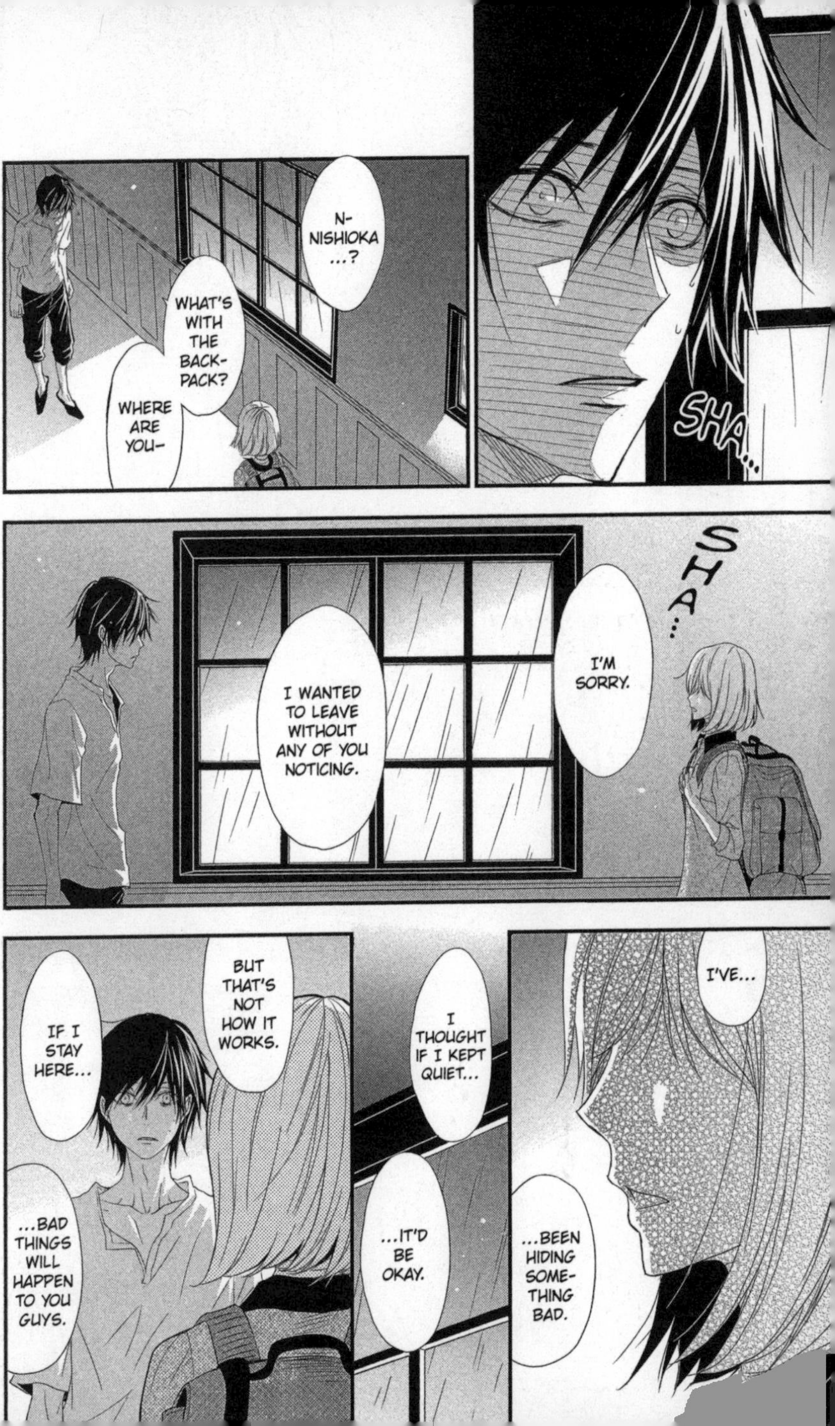
SHA...
N-NISHIOKA...?
WHAT'S WITH THE BACKPACK?
WHERE ARE YOU-
SHA...
I'M SORRY.
I WANTED TO LEAVE WITHOUT ANY OF YOU NOTICING.
I'VE...
...BEEN HIDING SOMETHING BAD.
I THOUGHT IF I KEPT QUIET...
...IT'D BE OKAY.
BUT THAT'S NOT HOW IT WORKS.
IF I STAY HERE...
...BAD THINGS WILL HAPPEN TO YOU GUYS.

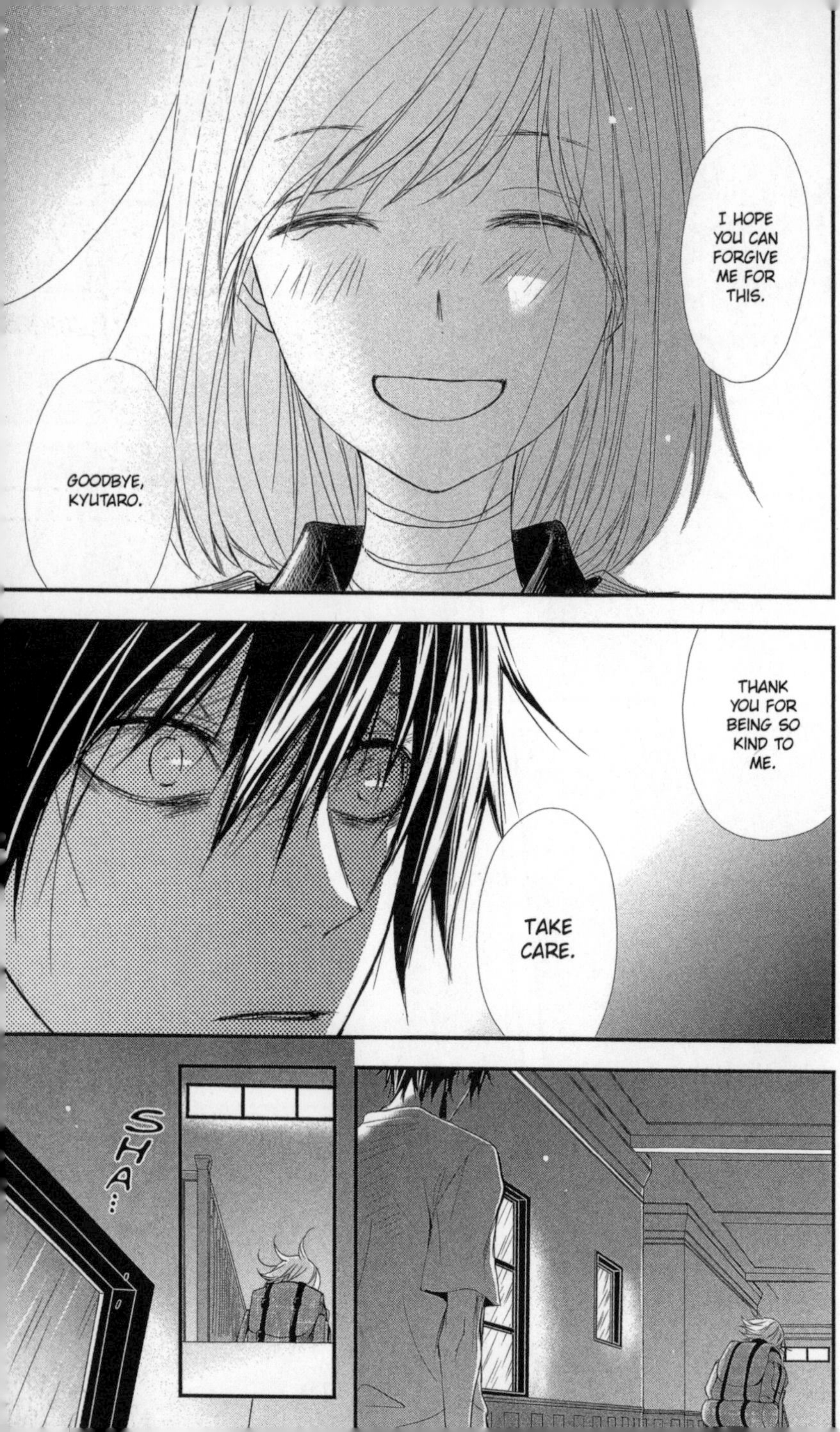
I HOPE YOU CAN FORGIVE ME FOR THIS.
GOODBYE, KYUTARO.
THANK YOU FOR BEING SO KIND TO ME.
TAKE CARE.
SHA...

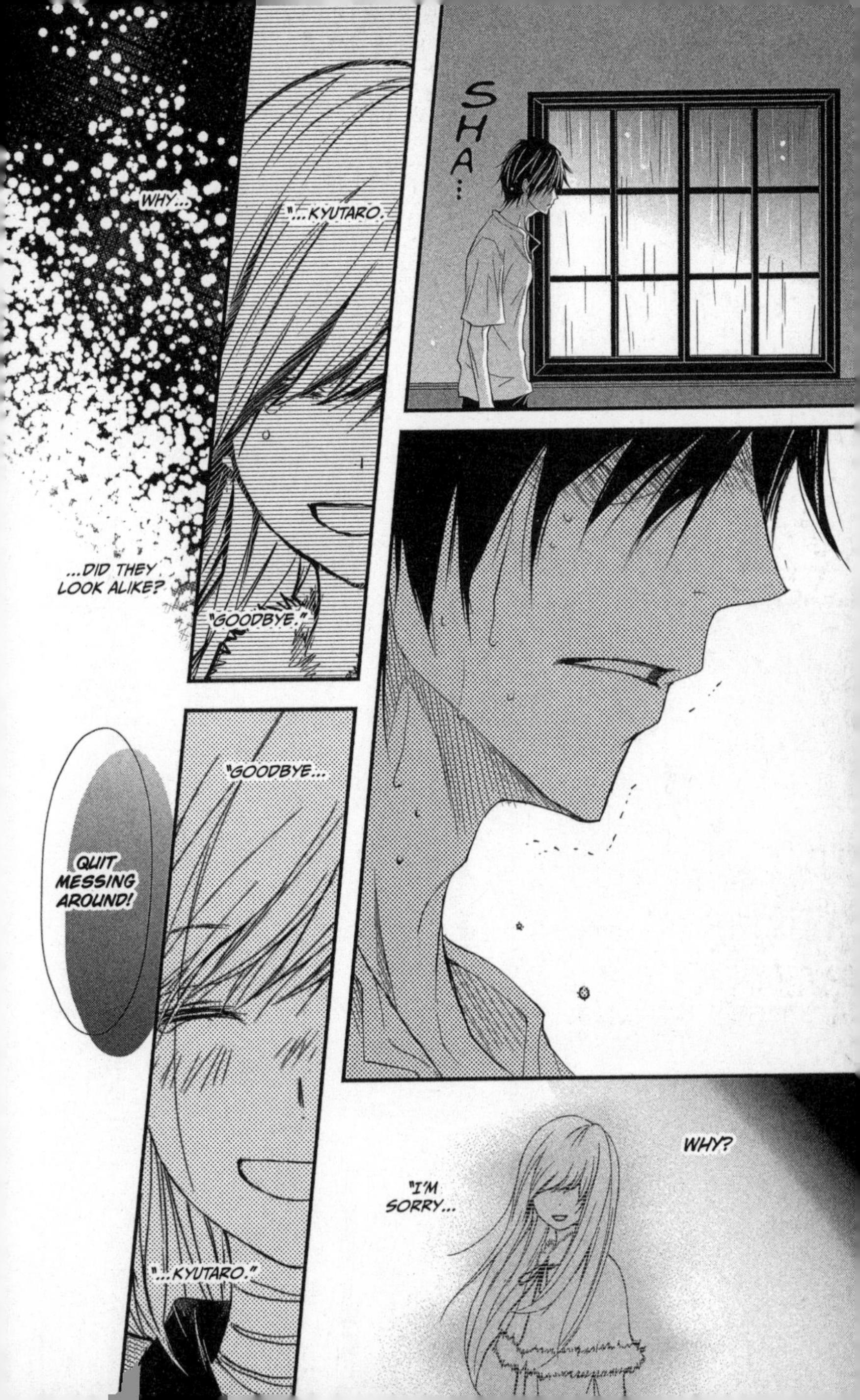
SHA...
"...KYUTARO.
"GOODBYE."
WHY...
...DID THEY LOOK ALIKE?
WHY?
"I'M SORRY...
"GOODBYE...
"...KYUTARO."
QUIT MESSING AROUND!

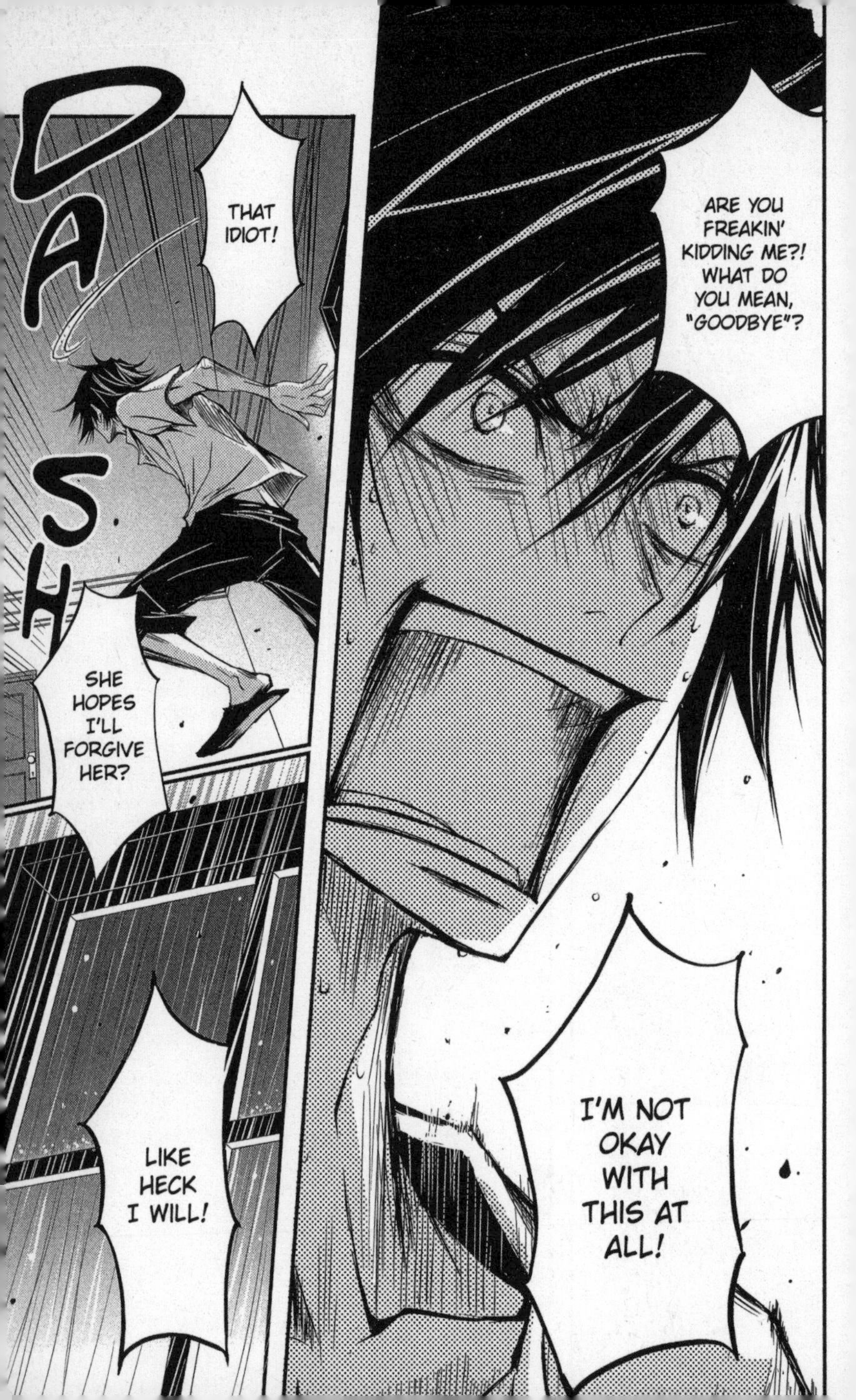
ARE YOU FREAKIN' KIDDING ME?! WHAT DO YOU MEAN, "GOODBYE"?
I'M NOT OKAY WITH THIS AT ALL!
THAT IDIOT!
DASH
SHE HOPES I'LL FORGIVE HER?
LIKE HECK I WILL!

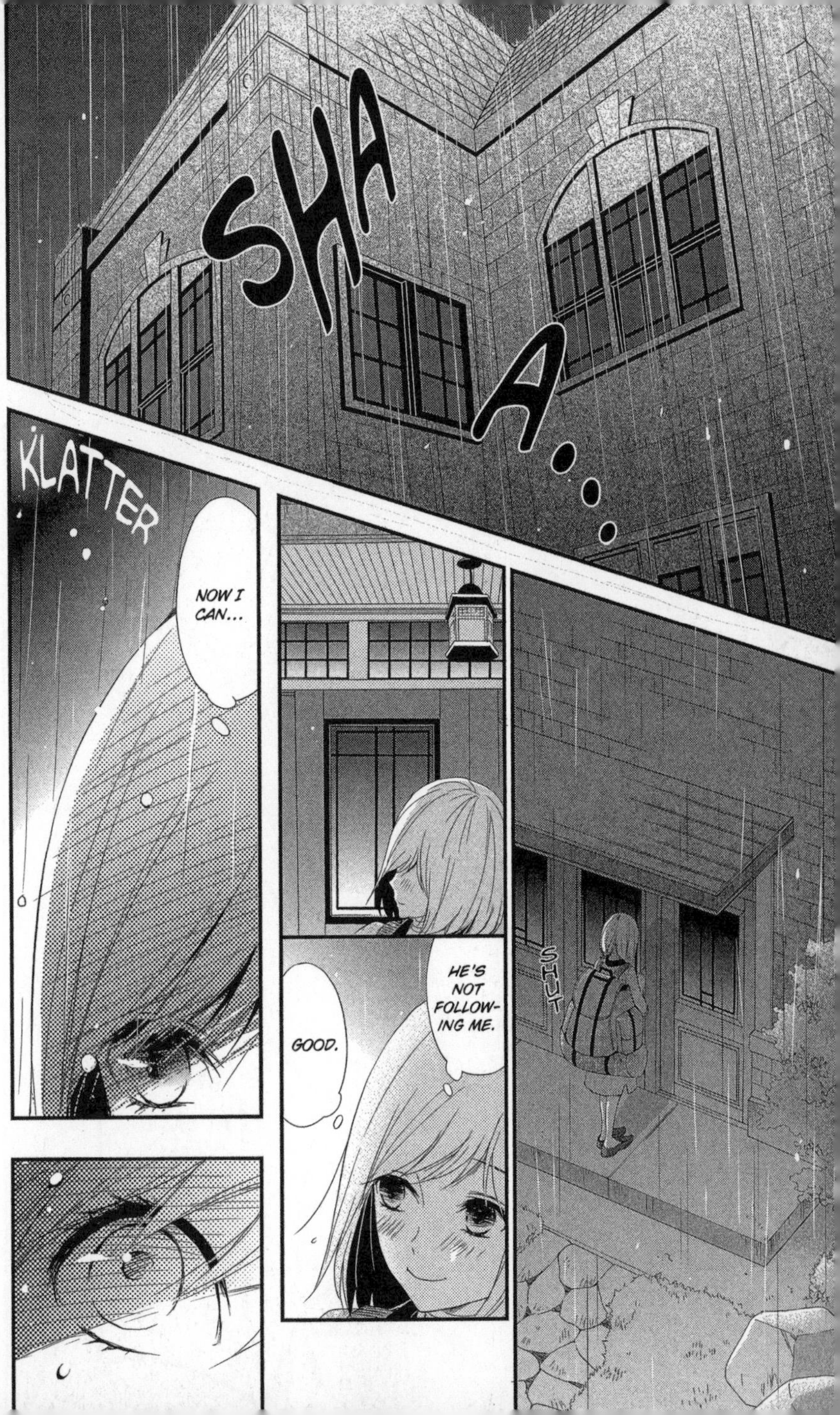
SHA
A...
SHUT
HE'S NOT FOLLOWING ME.
GOOD.
KLATTER
NOW I CAN...

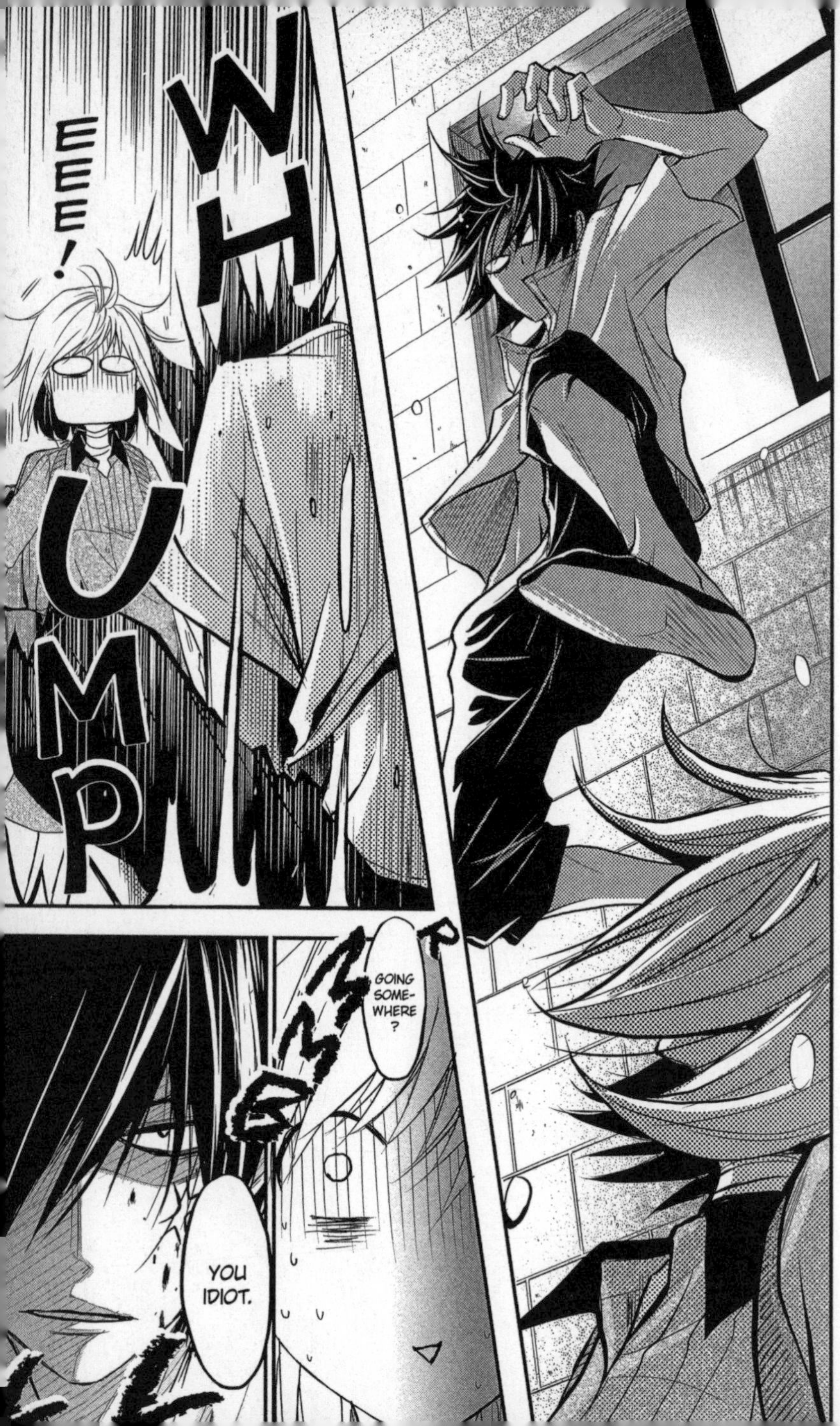
WHUMP
EEEE!
GOING SOME-WHERE?
YOU IDIOT.

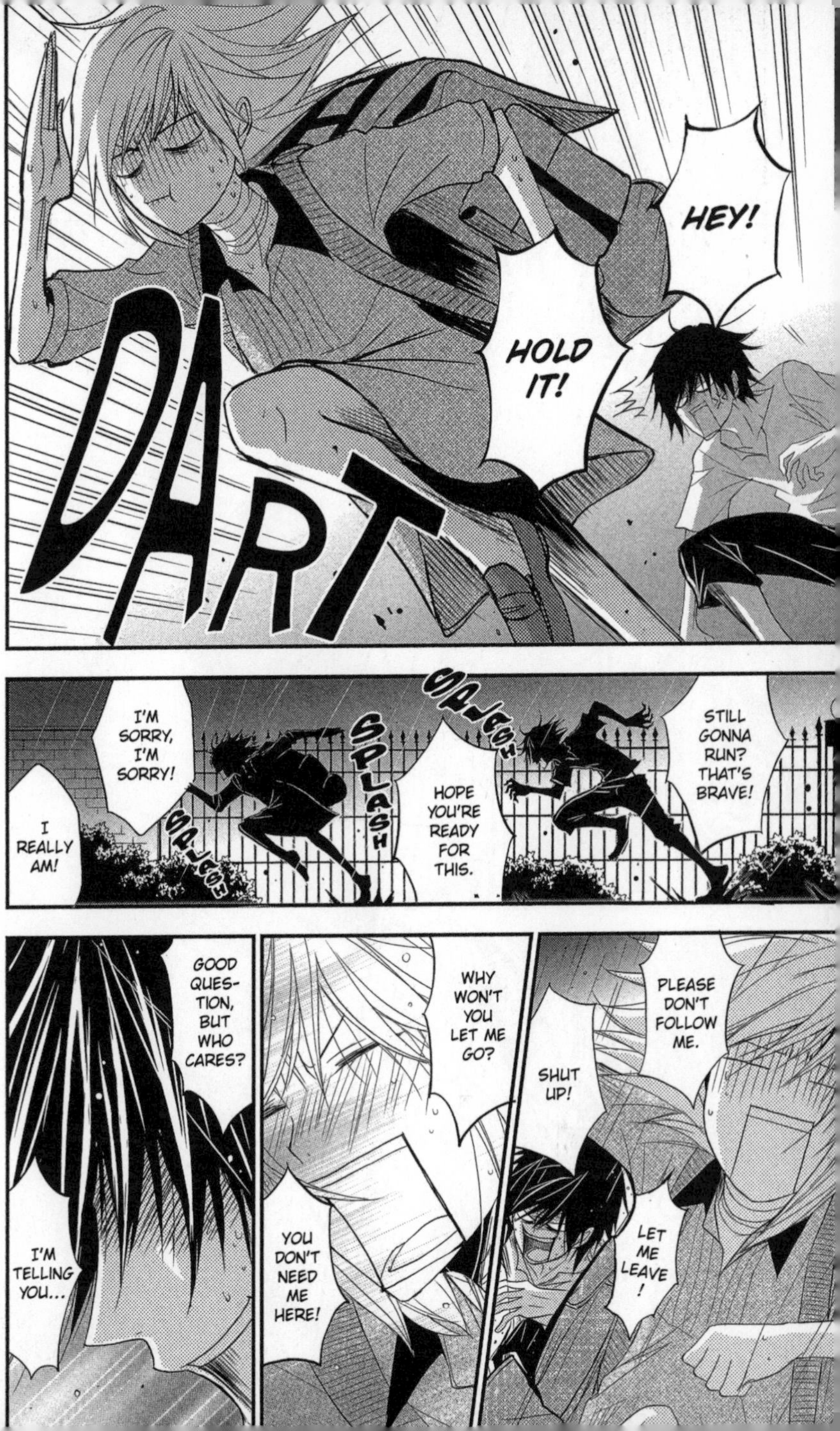

HEY!
HOLD IT!
DART
STILL GONNA RUN? THAT'S BRAVE!
SPLASH
HOPE YOU'RE READY FOR THIS.
SPLASH
I'M SORRY, I'M SORRY!
SPLASH
I REALLY AM!
PLEASE DON'T FOLLOW ME.
SHUT UP!
LET ME LEAVE!
WHY WON'T YOU LET ME GO?
YOU DON'T NEED ME HERE!
GOOD QUES-TION, BUT WHO CARES?
I'M TELLING YOU...

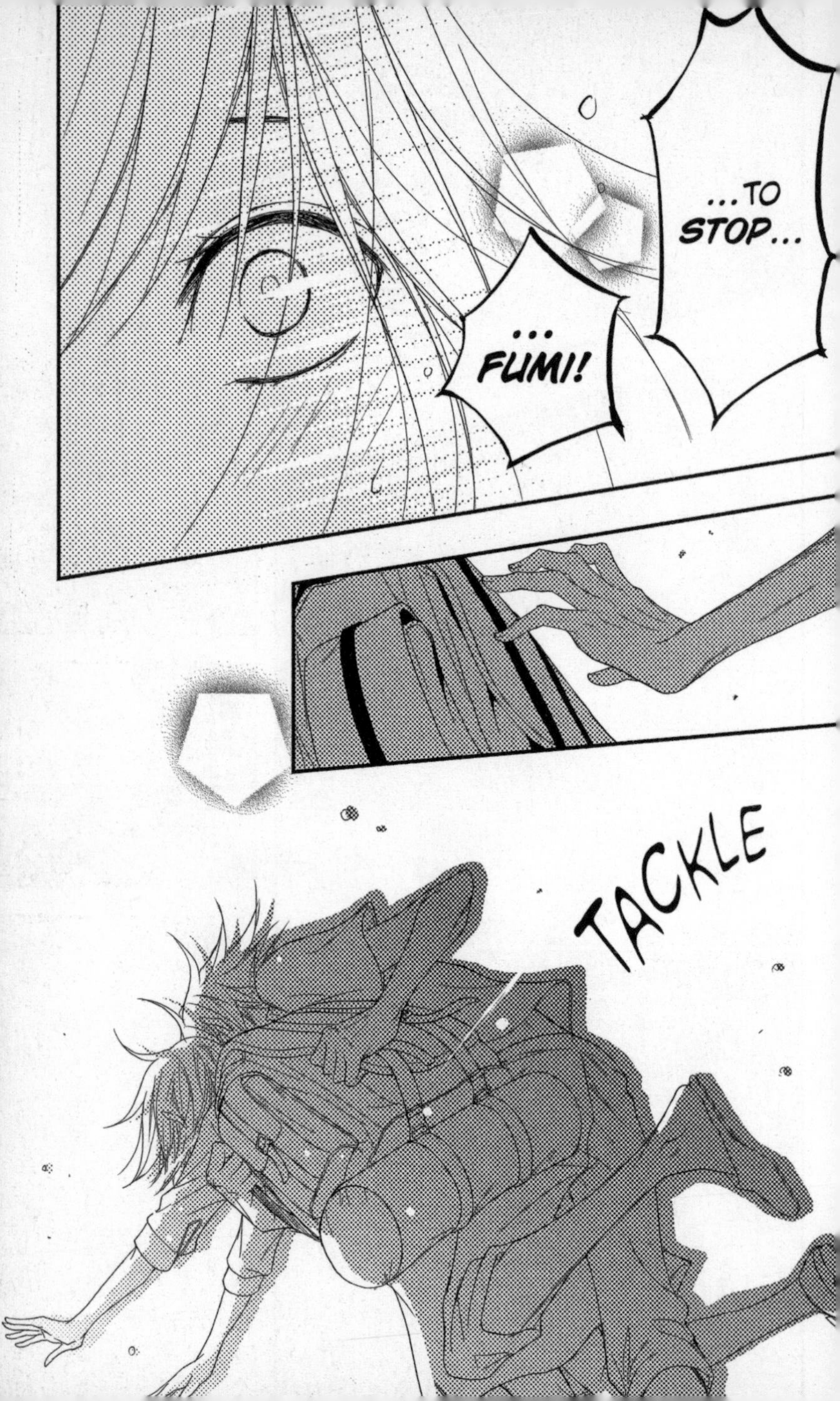
...TO STOP...
...FUMI!
TACKLE

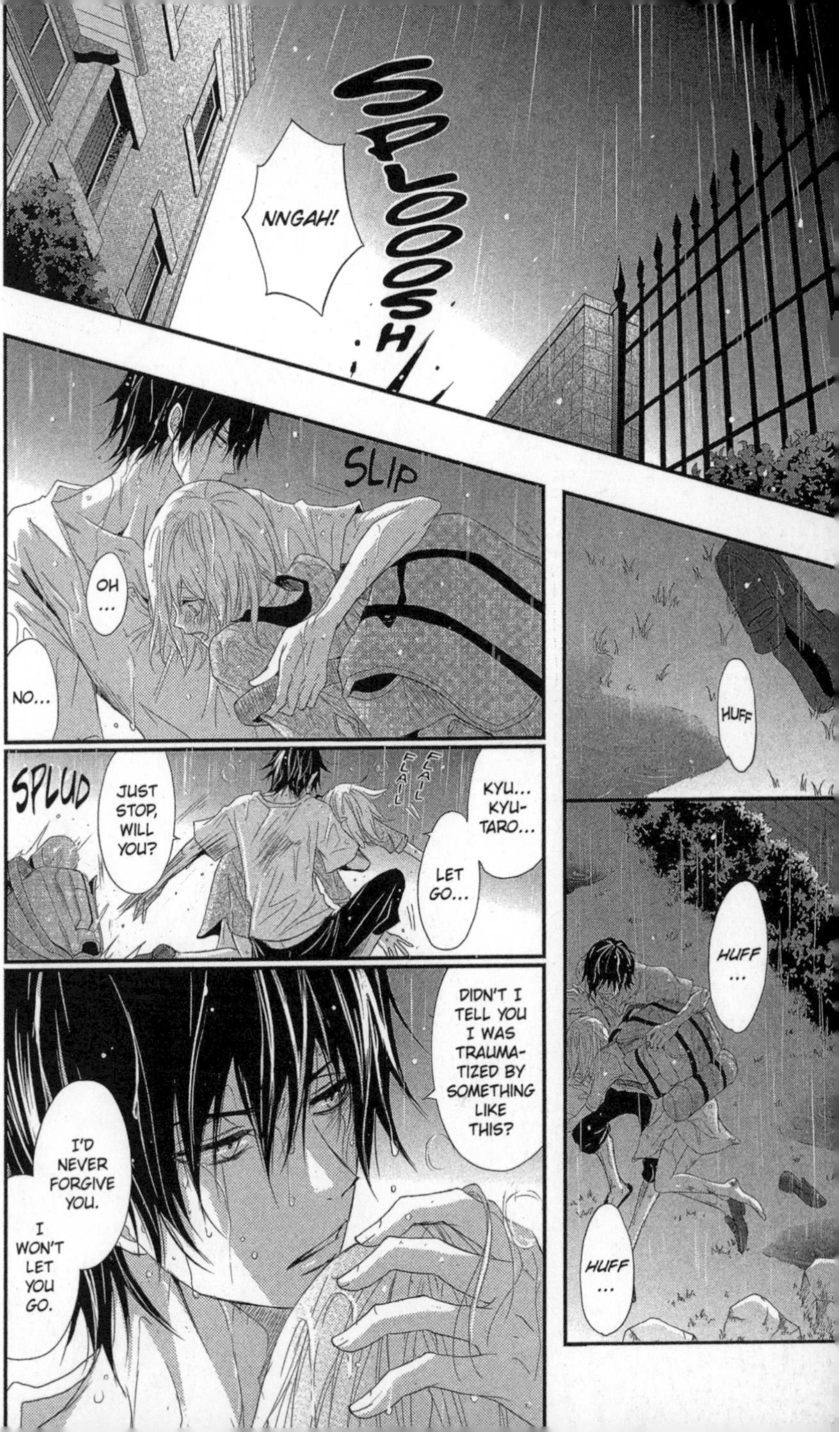
SPLOOOOSH
NNGAH!
HUFF
SLIP
OH...
NO...
KYU... KYU-TARO...
LET GO...
FLAIL FLAIL
JUST STOP, WILL YOU?
SPLUD
HUFF...
HUFF...
DIDN'T I TELL YOU I WAS TRAUMATIZED BY SOMETHING LIKE THIS?
I'D NEVER FORGIVE YOU.
I WON'T LET YOU GO.

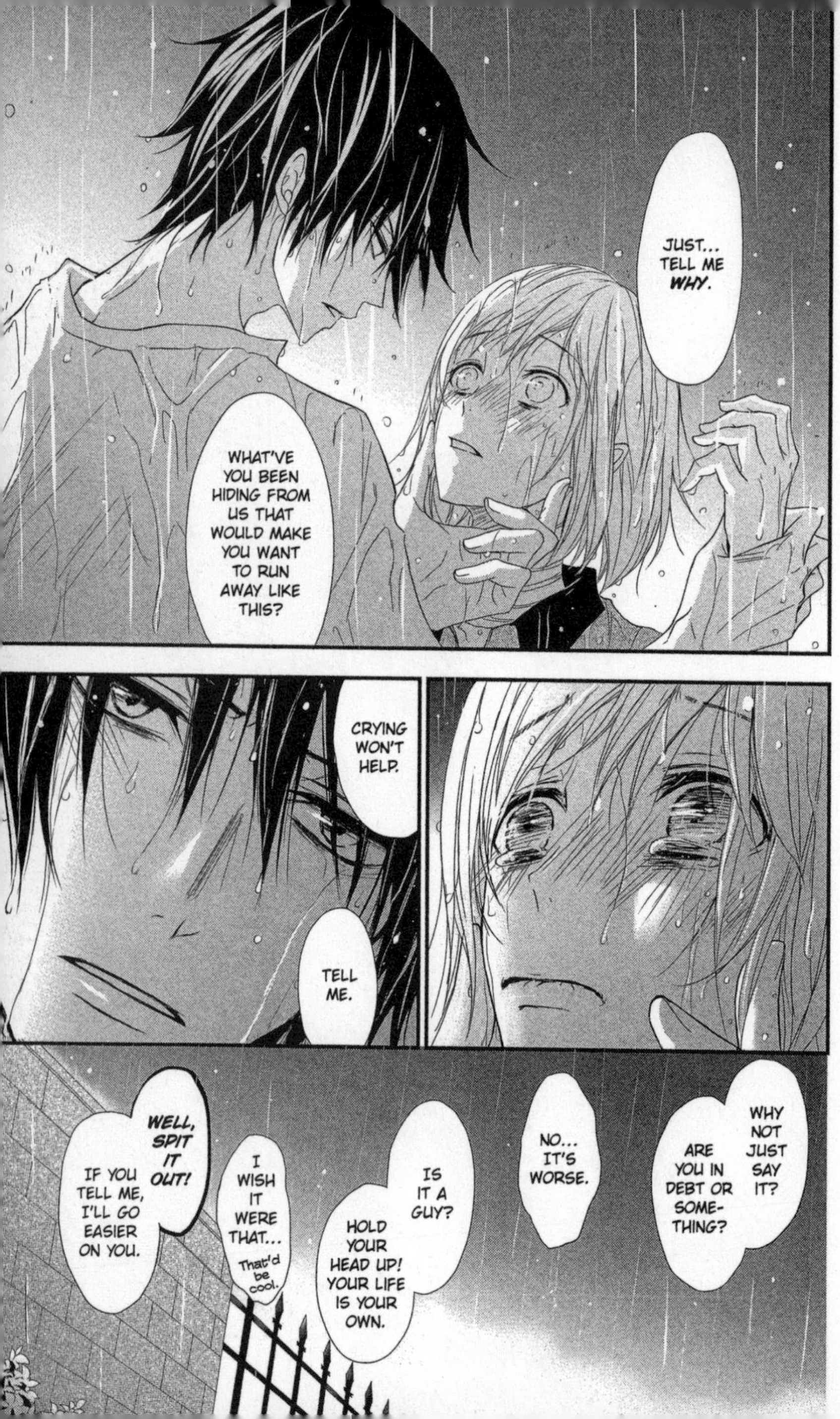
JUST... TELL ME WHY.
WHAT'VE YOU BEEN HIDING FROM US THAT WOULD MAKE YOU WANT TO RUN AWAY LIKE THIS?
CRYING WON'T HELP.
TELL ME.
WHY NOT JUST SAY IT?
ARE YOU IN DEBT OR SOME-THING?
NO... IT'S WORSE.
IS IT A GUY?
HOLD YOUR HEAD UP! YOUR LIFE IS YOUR OWN.
I WISH IT WERE THAT...
That'd be cool.
WELL, SPIT IT OUT!
IF YOU TELL ME, I'LL GO EASIER ON YOU.

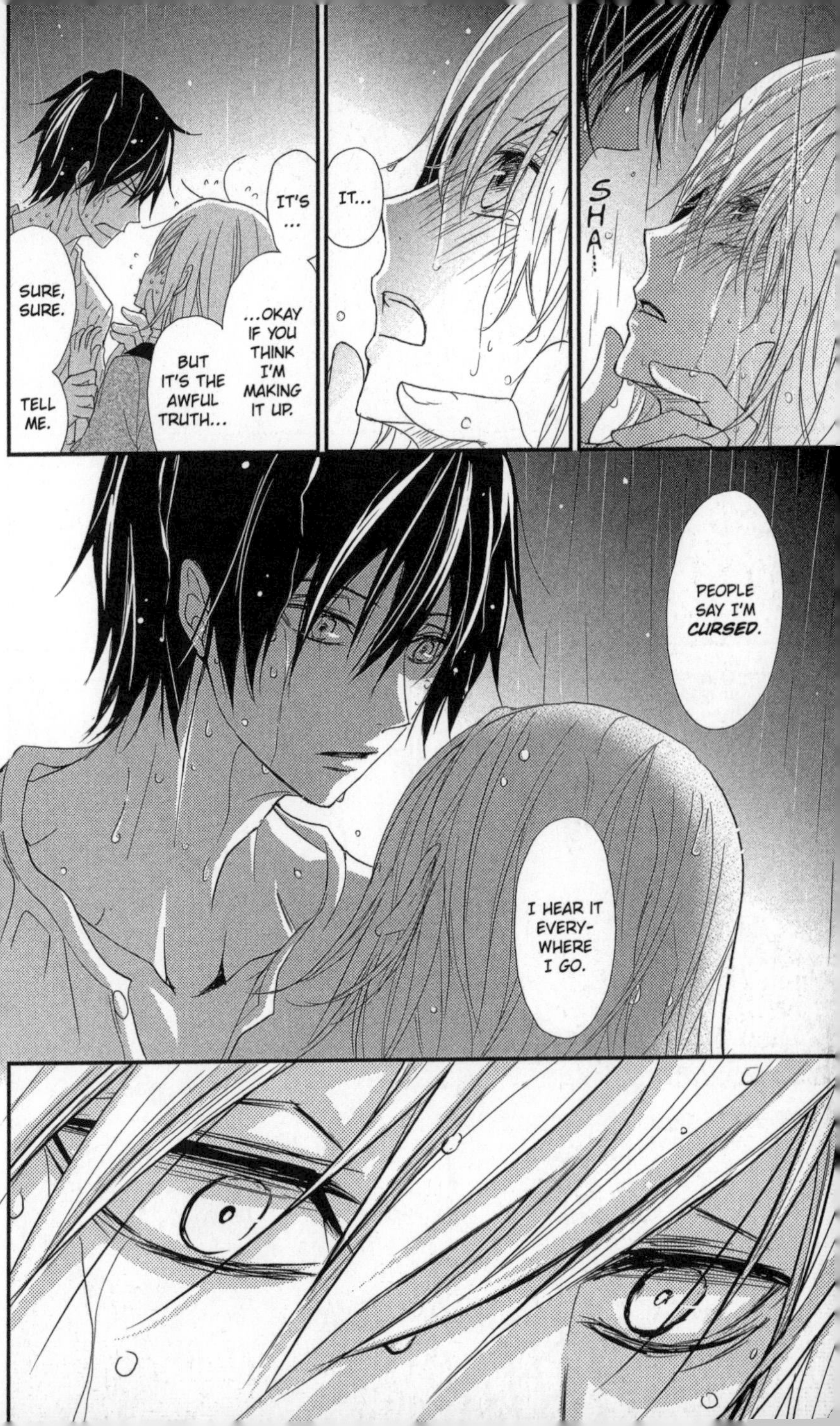
SHA...
IT...
IT'S ...
...OKAY IF YOU THINK I'M MAKING IT UP.
BUT IT'S THE AWFUL TRUTH...
SURE, SURE.
TELL ME.
PEOPLE SAY I'M **CURSED**.
I HEAR IT EVERY-WHERE I GO.

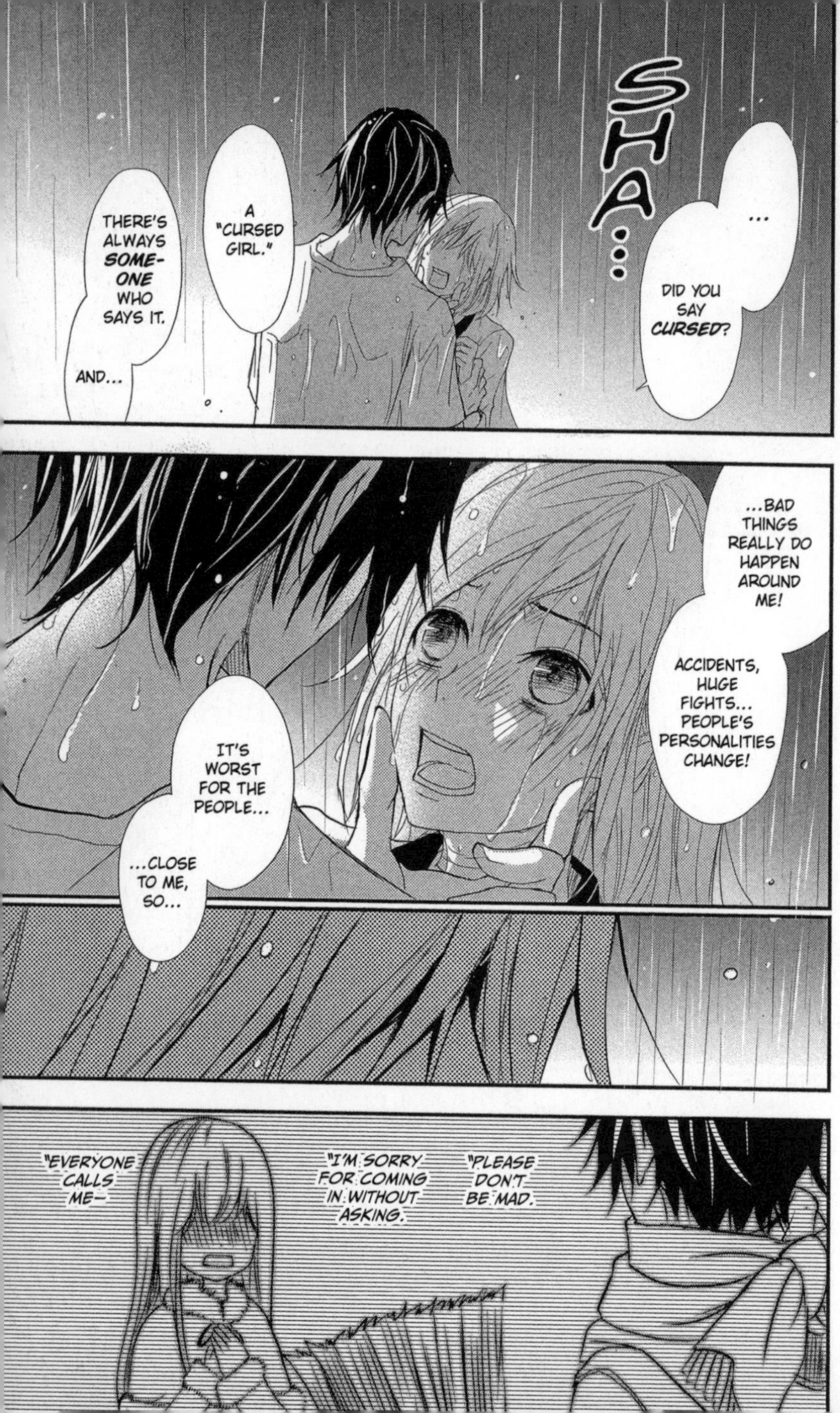
SHA...
... DID YOU SAY *CURSED*?
A "CURSED GIRL."
THERE'S ALWAYS *SOMEONE* WHO SAYS IT.
AND...
...BAD THINGS REALLY DO HAPPEN AROUND ME!
ACCIDENTS, HUGE FIGHTS... PEOPLE'S PERSONALITIES CHANGE!
IT'S WORST FOR THE PEOPLE...
...CLOSE TO ME, SO...
"PLEASE DON'T BE MAD.
"I'M SORRY FOR COMING IN WITHOUT ASKING.
"EVERYONE CALLS ME—

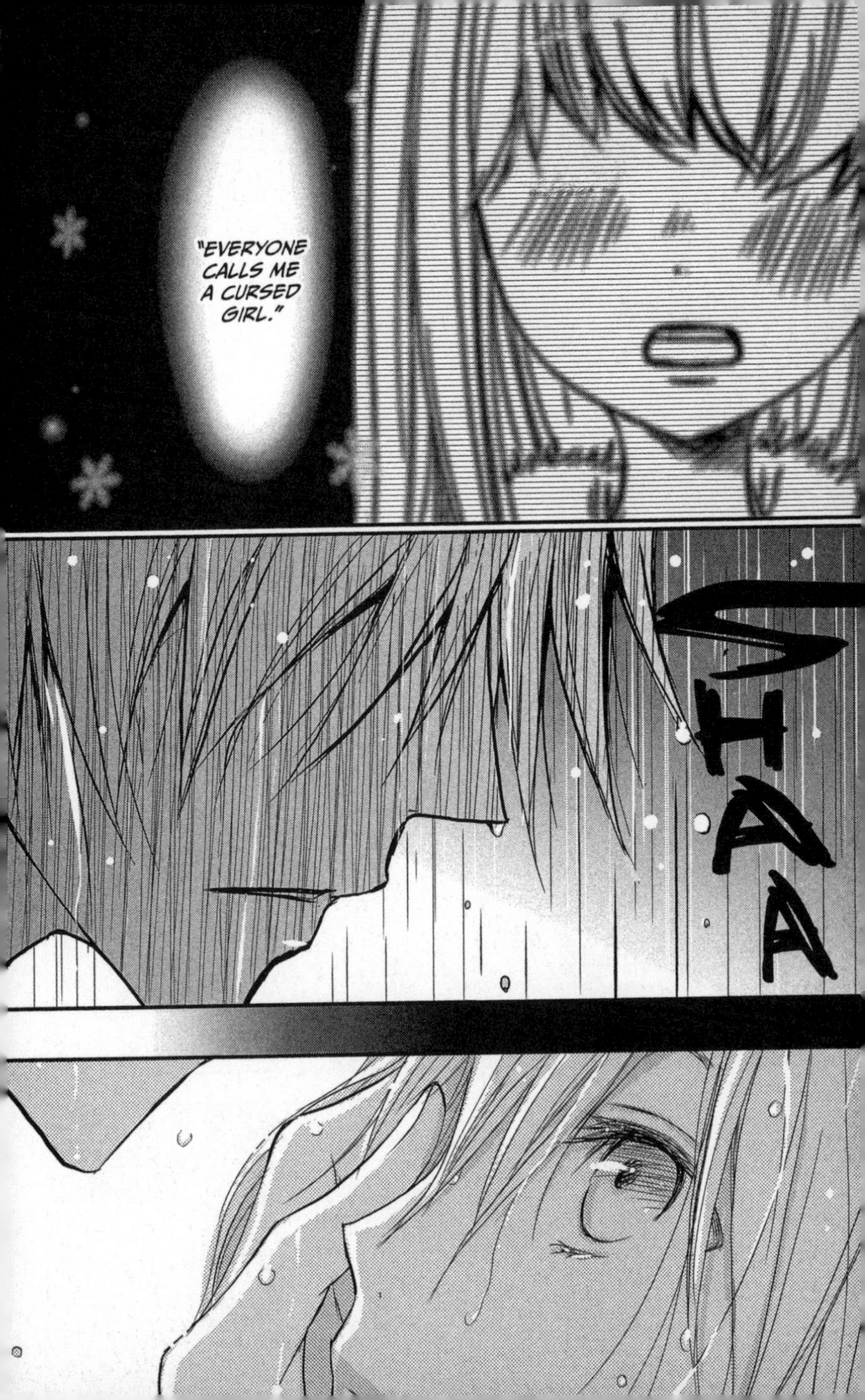
"EVERYONE CALLS ME A CURSED GIRL."
SHAA

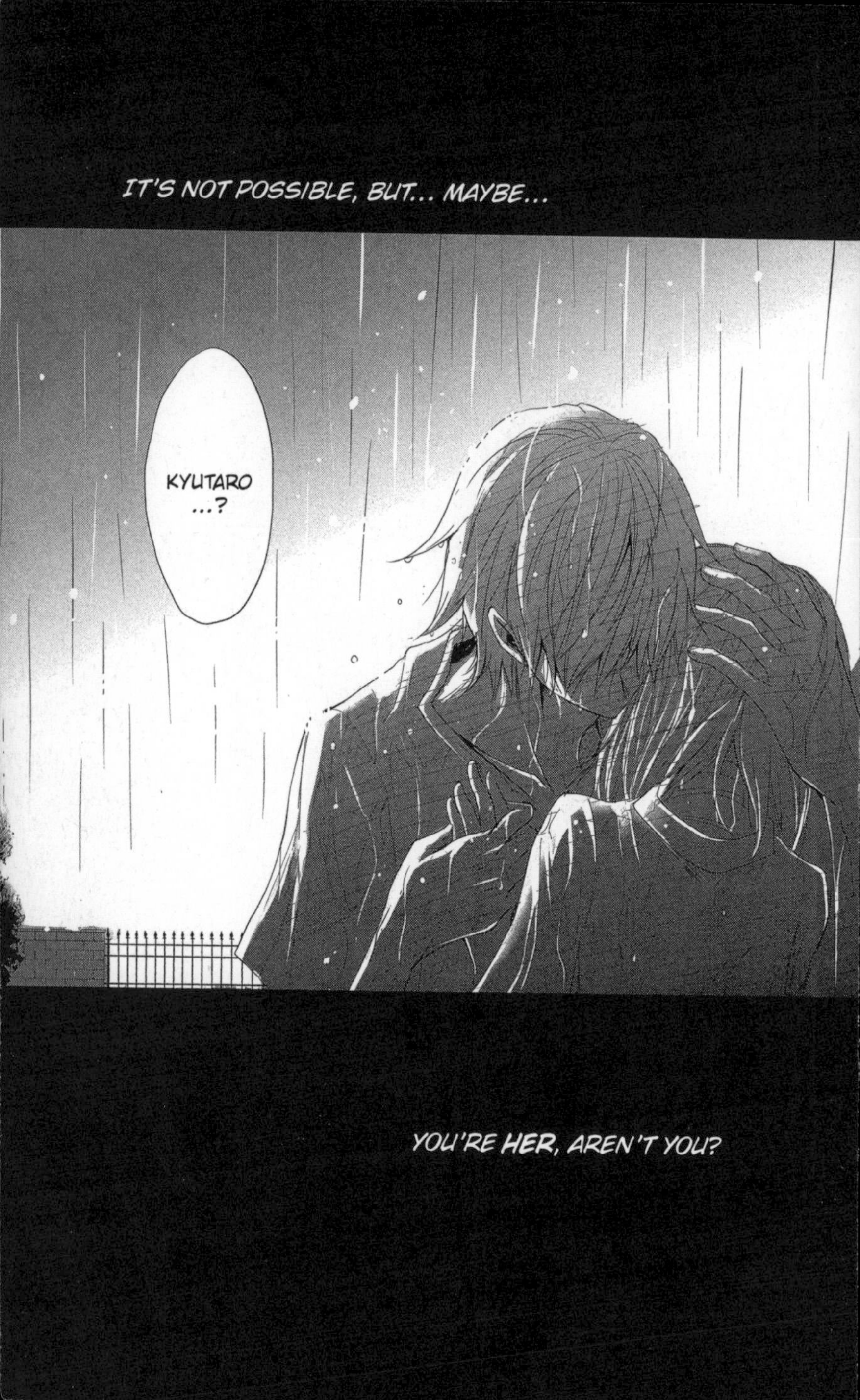
IT'S NOT POSSIBLE, BUT... MAYBE...
KYUTARO ...?
YOU'RE **HER**, AREN'T YOU?

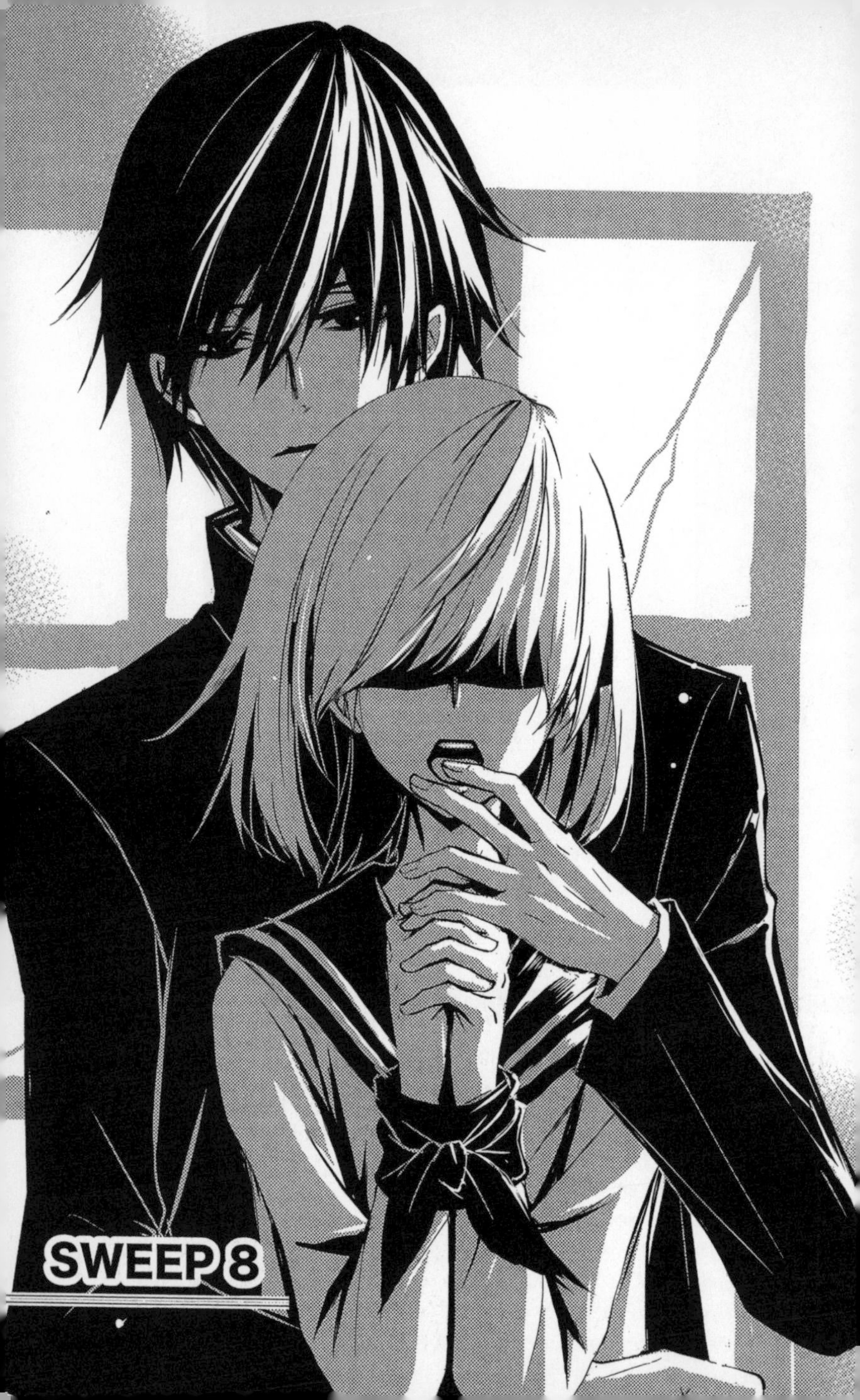
SWEEP 8

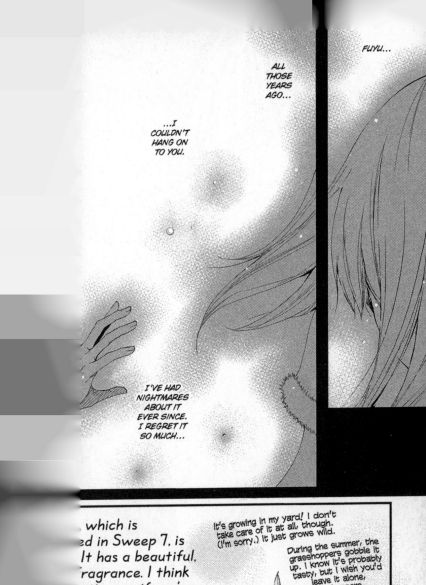

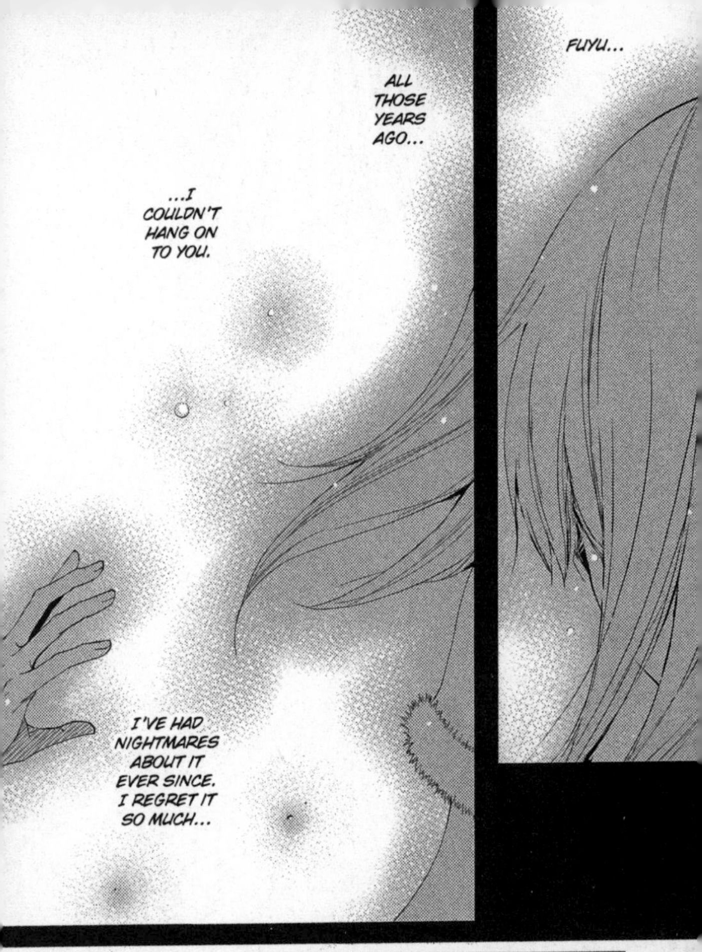
FUYU...
ALL THOSE YEARS AGO...
...I COULDN'T HANG ON TO YOU.
I'VE HAD NIGHTMARES ABOUT IT EVER SINCE. I REGRET IT SO MUCH...

which is
ed in Sweep 7, is
It has a beautiful,
fragrance. I think
e it, even if you're
to herbal teas. I
t it's very popular
e! (It's also called
I wish they'd sell it
upermarkets here
.

It's growing in my yard! I don't take care of it at all, though. (I'm sorry.) It just grows wild.

During the summer, the grasshoppers gobble it up. I know it's probably tasty, but I wish you'd leave it alone, grasshoppers...

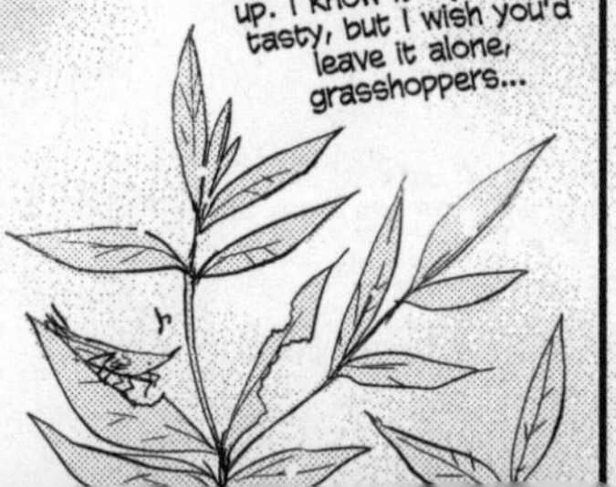

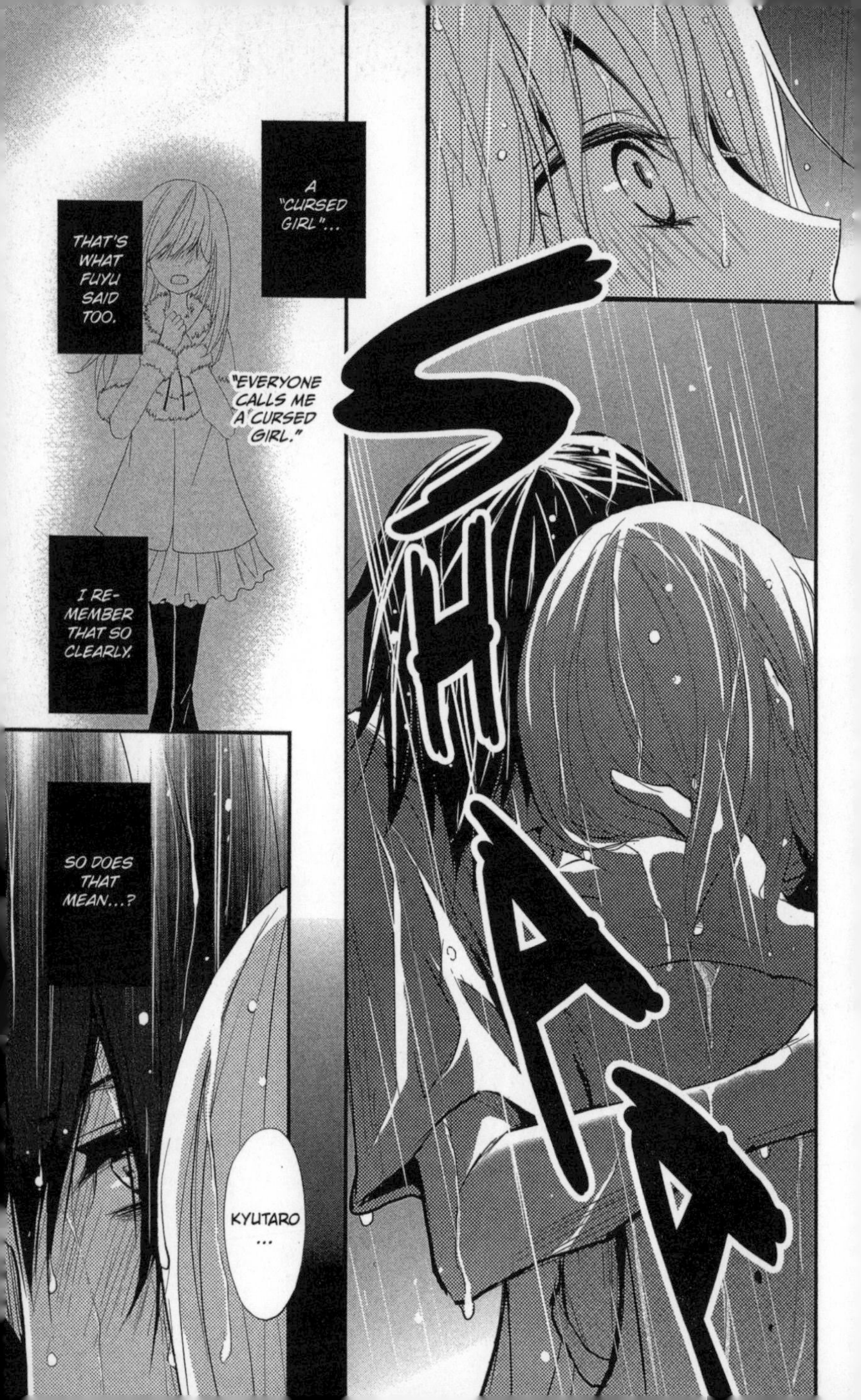

SHAA
A "CURSED GIRL"...
THAT'S WHAT FUYU SAID TOO.
"EVERYONE CALLS ME A CURSED GIRL."
I REMEMBER THAT SO CLEARLY.
SO DOES THAT MEAN...?
KYUTARO...

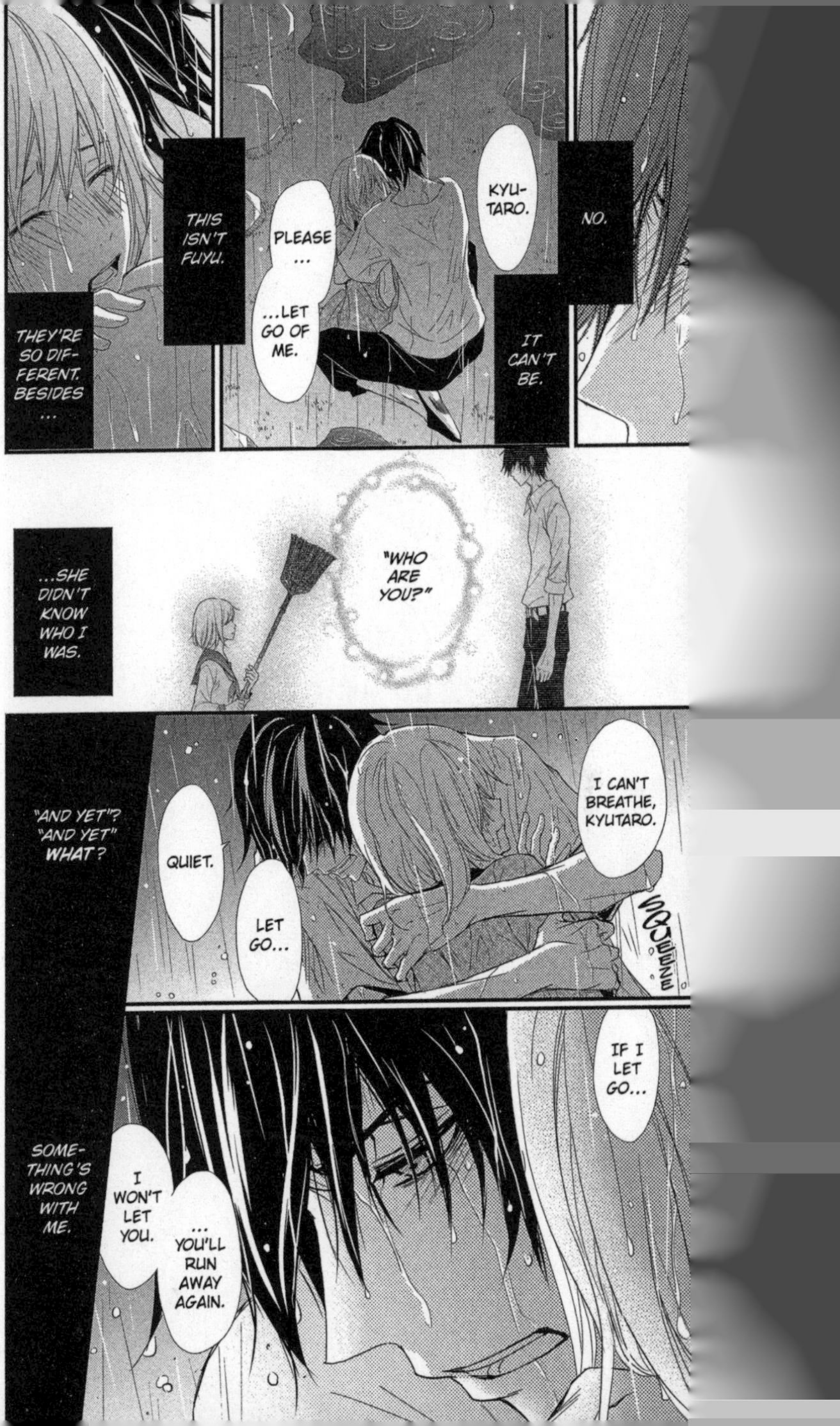
NO.
KYU-TARO.
IT CAN'T BE.
PLEASE...
...LET GO OF ME.
THIS ISN'T FUYU.
THEY'RE SO DIF-FERENT. BESIDES...
"WHO ARE YOU?"
...SHE DIDN'T KNOW WHO I WAS.
I CAN'T BREATHE, KYUTARO.
SQUEEZE
QUIET.
LET GO...
"AND YET"? "AND YET" WHAT?
IF I LET GO...
...YOU'LL RUN AWAY AGAIN.
I WON'T LET YOU.
SOME-THING'S WRONG WITH ME.

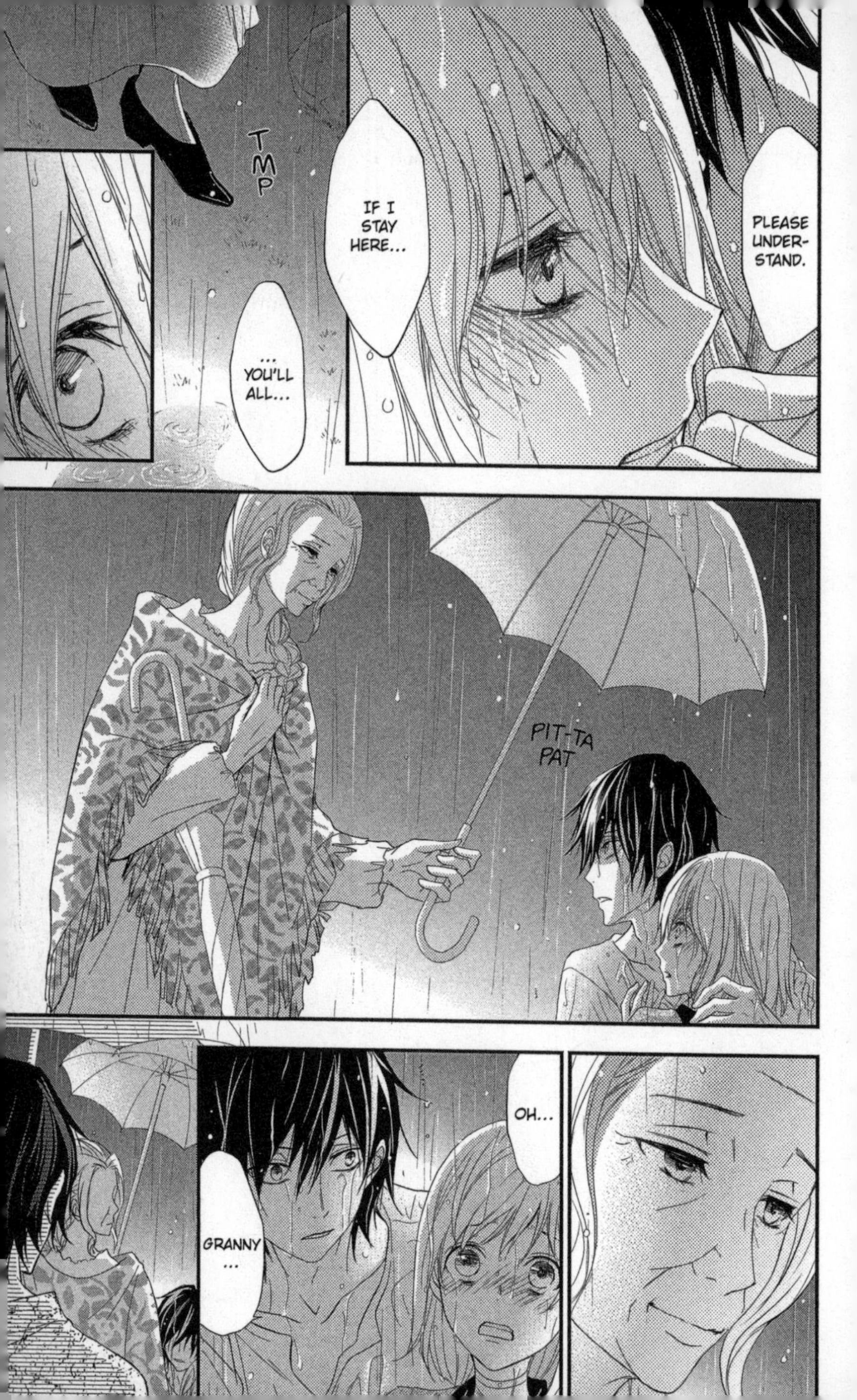
PLEASE UNDER-STAND.
IF I STAY HERE...
...YOU'LL ALL...
TMP
PIT-TA PAT
OH...
GRANNY...

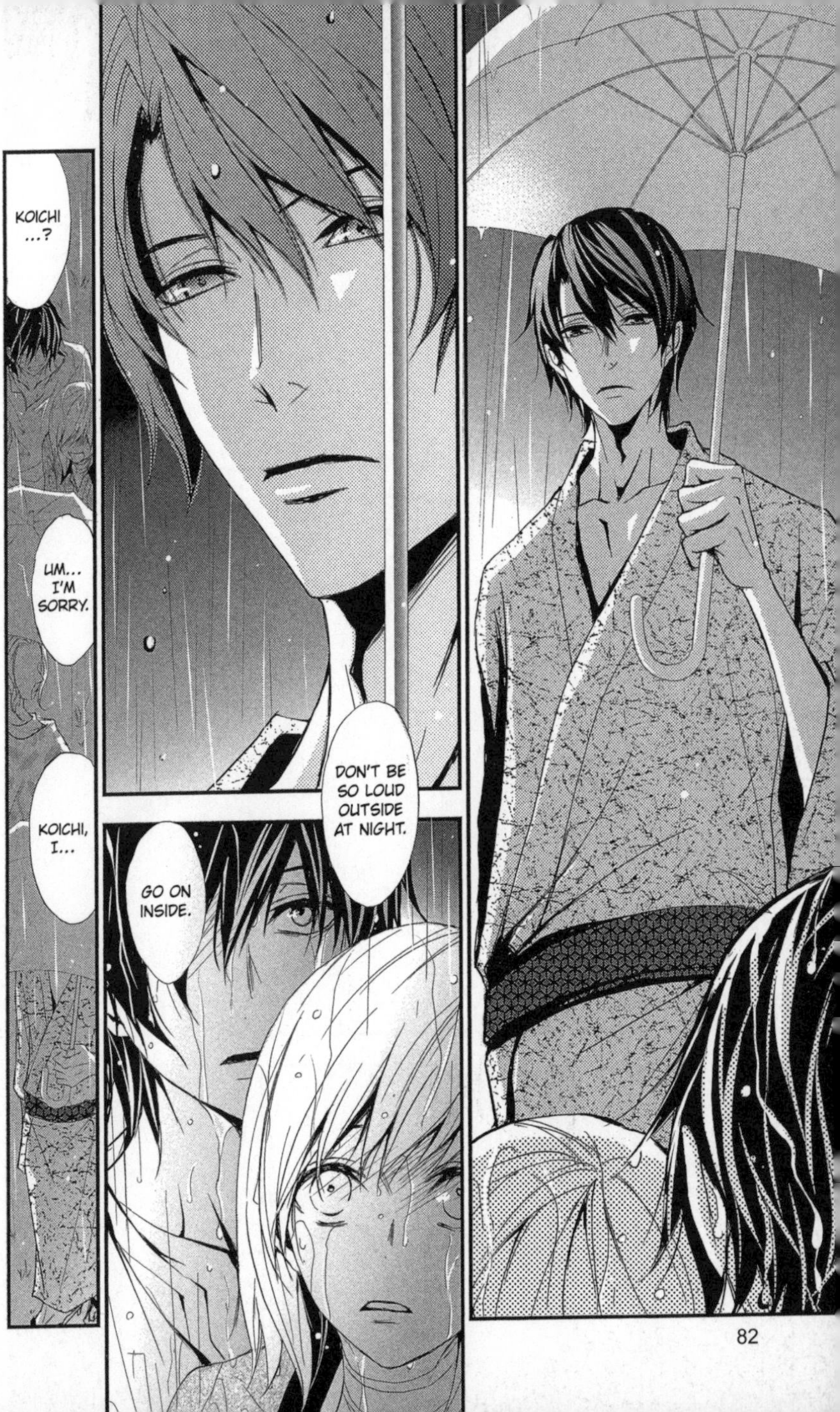
DON'T BE SO LOUD OUTSIDE AT NIGHT.
GO ON INSIDE.
KOICHI ...?
UM... I'M SORRY.
KOICHI, I...

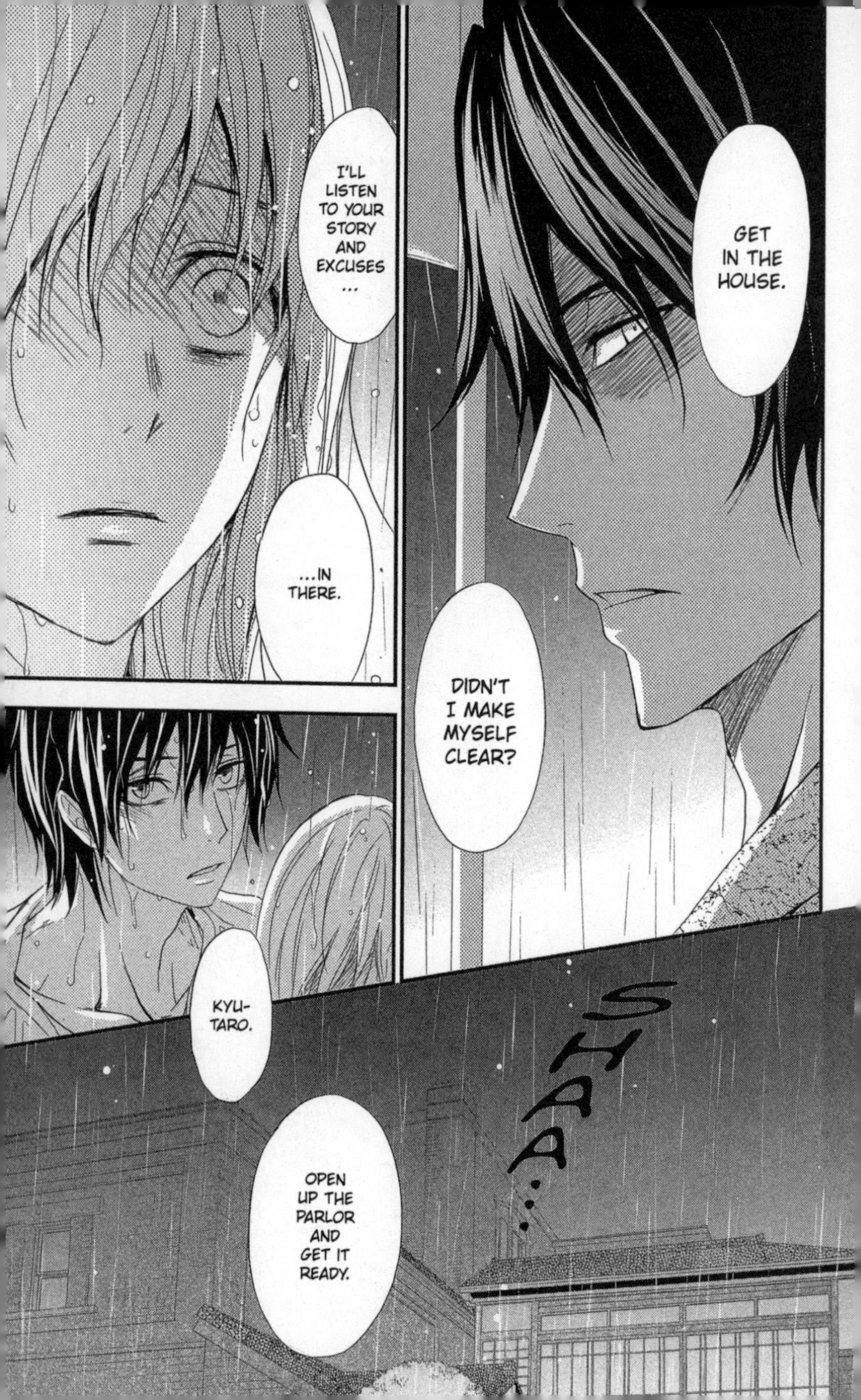
GET IN THE HOUSE.
DIDN'T I MAKE MYSELF CLEAR?
I'LL LISTEN TO YOUR STORY AND EXCUSES...
...IN THERE.
SHAA...
KYU-TARO.
OPEN UP THE PARLOR AND GET IT READY.

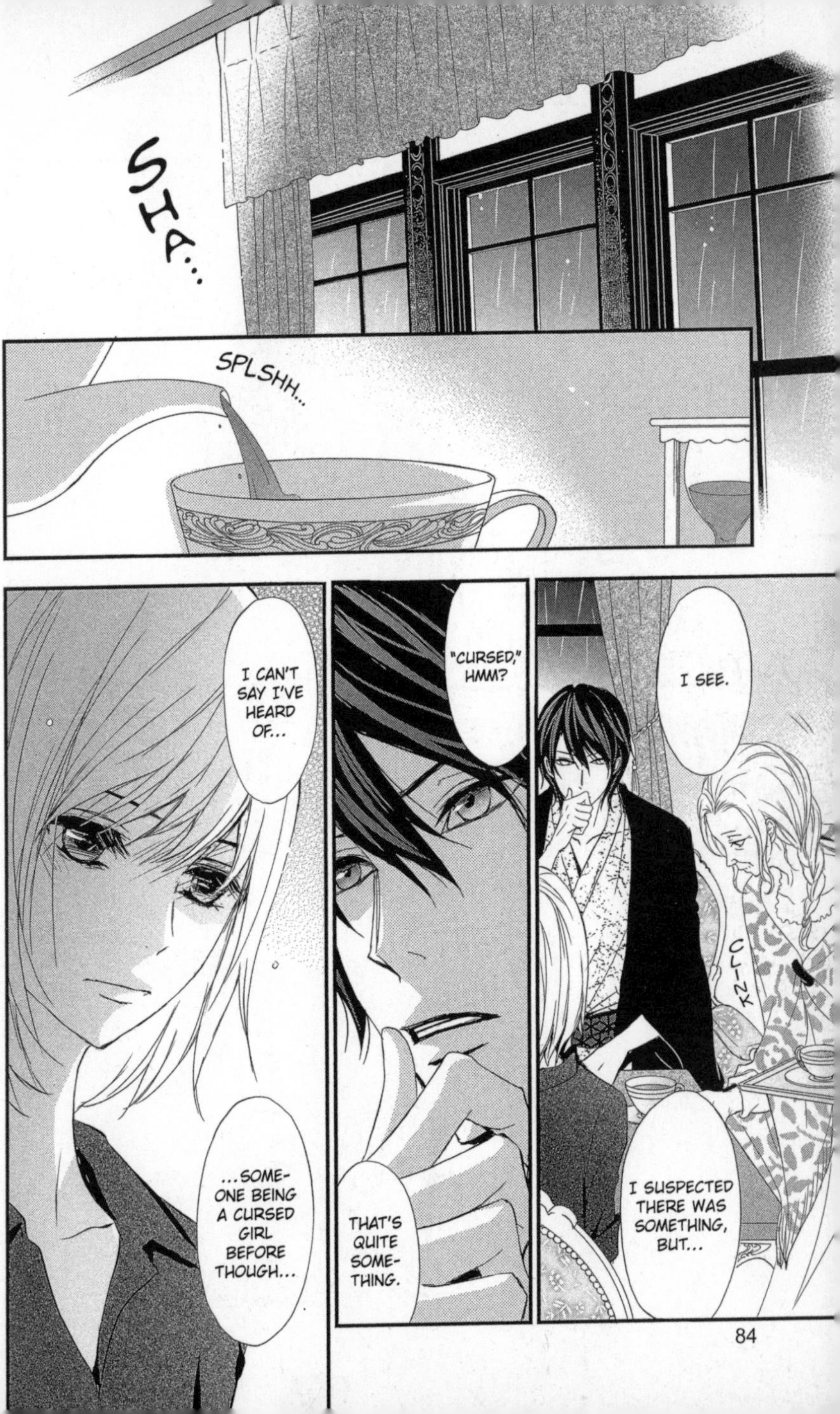
SHA...
SPLSHH...
I SEE.
CLINK
I SUSPECTED THERE WAS SOMETHING, BUT...
"CURSED," HMM?
THAT'S QUITE SOME-THING.
I CAN'T SAY I'VE HEARD OF...
...SOME-ONE BEING A CURSED GIRL BEFORE THOUGH...

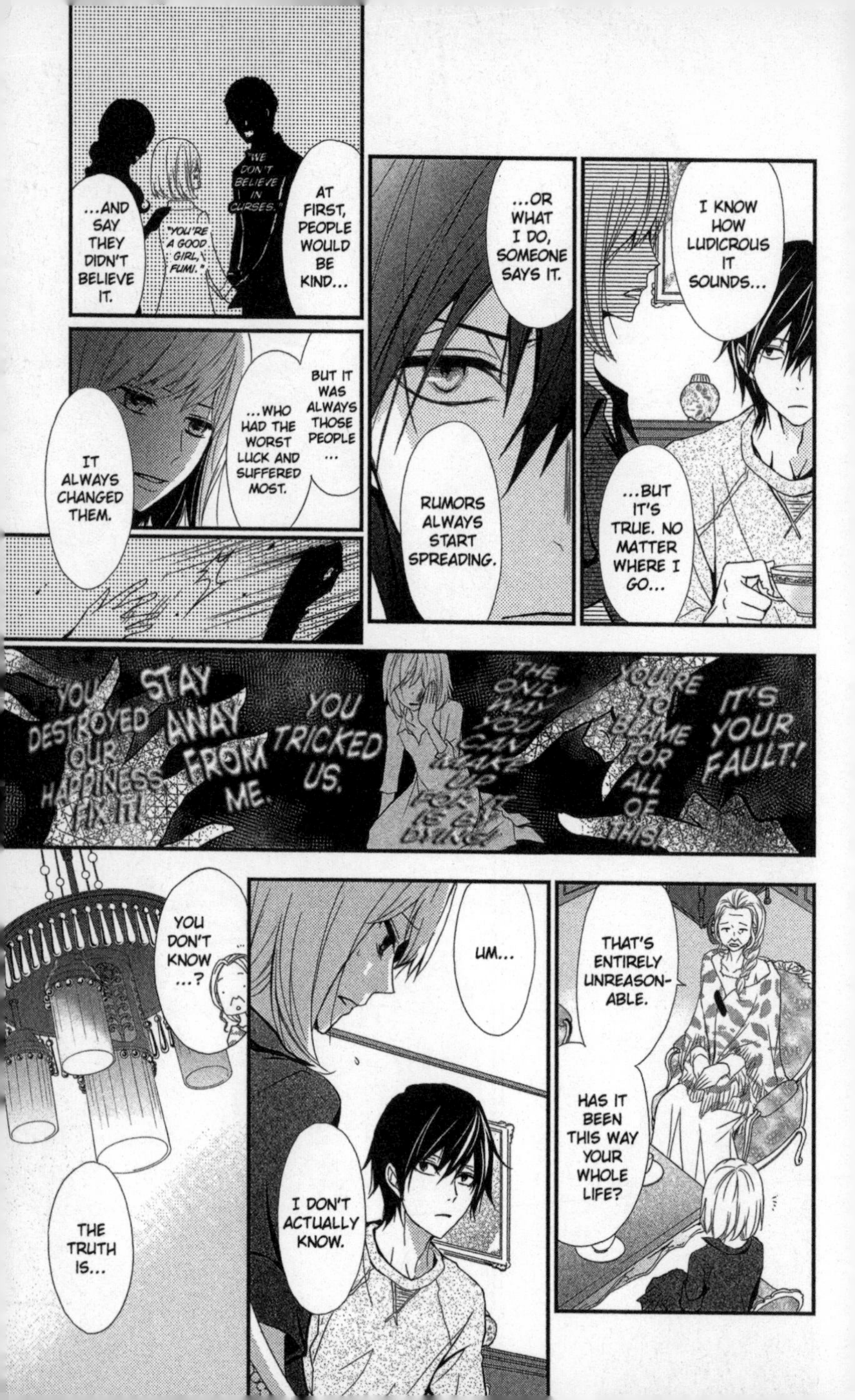
I KNOW HOW LUDICROUS IT SOUNDS...
...BUT IT'S TRUE. NO MATTER WHERE I GO...
...OR WHAT I DO, SOMEONE SAYS IT.
RUMORS ALWAYS START SPREADING.
AT FIRST, PEOPLE WOULD BE KIND...
"WE DON'T BELIEVE IN CURSES."
"YOU'RE A GOOD GIRL, FUMI."
...AND SAY THEY DIDN'T BELIEVE IT.
BUT IT WAS ALWAYS THOSE PEOPLE...
...WHO HAD THE WORST LUCK AND SUFFERED MOST.
IT ALWAYS CHANGED THEM.
IT'S YOUR FAULT!
YOU'RE TO BLAME FOR ALL OF THIS!
THE ONLY WAY YOU CAN MAKE UP FOR IT IS BY DYING!
YOU TRICKED US.
STAY AWAY FROM ME.
YOU DESTROYED OUR HAPPINESS. FIX IT!
THAT'S ENTIRELY UNREASON-ABLE.
HAS IT BEEN THIS WAY YOUR WHOLE LIFE?
UM...
I DON'T ACTUALLY KNOW.
YOU DON'T KNOW...?
THE TRUTH IS...

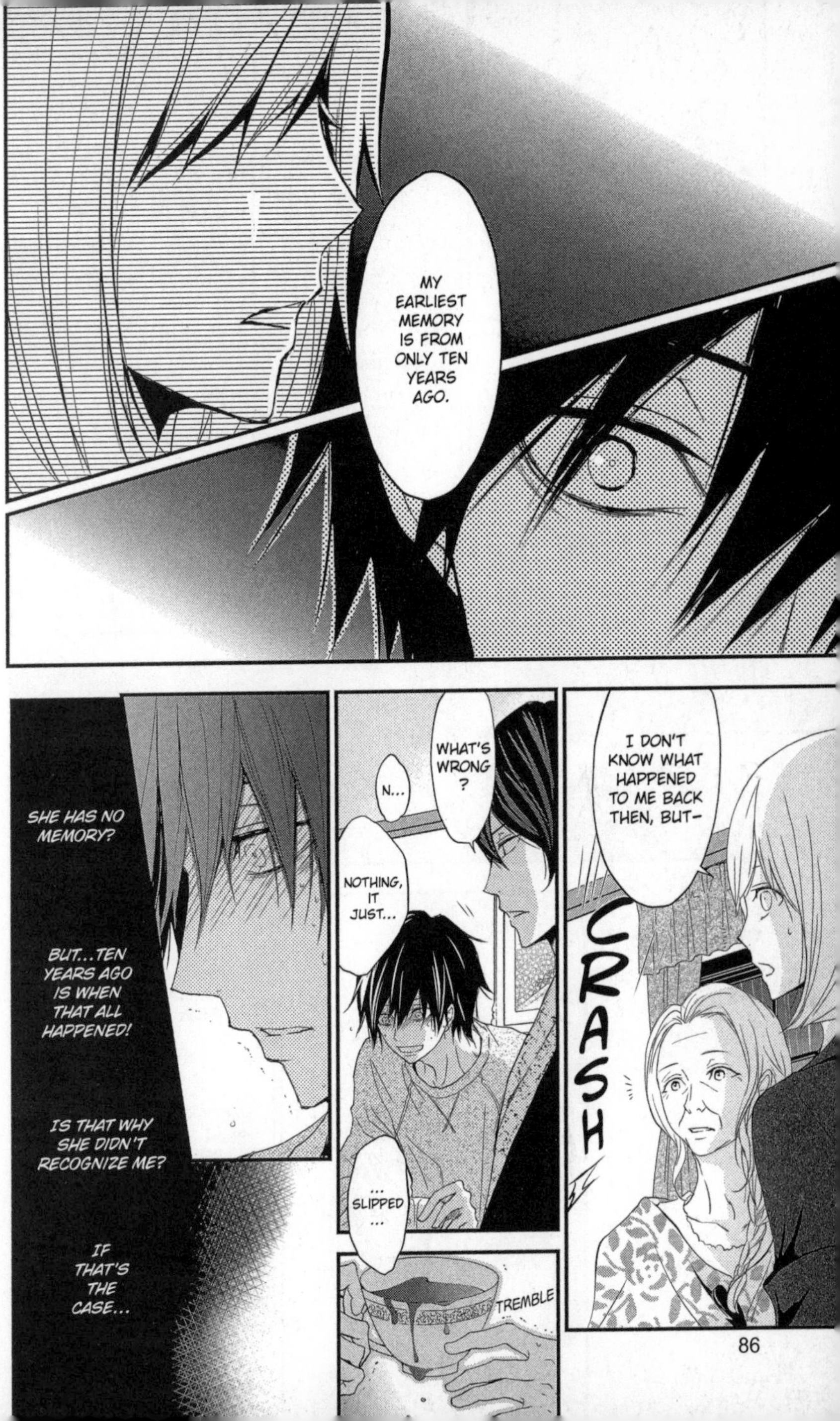
MY EARLIEST MEMORY IS FROM ONLY TEN YEARS AGO.
I DON'T KNOW WHAT HAPPENED TO ME BACK THEN, BUT—
CRASH
WHAT'S WRONG?
N...
NOTHING, IT JUST...
...SLIPPED...
TREMBLE
SHE HAS NO MEMORY?
BUT...TEN YEARS AGO IS WHEN THAT ALL HAPPENED!
IS THAT WHY SHE DIDN'T RECOGNIZE ME?
IF THAT'S THE CASE...

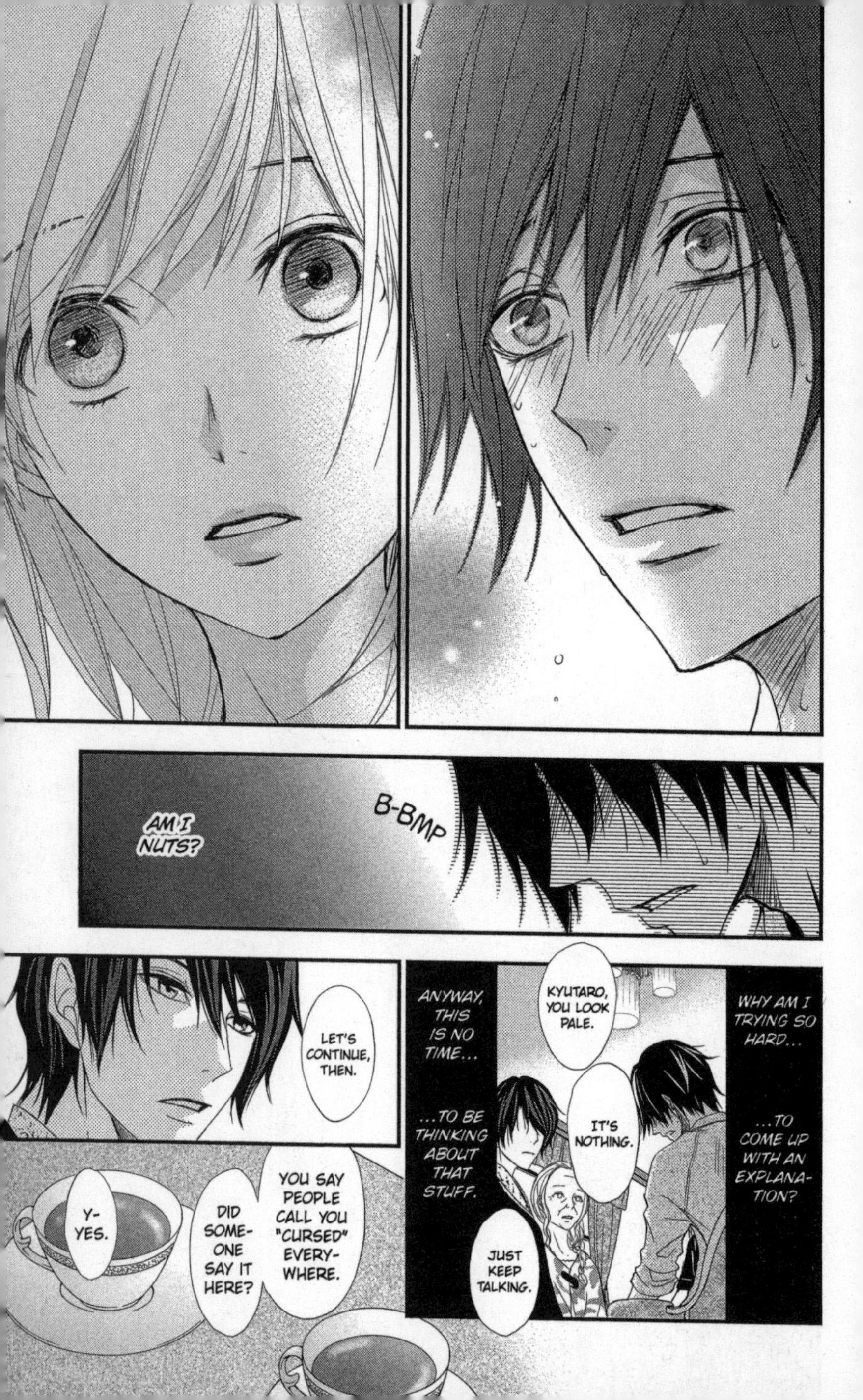
B-BMP
AM I NUTS?
WHY AM I TRYING SO HARD...
...TO COME UP WITH AN EXPLANATION?
KYUTARO, YOU LOOK PALE.
IT'S NOTHING.
ANYWAY, THIS IS NO TIME...
...TO BE THINKING ABOUT THAT STUFF.
JUST KEEP TALKING.
LET'S CONTINUE, THEN.
YOU SAY PEOPLE CALL YOU "CURSED" EVERYWHERE.
DID SOMEONE SAY IT HERE?
Y-YES.

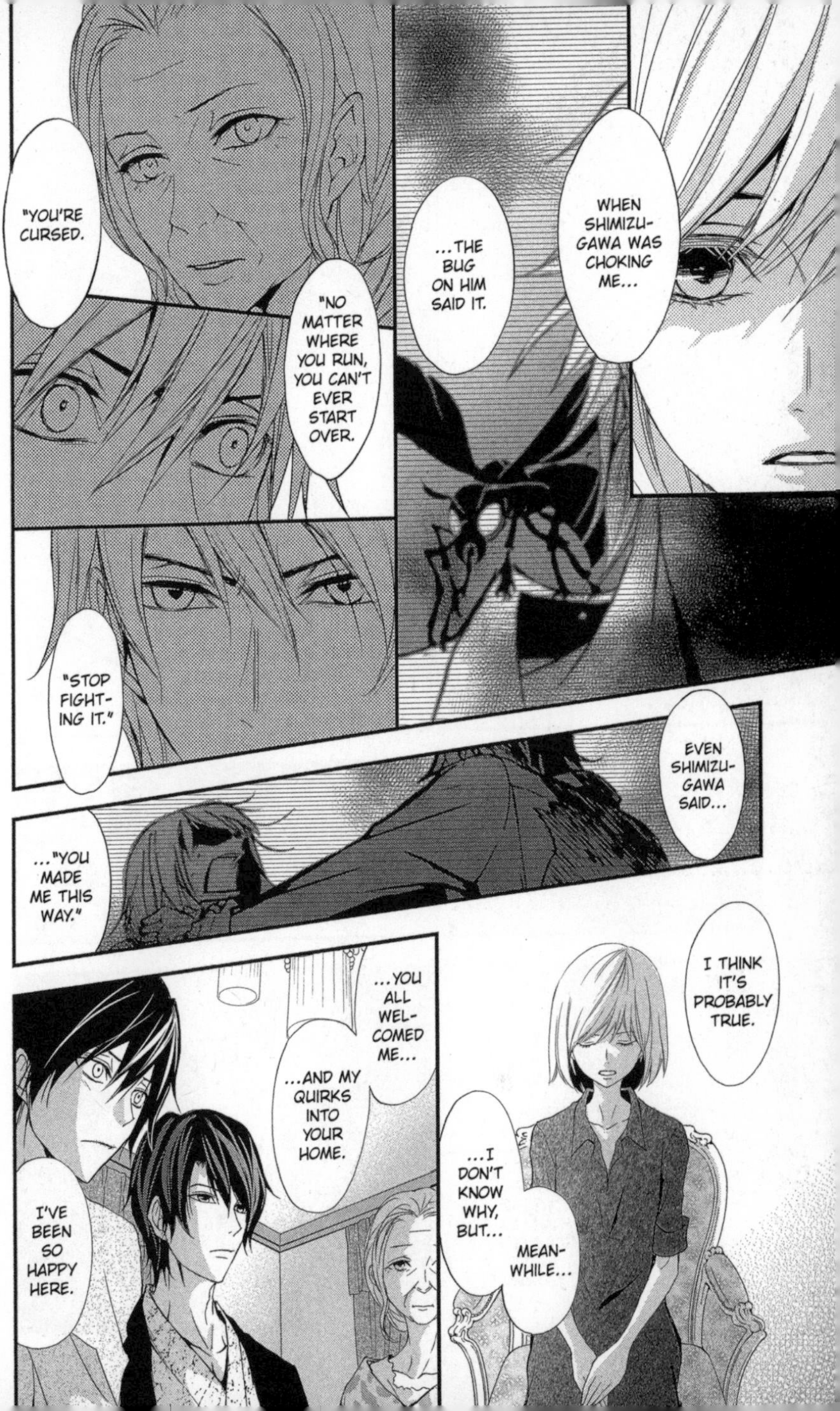
WHEN SHIMIZU-GAWA WAS CHOKING ME...
...THE BUG ON HIM SAID IT.
"YOU'RE CURSED.
"NO MATTER WHERE YOU RUN, YOU CAN'T EVER START OVER.
"STOP FIGHT-ING IT."
EVEN SHIMIZU-GAWA SAID...
..."YOU MADE ME THIS WAY."
I THINK IT'S PROBABLY TRUE.
...I DON'T KNOW WHY, BUT...
MEAN-WHILE...
...YOU ALL WEL-COMED ME...
...AND MY QUIRKS INTO YOUR HOME.
I'VE BEEN SO HAPPY HERE.

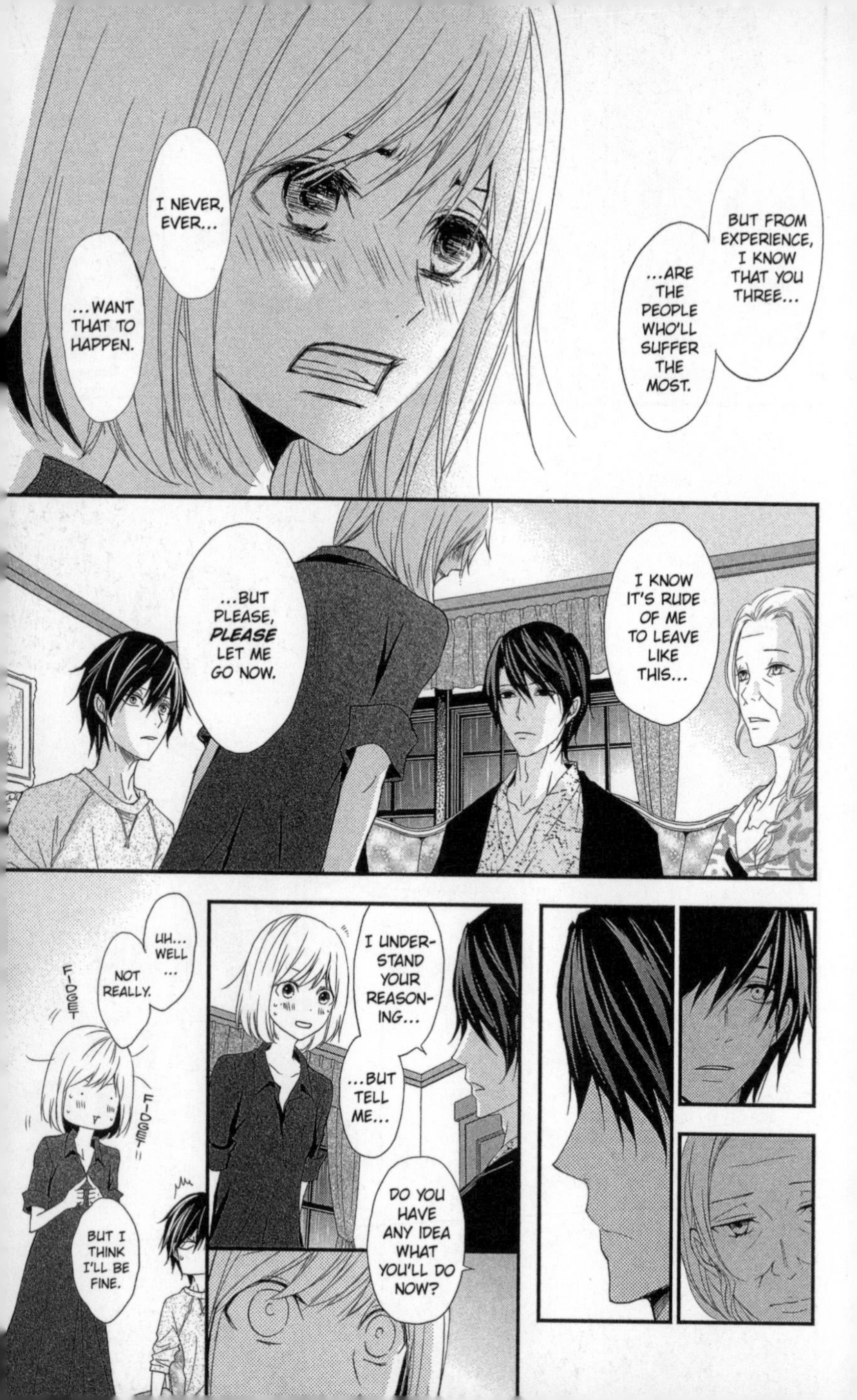
BUT FROM EXPERIENCE, I KNOW THAT YOU THREE...
...ARE THE PEOPLE WHO'LL SUFFER THE MOST.
I NEVER, EVER...
...WANT THAT TO HAPPEN.
I KNOW IT'S RUDE OF ME TO LEAVE LIKE THIS...
...BUT PLEASE, *PLEASE* LET ME GO NOW.
I UNDER-STAND YOUR REASON-ING...
...BUT TELL ME...
DO YOU HAVE ANY IDEA WHAT YOU'LL DO NOW?
UH... WELL...
NOT REALLY.
FIDGET
FIDGET
BUT I THINK I'LL BE FINE.

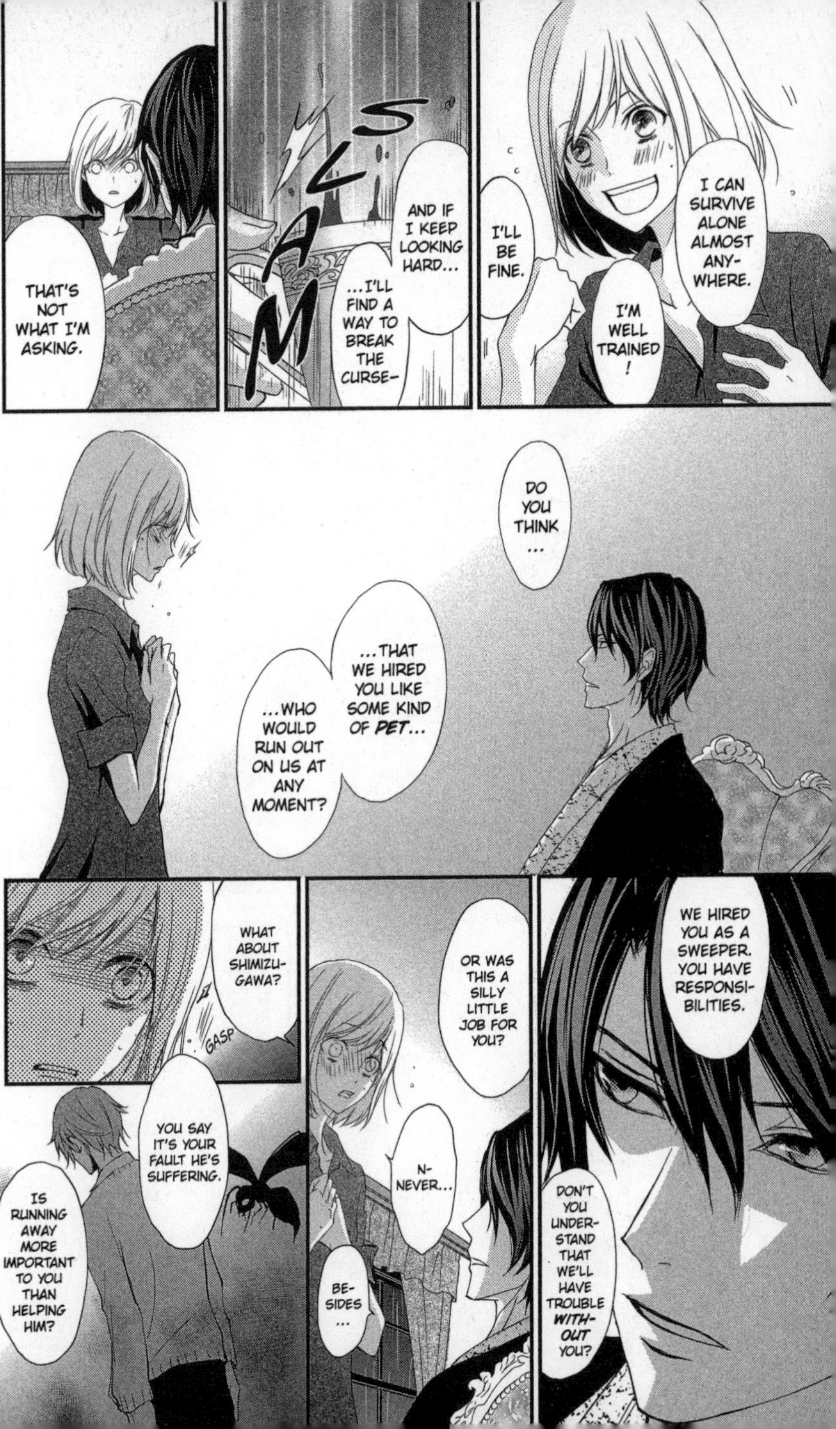
I CAN SURVIVE ALONE ALMOST ANYWHERE.
I'M WELL TRAINED!
I'LL BE FINE.
AND IF I KEEP LOOKING HARD...
...I'LL FIND A WAY TO BREAK THE CURSE-
SLAM
THAT'S NOT WHAT I'M ASKING.
DO YOU THINK...
...THAT WE HIRED YOU LIKE SOME KIND OF *PET*...
...WHO WOULD RUN OUT ON US AT ANY MOMENT?
WE HIRED YOU AS A SWEEPER. YOU HAVE RESPONSIBILITIES.
DON'T YOU UNDERSTAND THAT WE'LL HAVE TROUBLE *WITHOUT* YOU?
OR WAS THIS A SILLY LITTLE JOB FOR YOU?
N-NEVER...
BESIDES...
WHAT ABOUT SHIMIZUGAWA?
GASP
YOU SAY IT'S YOUR FAULT HE'S SUFFERING.
IS RUNNING AWAY MORE IMPORTANT TO YOU THAN HELPING HIM?

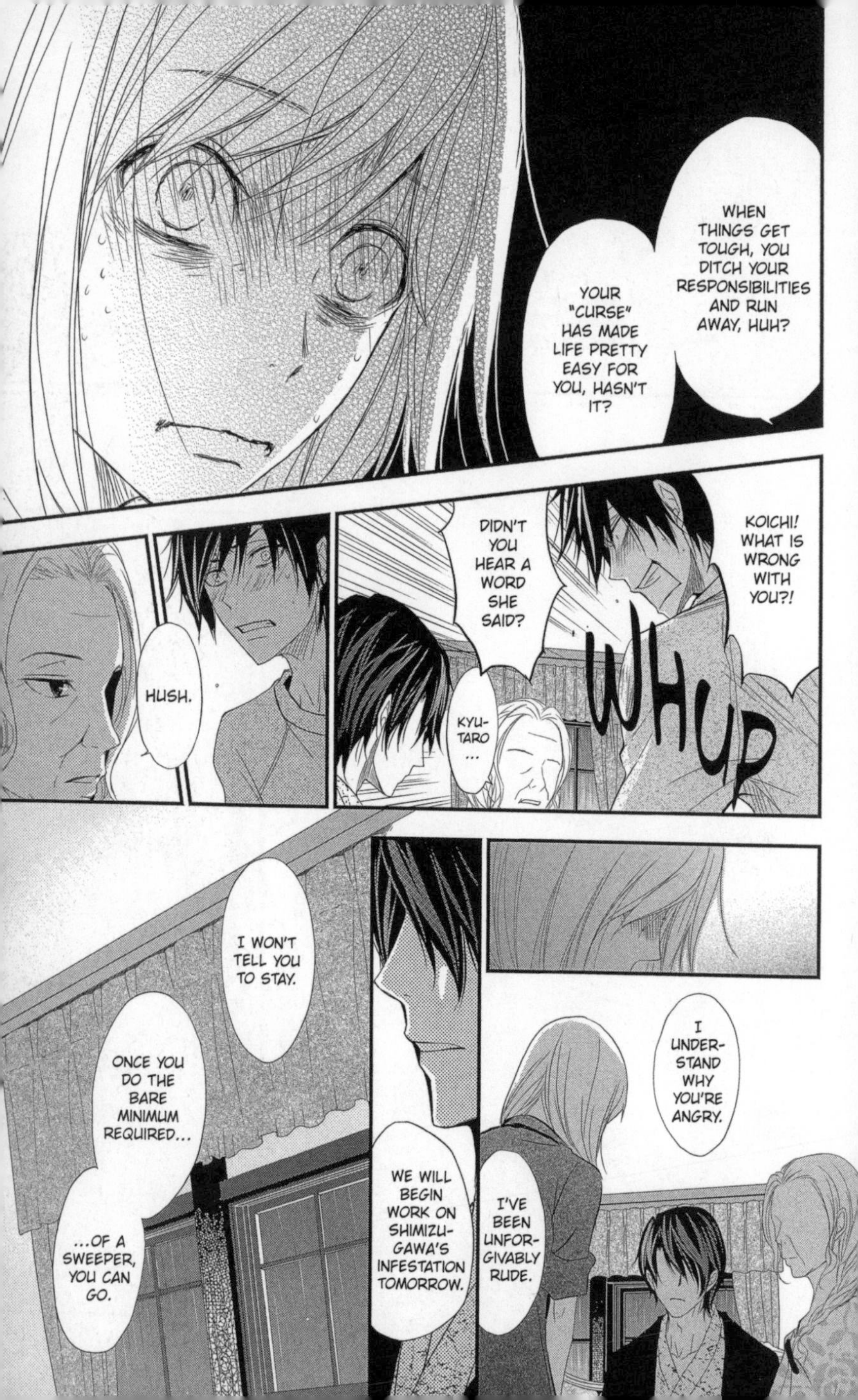
WHEN THINGS GET TOUGH, YOU DITCH YOUR RESPONSIBILITIES AND RUN AWAY, HUH?
YOUR "CURSE" HAS MADE LIFE PRETTY EASY FOR YOU, HASN'T IT?
KOICHI! WHAT IS WRONG WITH YOU?!
WHUP
DIDN'T YOU HEAR A WORD SHE SAID?
KYU-TARO...
HUSH.
I UNDER-STAND WHY YOU'RE ANGRY.
I'VE BEEN UNFOR-GIVABLY RUDE.
WE WILL BEGIN WORK ON SHIMIZU-GAWA'S INFESTATION TOMORROW.
I WON'T TELL YOU TO STAY.
ONCE YOU DO THE BARE MINIMUM REQUIRED...
...OF A SWEEPER, YOU CAN GO.

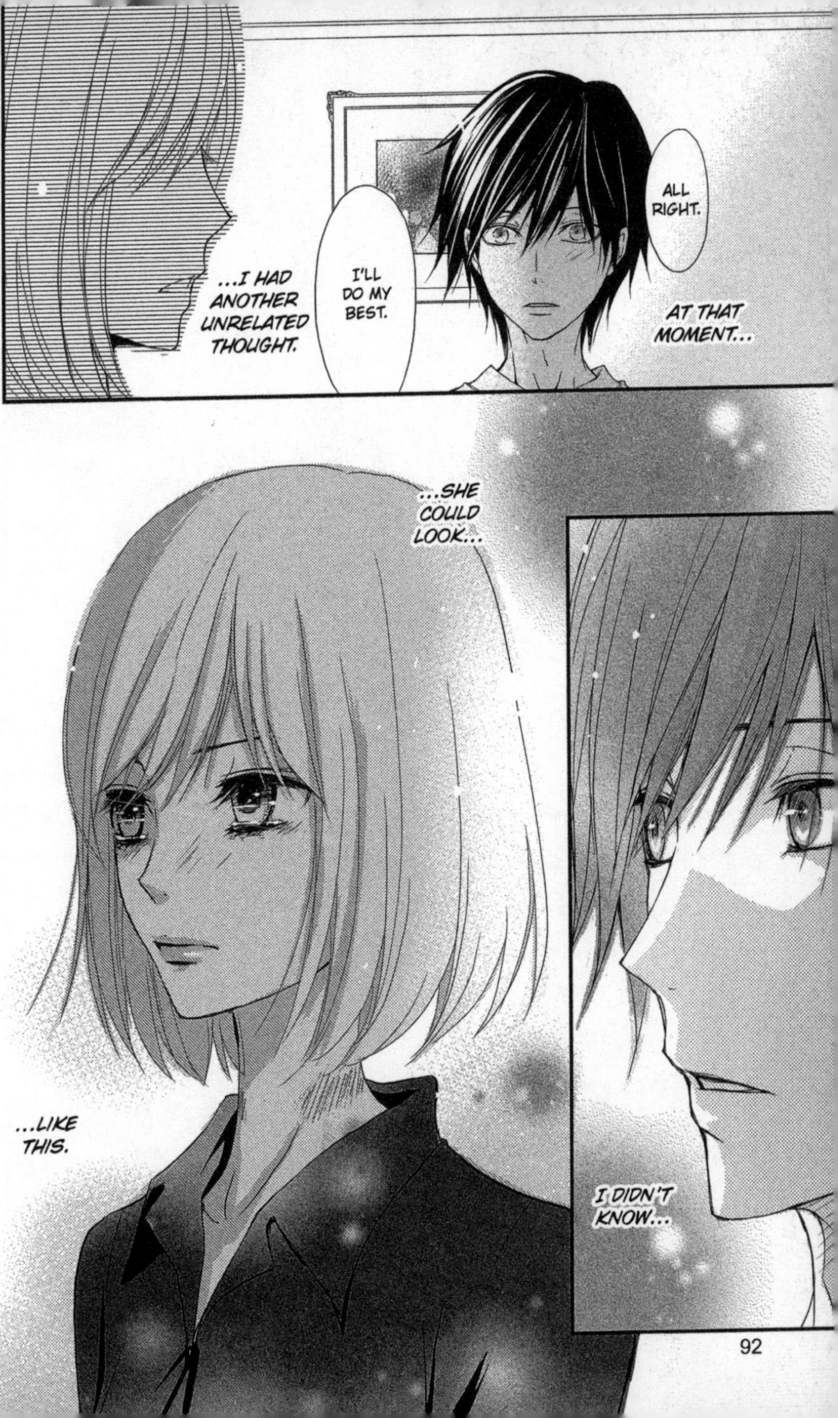
ALL RIGHT.
AT THAT MOMENT...
I'LL DO MY BEST.
...I HAD ANOTHER UNRELATED THOUGHT.
I DIDN'T KNOW...
...SHE COULD LOOK...
...LIKE THIS.

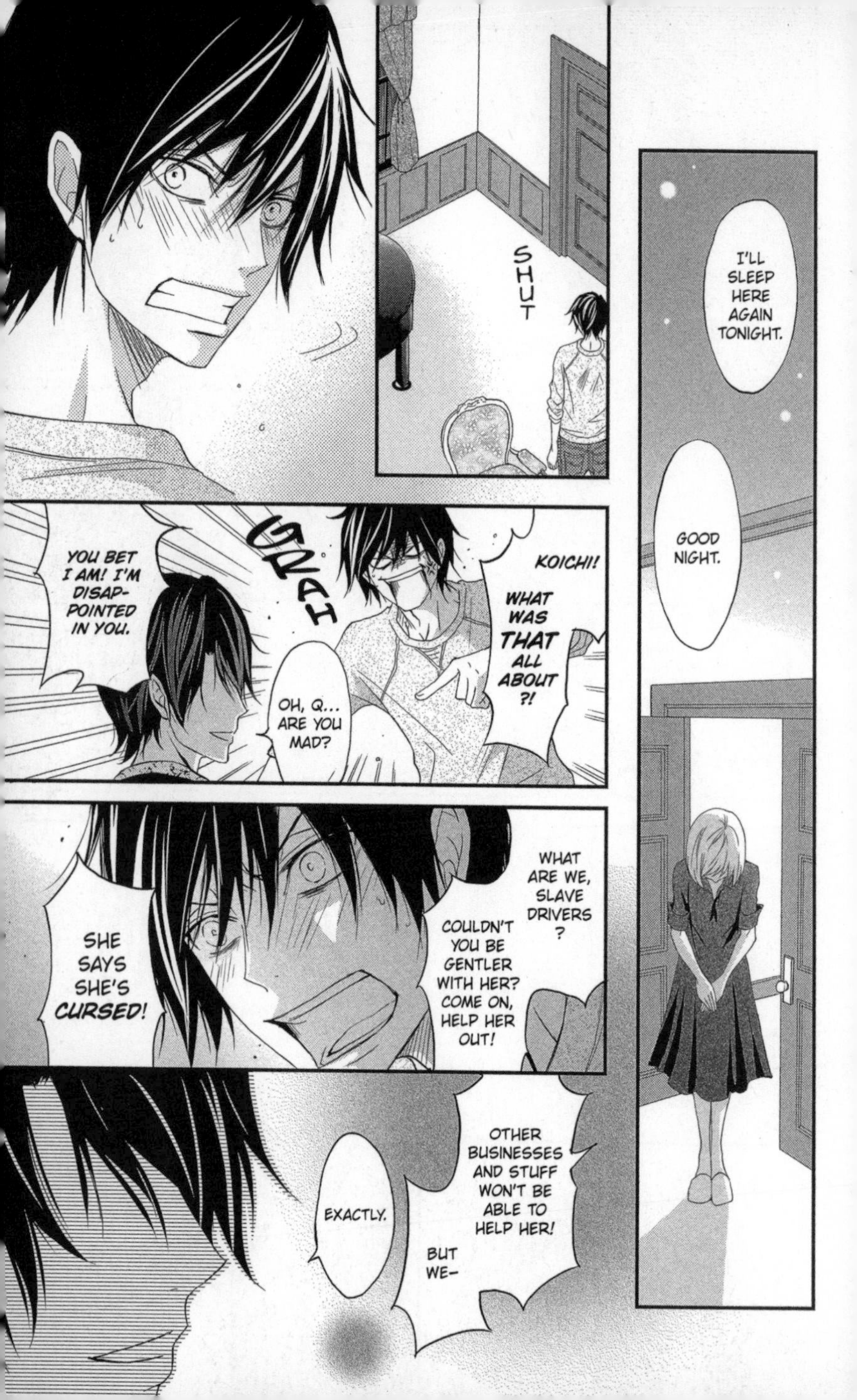
I'LL SLEEP HERE AGAIN TONIGHT.
GOOD NIGHT.
SHUT
KOICHI!
WHAT WAS THAT ALL ABOUT?!
GRAH
OH, Q... ARE YOU MAD?
YOU BET I AM! I'M DISAP-POINTED IN YOU.
WHAT ARE WE, SLAVE DRIVERS?
COULDN'T YOU BE GENTLER WITH HER? COME ON, HELP HER OUT!
SHE SAYS SHE'S CURSED!
OTHER BUSINESSES AND STUFF WON'T BE ABLE TO HELP HER!
BUT WE-
EXACTLY.

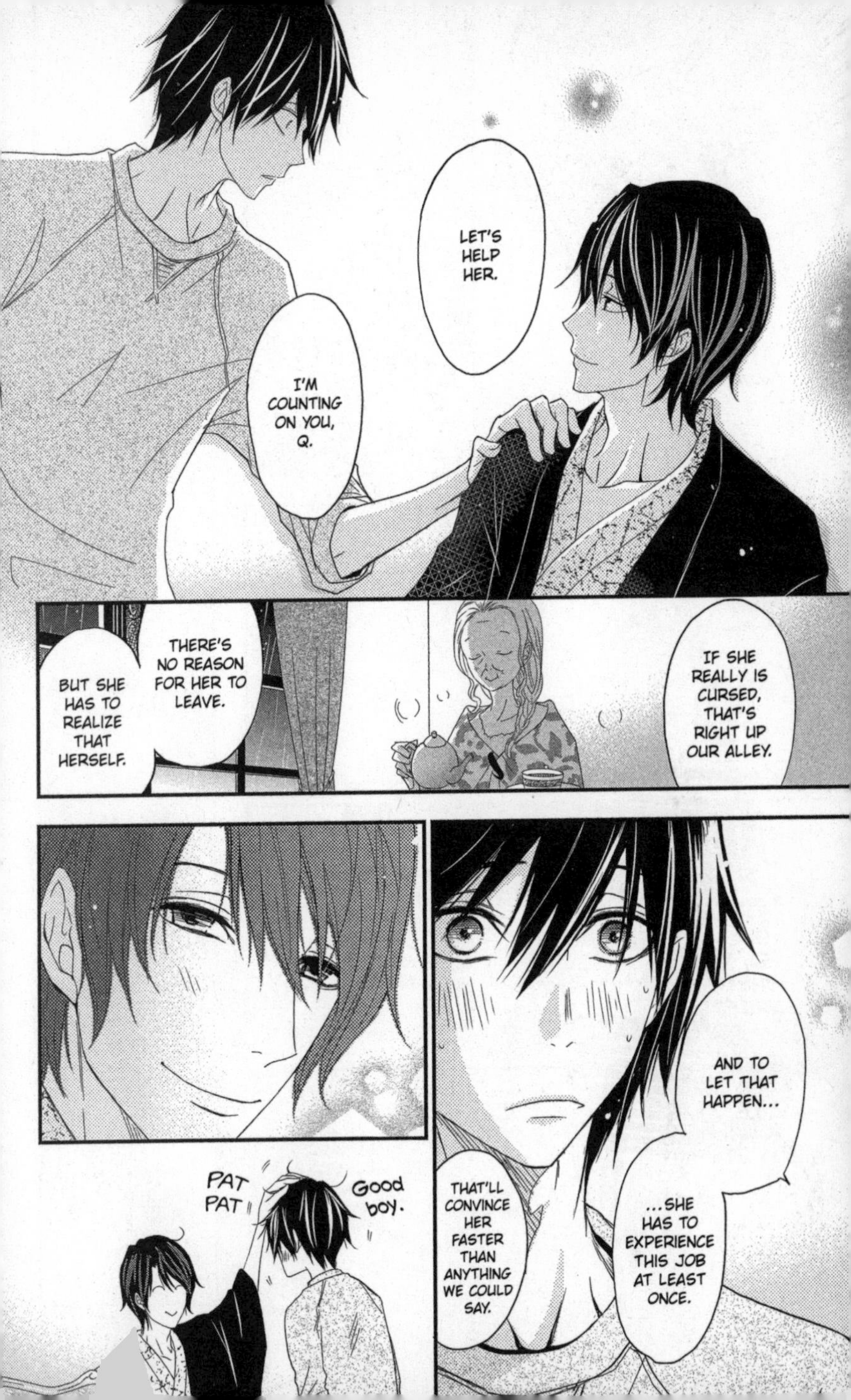
LET'S HELP HER.
I'M COUNTING ON YOU, Q.
IF SHE REALLY IS CURSED, THAT'S RIGHT UP OUR ALLEY.
THERE'S NO REASON FOR HER TO LEAVE.
BUT SHE HAS TO REALIZE THAT HERSELF.
AND TO LET THAT HAPPEN...
...SHE HAS TO EXPERIENCE THIS JOB AT LEAST ONCE.
THAT'LL CONVINCE HER FASTER THAN ANYTHING WE COULD SAY.
Good boy.
PAT PAT

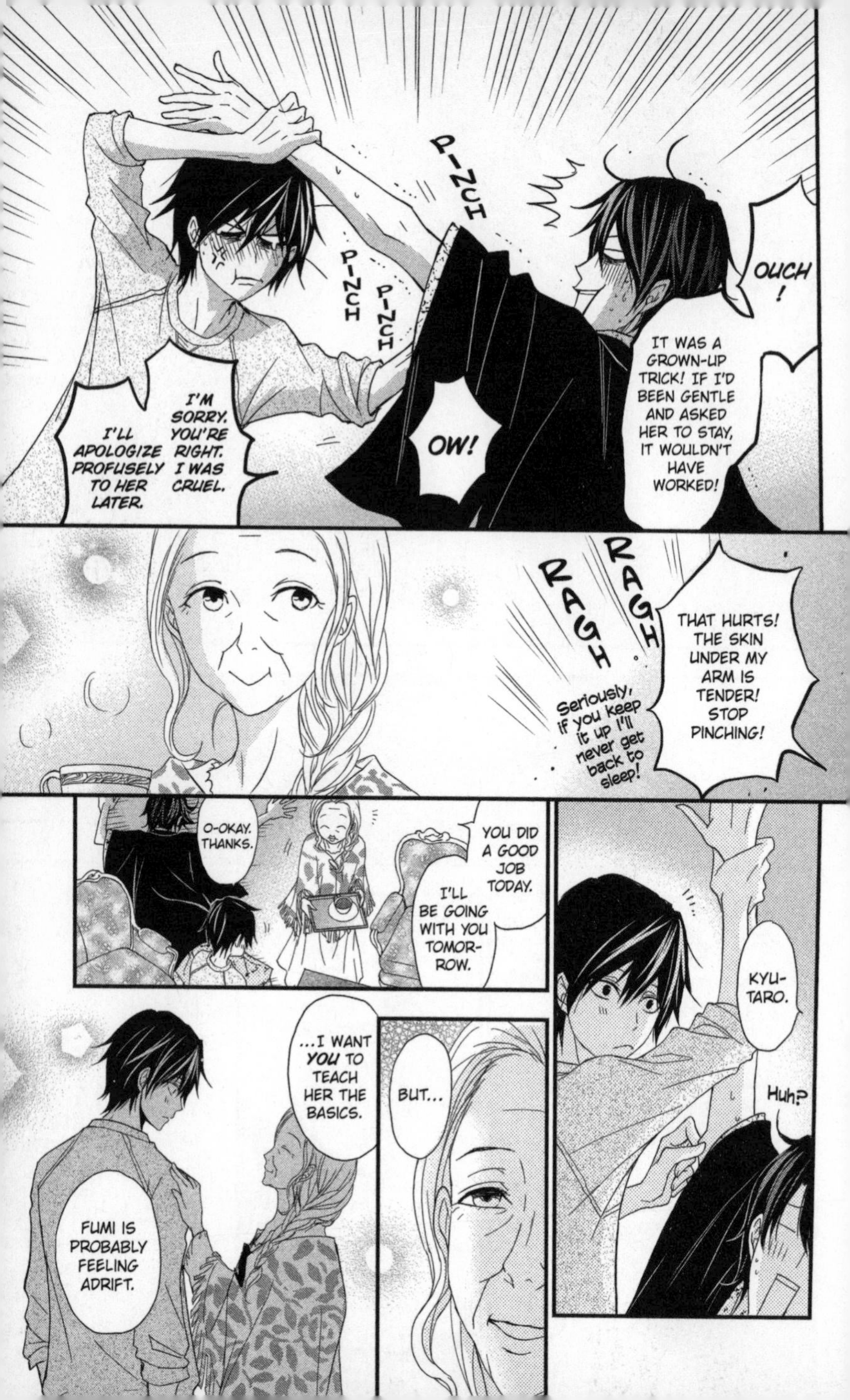
OUCH!
IT WAS A GROWN-UP TRICK! IF I'D BEEN GENTLE AND ASKED HER TO STAY, IT WOULDN'T HAVE WORKED!
PINCH
OW!
PINCH PINCH
I'M SORRY. YOU'RE RIGHT. I WAS CRUEL.
I'LL APOLOGIZE PROFUSELY TO HER LATER.
THAT HURTS! THE SKIN UNDER MY ARM IS TENDER! STOP PINCHING!
Seriously, if you keep it up I'll never get back to sleep!
RAGH RAGH
KYU-TARO.
Huh?
YOU DID A GOOD JOB TODAY.
I'LL BE GOING WITH YOU TOMORROW.
O-OKAY. THANKS.
BUT...
...I WANT YOU TO TEACH HER THE BASICS.
FUMI IS PROBABLY FEELING ADRIFT.

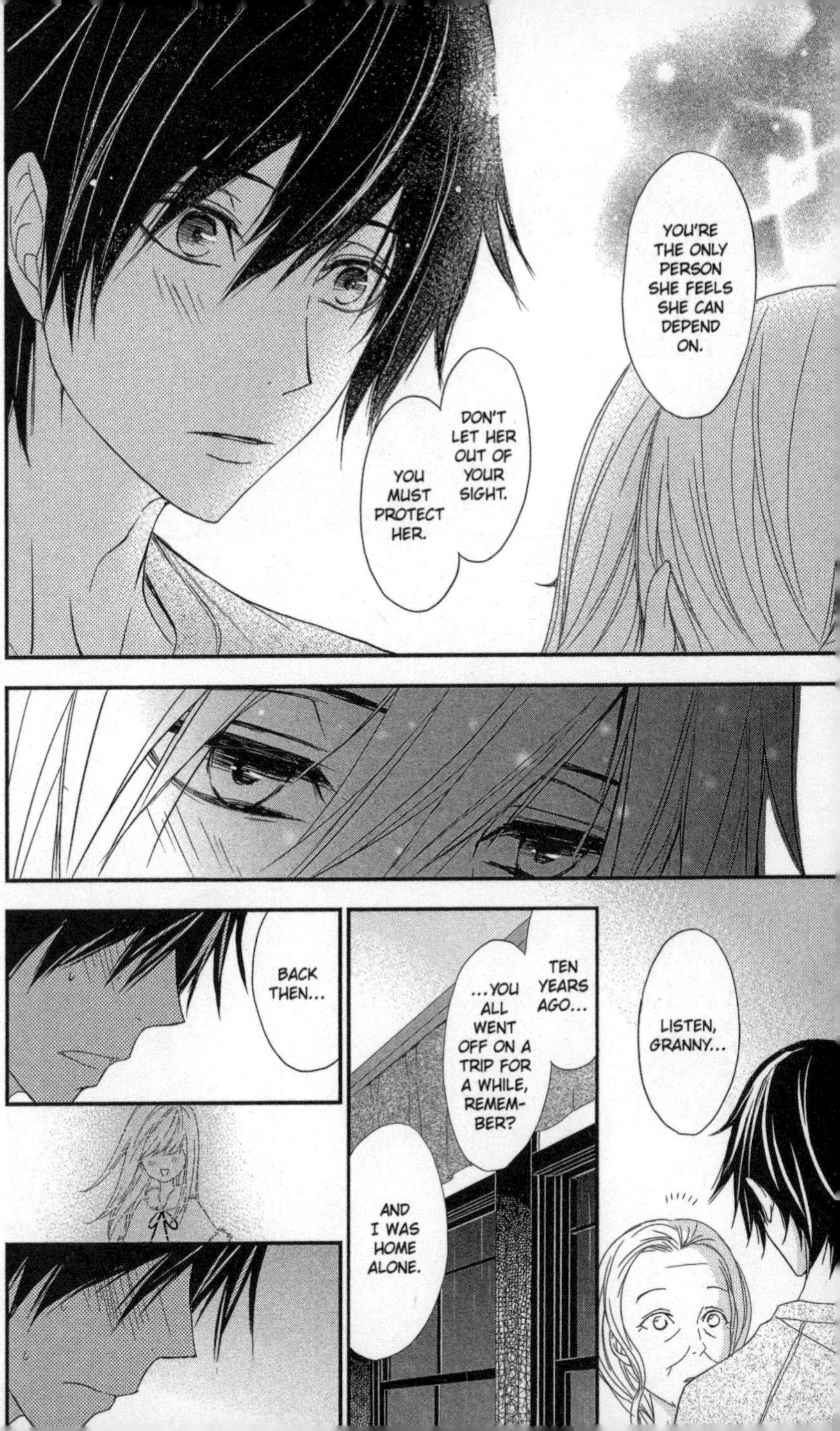
YOU'RE THE ONLY PERSON SHE FEELS SHE CAN DEPEND ON.
DON'T LET HER OUT OF YOUR SIGHT.
YOU MUST PROTECT HER.
LISTEN, GRANNY...
TEN YEARS AGO...
...YOU ALL WENT OFF ON A TRIP FOR A WHILE, REMEMBER?
AND I WAS HOME ALONE.
BACK THEN...

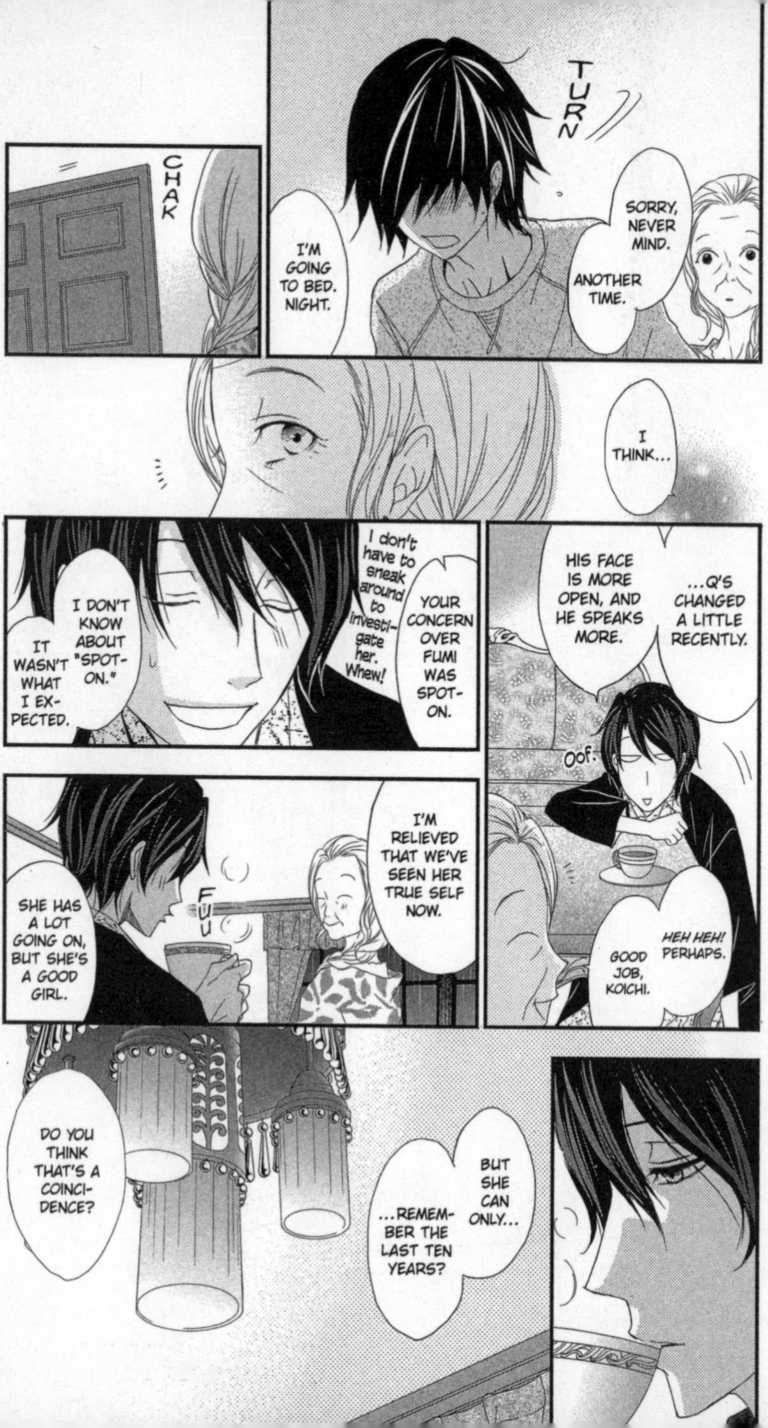
TURN
SORRY, NEVER MIND.
ANOTHER TIME.
I'M GOING TO BED. NIGHT.
CHAK
I THINK...
...Q'S CHANGED A LITTLE RECENTLY.
HIS FACE IS MORE OPEN, AND HE SPEAKS MORE.
Oof.
HEH HEH! PERHAPS.
GOOD JOB, KOICHI.
YOUR CONCERN OVER FUMI WAS SPOT-ON.
I don't have to sneak around to investigate her. Whew!
I DON'T KNOW ABOUT "SPOT-ON."
IT WASN'T WHAT I EXPECTED.
I'M RELIEVED THAT WE'VE SEEN HER TRUE SELF NOW.
FUU
SHE HAS A LOT GOING ON, BUT SHE'S A GOOD GIRL.
BUT SHE CAN ONLY...
...REMEMBER THE LAST TEN YEARS?
DO YOU THINK THAT'S A COINCIDENCE?

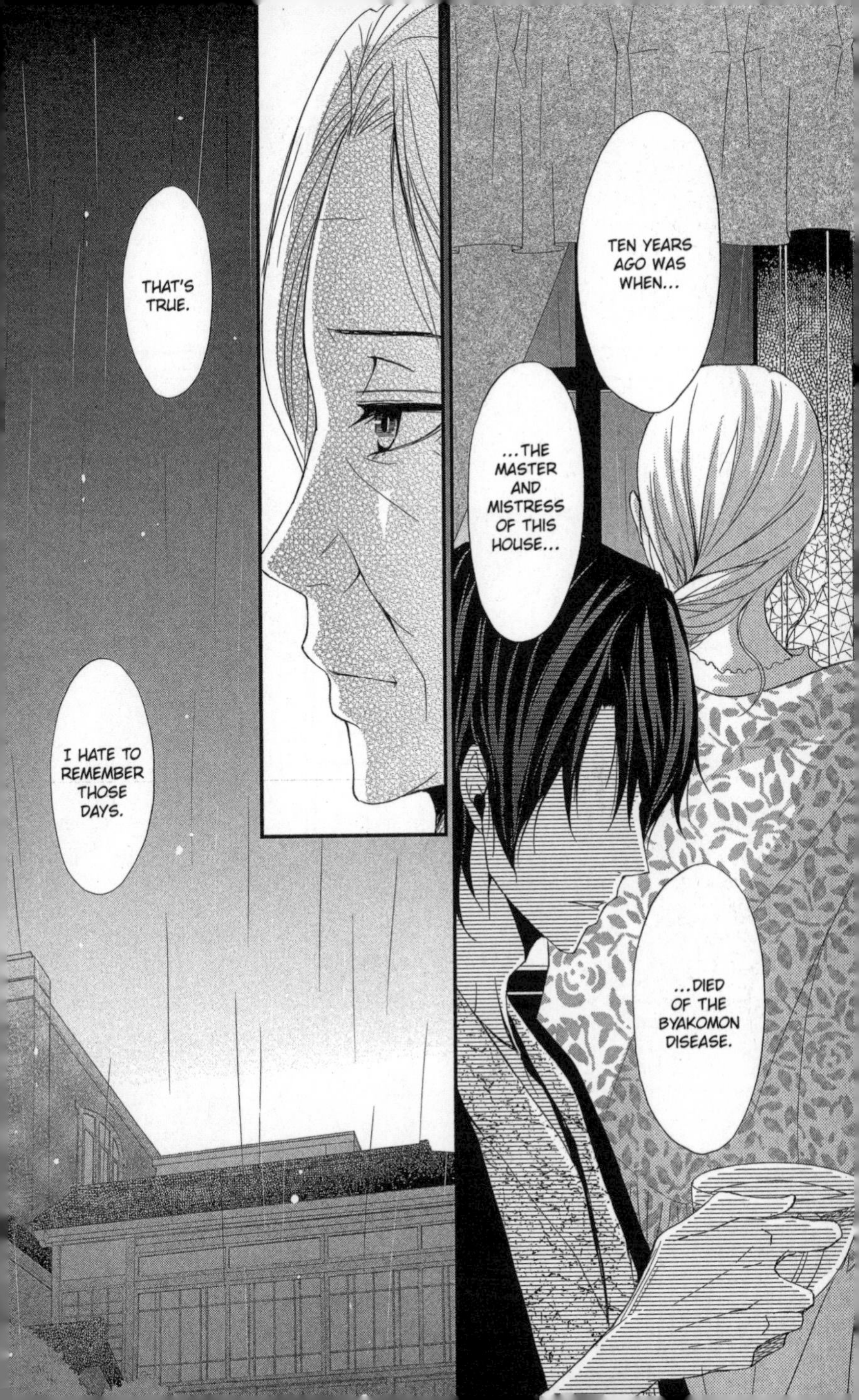
TEN YEARS AGO WAS WHEN...
...THE MASTER AND MISTRESS OF THIS HOUSE...
...DIED OF THE BYAKOMON DISEASE.
THAT'S TRUE.
I HATE TO REMEMBER THOSE DAYS.

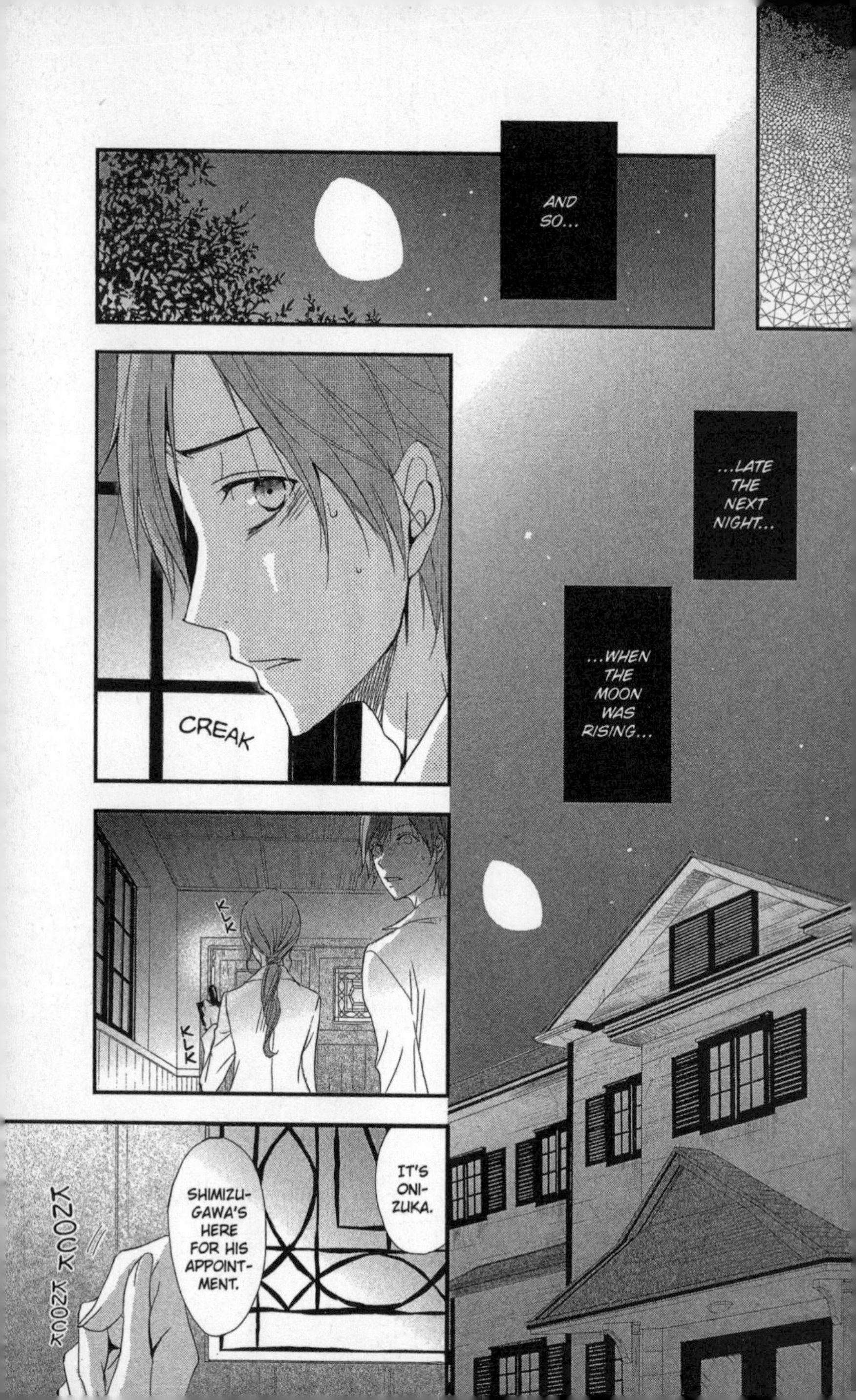
AND SO...
...LATE THE NEXT NIGHT...
...WHEN THE MOON WAS RISING...
CREAK
KLK KLK
IT'S ONI-ZUKA.
SHIMIZU-GAWA'S HERE FOR HIS APPOINT-MENT.
KNOCK KNOCK

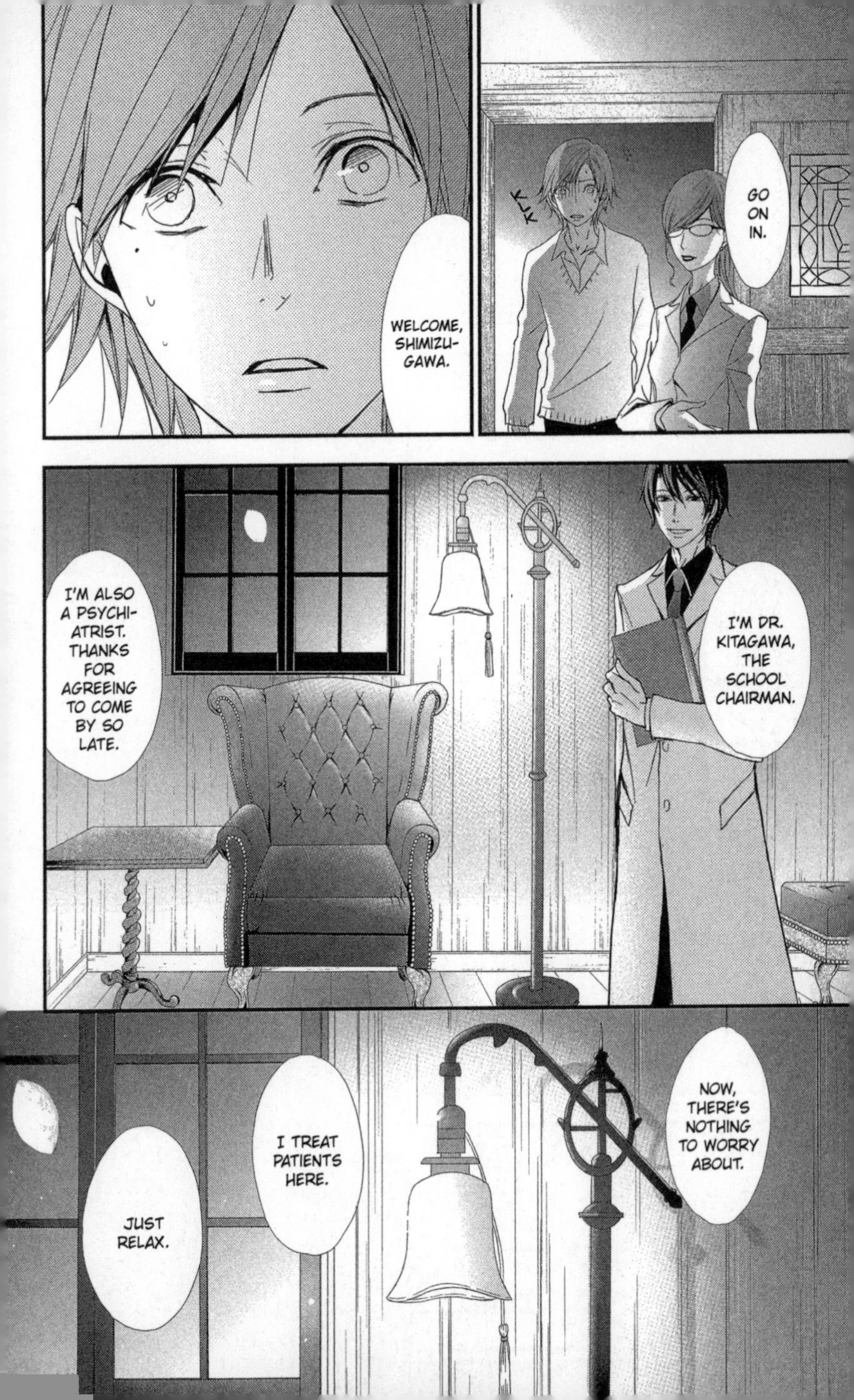
GO ON IN.
KLIK
WELCOME, SHIMIZU-GAWA.
I'M DR. KITAGAWA, THE SCHOOL CHAIRMAN.
I'M ALSO A PSYCHI-ATRIST. THANKS FOR AGREEING TO COME BY SO LATE.
NOW, THERE'S NOTHING TO WORRY ABOUT.
I TREAT PATIENTS HERE.
JUST RELAX.

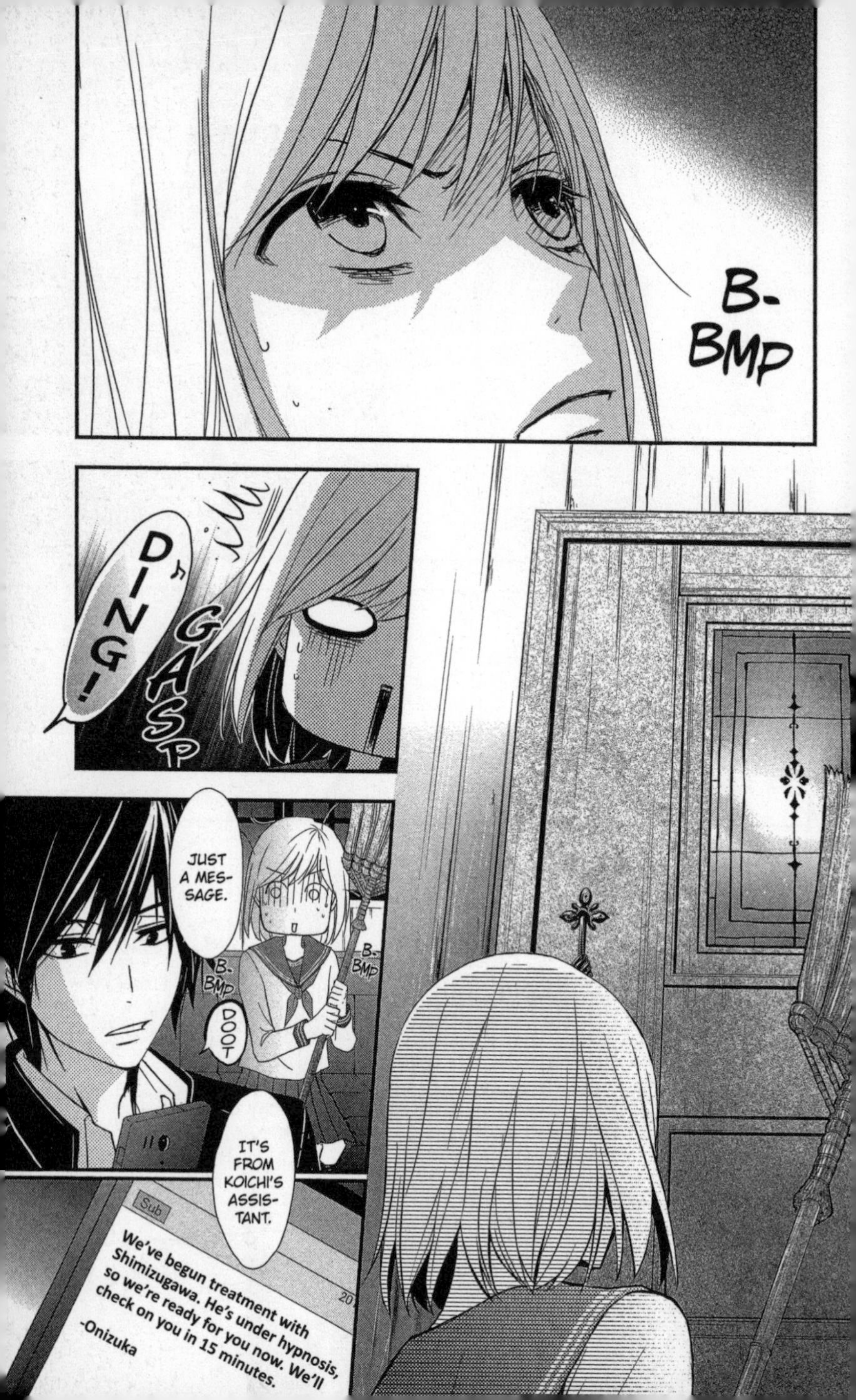
B-BMP
DING!
GASP
JUST A MES-SAGE.
B-BMP
B-BMP
DOOT
IT'S FROM KOICHI'S ASSIS-TANT.
Sub
We've begun treatment with Shimizugawa. He's under hypnosis, so we're ready for you now. We'll check on you in 15 minutes.
-Onizuka

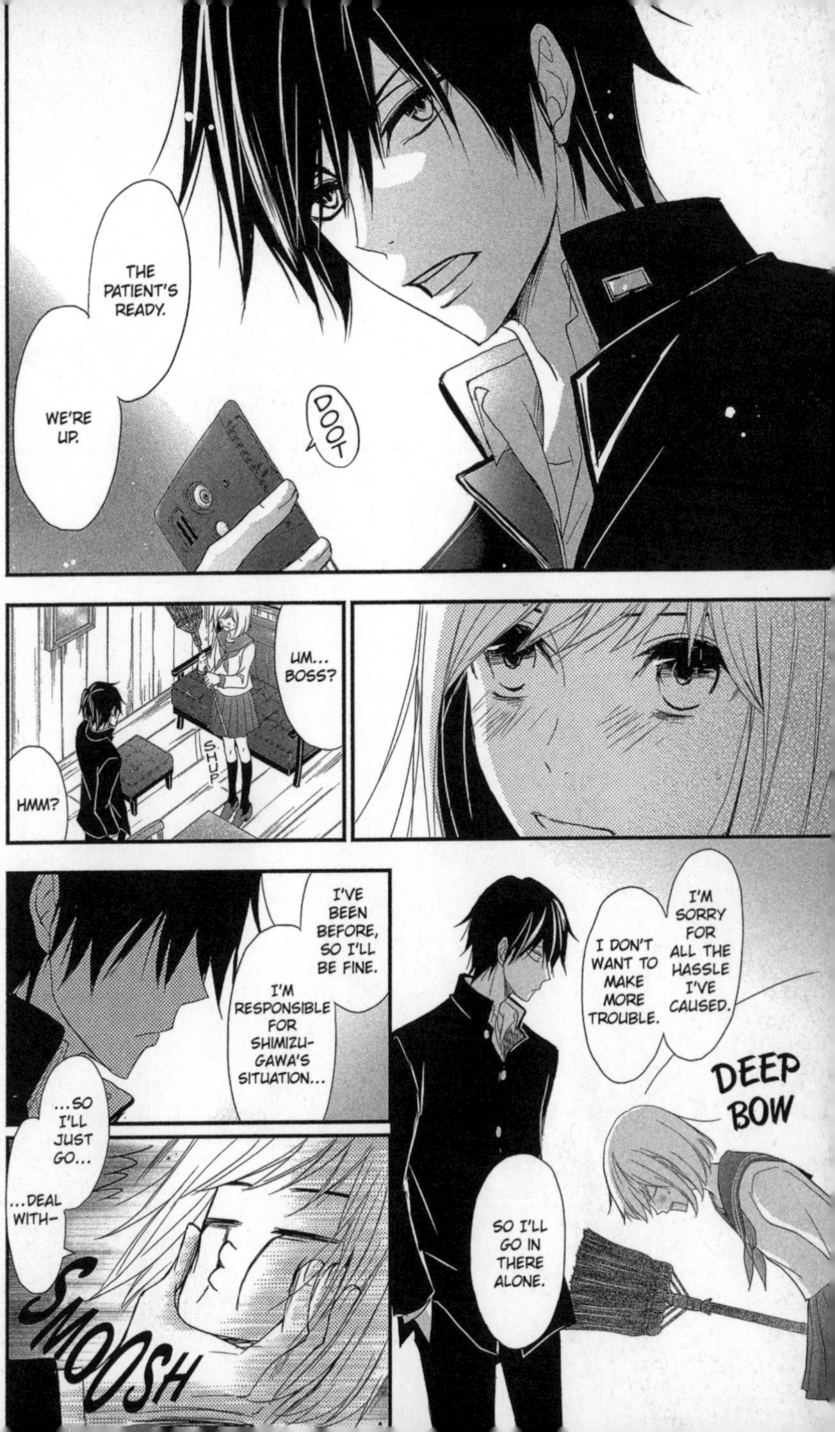
THE PATIENT'S READY.
WE'RE UP.
DOOT
UM... BOSS?
SHUP
HMM?
I'M SORRY FOR ALL THE HASSLE I'VE CAUSED.
I DON'T WANT TO MAKE MORE TROUBLE.
DEEP BOW
SO I'LL GO IN THERE ALONE.
I'VE BEEN BEFORE, SO I'LL BE FINE.
I'M RESPONSIBLE FOR SHIMIZU-GAWA'S SITUATION...
...SO I'LL JUST GO...
...DEAL WITH-
SMOOSH

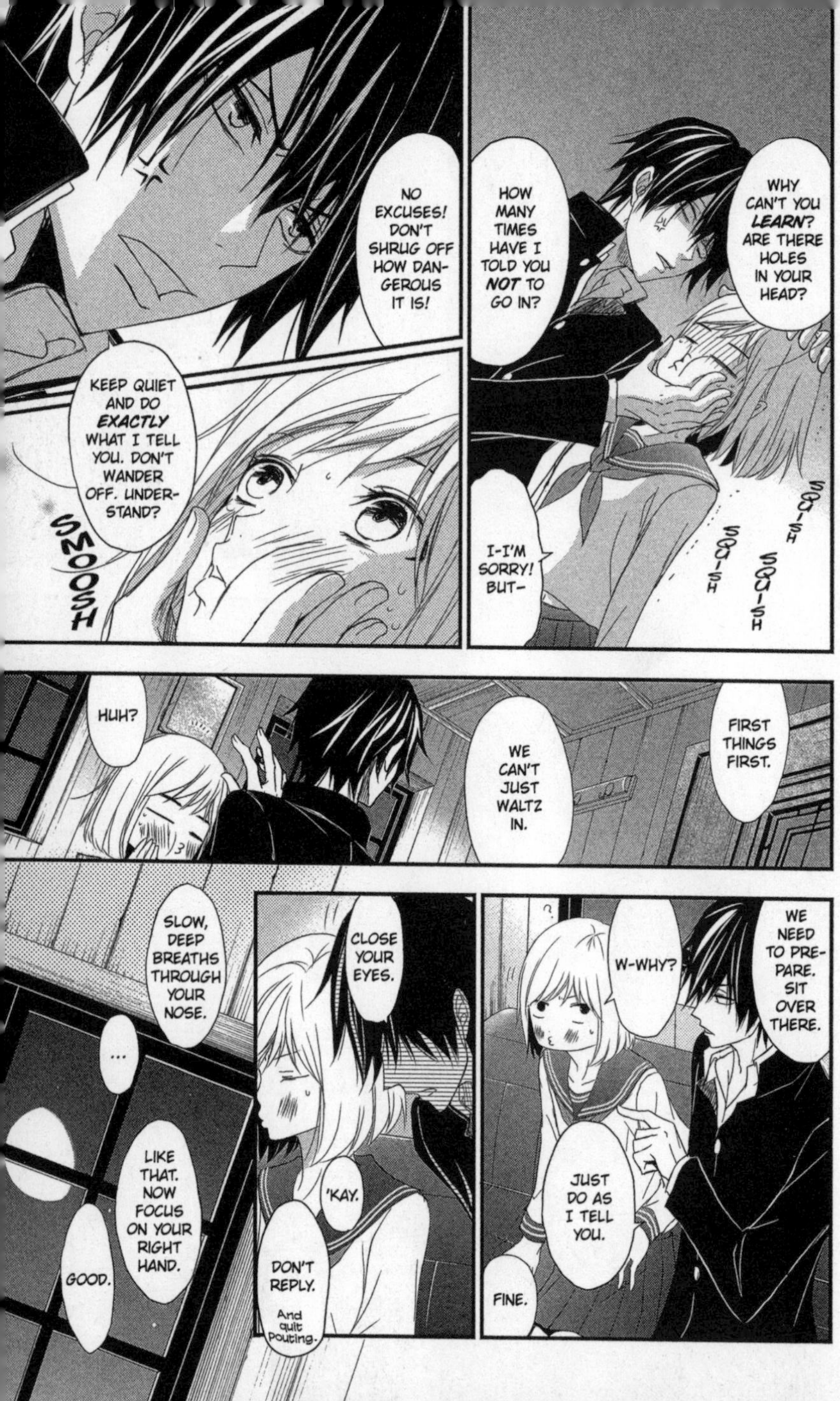
WHY CAN'T YOU *LEARN*? ARE THERE HOLES IN YOUR HEAD?
HOW MANY TIMES HAVE I TOLD YOU *NOT* TO GO IN?
SQUISH SQUISH
SQUISH SQUISH
I-I'M SORRY! BUT-
NO EXCUSES! DON'T SHRUG OFF HOW DANGEROUS IT IS!
KEEP QUIET AND DO *EXACTLY* WHAT I TELL YOU. DON'T WANDER OFF. UNDERSTAND?
SMOOSH
FIRST THINGS FIRST.
WE CAN'T JUST WALTZ IN.
HUH?
WE NEED TO PREPARE. SIT OVER THERE.
W-WHY?
JUST DO AS I TELL YOU.
FINE.
CLOSE YOUR EYES.
'KAY.
DON'T REPLY.
And quit pouting.
SLOW, DEEP BREATHS THROUGH YOUR NOSE.
...
LIKE THAT. NOW FOCUS ON YOUR RIGHT HAND.
GOOD.

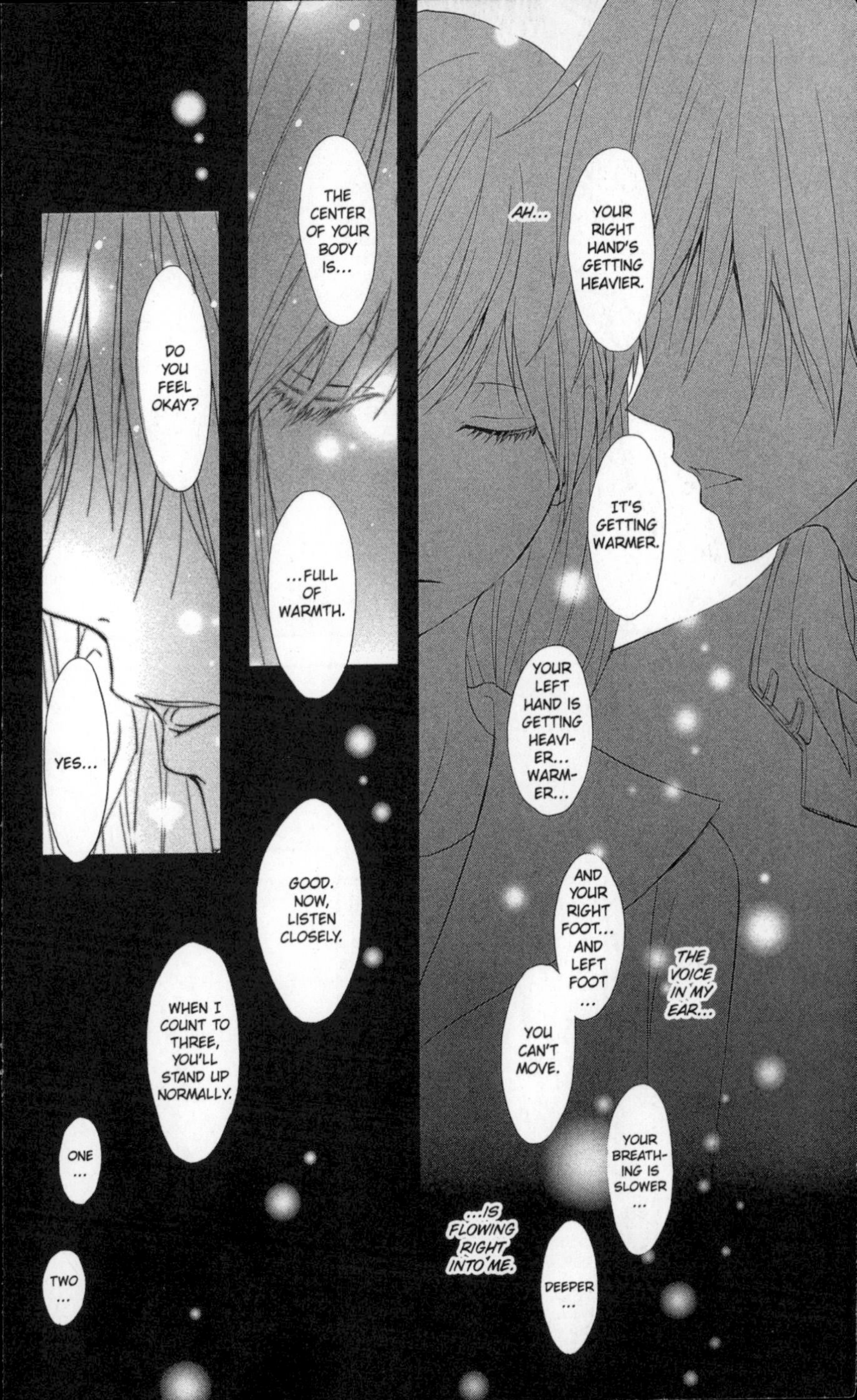
YOUR RIGHT HAND'S GETTING HEAVIER.
AH...
IT'S GETTING WARMER.
YOUR LEFT HAND IS GETTING HEAVI-ER... WARM-ER...
AND YOUR RIGHT FOOT... AND LEFT FOOT...
THE VOICE IN MY EAR...
YOU CAN'T MOVE.
YOUR BREATH-ING IS SLOWER...
...IS FLOWING RIGHT INTO ME.
DEEPER...
THE CENTER OF YOUR BODY IS...
...FULL OF WARMTH.
DO YOU FEEL OKAY?
YES...
GOOD. NOW, LISTEN CLOSELY.
WHEN I COUNT TO THREE, YOU'LL STAND UP NORMALLY.
ONE...
TWO...

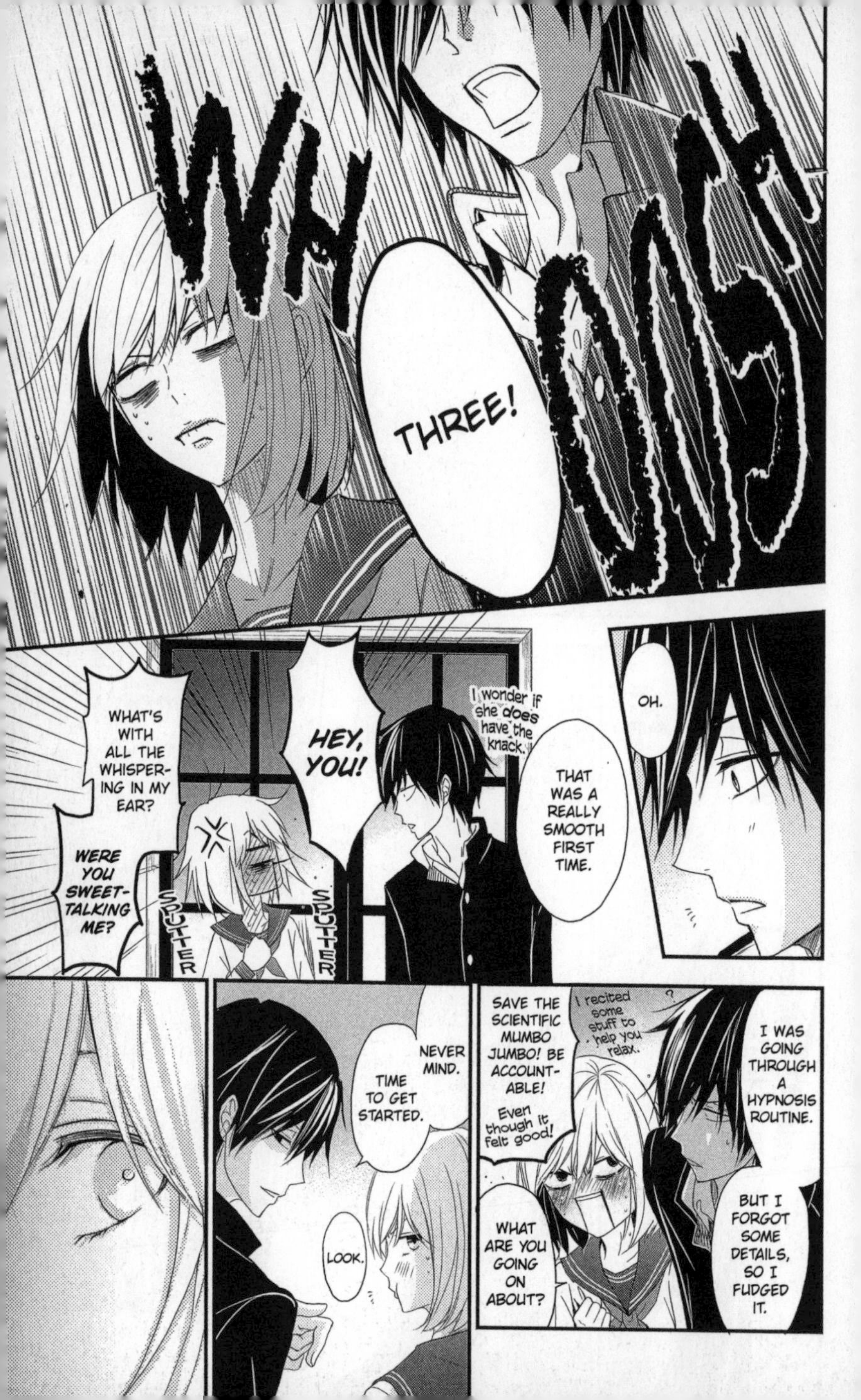
WHOOSH
THREE!
OH.
THAT WAS A REALLY SMOOTH FIRST TIME.
I wonder if she does have the knack.
HEY, YOU!
SPUTTER
SPUTTER
WHAT'S WITH ALL THE WHISPERING IN MY EAR?
WERE YOU SWEET-TALKING ME?
I WAS GOING THROUGH A HYPNOSIS ROUTINE.
BUT I FORGOT SOME DETAILS, SO I FUDGED IT.
I recited some stuff to help you relax.
SAVE THE SCIENTIFIC MUMBO JUMBO! BE ACCOUNTABLE!
Even though it felt good!
WHAT ARE YOU GOING ON ABOUT?
NEVER MIND.
TIME TO GET STARTED.
LOOK.

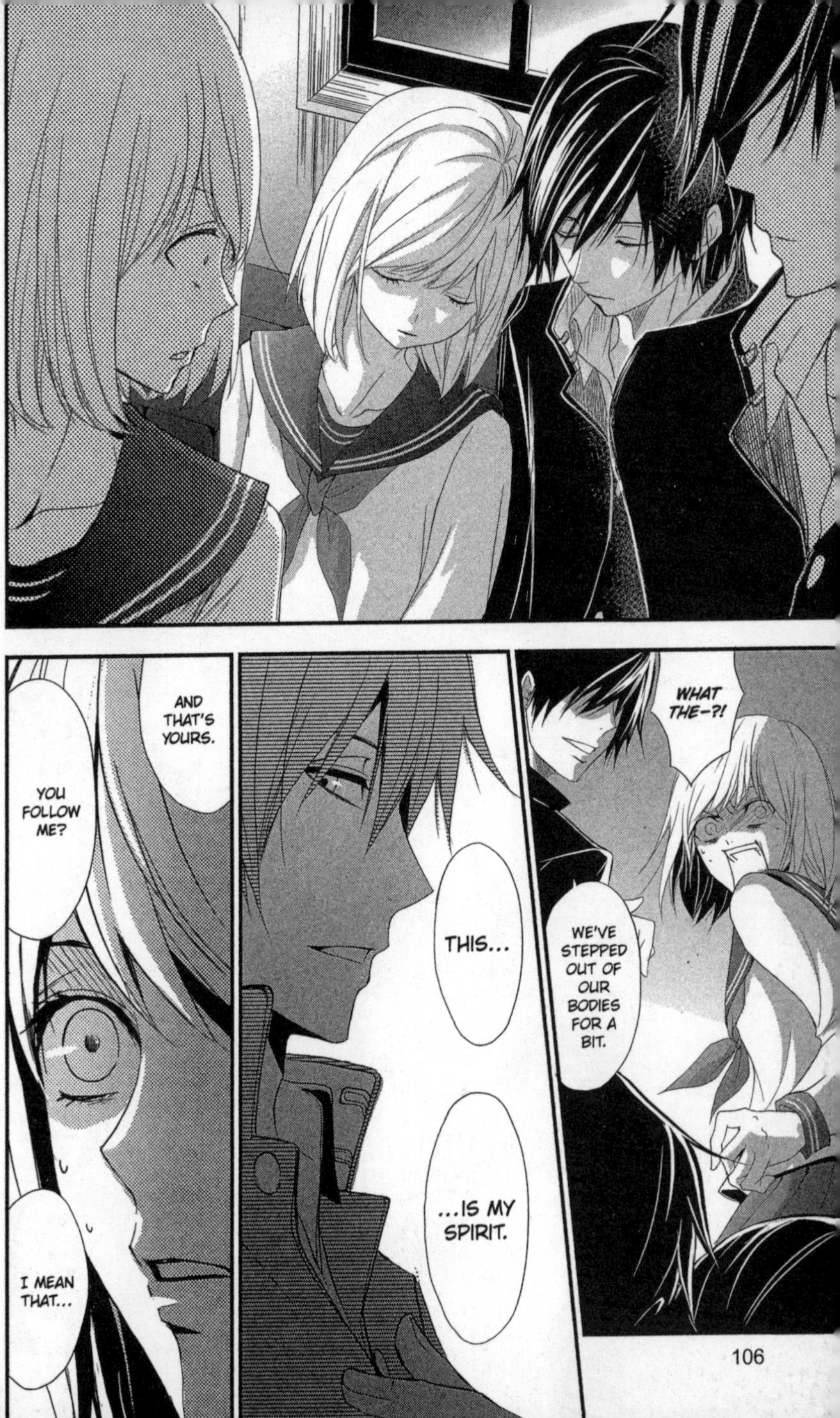
WHAT THE–?!
WE'VE STEPPED OUT OF OUR BODIES FOR A BIT.
THIS...
...IS MY SPIRIT.
AND THAT'S YOURS.
YOU FOLLOW ME?
I MEAN THAT...

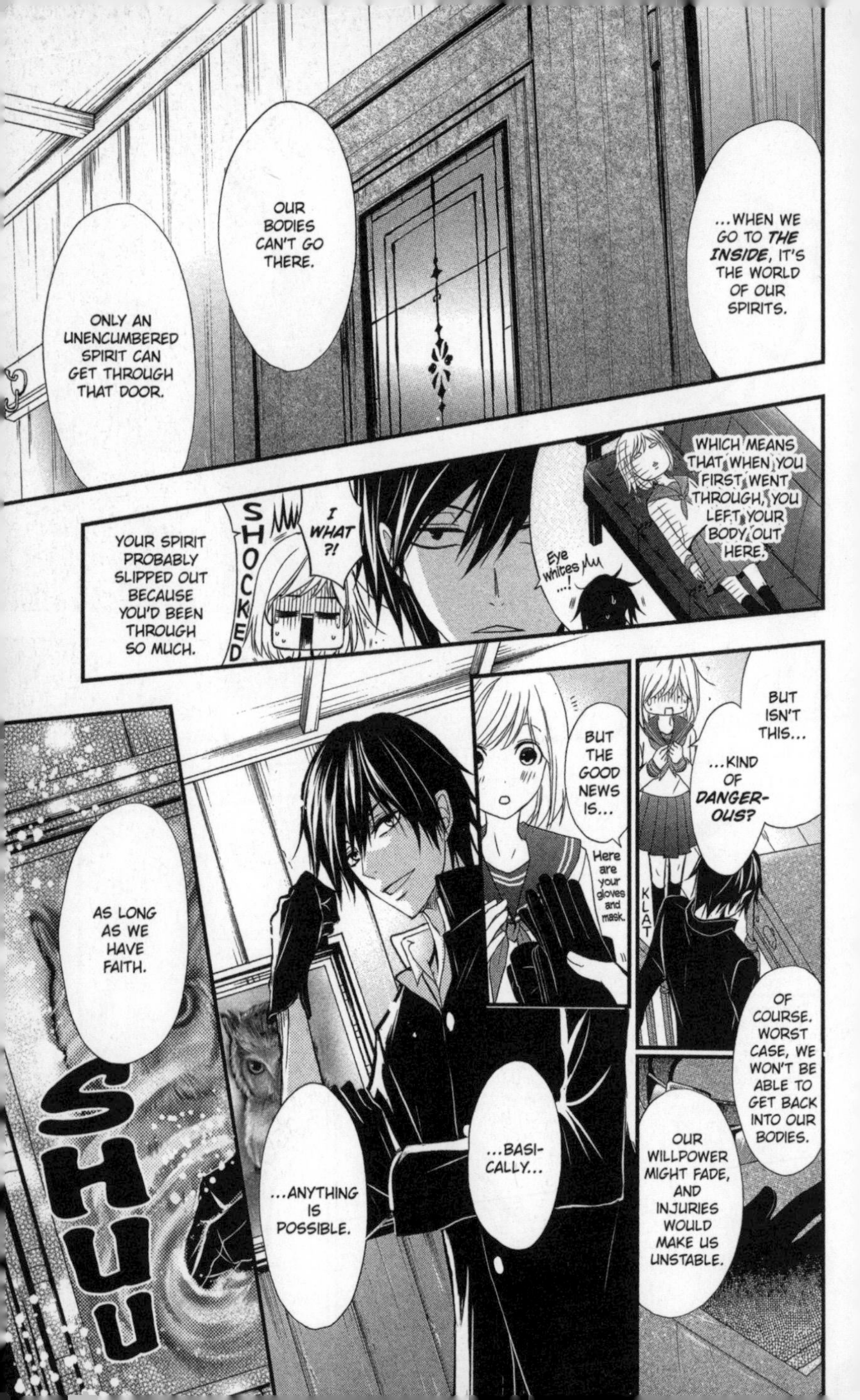
...WHEN WE GO TO *THE INSIDE*, IT'S THE WORLD OF OUR SPIRITS.
OUR BODIES CAN'T GO THERE.
ONLY AN UNENCUMBERED SPIRIT CAN GET THROUGH THAT DOOR.
WHICH MEANS THAT WHEN YOU FIRST WENT THROUGH, YOU LEFT YOUR BODY OUT HERE.
Eye whites ...!
I *WHAT* ?!
SHOCKED
YOUR SPIRIT PROBABLY SLIPPED OUT BECAUSE YOU'D BEEN THROUGH SO MUCH.
BUT ISN'T THIS...
...KIND OF *DANGER-OUS?*
KLAT
OF COURSE. WORST CASE, WE WON'T BE ABLE TO GET BACK INTO OUR BODIES.
OUR WILLPOWER MIGHT FADE, AND INJURIES WOULD MAKE US UNSTABLE.
BUT THE GOOD NEWS IS...
Here are your gloves and mask.
...BASI-CALLY...
...ANYTHING IS POSSIBLE.
AS LONG AS WE HAVE FAITH.
SHUU

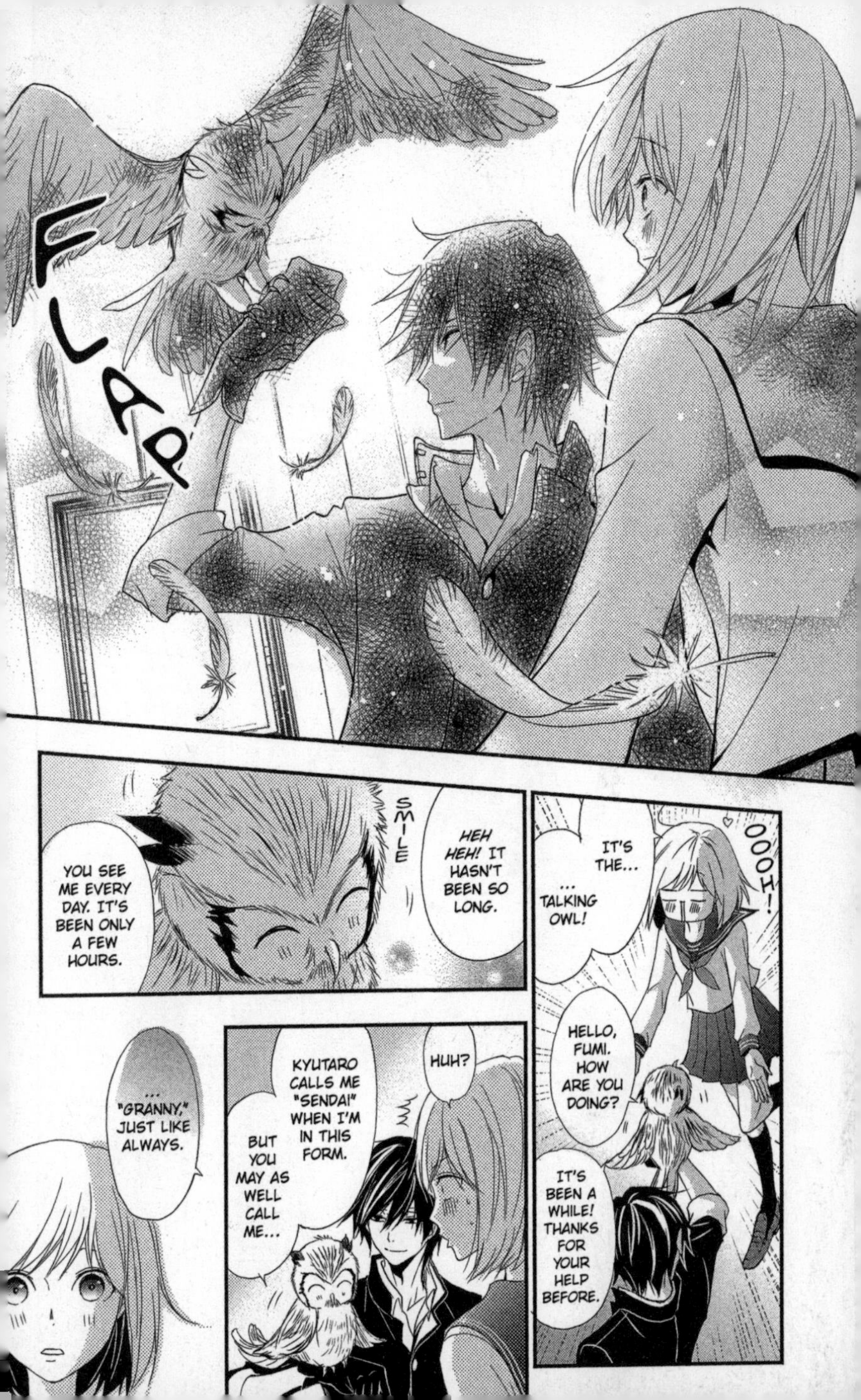
FLAP
IT'S THE...
...TALKING OWL!
OOOH!
HELLO, FUMI. HOW ARE YOU DOING?
IT'S BEEN A WHILE! THANKS FOR YOUR HELP BEFORE.
SMILE
HEH HEH! IT HASN'T BEEN SO LONG.
YOU SEE ME EVERY DAY. IT'S BEEN ONLY A FEW HOURS.
HUH?
KYUTARO CALLS ME "SENDAI" WHEN I'M IN THIS FORM.
BUT YOU MAY AS WELL CALL ME...
..."GRANNY," JUST LIKE ALWAYS.

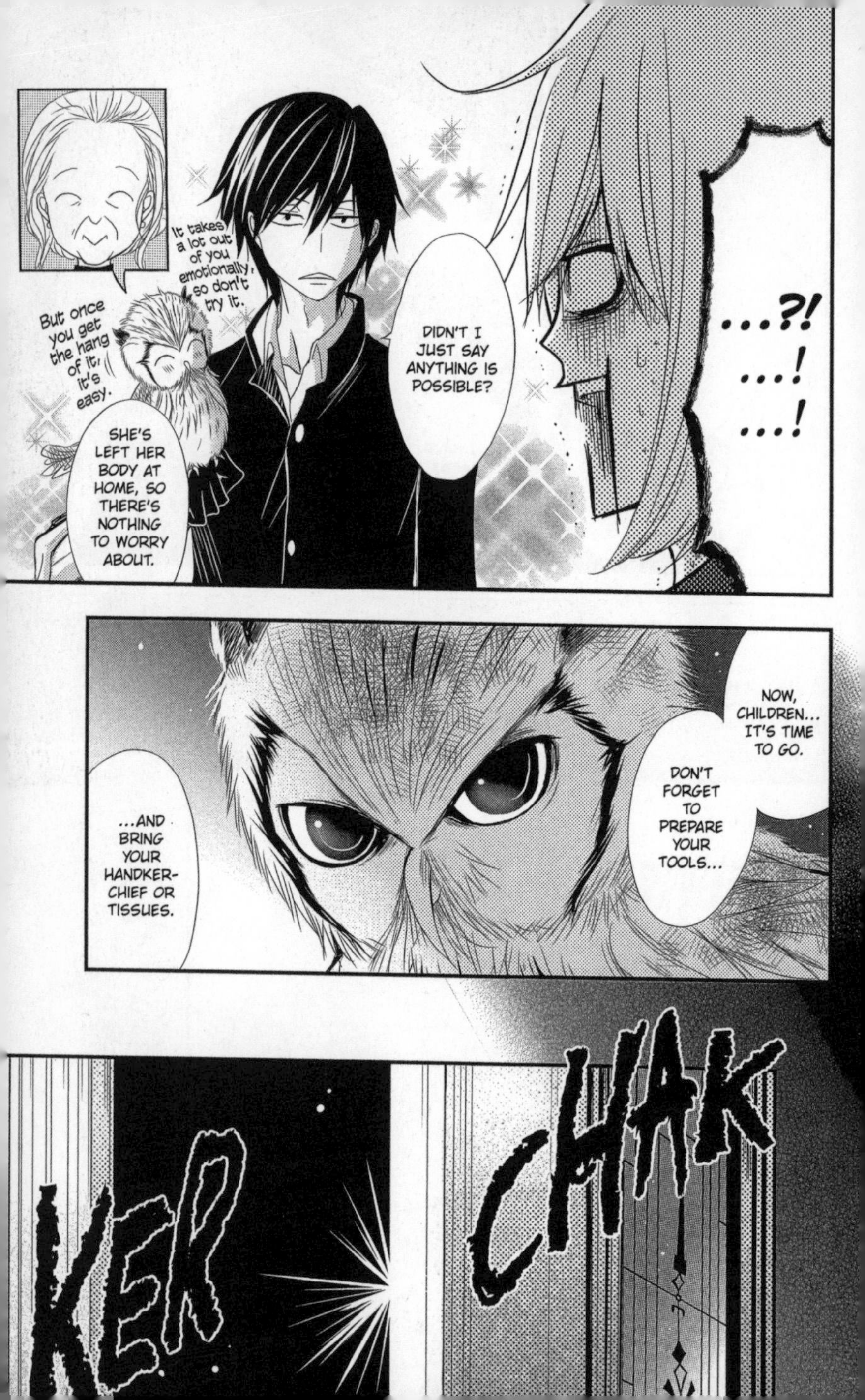
...?!
...!
...!
DIDN'T I JUST SAY ANYTHING IS POSSIBLE?
It takes a lot out of you emotionally, so don't try it.
But once you get the hang of it, it's easy.
SHE'S LEFT HER BODY AT HOME, SO THERE'S NOTHING TO WORRY ABOUT.
NOW, CHILDREN... IT'S TIME TO GO.
DON'T FORGET TO PREPARE YOUR TOOLS...
...AND BRING YOUR HANDKER-CHIEF OR TISSUES.
CHAK
KER

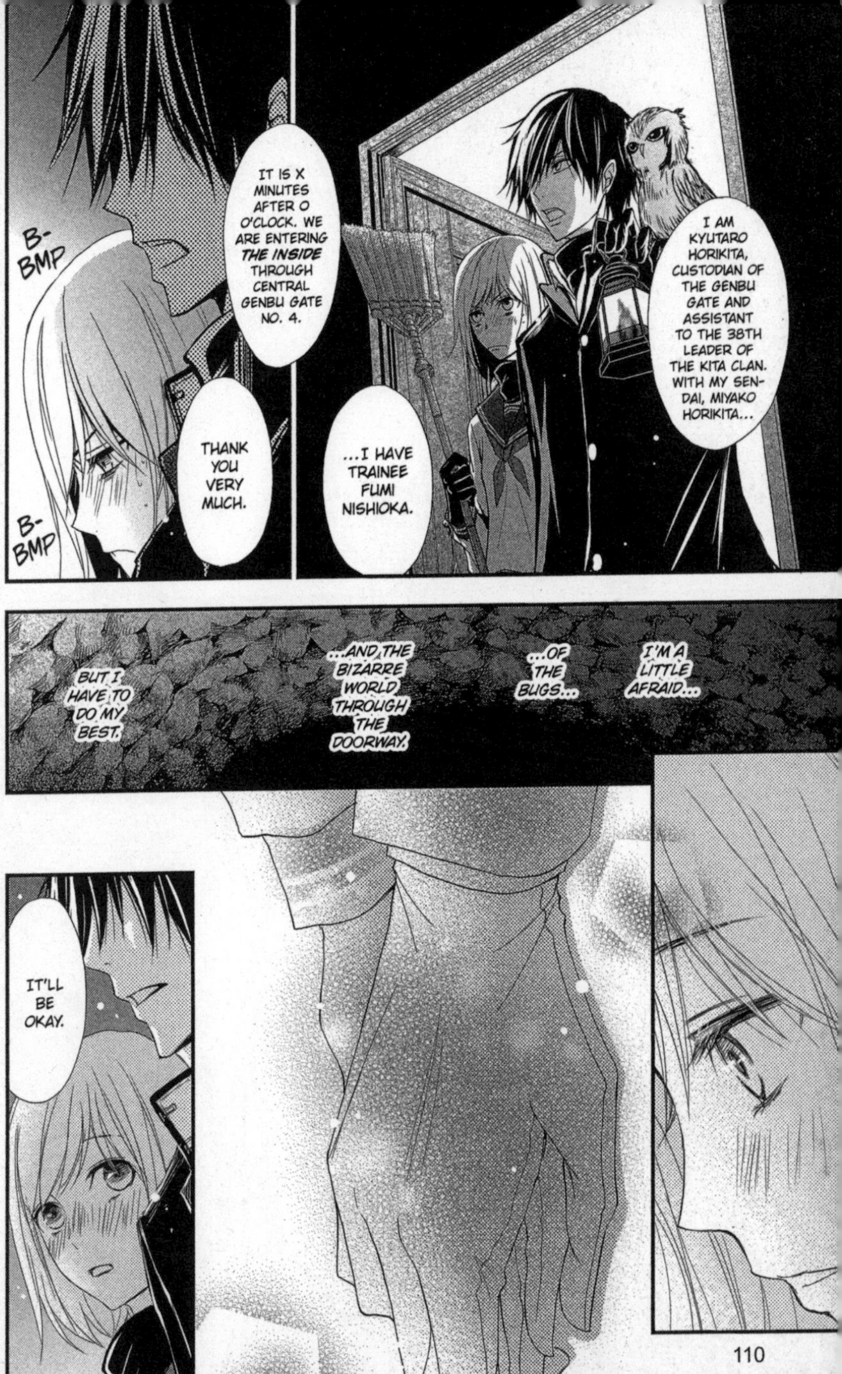
I AM KYUTARO HORIKITA, CUSTODIAN OF THE GENBU GATE AND ASSISTANT TO THE 38TH LEADER OF THE KITA CLAN. WITH MY SEN-DAI, MIYAKO HORIKITA...
...I HAVE TRAINEE FUMI NISHIOKA.
IT IS X MINUTES AFTER O O'CLOCK. WE ARE ENTERING ***THE INSIDE*** THROUGH CENTRAL GENBU GATE NO. 4.
B-BMP
THANK YOU VERY MUCH.
B-BMP
I'M A LITTLE AFRAID...
...OF THE BUGS...
...AND THE BIZARRE WORLD THROUGH THE DOORWAY.
BUT I HAVE TO DO MY BEST.
IT'LL BE OKAY.

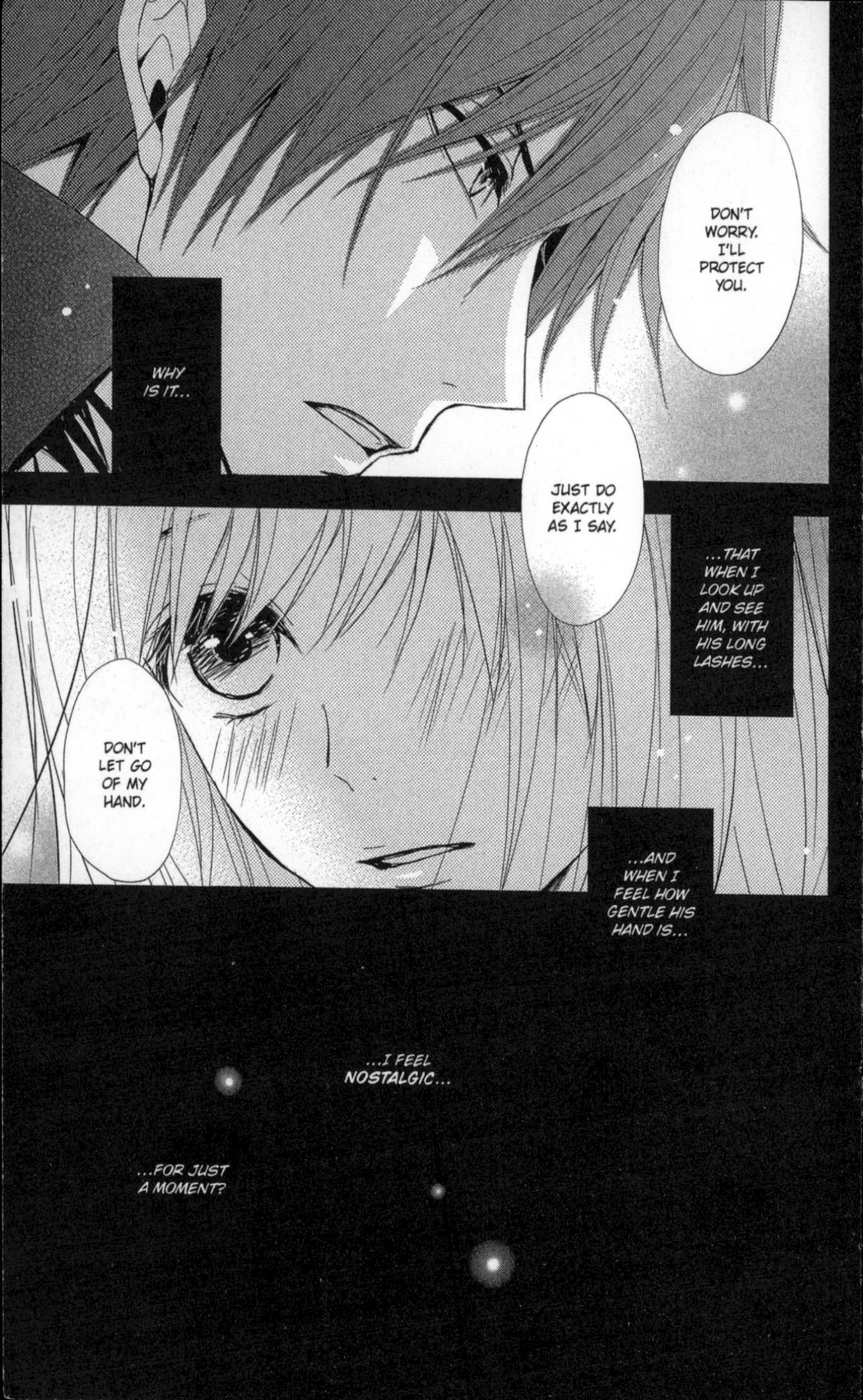

DON'T WORRY. I'LL PROTECT YOU.
JUST DO EXACTLY AS I SAY.
WHY IS IT...
...THAT WHEN I LOOK UP AND SEE HIM, WITH HIS LONG LASHES...
DON'T LET GO OF MY HAND.
...AND WHEN I FEEL HOW GENTLE HIS HAND IS...
...I FEEL NOSTALGIC...
...FOR JUST A MOMENT?

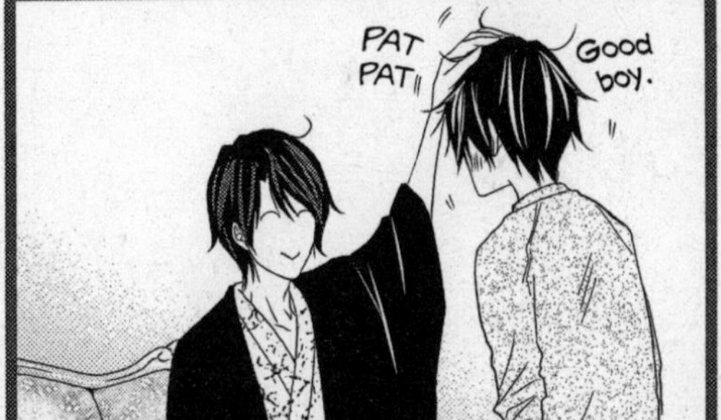
Good boy.
PAT PAT

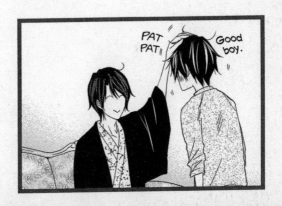

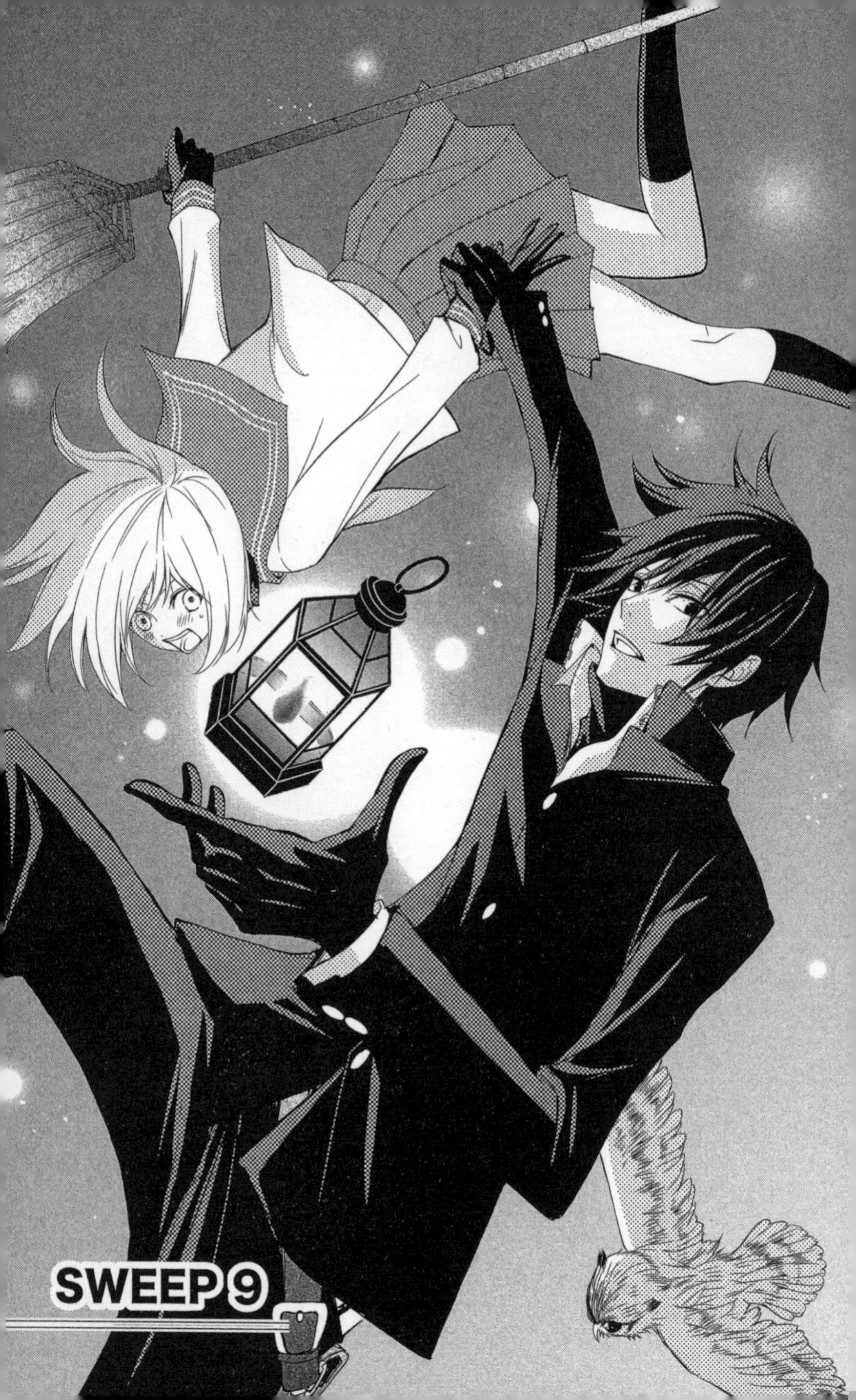
SWEEP 9

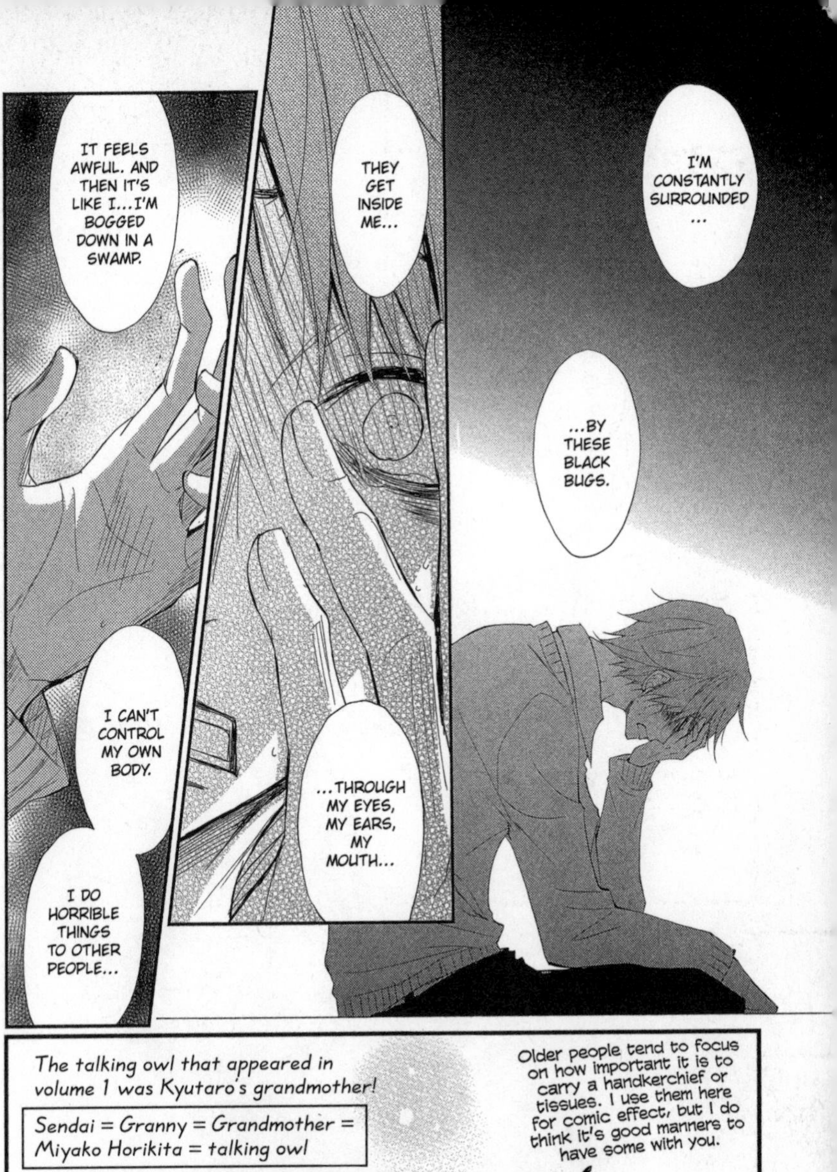
I'M CONSTANTLY SURROUNDED...
...BY THESE BLACK BUGS.
THEY GET INSIDE ME...
...THROUGH MY EYES, MY EARS, MY MOUTH...
IT FEELS AWFUL. AND THEN IT'S LIKE I...I'M BOGGED DOWN IN A SWAMP.
I CAN'T CONTROL MY OWN BODY.
I DO HORRIBLE THINGS TO OTHER PEOPLE...

The talking owl that appeared in volume 1 was Kyutaro's grandmother!

Sendai = Granny = Grandmother = Miyako Horikita = talking owl

I'm sorry she has so many names.

You may wonder why I've been referring to her using the term for an owl without ears, since she does have tufts, instead of using the word for a horned owl. From what I've learned, there isn't actually much of a difference! And in the world of this story, where anything is possible, this owl's coloring and size varies with each appearance. There's no deep meaning. It's just an artistic weakness.

Older people tend to focus on how important it is to carry a handkerchief or tissues. I use them here for comic effect, but I do think it's good manners to have some with you.

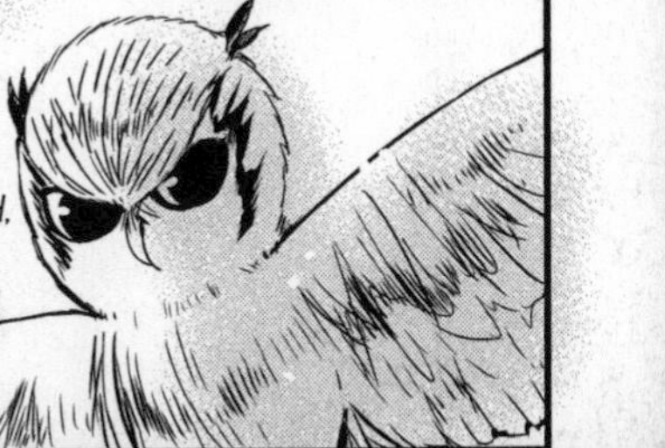

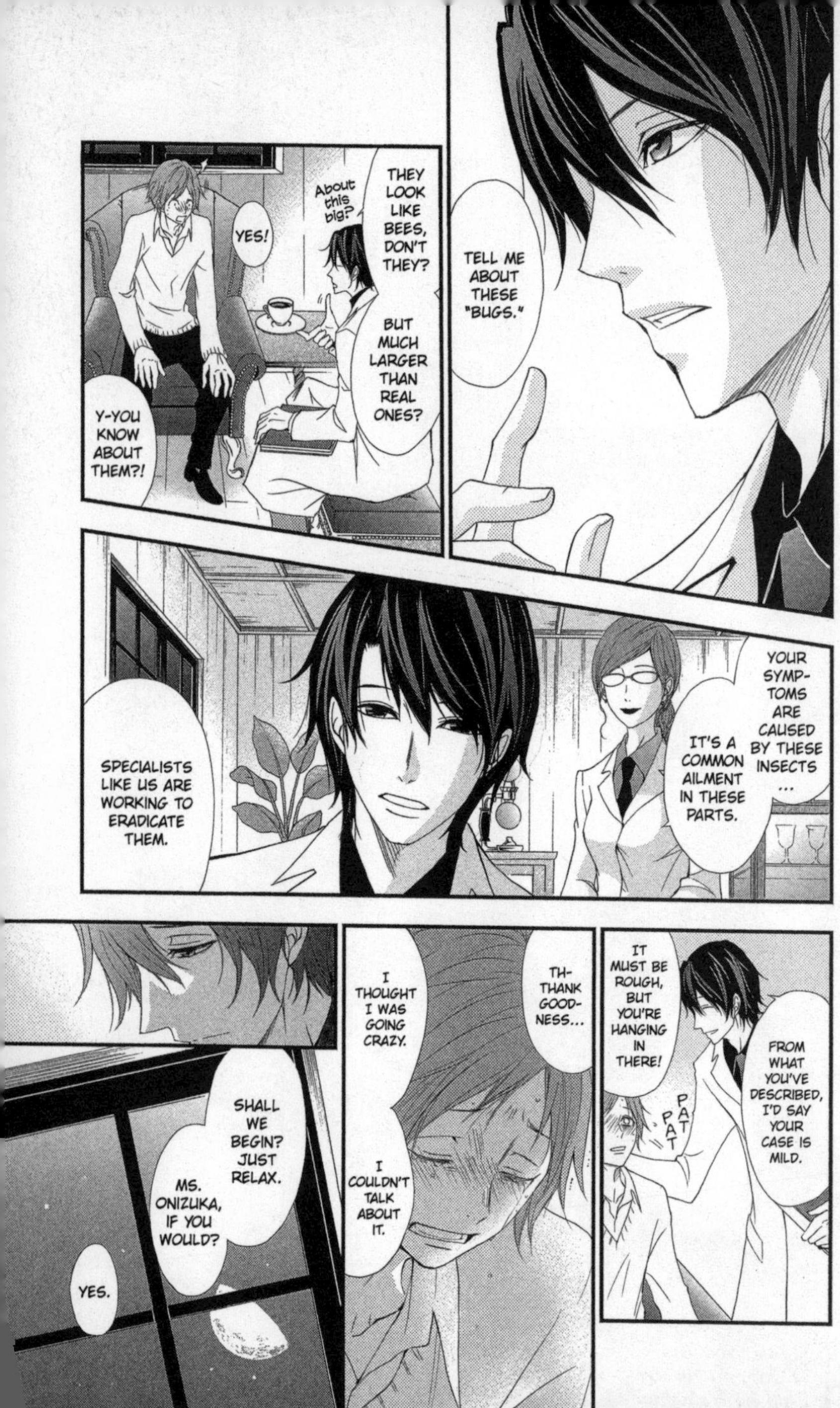
TELL ME ABOUT THESE "BUGS."
THEY LOOK LIKE BEES, DON'T THEY?
About this big?
BUT MUCH LARGER THAN REAL ONES?
YES!
Y-YOU KNOW ABOUT THEM?!
YOUR SYMPTOMS ARE CAUSED BY THESE INSECTS...
IT'S A COMMON AILMENT IN THESE PARTS.
SPECIALISTS LIKE US ARE WORKING TO ERADICATE THEM.
FROM WHAT YOU'VE DESCRIBED, I'D SAY YOUR CASE IS MILD.
PAT PAT
IT MUST BE ROUGH, BUT YOU'RE HANGING IN THERE!
TH-THANK GOODNESS...
I THOUGHT I WAS GOING CRAZY.
I COULDN'T TALK ABOUT IT.
SHALL WE BEGIN? JUST RELAX.
MS. ONIZUKA, IF YOU WOULD?
YES.

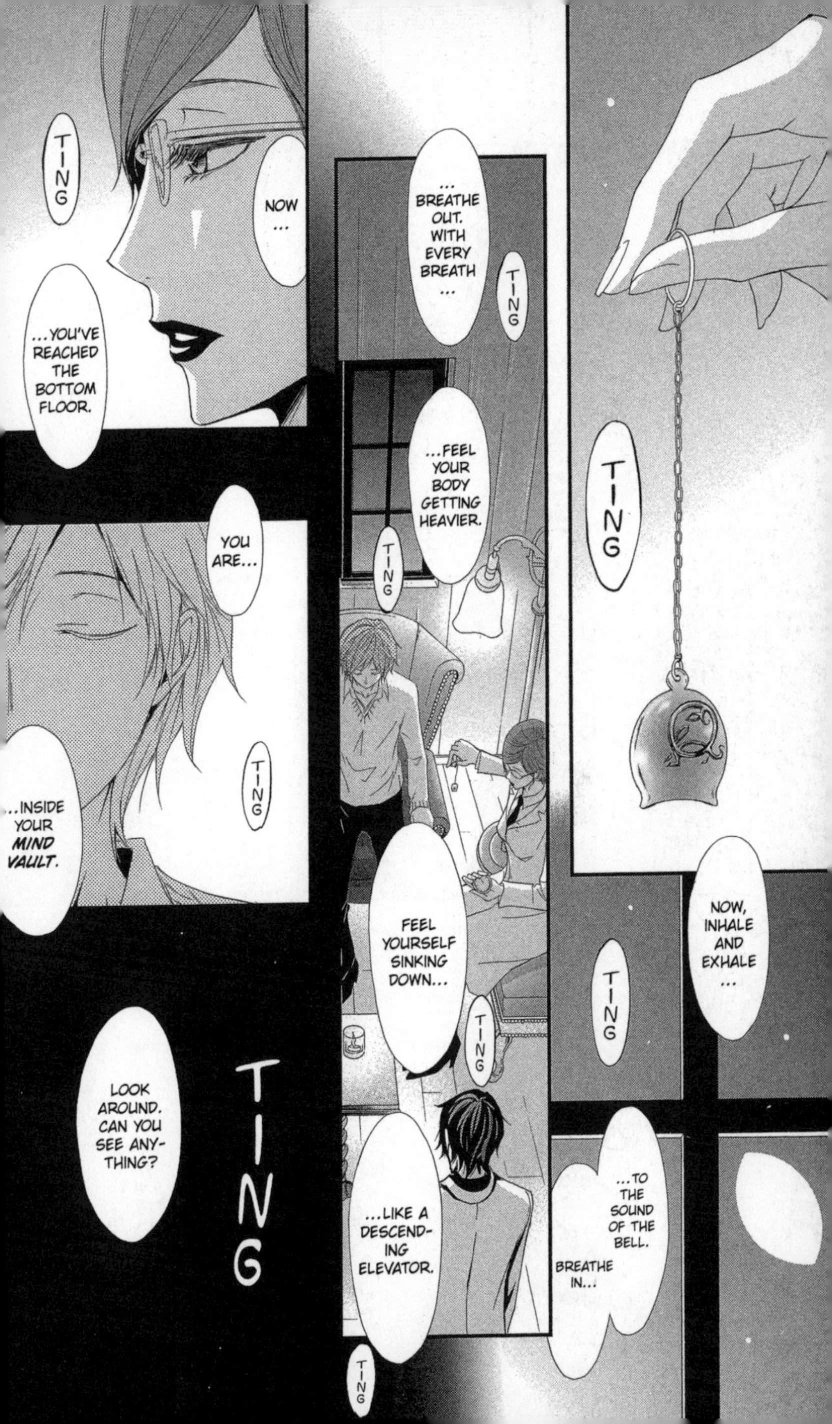
TING
NOW, INHALE AND EXHALE...
TING
...TO THE SOUND OF THE BELL.
BREATHE IN...
...BREATHE OUT. WITH EVERY BREATH...
TING
...FEEL YOUR BODY GETTING HEAVIER.
TING
FEEL YOURSELF SINKING DOWN...
TING
...LIKE A DESCENDING ELEVATOR.
TING
NOW...
TING
...YOU'VE REACHED THE BOTTOM FLOOR.
YOU ARE...
TING
...INSIDE YOUR *MIND VAULT*.
TING
LOOK AROUND. CAN YOU SEE ANYTHING?

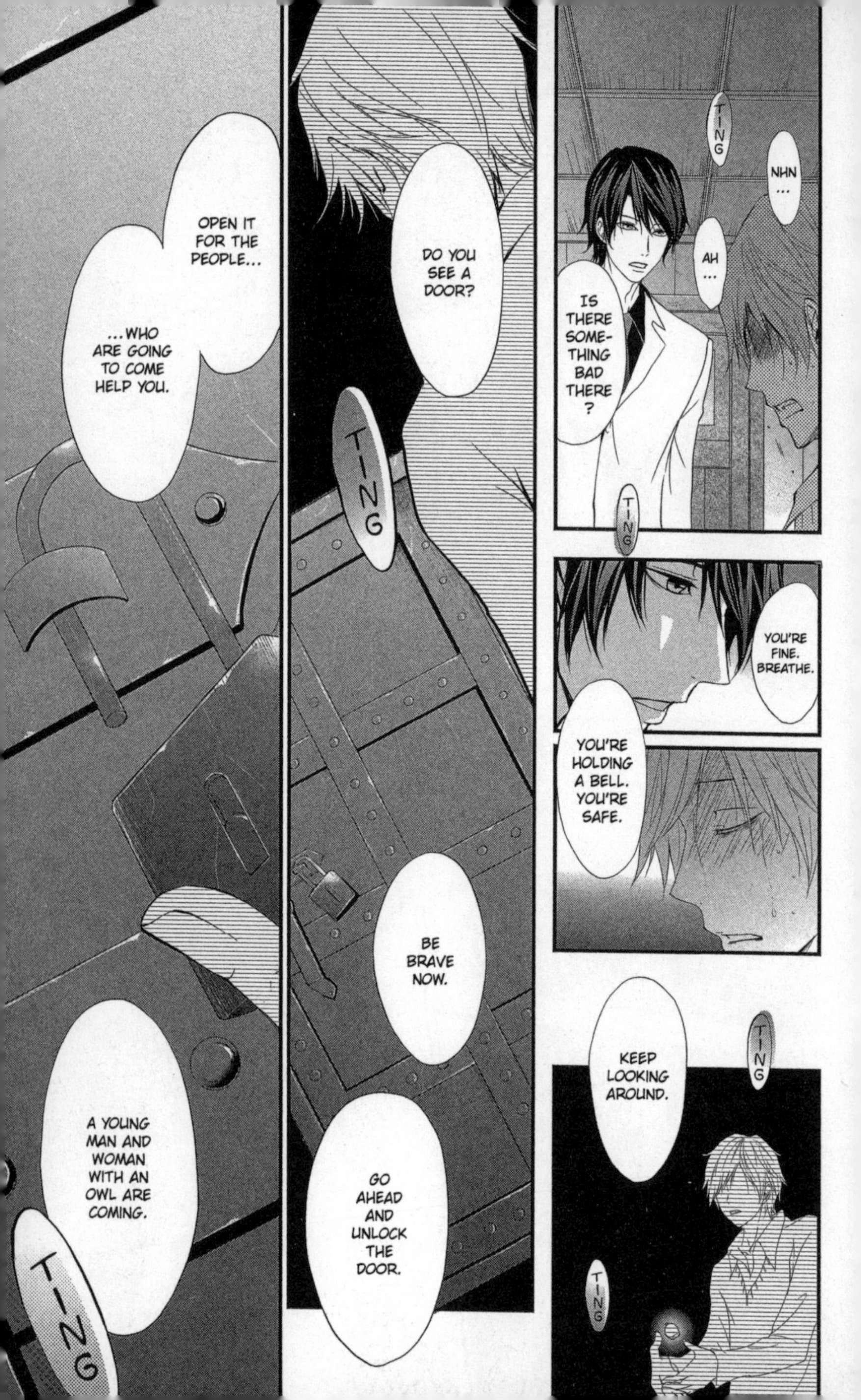
NHN...
TING
AH...
IS THERE SOMETHING BAD THERE?
TING
YOU'RE FINE. BREATHE.
YOU'RE HOLDING A BELL. YOU'RE SAFE.
TING
KEEP LOOKING AROUND.
TING
DO YOU SEE A DOOR?
TING
BE BRAVE NOW.
GO AHEAD AND UNLOCK THE DOOR.
OPEN IT FOR THE PEOPLE...
...WHO ARE GOING TO COME HELP YOU.
A YOUNG MAN AND WOMAN WITH AN OWL ARE COMING.
TING

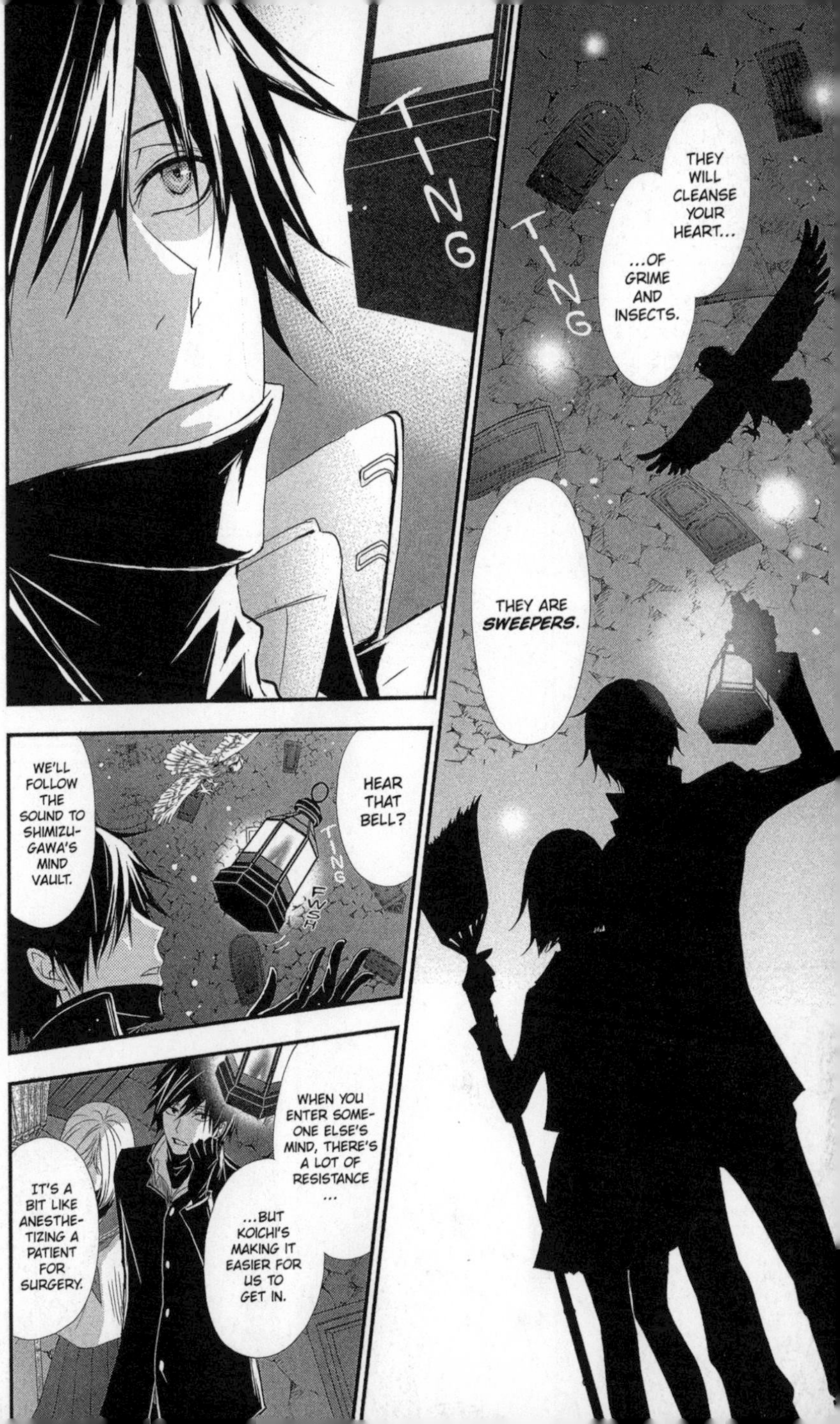
THEY WILL CLEANSE YOUR HEART...
...OF GRIME AND INSECTS.
TING
THEY ARE SWEEPERS.
TING
HEAR THAT BELL?
TING
FWSH
WE'LL FOLLOW THE SOUND TO SHIMIZU-GAWA'S MIND VAULT.
WHEN YOU ENTER SOME-ONE ELSE'S MIND, THERE'S A LOT OF RESISTANCE ...
...BUT KOICHI'S MAKING IT EASIER FOR US TO GET IN.
IT'S A BIT LIKE ANESTHE-TIZING A PATIENT FOR SURGERY.

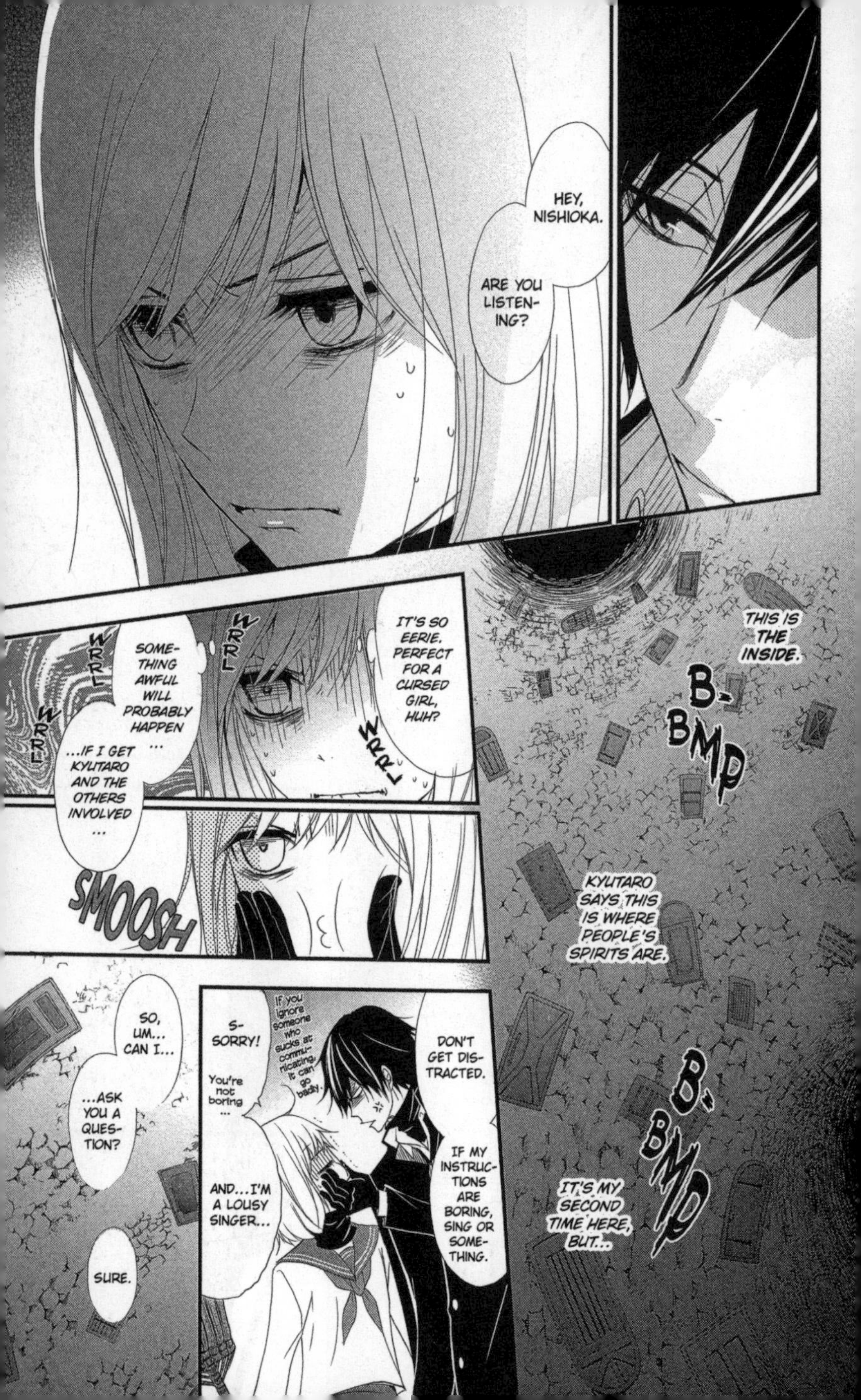
HEY, NISHIOKA.
ARE YOU LISTENING?
THIS IS THE INSIDE.
B-BMP
KYUTARO SAYS THIS IS WHERE PEOPLE'S SPIRITS ARE.
B-BMP
IT'S MY SECOND TIME HERE, BUT...
IT'S SO EERIE. PERFECT FOR A CURSED GIRL, HUH?
WRRL
SOMETHING AWFUL WILL PROBABLY HAPPEN...
WRRL
...IF I GET KYUTARO AND THE OTHERS INVOLVED...
WRRL
SMOOSH
DON'T GET DISTRACTED.
IF MY INSTRUCTIONS ARE BORING, SING OR SOMETHING.
S-SORRY!
If you ignore someone who sucks at communicating, it can go badly.
You're not boring...
AND...I'M A LOUSY SINGER...
SO, UM... CAN I...
...ASK YOU A QUESTION?
SURE.

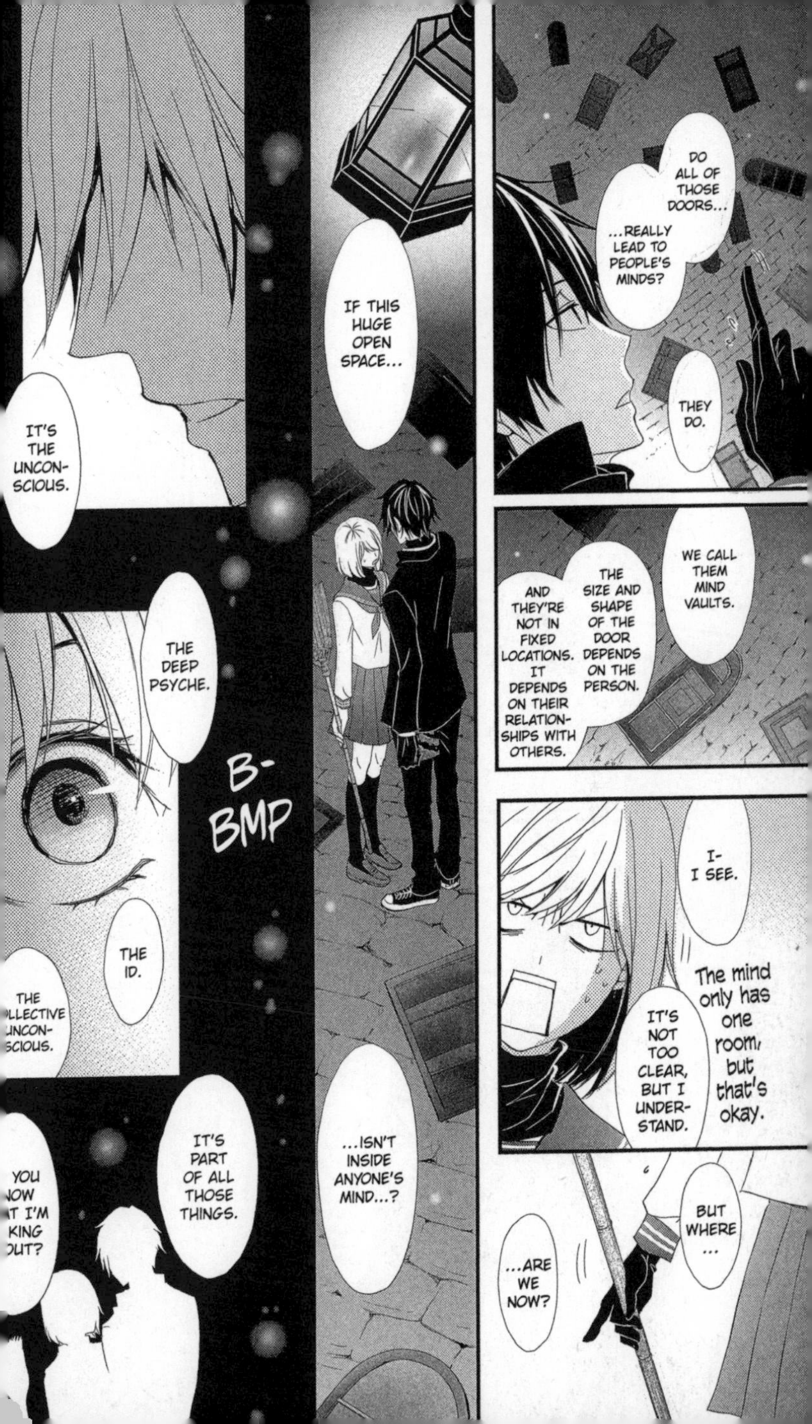
DO ALL OF THOSE DOORS...
...REALLY LEAD TO PEOPLE'S MINDS?
THEY DO.
WE CALL THEM MIND VAULTS.
THE SIZE AND SHAPE OF THE DOOR DEPENDS ON THE PERSON.
AND THEY'RE NOT IN FIXED LOCATIONS. IT DEPENDS ON THEIR RELATIONSHIPS WITH OTHERS.
I- I SEE.
The mind only has one room, but that's okay.
IT'S NOT TOO CLEAR, BUT I UNDERSTAND.
BUT WHERE...
...ARE WE NOW?
IF THIS HUGE OPEN SPACE...
...ISN'T INSIDE ANYONE'S MIND...?
B-BMP
IT'S THE UNCONSCIOUS.
THE DEEP PSYCHE.
THE ID.
THE LLECTIVE UNCON- SCIOUS.
IT'S PART OF ALL THOSE THINGS.
YOU NOW T I'M KING OUT?

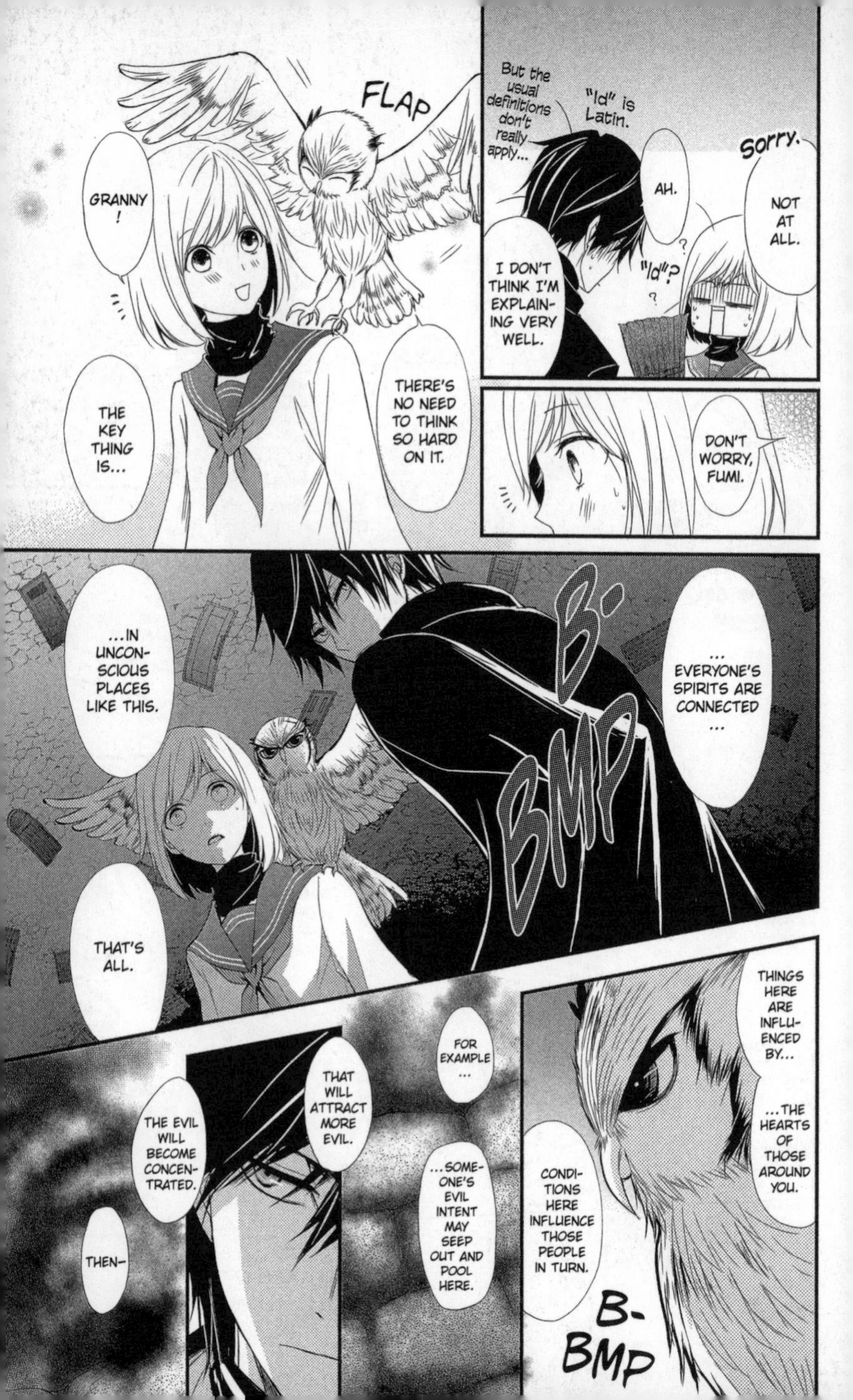
Sorry.
NOT AT ALL.
AH.
"Id" is Latin.
But the usual definitions don't really apply...
"Id"?
I DON'T THINK I'M EXPLAINING VERY WELL.
DON'T WORRY, FUMI.
FLAP
GRANNY!
THERE'S NO NEED TO THINK SO HARD ON IT.
THE KEY THING IS...
...EVERYONE'S SPIRITS ARE CONNECTED...
B-BMP
...IN UNCONSCIOUS PLACES LIKE THIS.
THAT'S ALL.
THINGS HERE ARE INFLUENCED BY...
...THE HEARTS OF THOSE AROUND YOU.
CONDITIONS HERE INFLUENCE THOSE PEOPLE IN TURN.
B-BMP
FOR EXAMPLE...
...SOMEONE'S EVIL INTENT MAY SEEP OUT AND POOL HERE.
THAT WILL ATTRACT MORE EVIL.
THE EVIL WILL BECOME CONCENTRATED.
THEN-

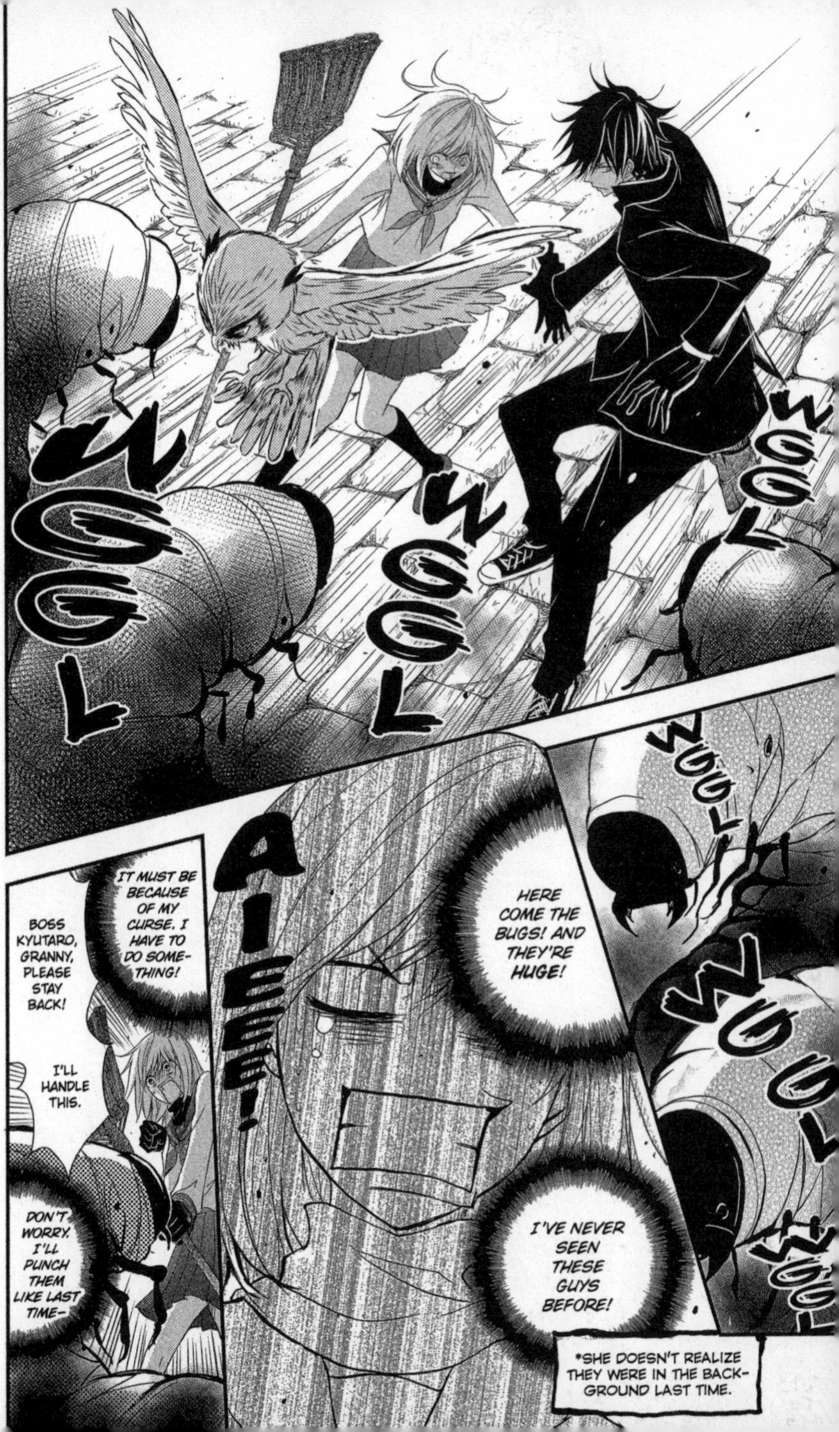
WGGL
WGGL
WGGL
WGGL
WGGL
AIEEE!
HERE COME THE BUGS! AND THEY'RE HUGE!
I'VE NEVER SEEN THESE GUYS BEFORE!
*SHE DOESN'T REALIZE THEY WERE IN THE BACK-GROUND LAST TIME.
IT MUST BE BECAUSE OF MY CURSE. I HAVE TO DO SOME-THING!
BOSS KYUTARO, GRANNY, PLEASE STAY BACK!
I'LL HANDLE THIS.
DON'T WORRY. I'LL PUNCH THEM LIKE LAST TIME-

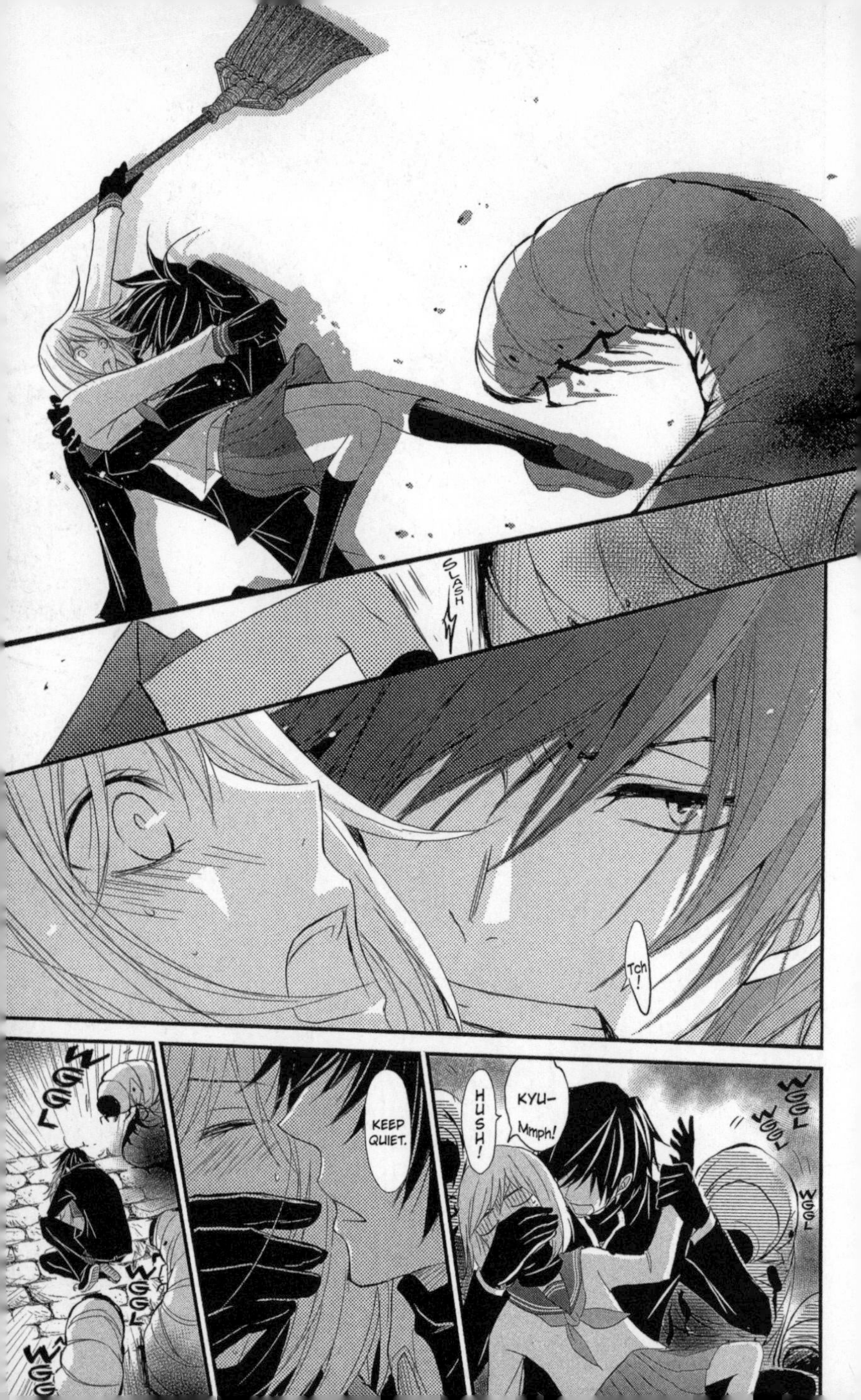
SLASH
Tch!
WGGL WGGL
KYU- Mmph!
HUSH!
WGGL
KEEP QUIET.
WGGL
WGGL
WGG

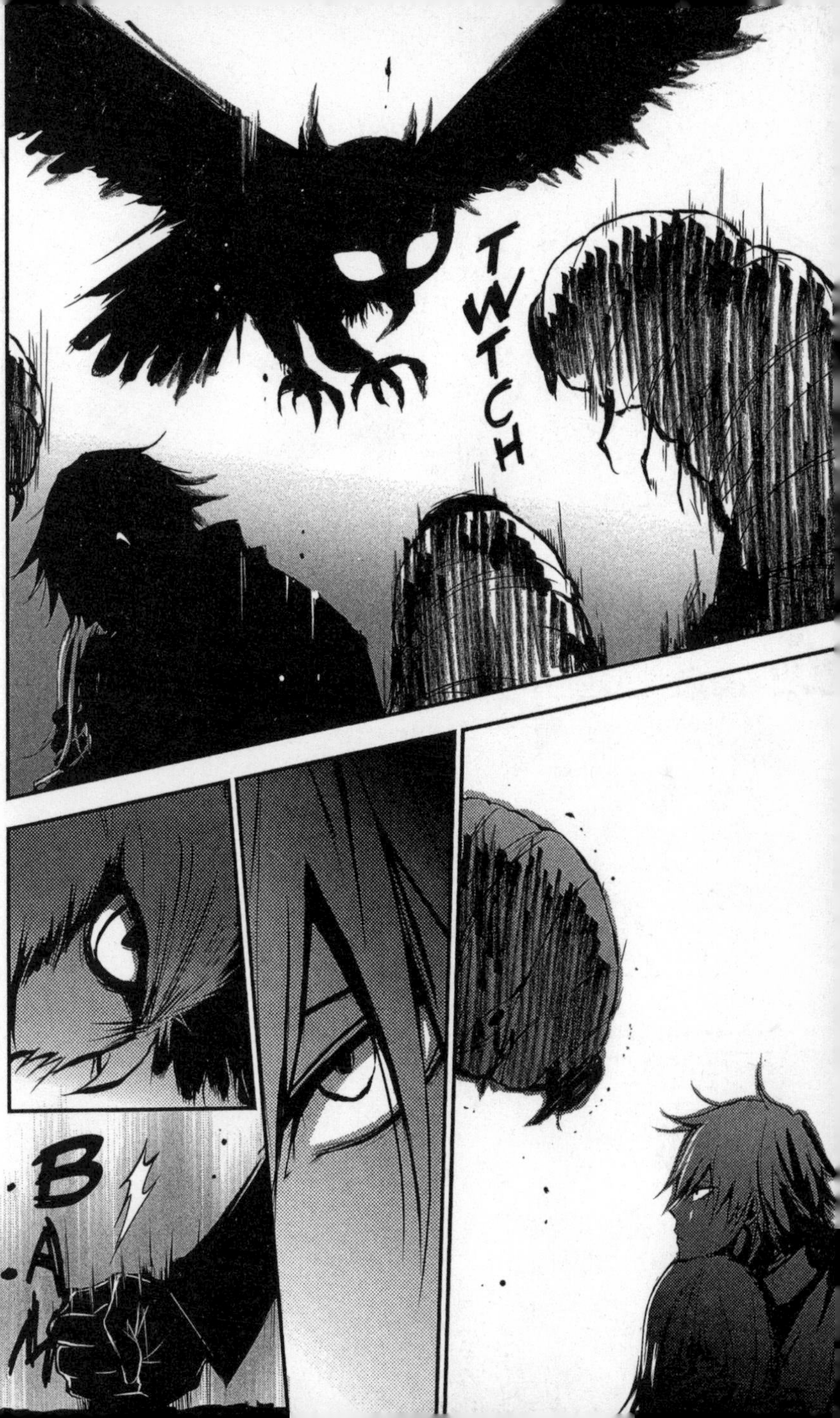
TWTCH
BAM

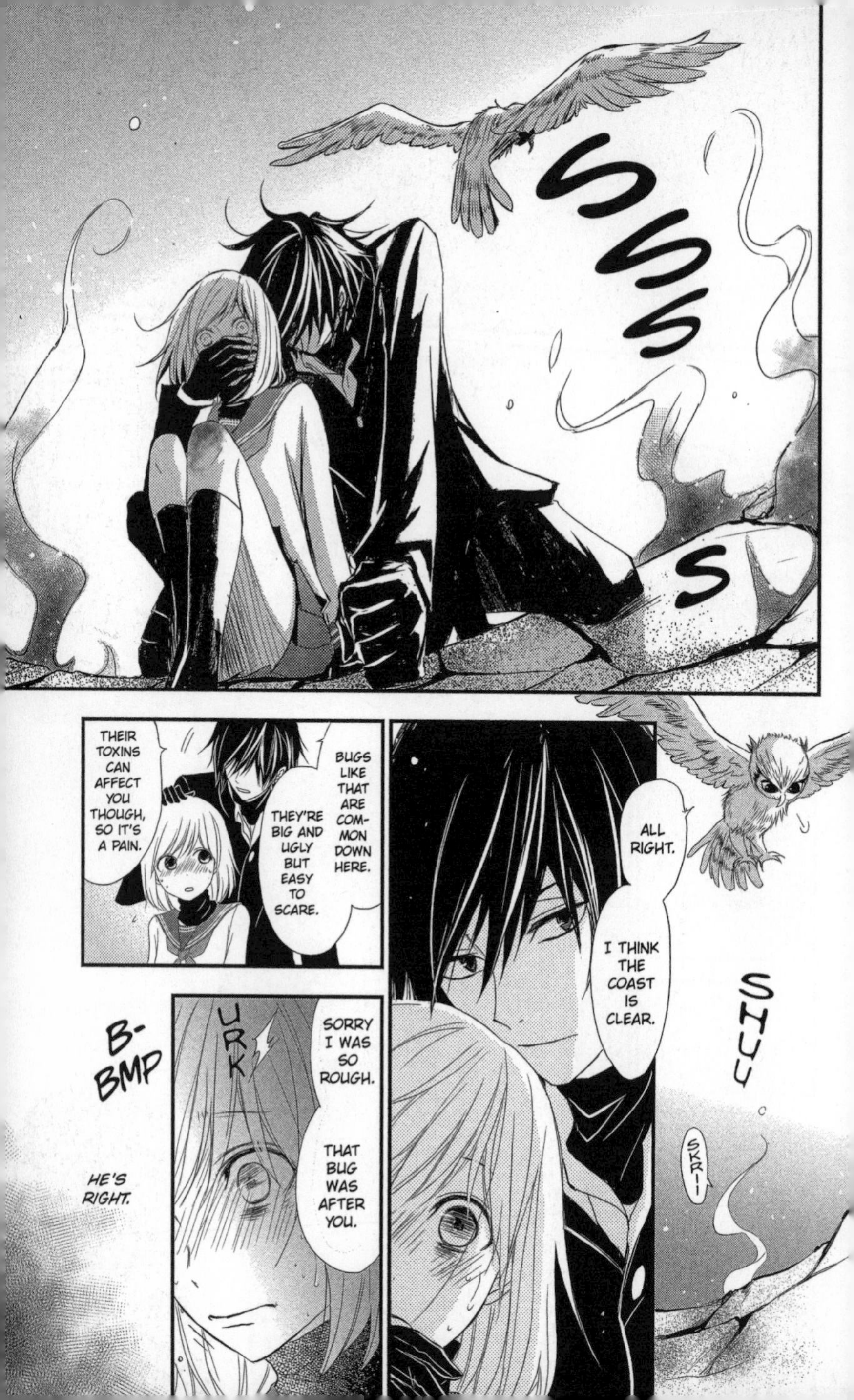
SSSS
S
ALL RIGHT.
I THINK THE COAST IS CLEAR.
SHUU
SKRI
BUGS LIKE THAT ARE COM-MON DOWN HERE.
THEY'RE BIG AND UGLY BUT EASY TO SCARE.
THEIR TOXINS CAN AFFECT YOU THOUGH, SO IT'S A PAIN.
SORRY I WAS SO ROUGH.
URK
THAT BUG WAS AFTER YOU.
B-BMP
HE'S RIGHT.

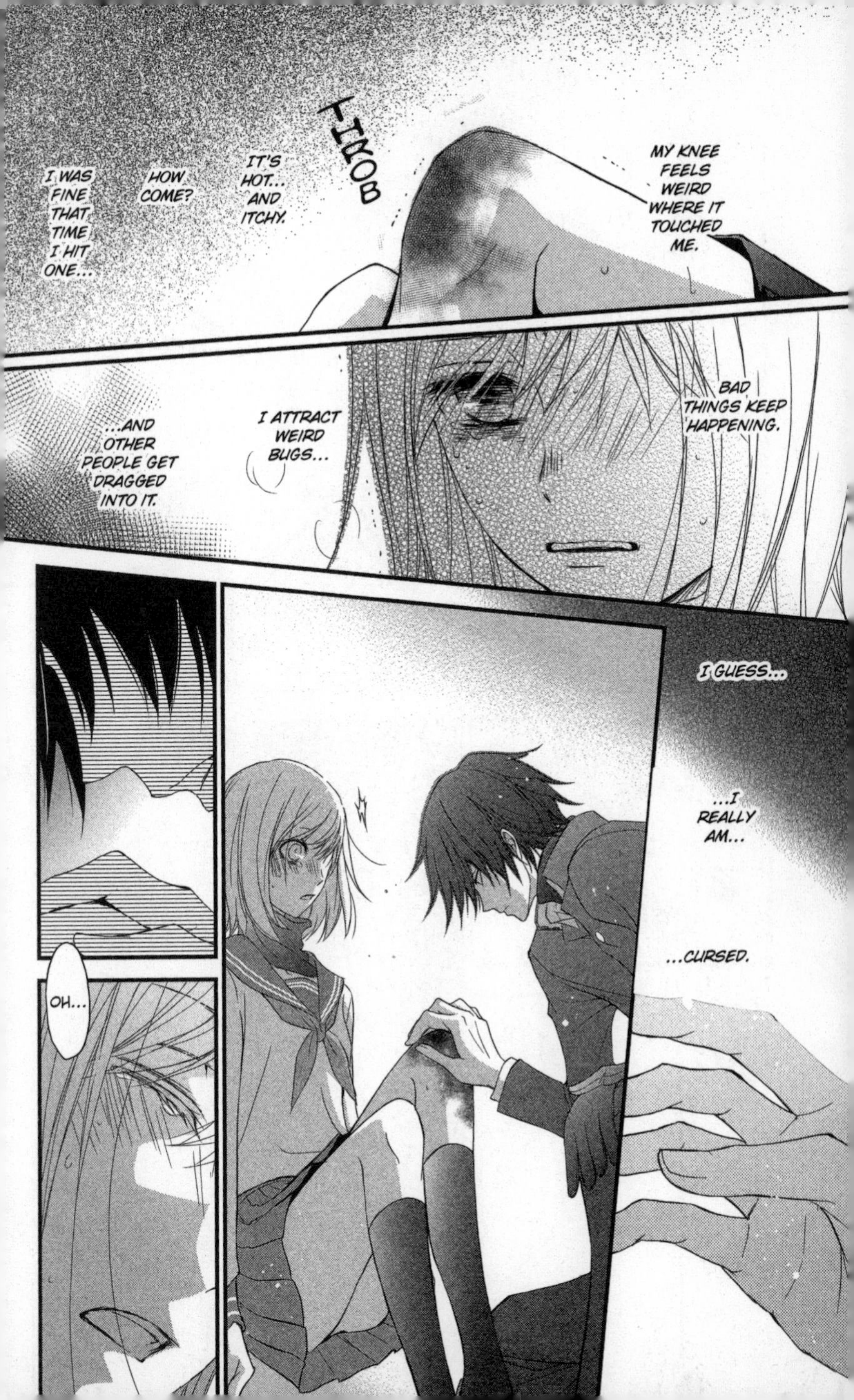
MY KNEE FEELS WEIRD WHERE IT TOUCHED ME.
THROB
IT'S HOT... AND ITCHY.
HOW COME?
I WAS FINE THAT TIME I HIT ONE...
BAD THINGS KEEP HAPPENING.
I ATTRACT WEIRD BUGS...
...AND OTHER PEOPLE GET DRAGGED INTO IT.
I GUESS...
...I REALLY AM...
...CURSED.
OH...

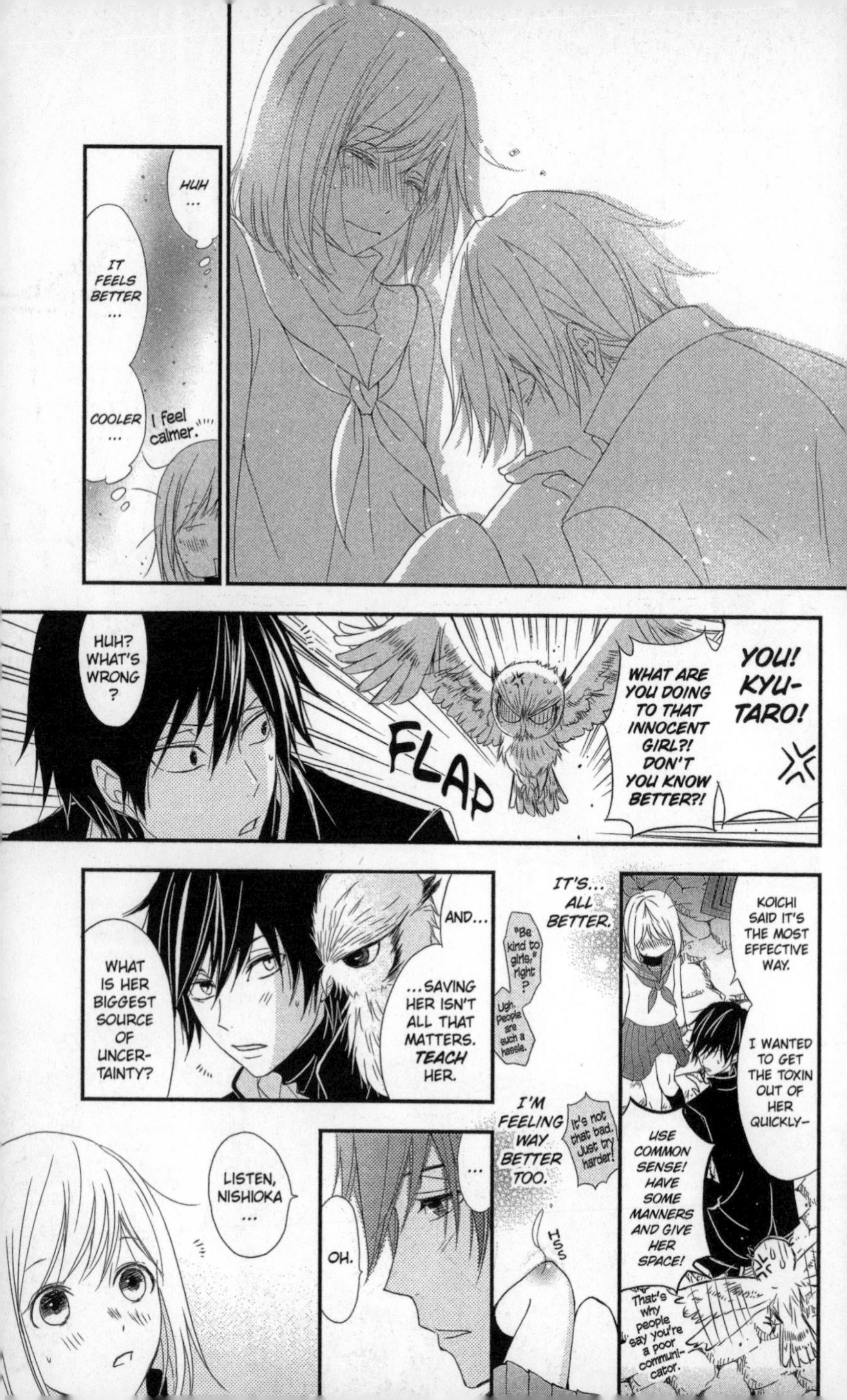
HUH ...
IT FEELS BETTER ...
COOLER ...
I feel calmer.
YOU! KYU-TARO!
WHAT ARE YOU DOING TO THAT INNOCENT GIRL?! DON'T YOU KNOW BETTER?!
FLAP
HUH? WHAT'S WRONG?
KOICHI SAID IT'S THE MOST EFFECTIVE WAY.
I WANTED TO GET THE TOXIN OUT OF HER QUICKLY–
USE COMMON SENSE! HAVE SOME MANNERS AND GIVE HER SPACE!
That's why people say you're a poor communi-cator.
IT'S... ALL BETTER.
"Be kind to girls," right?
Ugh. People are such a hassle.
I'M FEELING WAY BETTER TOO.
It's not that bad. Just try harder!
HSS
AND...
...SAVING HER ISN'T ALL THAT MATTERS. TEACH HER.
WHAT IS HER BIGGEST SOURCE OF UNCER-TAINTY?
...
OH.
LISTEN, NISHIOKA ...

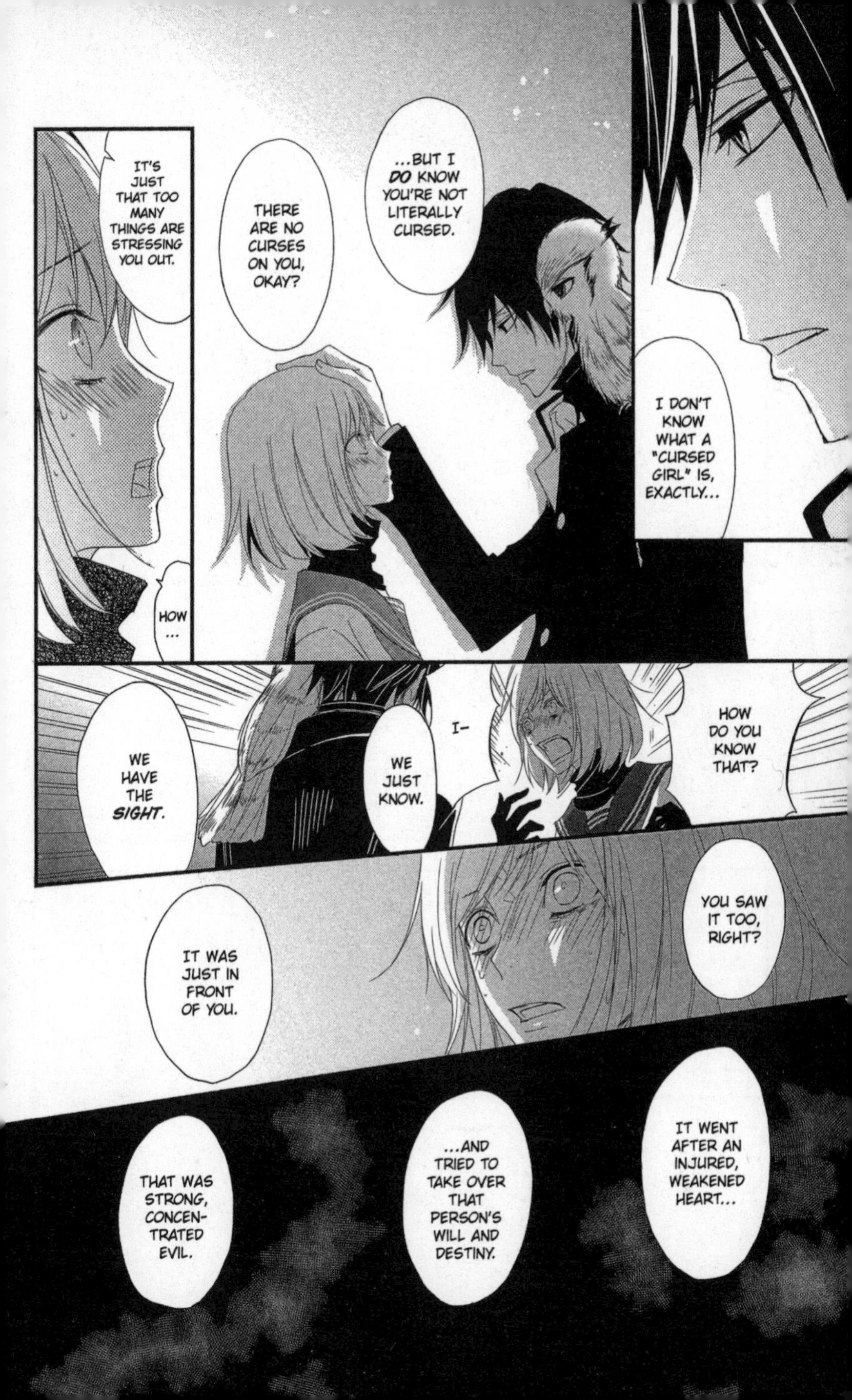
I DON'T KNOW WHAT A "CURSED GIRL" IS, EXACTLY...
...BUT I DO KNOW YOU'RE NOT LITERALLY CURSED.
THERE ARE NO CURSES ON YOU, OKAY?
IT'S JUST THAT TOO MANY THINGS ARE STRESSING YOU OUT.
HOW ...
HOW DO YOU KNOW THAT?
I–
WE JUST KNOW.
WE HAVE THE SIGHT.
YOU SAW IT TOO, RIGHT?
IT WAS JUST IN FRONT OF YOU.
IT WENT AFTER AN INJURED, WEAKENED HEART...
...AND TRIED TO TAKE OVER THAT PERSON'S WILL AND DESTINY.
THAT WAS STRONG, CONCEN-TRATED EVIL.

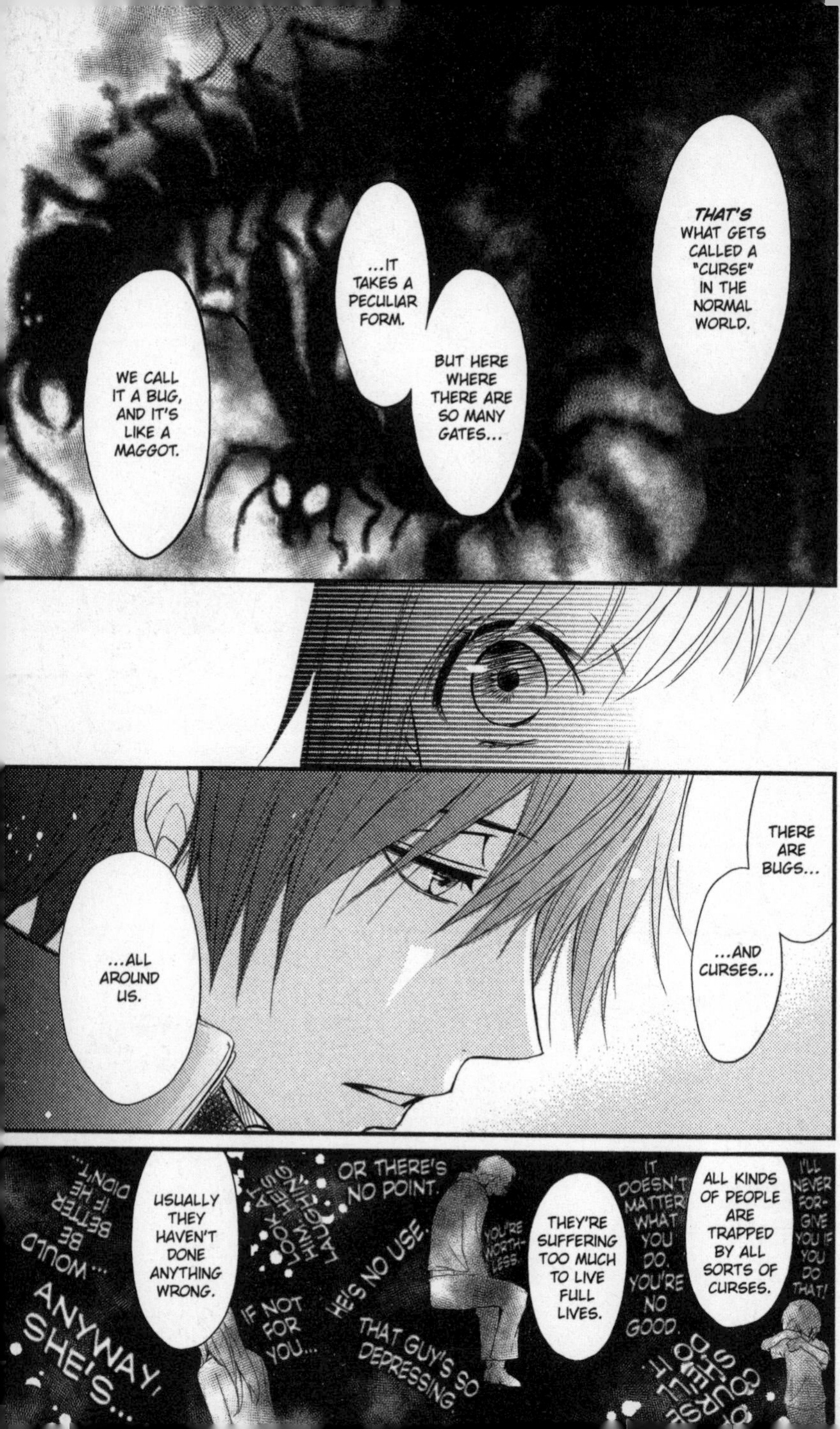
THAT'S WHAT GETS CALLED A "CURSE" IN THE NORMAL WORLD.
BUT HERE WHERE THERE ARE SO MANY GATES...
...IT TAKES A PECULIAR FORM.
WE CALL IT A BUG, AND IT'S LIKE A MAGGOT.
THERE ARE BUGS...
...AND CURSES...
...ALL AROUND US.
I'LL NEVER FORGIVE YOU IF YOU DO THAT!
ALL KINDS OF PEOPLE ARE TRAPPED BY ALL SORTS OF CURSES.
OF COURSE SHE'LL DO IT.
IT DOESN'T MATTER WHAT YOU DO. YOU'RE NO GOOD.
THEY'RE SUFFERING TOO MUCH TO LIVE FULL LIVES.
YOU'RE WORTHLESS.
OR THERE'S NO POINT.
HE'S NO USE.
THAT GUY'S SO DEPRESSING
LOOK AT HIM. HE'S LAUGHING.
IF NOT FOR YOU...
USUALLY THEY HAVEN'T DONE ANYTHING WRONG.
...WOULD BE BETTER IF HE DIDN'T...
ANYWAY, SHE'S...

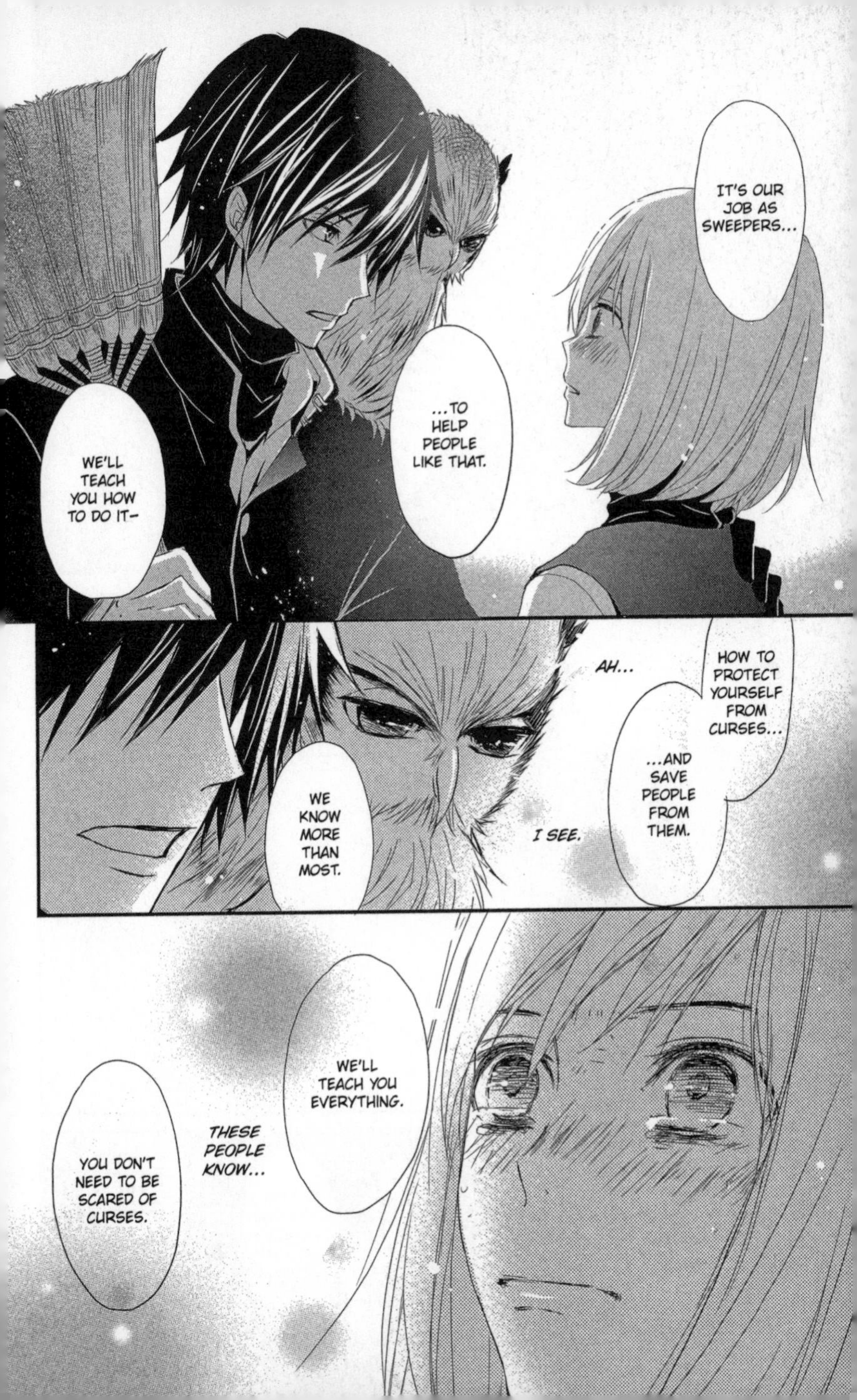
IT'S OUR JOB AS SWEEPERS...
...TO HELP PEOPLE LIKE THAT.
WE'LL TEACH YOU HOW TO DO IT—
HOW TO PROTECT YOURSELF FROM CURSES...
AH...
...AND SAVE PEOPLE FROM THEM.
I SEE.
WE KNOW MORE THAN MOST.
WE'LL TEACH YOU EVERYTHING.
THESE PEOPLE KNOW...
YOU DON'T NEED TO BE SCARED OF CURSES.

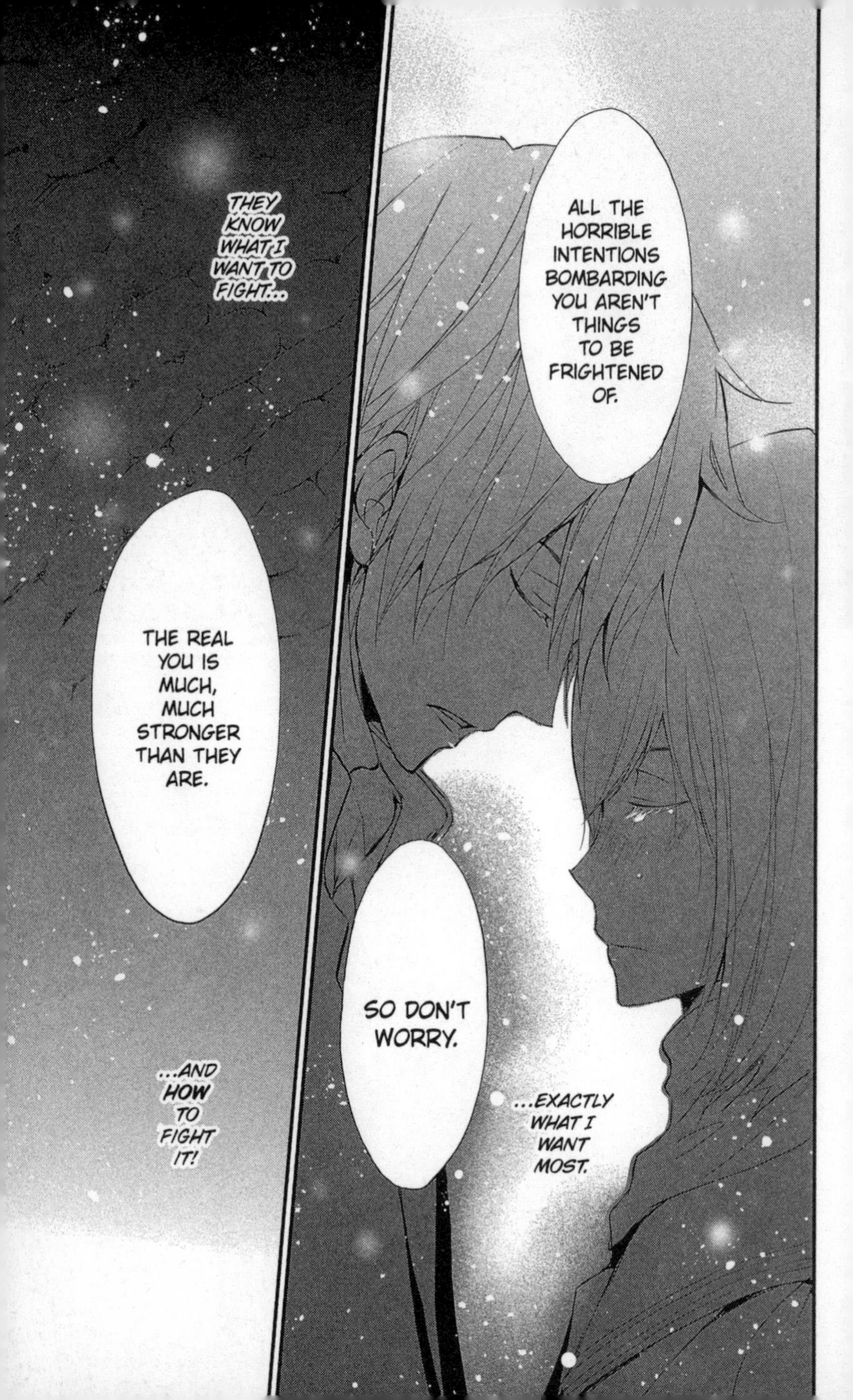
ALL THE HORRIBLE INTENTIONS BOMBARDING YOU AREN'T THINGS TO BE FRIGHTENED OF.
SO DON'T WORRY.
...EXACTLY WHAT I WANT MOST.
THEY KNOW WHAT I WANT TO FIGHT...
THE REAL YOU IS MUCH, MUCH STRONGER THAN THEY ARE.
...AND HOW TO FIGHT IT!

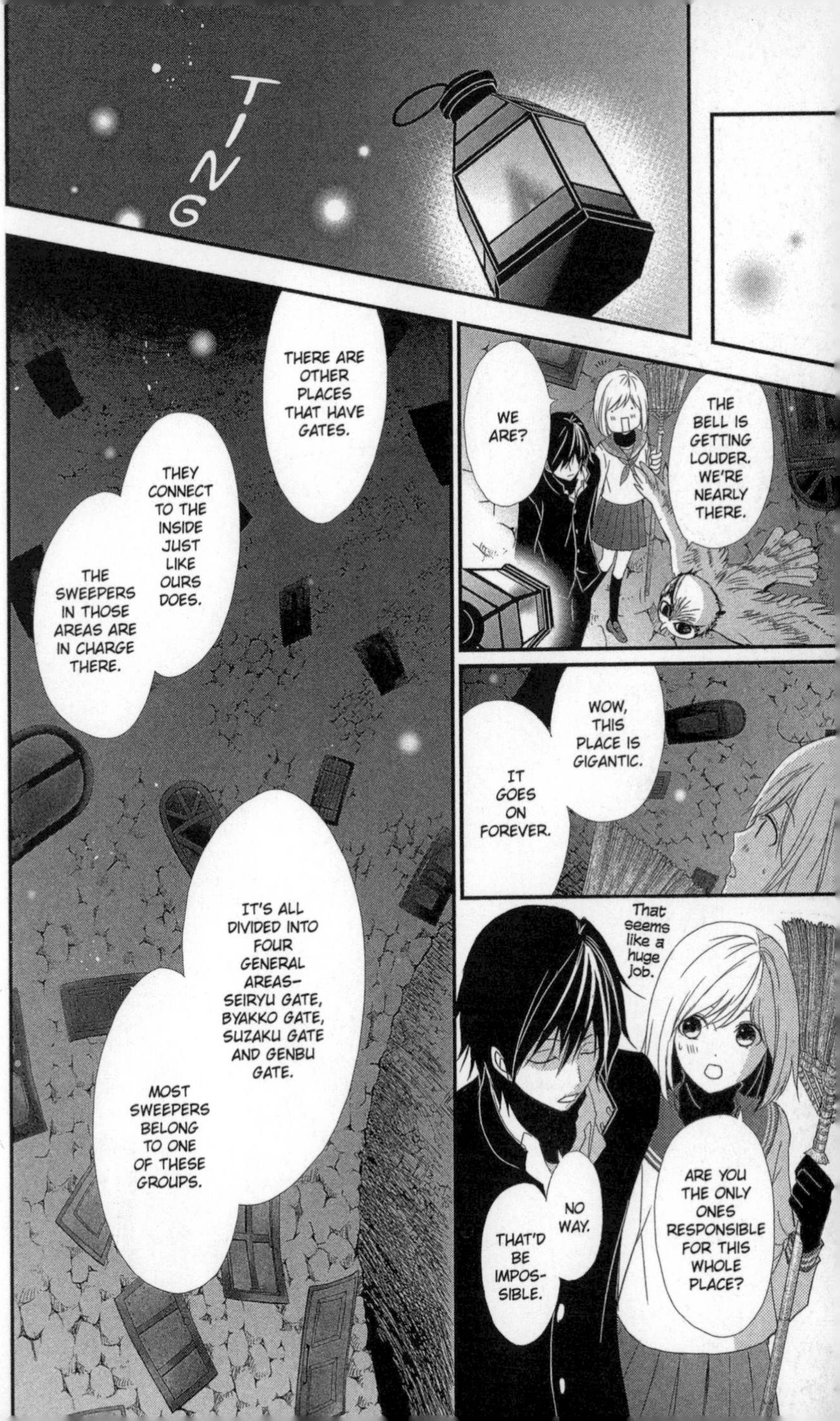
TING
THE BELL IS GETTING LOUDER. WE'RE NEARLY THERE.
WE ARE?
WOW, THIS PLACE IS GIGANTIC.
IT GOES ON FOREVER.
That seems like a huge job.
ARE YOU THE ONLY ONES RESPONSIBLE FOR THIS WHOLE PLACE?
NO WAY.
THAT'D BE IMPOSSIBLE.
THERE ARE OTHER PLACES THAT HAVE GATES.
THEY CONNECT TO THE INSIDE JUST LIKE OURS DOES.
THE SWEEPERS IN THOSE AREAS ARE IN CHARGE THERE.
IT'S ALL DIVIDED INTO FOUR GENERAL AREAS- SEIRYU GATE, BYAKKO GATE, SUZAKU GATE AND GENBU GATE.
MOST SWEEPERS BELONG TO ONE OF THESE GROUPS.

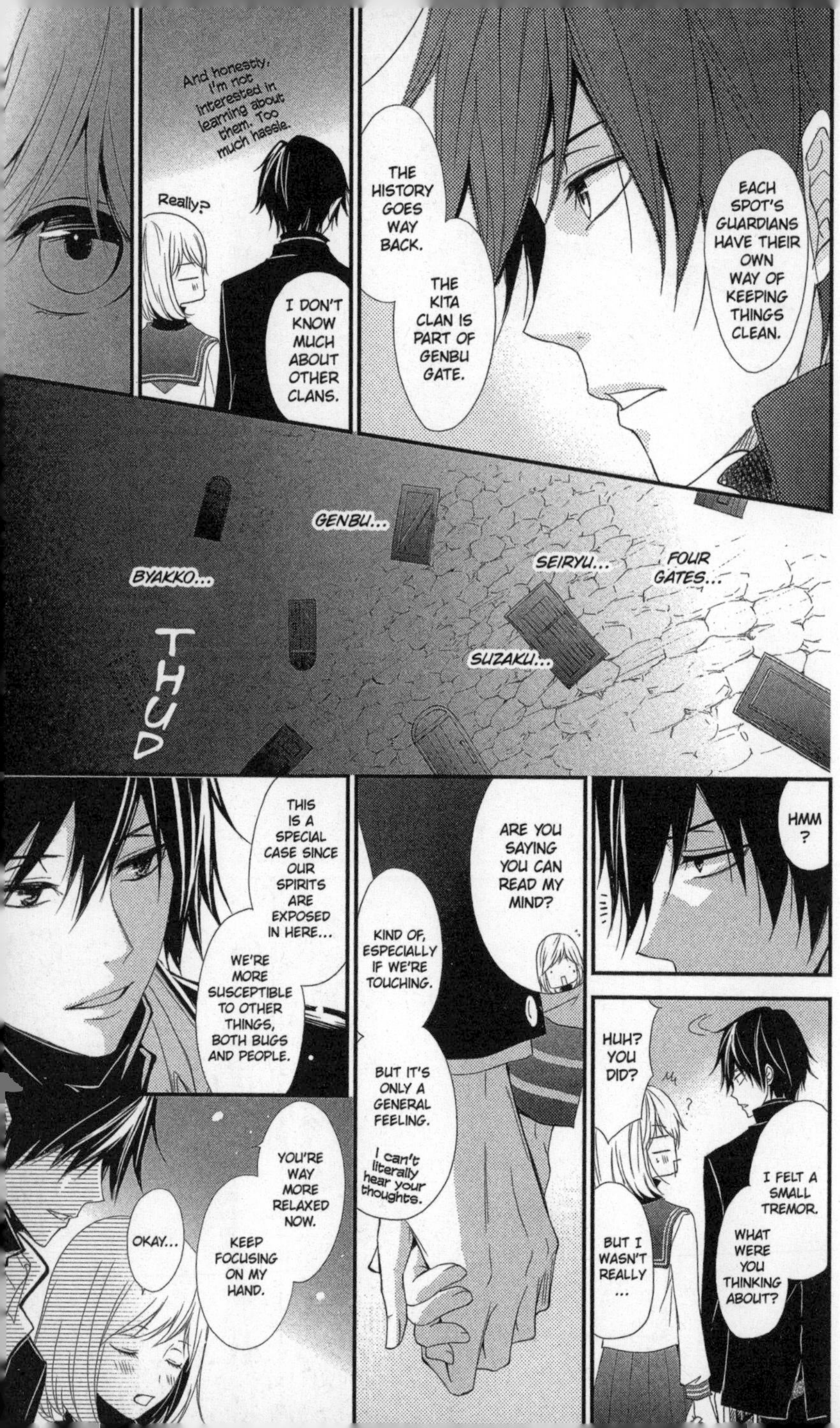
EACH SPOT'S GUARDIANS HAVE THEIR OWN WAY OF KEEPING THINGS CLEAN.
THE HISTORY GOES WAY BACK.
THE KITA CLAN IS PART OF GENBU GATE.
I DON'T KNOW MUCH ABOUT OTHER CLANS.
Really?
And honesty, I'm not interested in learning about them. Too much hassle.
FOUR GATES...
SEIRYU...
GENBU...
SUZAKU...
BYAKKO...
THUD
HMM?
I FELT A SMALL TREMOR.
HUH? YOU DID?
WHAT WERE YOU THINKING ABOUT?
BUT I WASN'T REALLY...
ARE YOU SAYING YOU CAN READ MY MIND?
KIND OF, ESPECIALLY IF WE'RE TOUCHING.
BUT IT'S ONLY A GENERAL FEELING.
I can't literally hear your thoughts.
THIS IS A SPECIAL CASE SINCE OUR SPIRITS ARE EXPOSED IN HERE...
WE'RE MORE SUSCEPTIBLE TO OTHER THINGS, BOTH BUGS AND PEOPLE.
YOU'RE WAY MORE RELAXED NOW.
KEEP FOCUSING ON MY HAND.
OKAY...

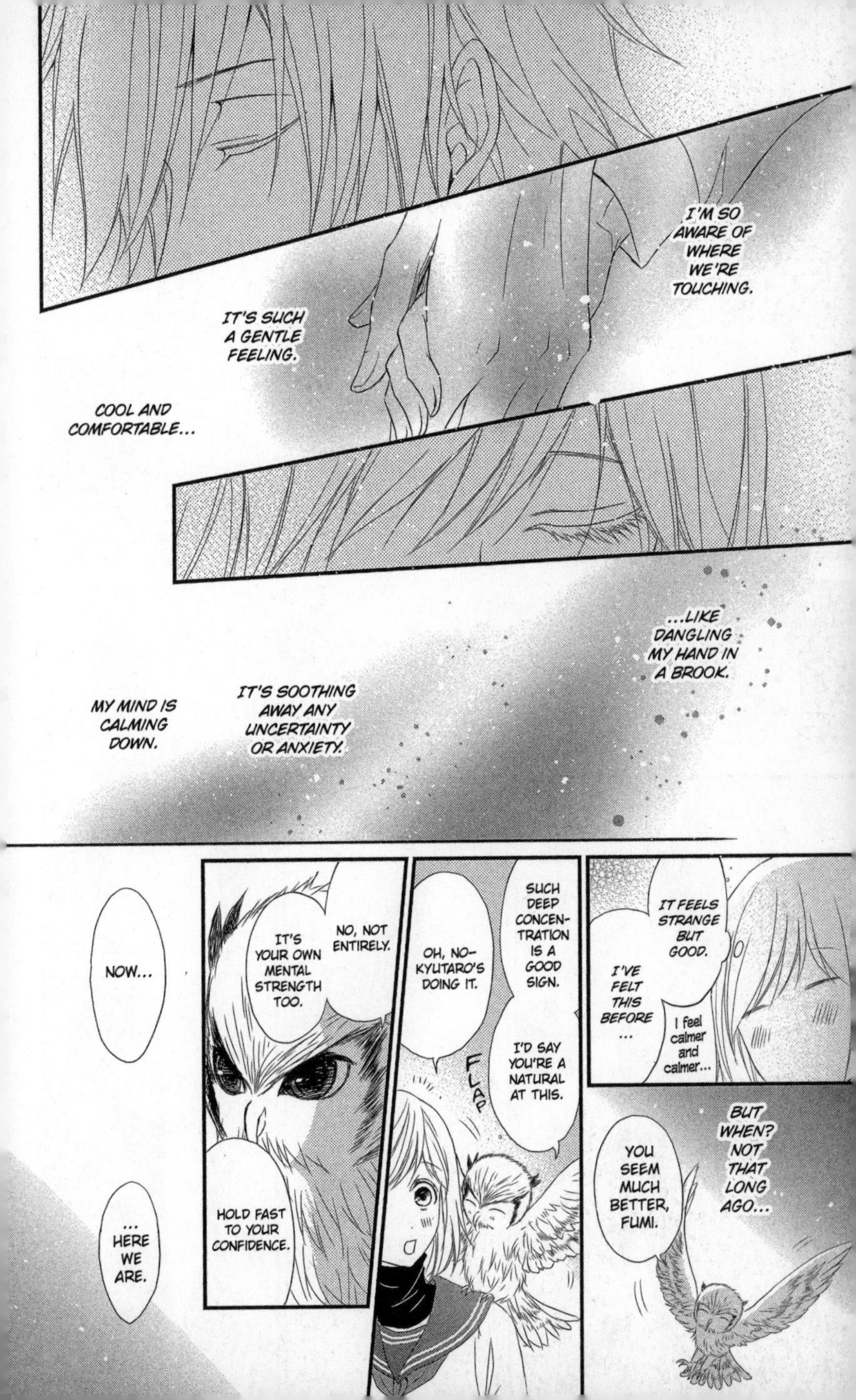
I'M SO AWARE OF WHERE WE'RE TOUCHING.
IT'S SUCH A GENTLE FEELING.
COOL AND COMFORTABLE...
...LIKE DANGLING MY HAND IN A BROOK.
IT'S SOOTHING AWAY ANY UNCERTAINTY OR ANXIETY.
MY MIND IS CALMING DOWN.
IT FEELS STRANGE BUT GOOD.
I'VE FELT THIS BEFORE...
I feel calmer and calmer...
BUT WHEN? NOT THAT LONG AGO...
YOU SEEM MUCH BETTER, FUMI.
SUCH DEEP CONCENTRATION IS A GOOD SIGN.
OH, NO-KYUTARO'S DOING IT.
I'D SAY YOU'RE A NATURAL AT THIS.
FLAP
NO, NOT ENTIRELY.
IT'S YOUR OWN MENTAL STRENGTH TOO.
HOLD FAST TO YOUR CONFIDENCE.
NOW...
...HERE WE ARE.

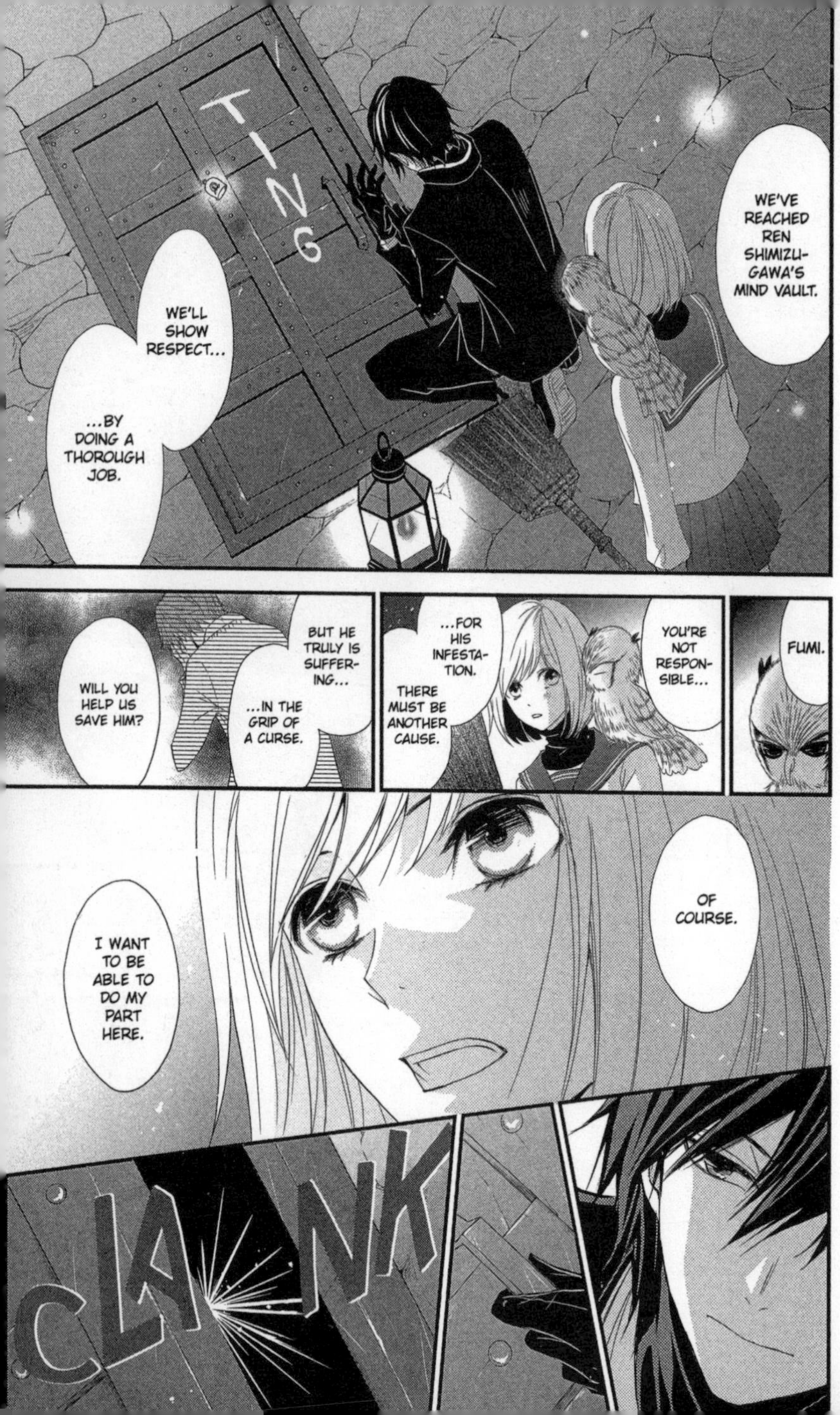
WE'VE REACHED REN SHIMIZUGAWA'S MIND VAULT.
TING
WE'LL SHOW RESPECT...
...BY DOING A THOROUGH JOB.
FUMI.
YOU'RE NOT RESPONSIBLE...
...FOR HIS INFESTATION.
THERE MUST BE ANOTHER CAUSE.
BUT HE TRULY IS SUFFERING...
...IN THE GRIP OF A CURSE.
WILL YOU HELP US SAVE HIM?
OF COURSE.
I WANT TO BE ABLE TO DO MY PART HERE.
CLANK

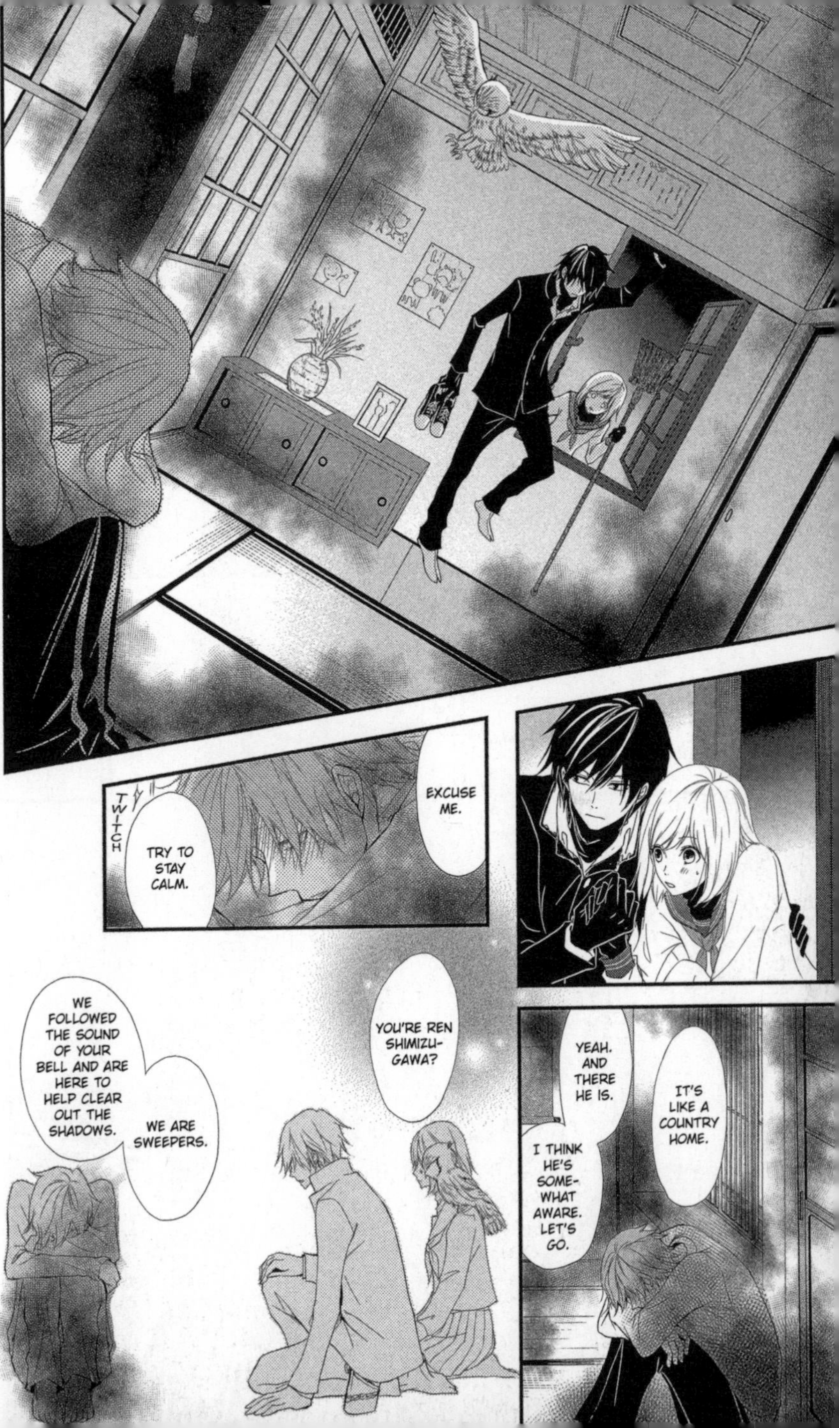
EXCUSE ME.
TWITCH
TRY TO STAY CALM.
IT'S LIKE A COUNTRY HOME.
YEAH. AND THERE HE IS.
I THINK HE'S SOME-WHAT AWARE. LET'S GO.
YOU'RE REN SHIMIZU-GAWA?
WE ARE SWEEPERS.
WE FOLLOWED THE SOUND OF YOUR BELL AND ARE HERE TO HELP CLEAR OUT THE SHADOWS.

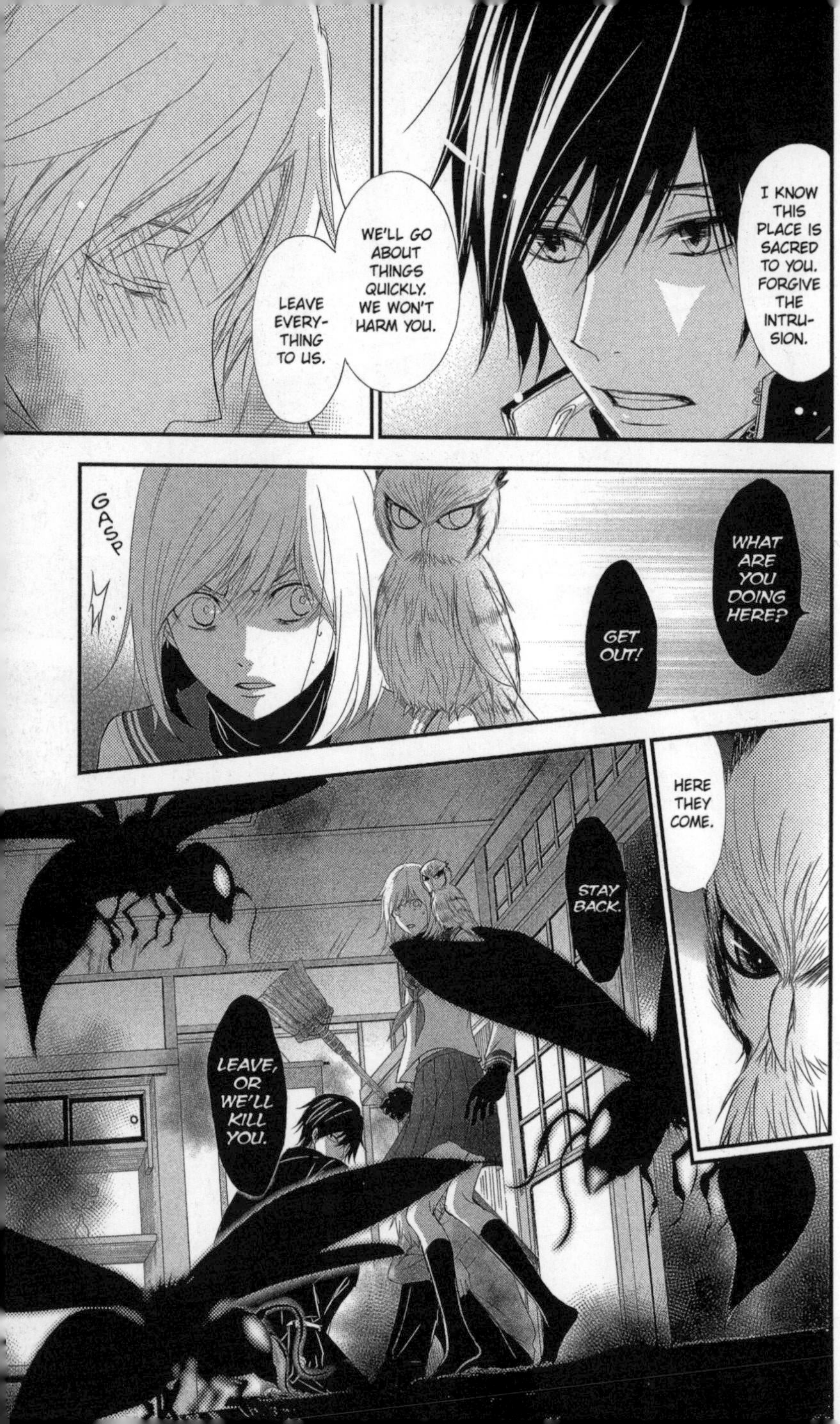
I KNOW THIS PLACE IS SACRED TO YOU. FORGIVE THE INTRUSION.
WE'LL GO ABOUT THINGS QUICKLY. WE WON'T HARM YOU.
LEAVE EVERYTHING TO US.
WHAT ARE YOU DOING HERE?
GET OUT!
GASP
HERE THEY COME.
STAY BACK.
LEAVE, OR WE'LL KILL YOU.

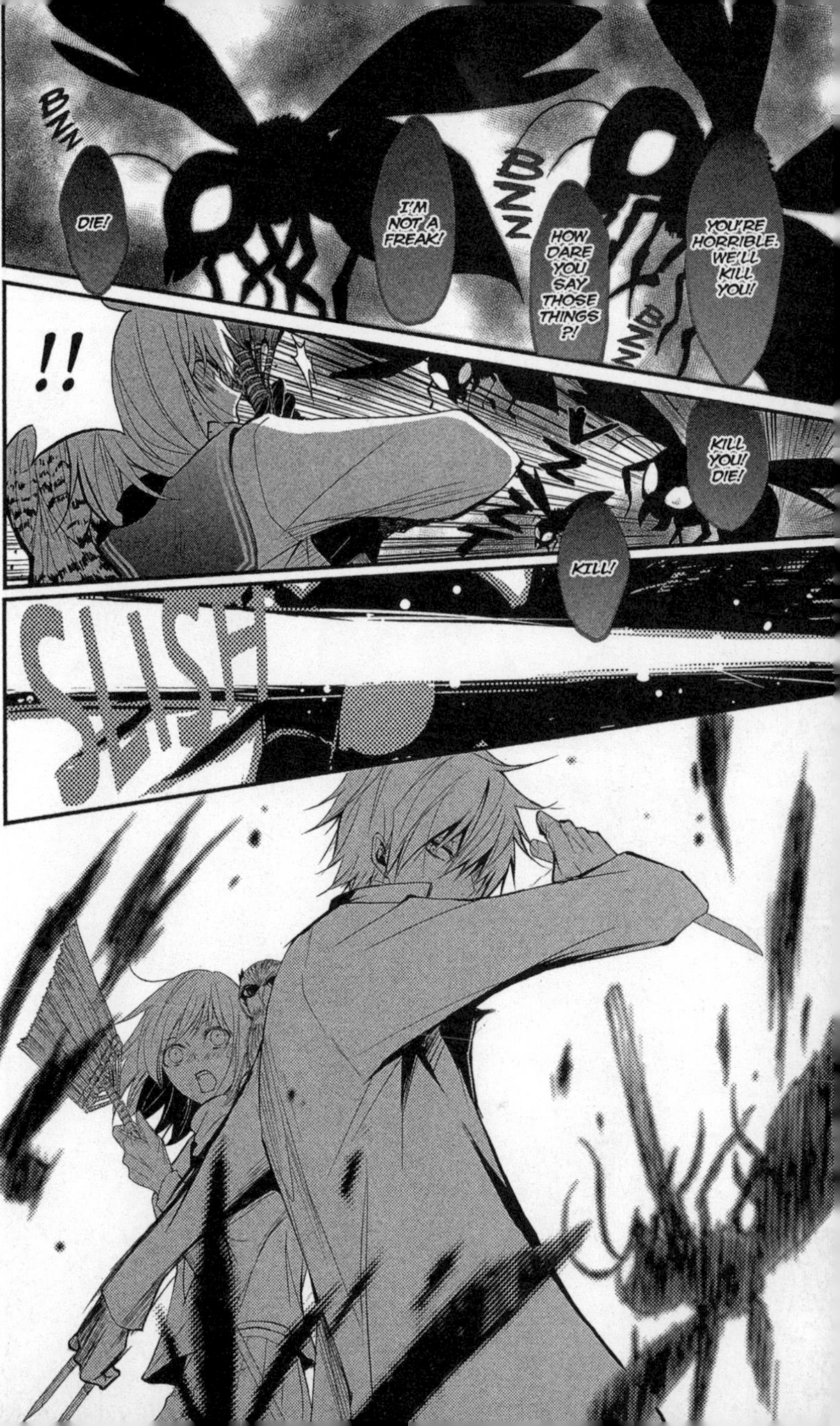
YOU'RE HORRIBLE. WE'LL KILL YOU!
BZZ
HOW DARE YOU SAY THOSE THINGS?!
BZZ
I'M NOT A FREAK!
BZZ
DIE!
BZZ
KILL YOU! DIE!
KILL!
!!
CLISH

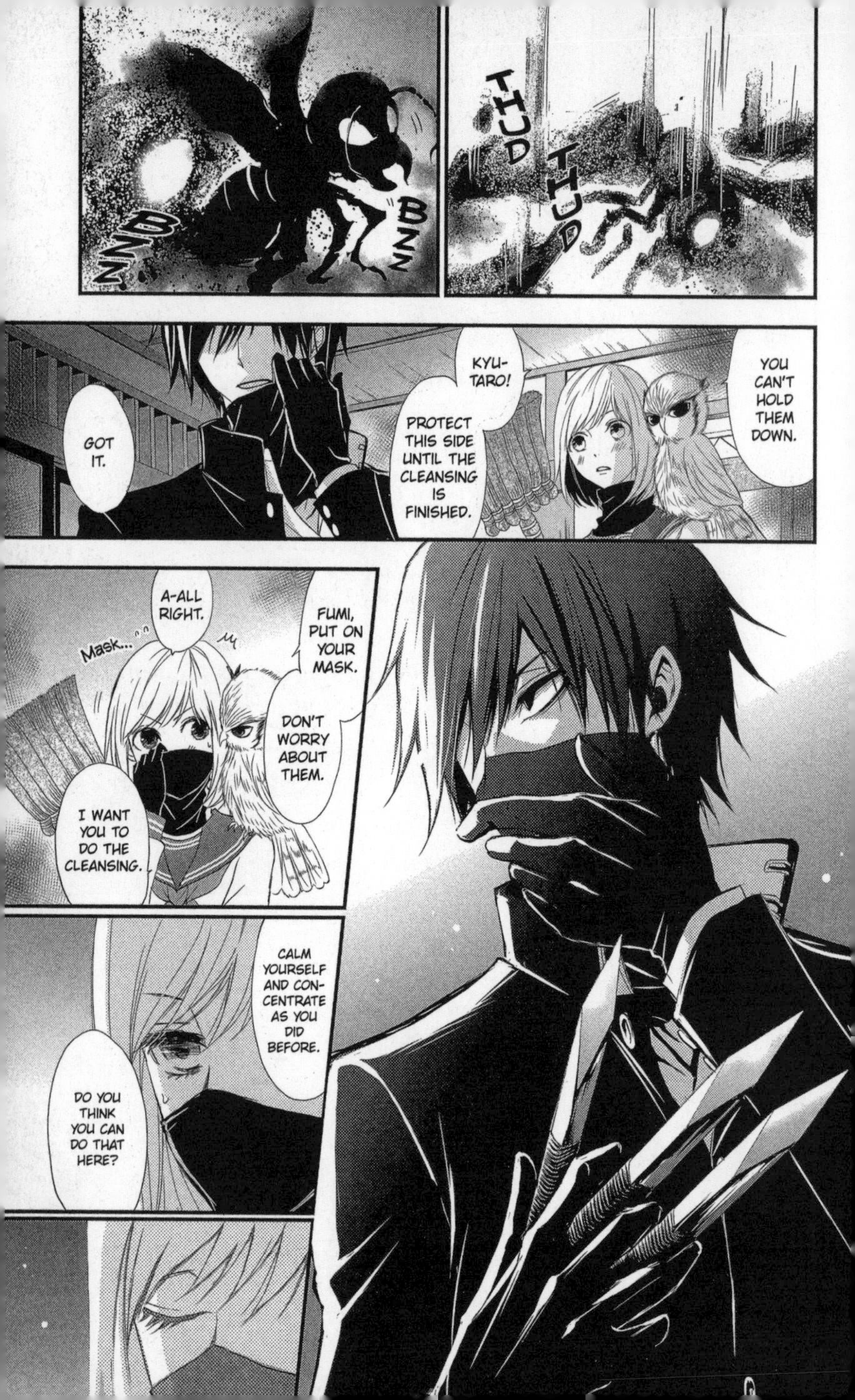
THUD
THUD
BZZ
BZZ
YOU CAN'T HOLD THEM DOWN.
KYU-TARO!
PROTECT THIS SIDE UNTIL THE CLEANSING IS FINISHED.
GOT IT.
FUMI, PUT ON YOUR MASK.
A-ALL RIGHT.
Mask...
DON'T WORRY ABOUT THEM.
I WANT YOU TO DO THE CLEANSING.
CALM YOURSELF AND CON-CENTRATE AS YOU DID BEFORE.
DO YOU THINK YOU CAN DO THAT HERE?

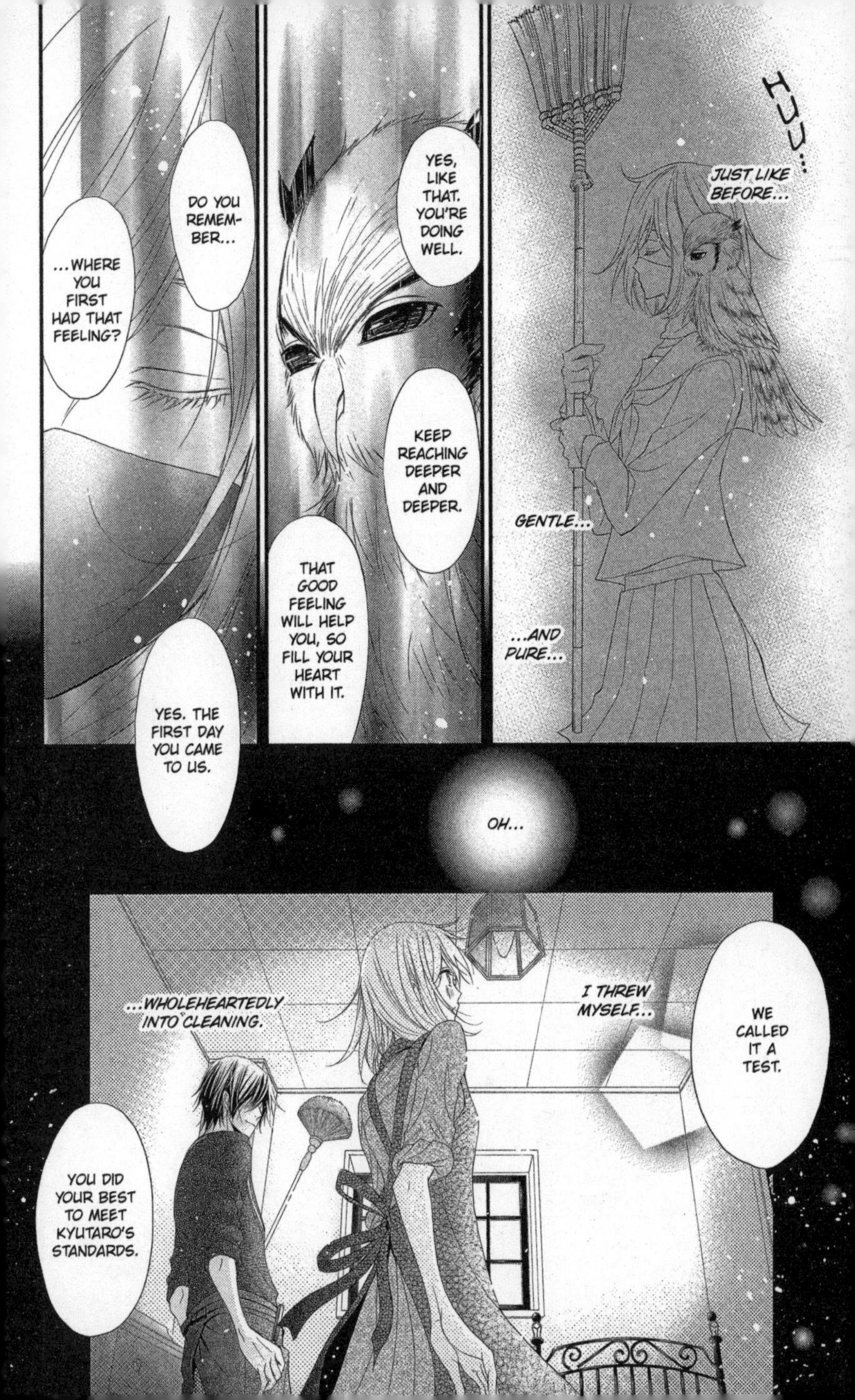
HUU...
JUST LIKE BEFORE...
GENTLE...
...AND PURE...
YES, LIKE THAT. YOU'RE DOING WELL.
KEEP REACHING DEEPER AND DEEPER.
THAT GOOD FEELING WILL HELP YOU, SO FILL YOUR HEART WITH IT.
DO YOU REMEMBER...
...WHERE YOU FIRST HAD THAT FEELING?
YES. THE FIRST DAY YOU CAME TO US.
OH...
WE CALLED IT A TEST.
I THREW MYSELF...
...WHOLEHEARTEDLY INTO CLEANING.
YOU DID YOUR BEST TO MEET KYUTARO'S STANDARDS.

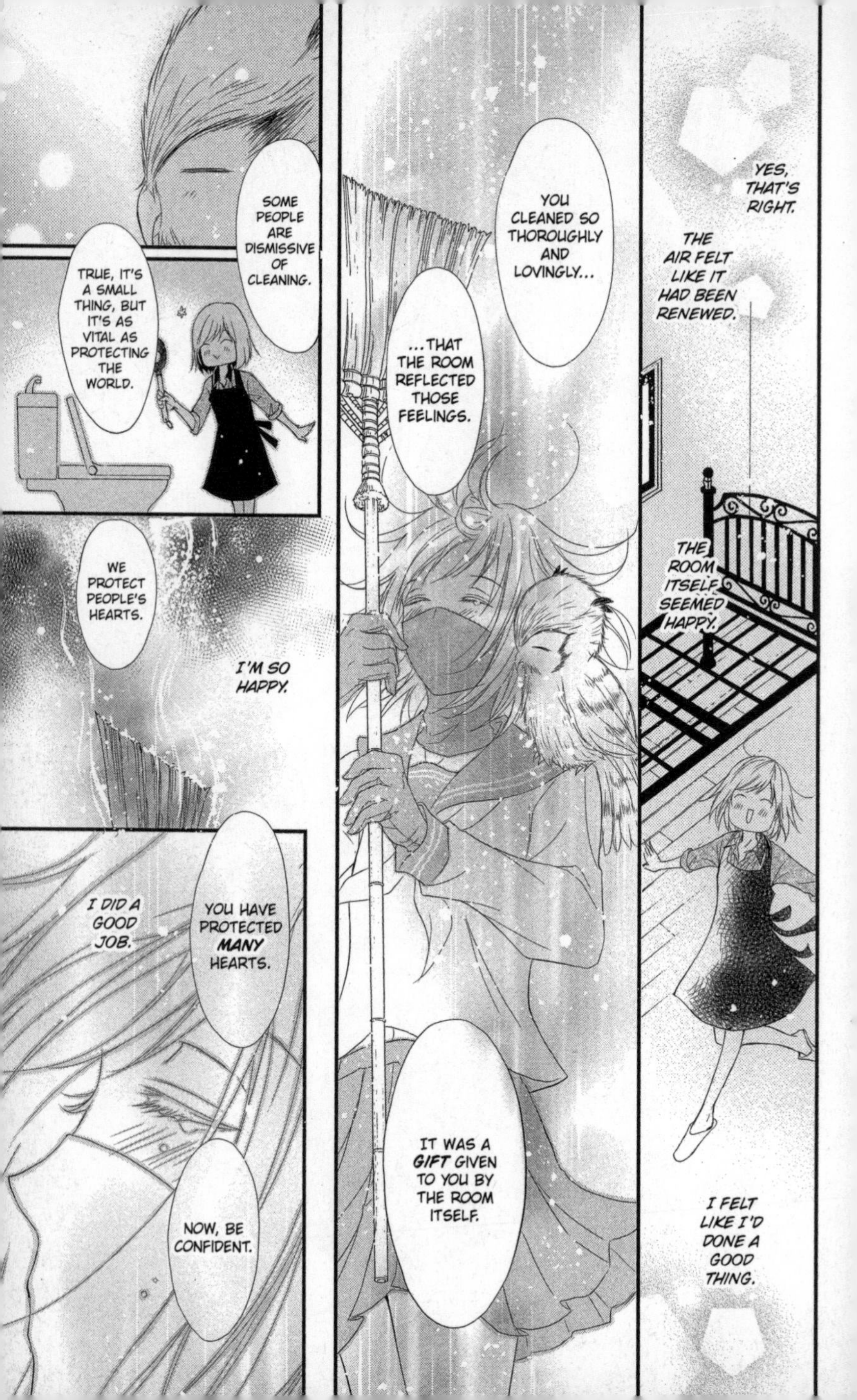
YES, THAT'S RIGHT.
THE AIR FELT LIKE IT HAD BEEN RENEWED.
THE ROOM ITSELF SEEMED HAPPY.
I FELT LIKE I'D DONE A GOOD THING.
YOU CLEANED SO THOROUGHLY AND LOVINGLY...
...THAT THE ROOM REFLECTED THOSE FEELINGS.
IT WAS A **GIFT** GIVEN TO YOU BY THE ROOM ITSELF.
SOME PEOPLE ARE DISMISSIVE OF CLEANING.
TRUE, IT'S A SMALL THING, BUT IT'S AS VITAL AS PROTECTING THE WORLD.
WE PROTECT PEOPLE'S HEARTS.
I'M SO HAPPY.
YOU HAVE PROTECTED **MANY** HEARTS.
I DID A GOOD JOB.
NOW, BE CONFIDENT.

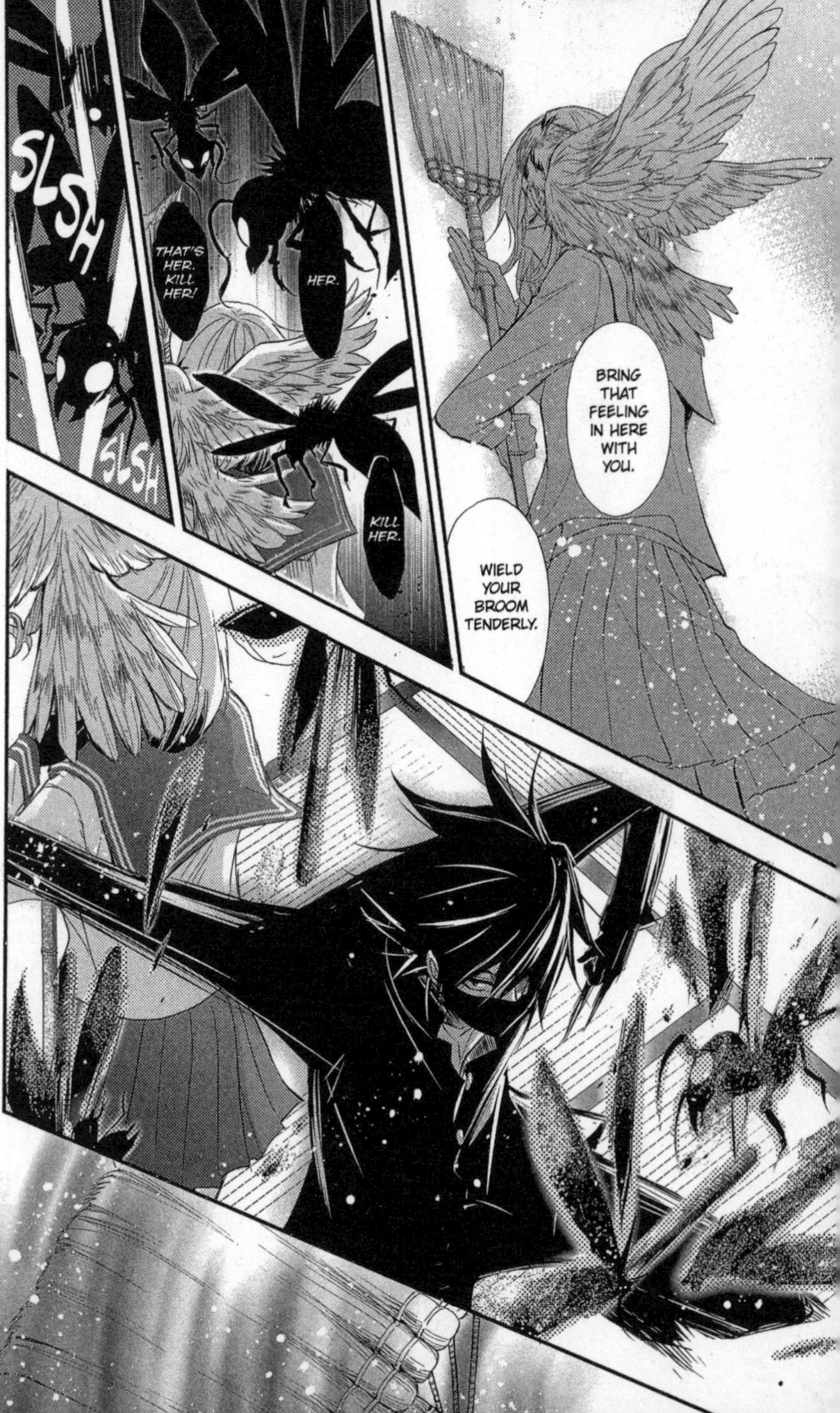
BRING THAT FEELING IN HERE WITH YOU.
WIELD YOUR BROOM TENDERLY.
HER.
KILL HER.
THAT'S HER. KILL HER!
SLSH
SLSH

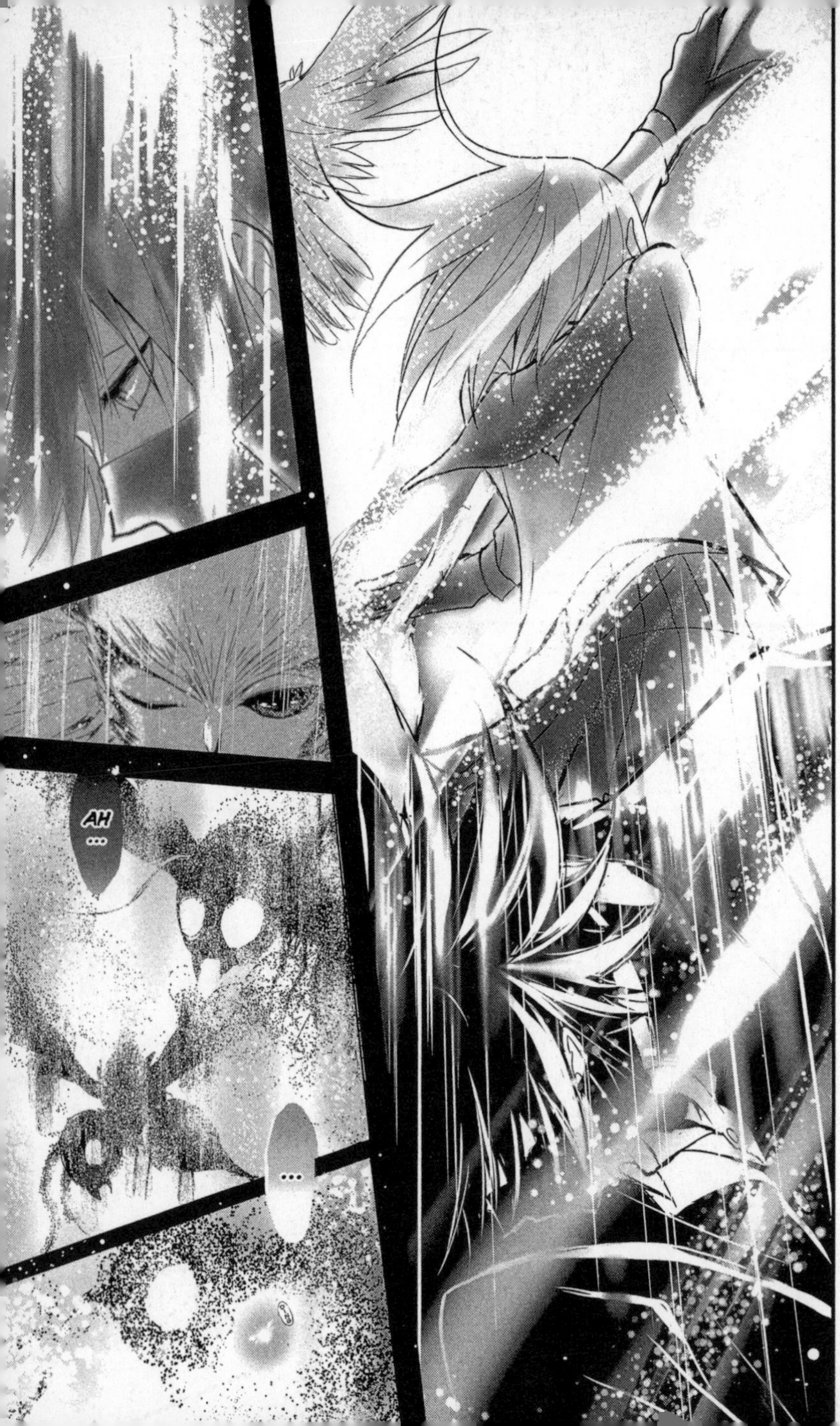
AH ...
...

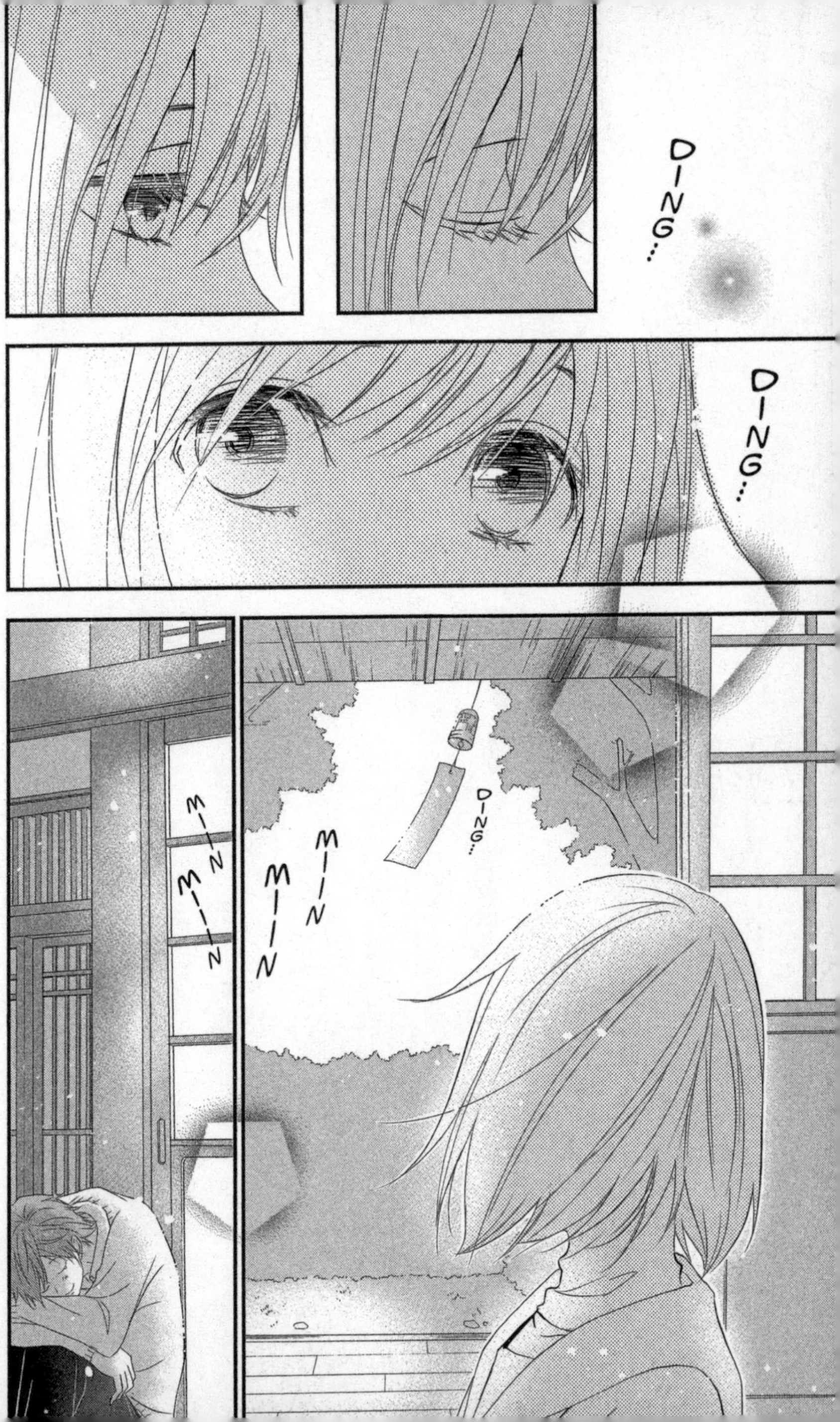
DING...
DING...
DING...
MI-N
MI-N
MI-N
MI-N

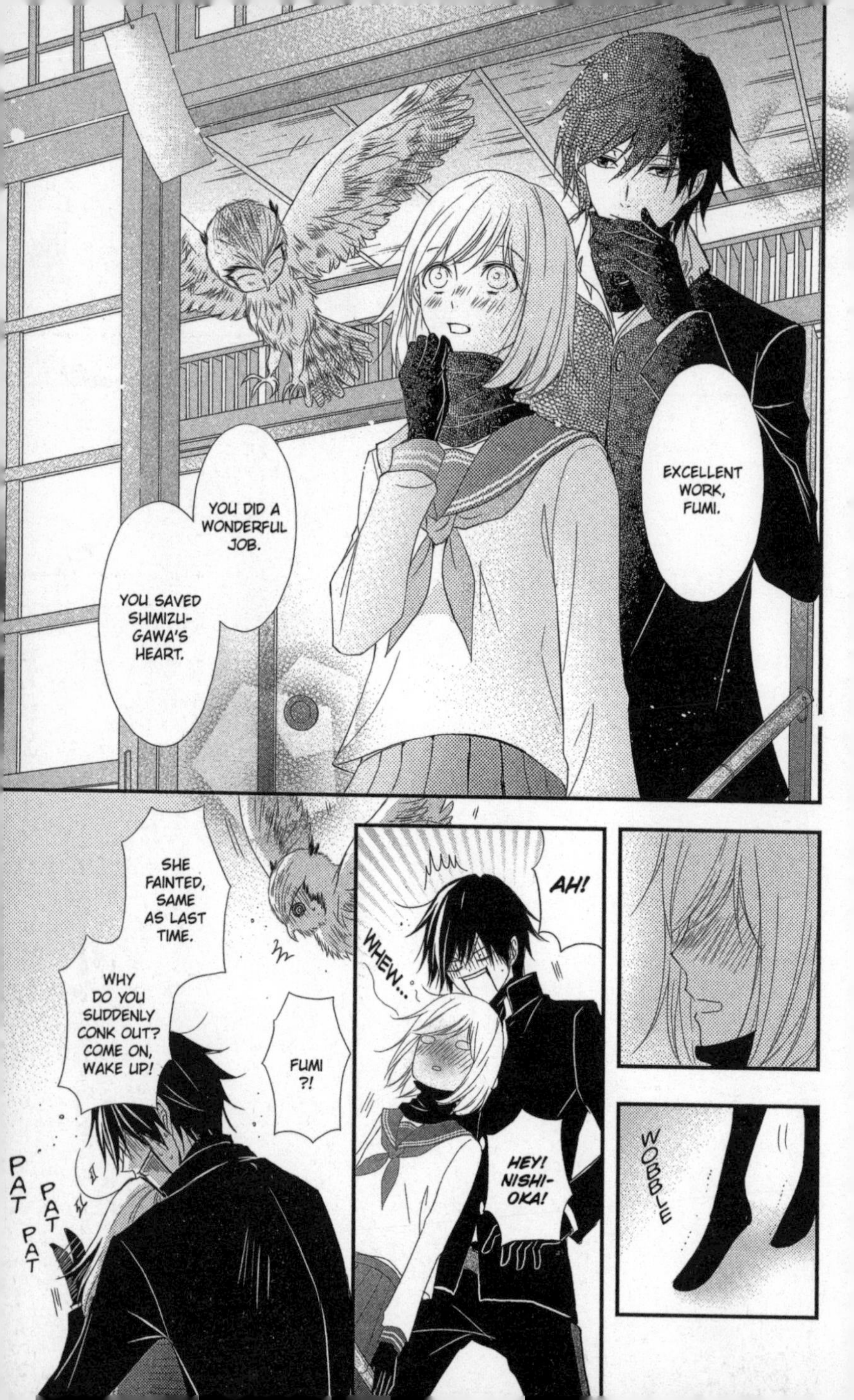
EXCELLENT WORK, FUMI.
YOU DID A WONDERFUL JOB.
YOU SAVED SHIMIZU-GAWA'S HEART.
WOBBLE
AH!
WHEW...
HEY! NISHI-OKA!
FUMI ?!
SHE FAINTED, SAME AS LAST TIME.
WHY DO YOU SUDDENLY CONK OUT? COME ON, WAKE UP!
PAT PAT
PAT PAT

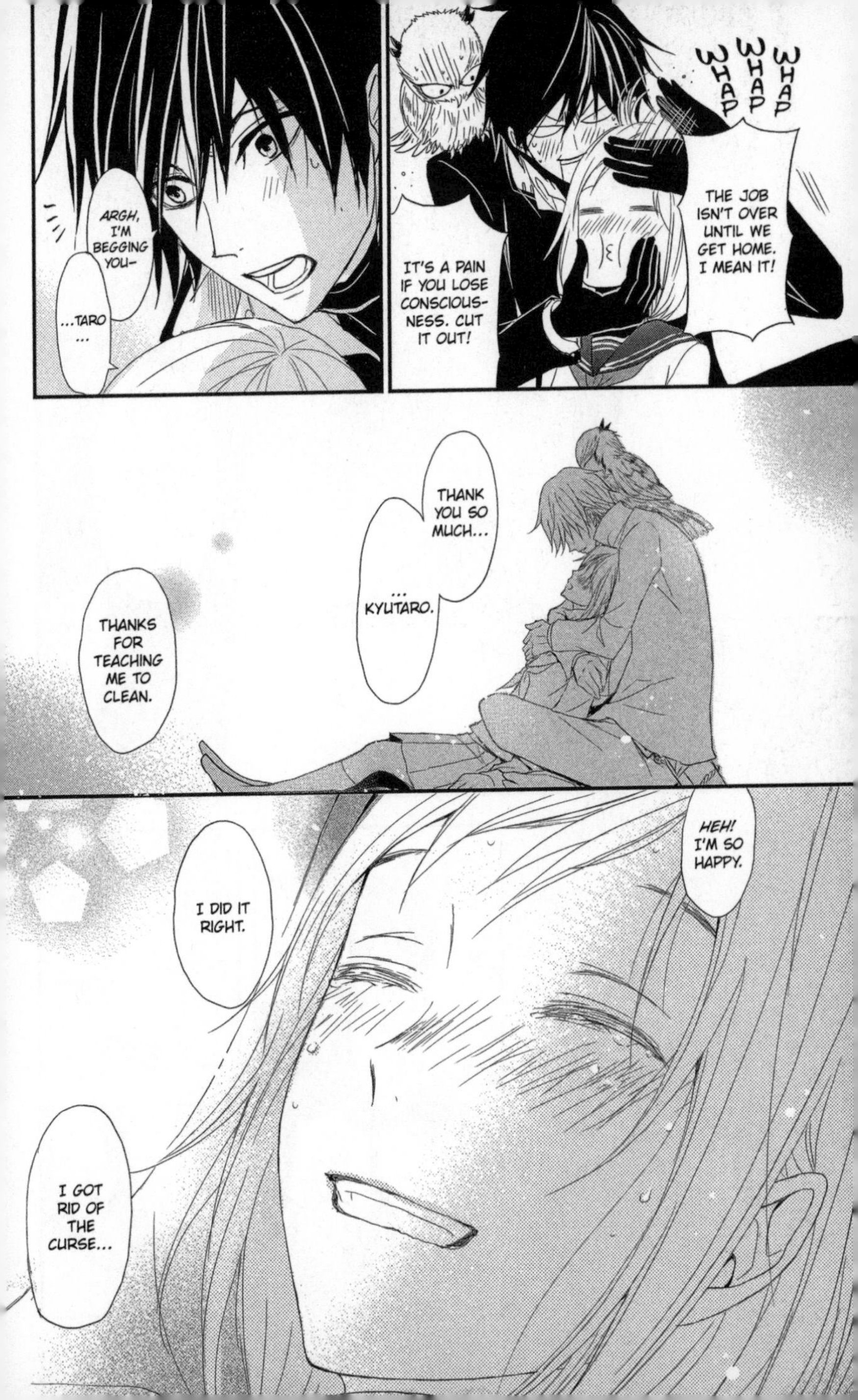
WHAP WHAP WHAP
THE JOB ISN'T OVER UNTIL WE GET HOME. I MEAN IT!
IT'S A PAIN IF YOU LOSE CONSCIOUS-NESS. CUT IT OUT!
ARGH, I'M BEGGING YOU—
...TARO...
THANK YOU SO MUCH...
...KYUTARO.
THANKS FOR TEACHING ME TO CLEAN.
HEH! I'M SO HAPPY.
I DID IT RIGHT.
I GOT RID OF THE CURSE...

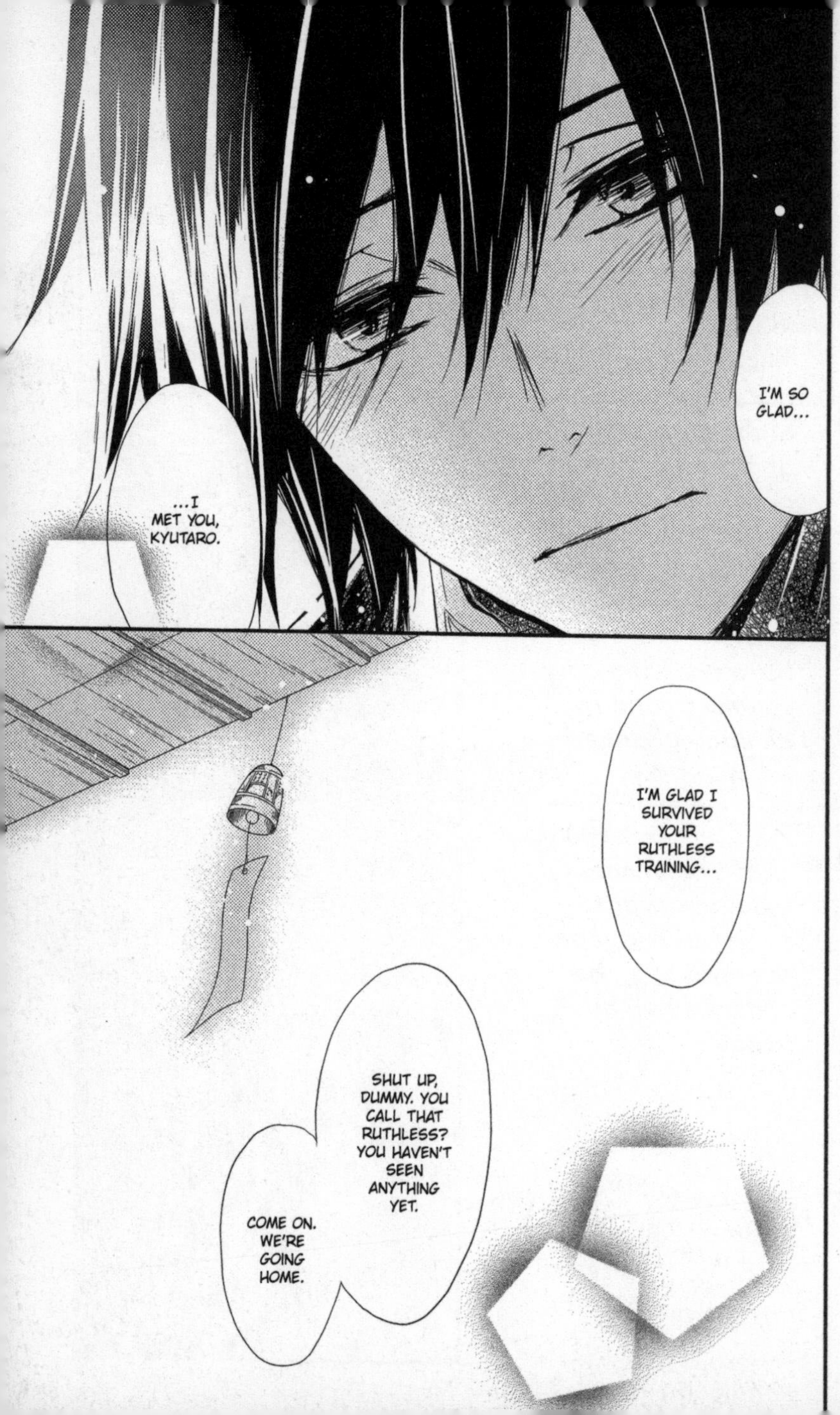
I'M SO GLAD...
...I MET YOU, KYUTARO.
I'M GLAD I SURVIVED YOUR RUTHLESS TRAINING...
SHUT UP, DUMMY. YOU CALL THAT RUTHLESS? YOU HAVEN'T SEEN ANYTHING YET.
COME ON. WE'RE GOING HOME.

QQ'S NONSENSE STORY

About this panel
in Sweep 8. ⟶

I debated long and hard (okay, about eight minutes) about whether to dress him like this. According to what I wrote in volume 1, he should have been dressed like this! I hate that it's only volume 2, and I've already changed my mind.

But...then I thought that she probably wouldn't want to listen if a man dressed like this ordered her back inside.

I love putting him in weird clothes, so I wish they wouldn't have such serious conversations.

SWEEP 10

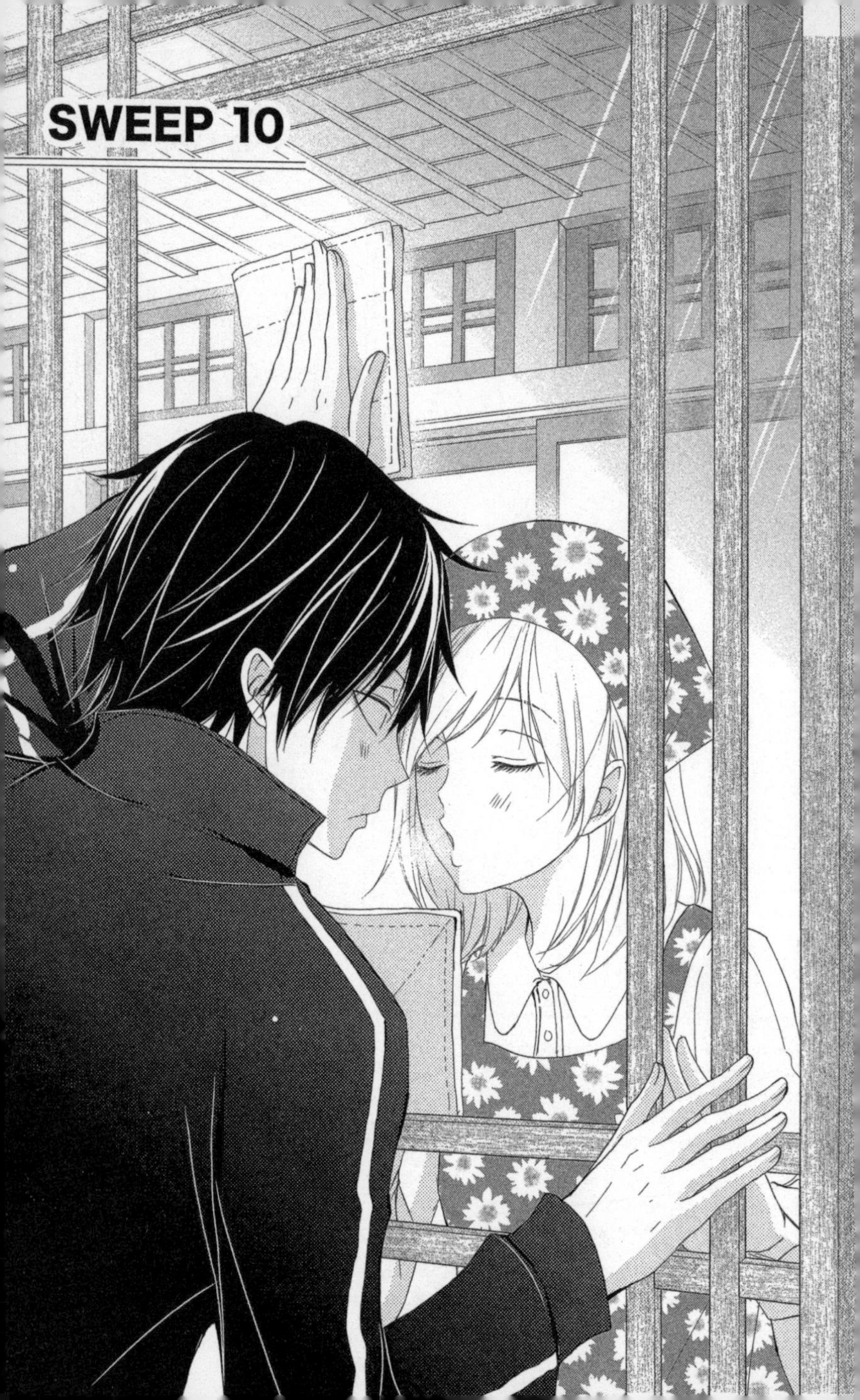

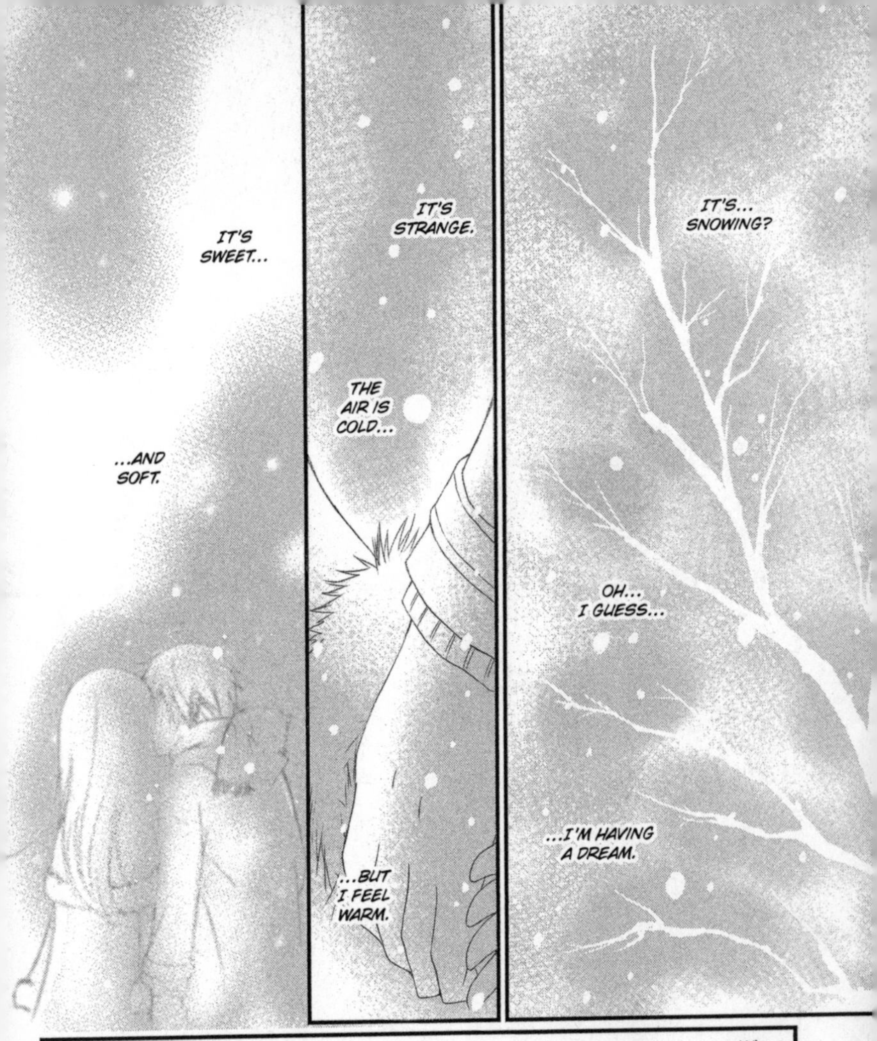
IT'S... SNOWING?
OH... I GUESS...
...I'M HAVING A DREAM.
IT'S STRANGE.
THE AIR IS COLD...
...BUT I FEEL WARM.
IT'S SWEET...
...AND SOFT.

What can I say? Until I began this series, I didn't think much about how lots of people hate bugs. I don't hate bugs personally (I kind of like them, actually), but I think I'm in the minority there.

If you're a bug-hater, I'm afraid there may be a lot of scenes that you'll find unpleasant. So I'm very grateful to those of you who read this story anyway! I'll do my very best to make the bugs look pretty from now on.

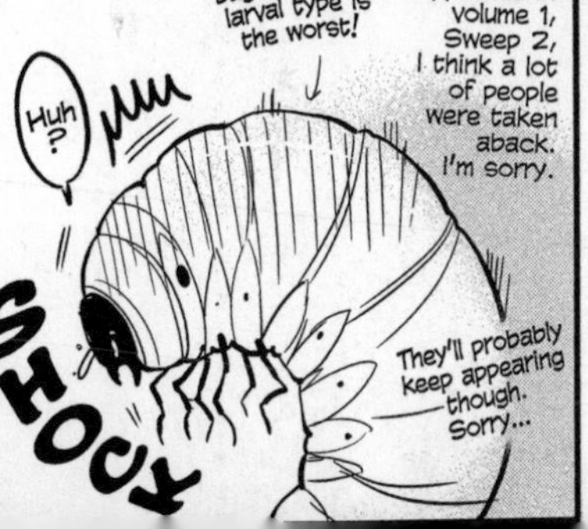
When it first appeared in volume 1, Sweep 2, I think a lot of people were taken aback. I'm sorry.
No one likes bugs, but this larval type is the worst!
Huh?
SHOCK
They'll probably keep appearing though. Sorry...
Is this so bad? I think it's cute...like a meat bun...

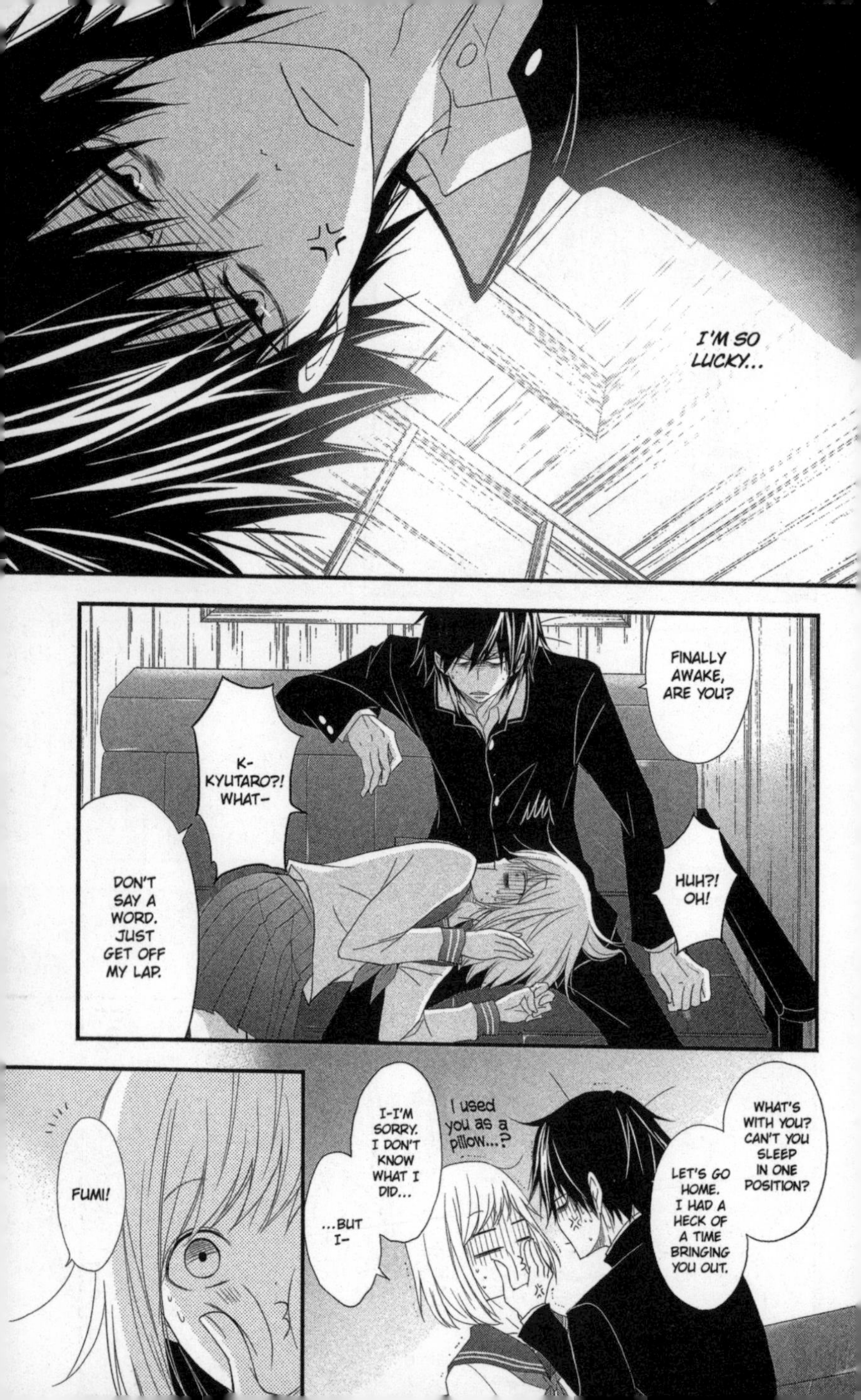
I'M SO LUCKY...
FINALLY AWAKE, ARE YOU?
HUH?! OH!
K-KYUTARO?! WHAT-
DON'T SAY A WORD. JUST GET OFF MY LAP.
WHAT'S WITH YOU? CAN'T YOU SLEEP IN ONE POSITION?
LET'S GO HOME. I HAD A HECK OF A TIME BRINGING YOU OUT.
I used you as a pillow...?
I-I'M SORRY. I DON'T KNOW WHAT I DID...
...BUT I-
FUMI!

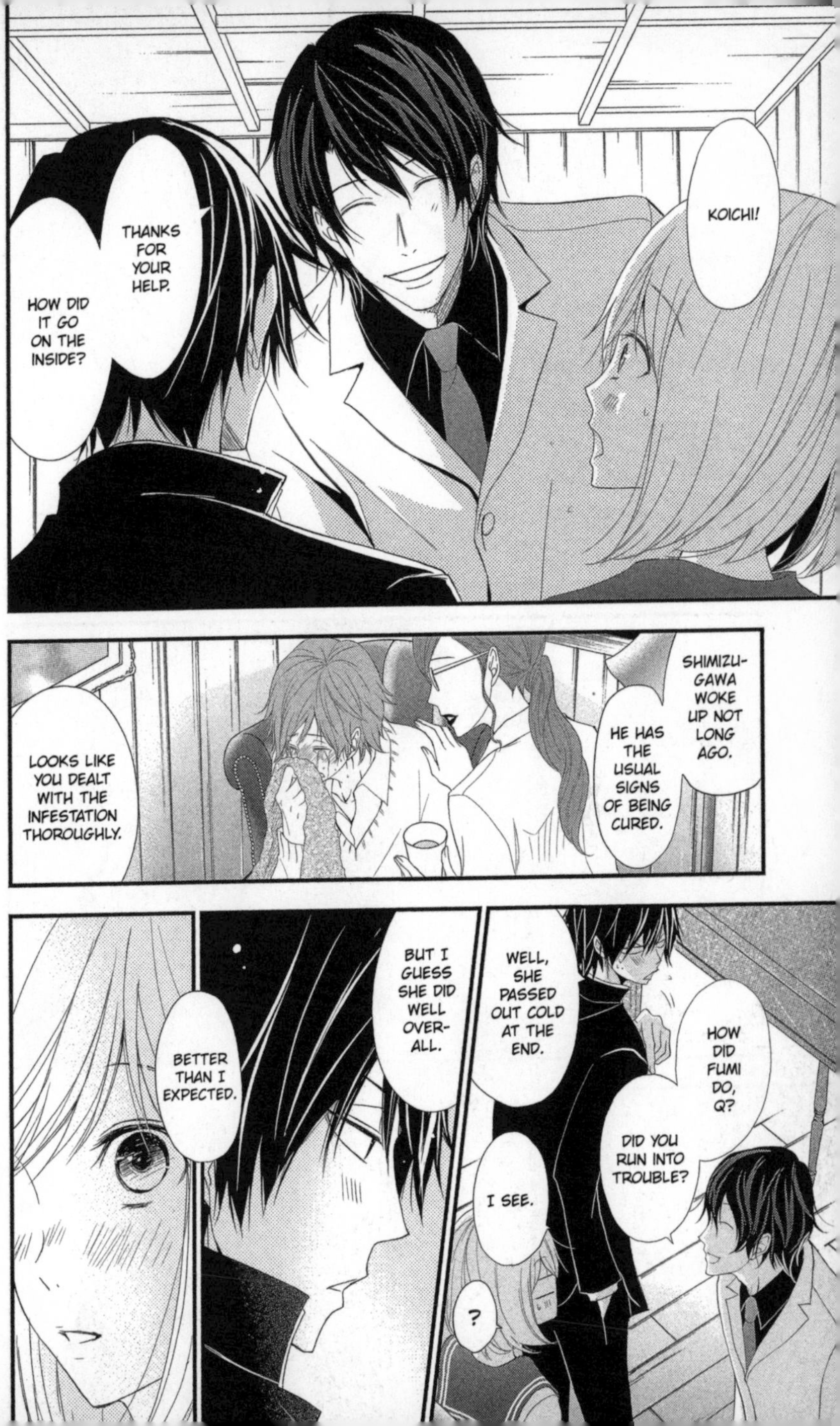
KOICHI!
THANKS FOR YOUR HELP.
HOW DID IT GO ON THE INSIDE?
SHIMIZU-GAWA WOKE UP NOT LONG AGO.
HE HAS THE USUAL SIGNS OF BEING CURED.
LOOKS LIKE YOU DEALT WITH THE INFESTATION THOROUGHLY.
HOW DID FUMI DO, Q?
DID YOU RUN INTO TROUBLE?
WELL, SHE PASSED OUT COLD AT THE END.
I SEE.
?
BUT I GUESS SHE DID WELL OVER-ALL.
BETTER THAN I EXPECTED.

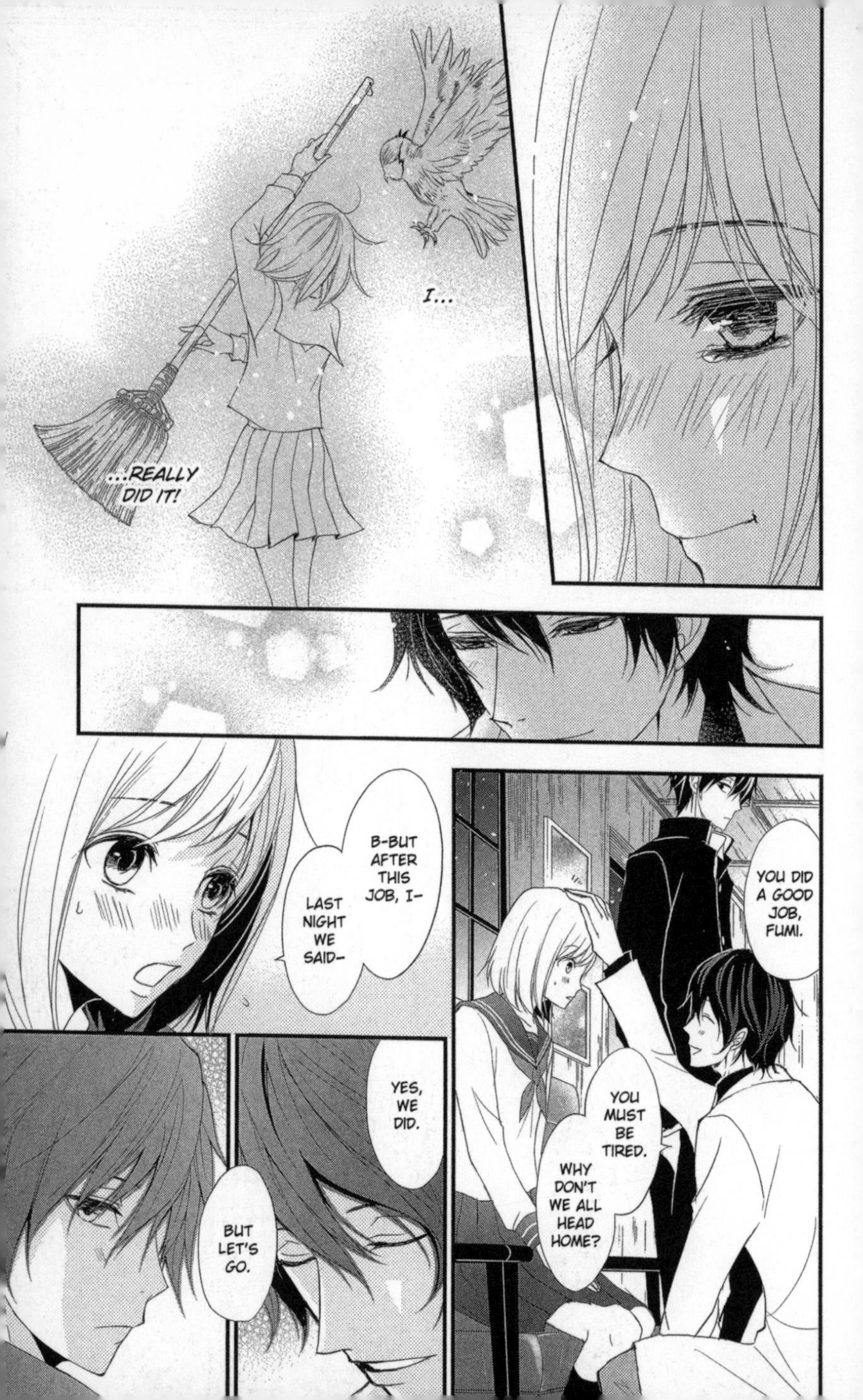
I...
...REALLY DID IT!
YOU DID A GOOD JOB, FUMI.
YOU MUST BE TIRED.
WHY DON'T WE ALL HEAD HOME?
B-BUT AFTER THIS JOB, I-
LAST NIGHT WE SAID-
YES, WE DID.
BUT LET'S GO.

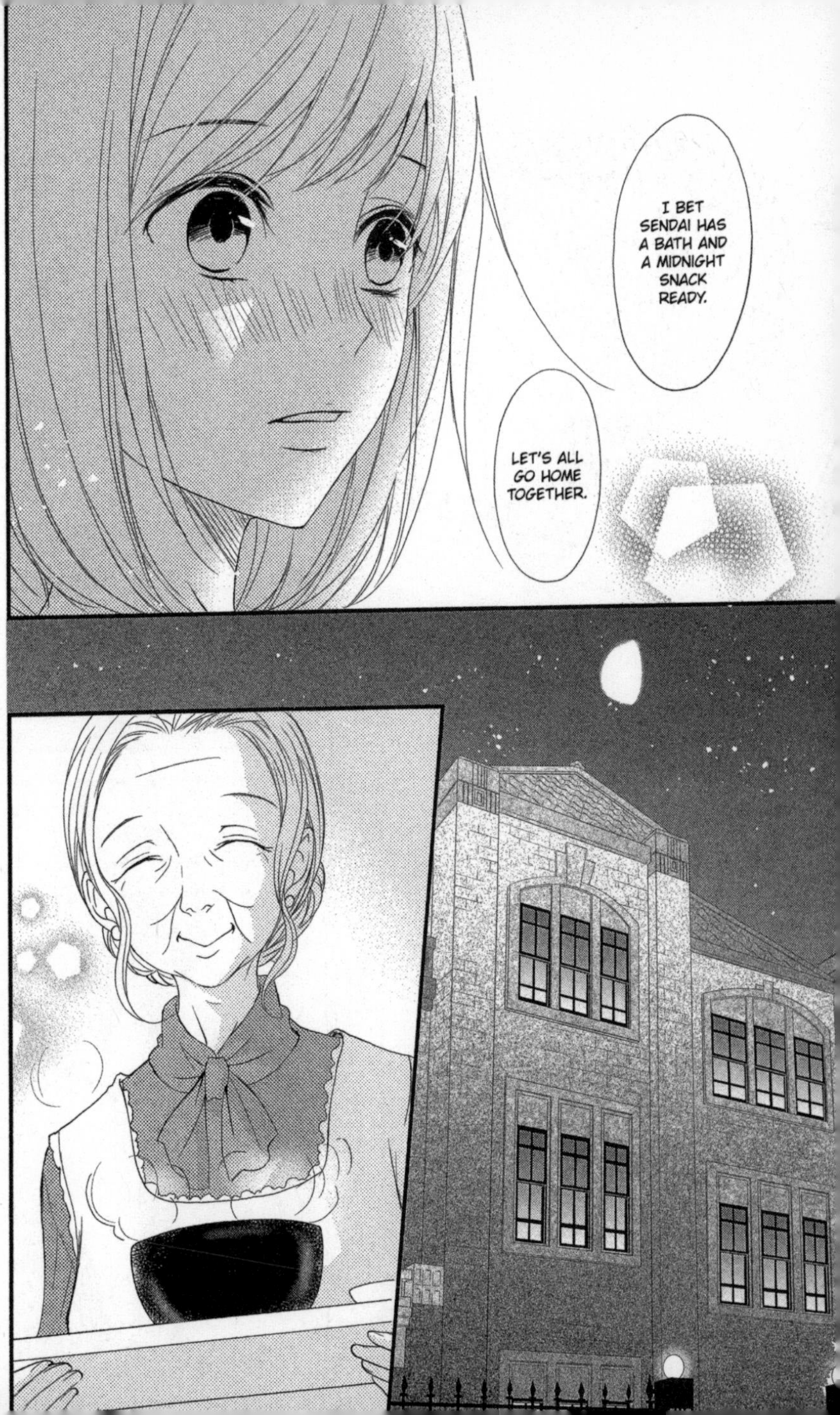
I BET SENDAI HAS A BATH AND A MIDNIGHT SNACK READY.
LET'S ALL GO HOME TOGETHER.

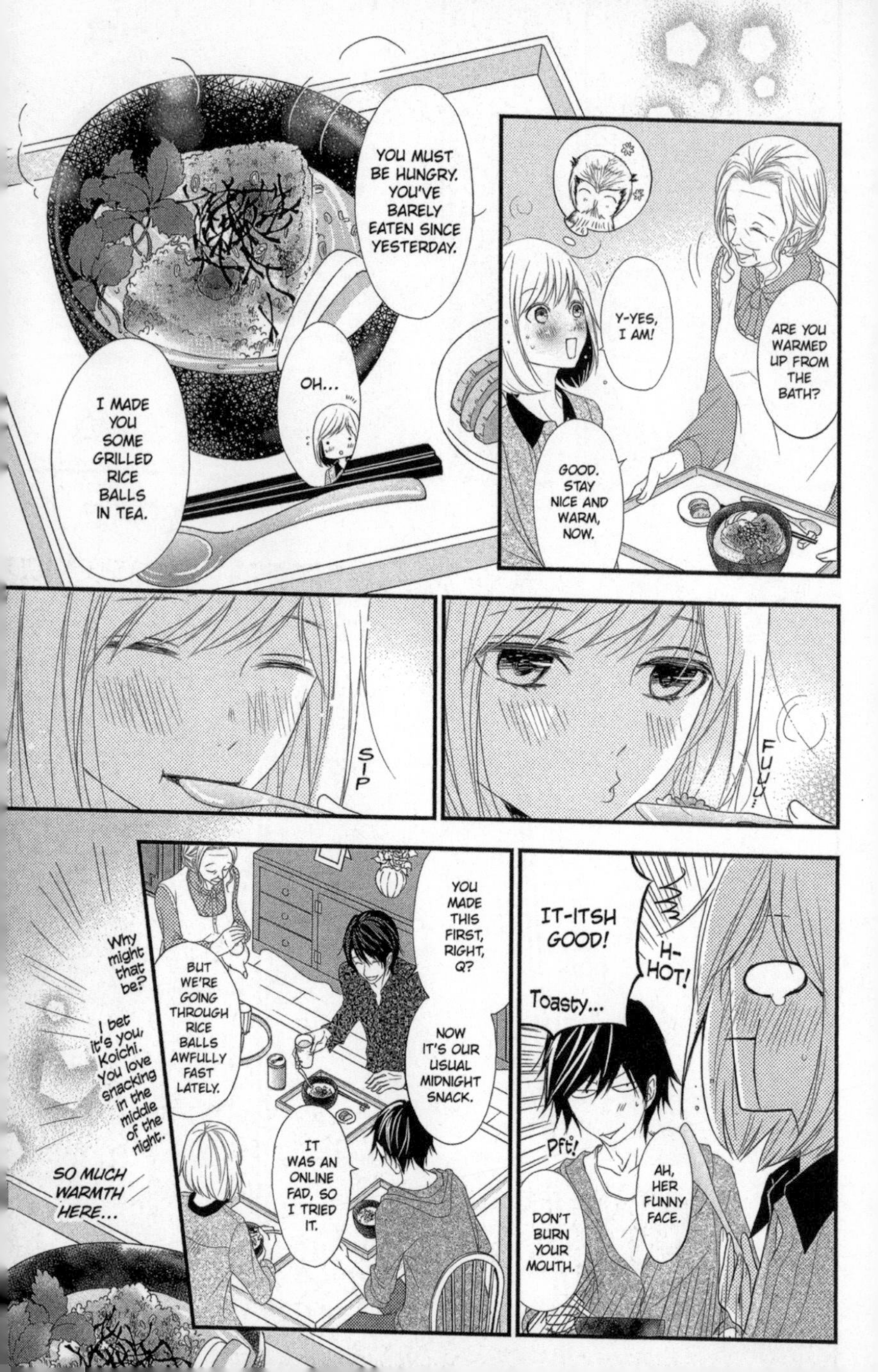
ARE YOU WARMED UP FROM THE BATH?
Y-YES, I AM!
GOOD. STAY NICE AND WARM, NOW.
YOU MUST BE HUNGRY. YOU'VE BARELY EATEN SINCE YESTERDAY.
OH...
I MADE YOU SOME GRILLED RICE BALLS IN TEA.
FUUU...
SIP
H-HOT!
IT-ITSH GOOD!
Toasty...
AH, HER FUNNY FACE.
Pft!
DON'T BURN YOUR MOUTH.
YOU MADE THIS FIRST, RIGHT, Q?
NOW IT'S OUR USUAL MIDNIGHT SNACK.
BUT WE'RE GOING THROUGH RICE BALLS AWFULLY FAST LATELY.
IT WAS AN ONLINE FAD, SO I TRIED IT.
Why might that be?
I bet it's you, Koichi. You love snacking in the middle of the night.
SO MUCH WARMTH HERE...

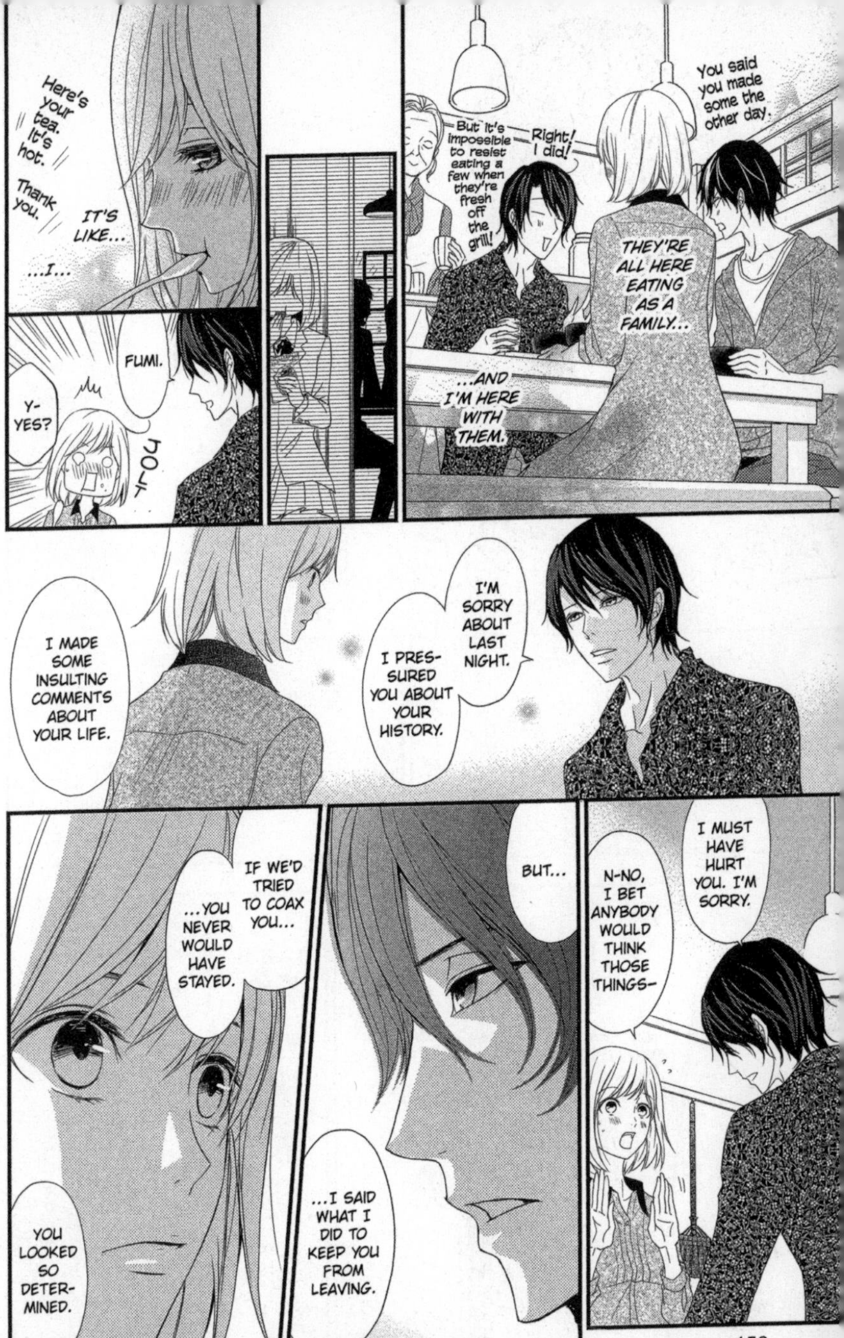
You said you made some the other day.
Right! I did!
But it's impossible to resist eating a few when they're fresh off the grill!
THEY'RE ALL HERE EATING AS A FAMILY...
...AND I'M HERE WITH THEM.
Here's your tea. It's hot.
Thank you.
IT'S LIKE...
...I...
FUMI.
Y-YES?
JOLT
I'M SORRY ABOUT LAST NIGHT.
I PRES-SURED YOU ABOUT YOUR HISTORY.
I MADE SOME INSULTING COMMENTS ABOUT YOUR LIFE.
I MUST HAVE HURT YOU. I'M SORRY.
N-NO, I BET ANYBODY WOULD THINK THOSE THINGS-
BUT...
...I SAID WHAT I DID TO KEEP YOU FROM LEAVING.
IF WE'D TRIED TO COAX YOU...
...YOU NEVER WOULD HAVE STAYED.
YOU LOOKED SO DETER-MINED.

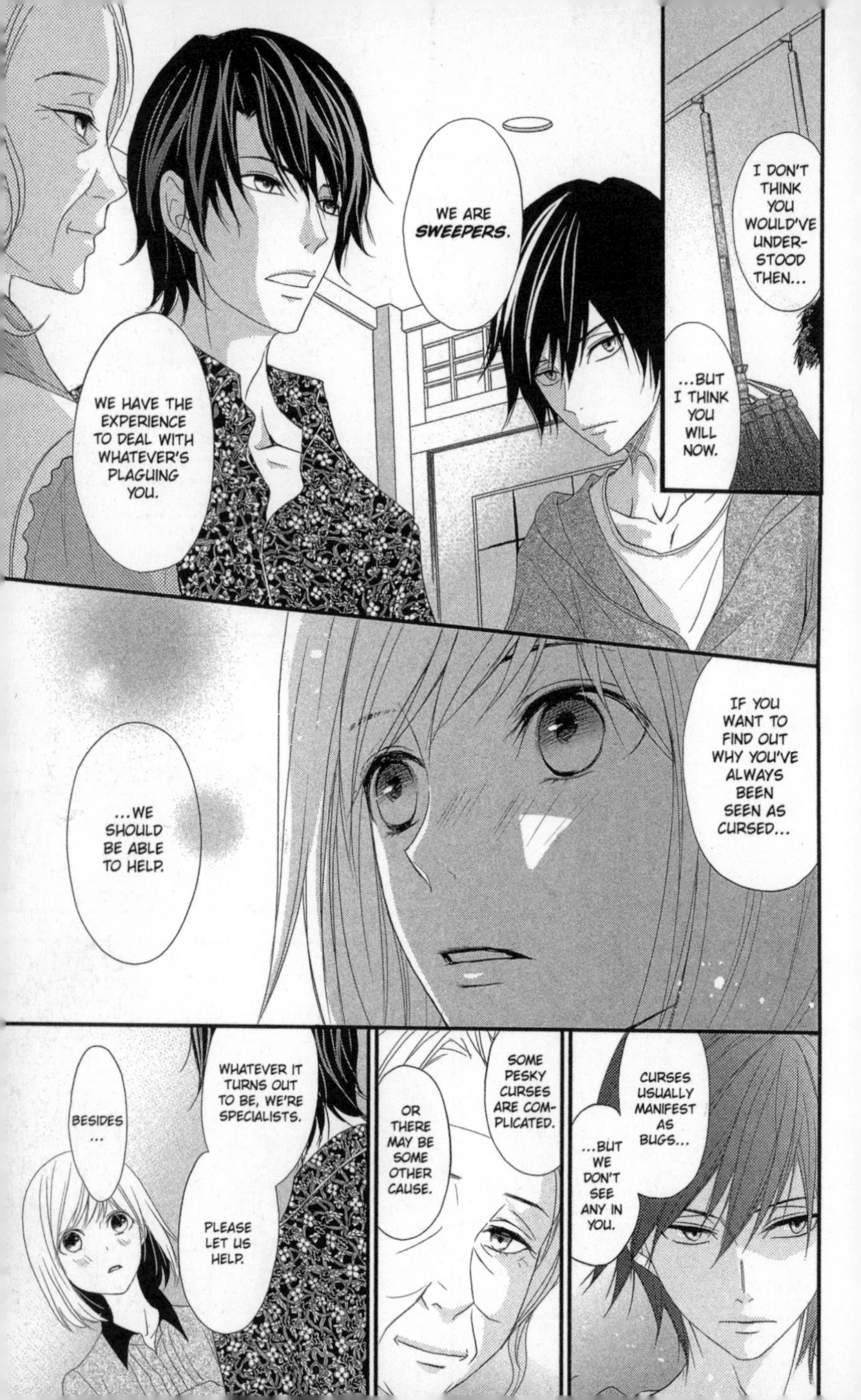
I DON'T THINK YOU WOULD'VE UNDERSTOOD THEN...
...BUT I THINK YOU WILL NOW.
WE ARE **SWEEPERS**.
WE HAVE THE EXPERIENCE TO DEAL WITH WHATEVER'S PLAGUING YOU.
IF YOU WANT TO FIND OUT WHY YOU'VE ALWAYS BEEN SEEN AS CURSED...
...WE SHOULD BE ABLE TO HELP.
CURSES USUALLY MANIFEST AS BUGS...
...BUT WE DON'T SEE ANY IN YOU.
SOME PESKY CURSES ARE COMPLICATED.
OR THERE MAY BE SOME OTHER CAUSE.
WHATEVER IT TURNS OUT TO BE, WE'RE SPECIALISTS.
BESIDES...
PLEASE LET US HELP.

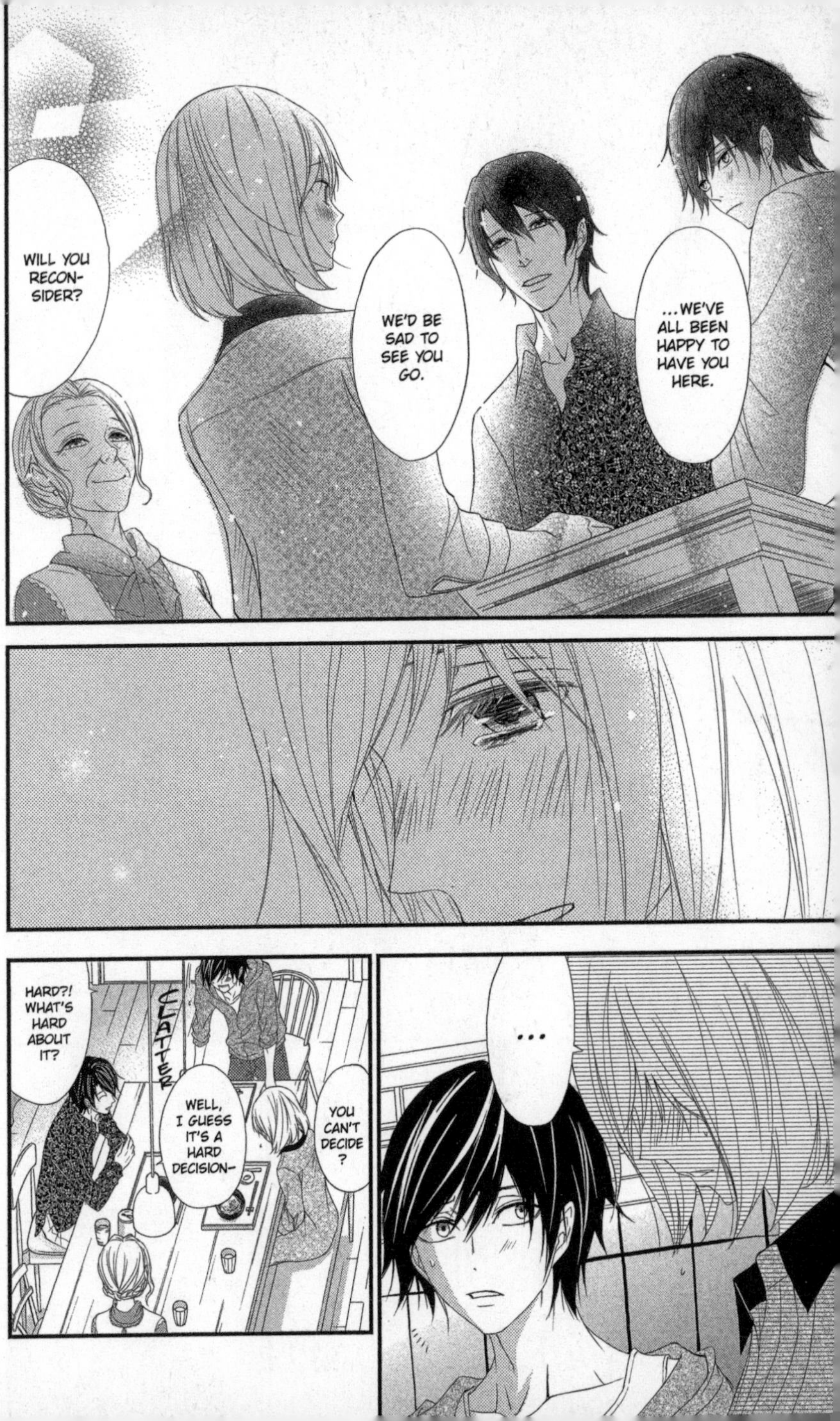
...WE'VE ALL BEEN HAPPY TO HAVE YOU HERE.
WE'D BE SAD TO SEE YOU GO.
WILL YOU RECONSIDER?
...
YOU CAN'T DECIDE?
WELL, I GUESS IT'S A HARD DECISION—
CLATTER
HARD?! WHAT'S HARD ABOUT IT?

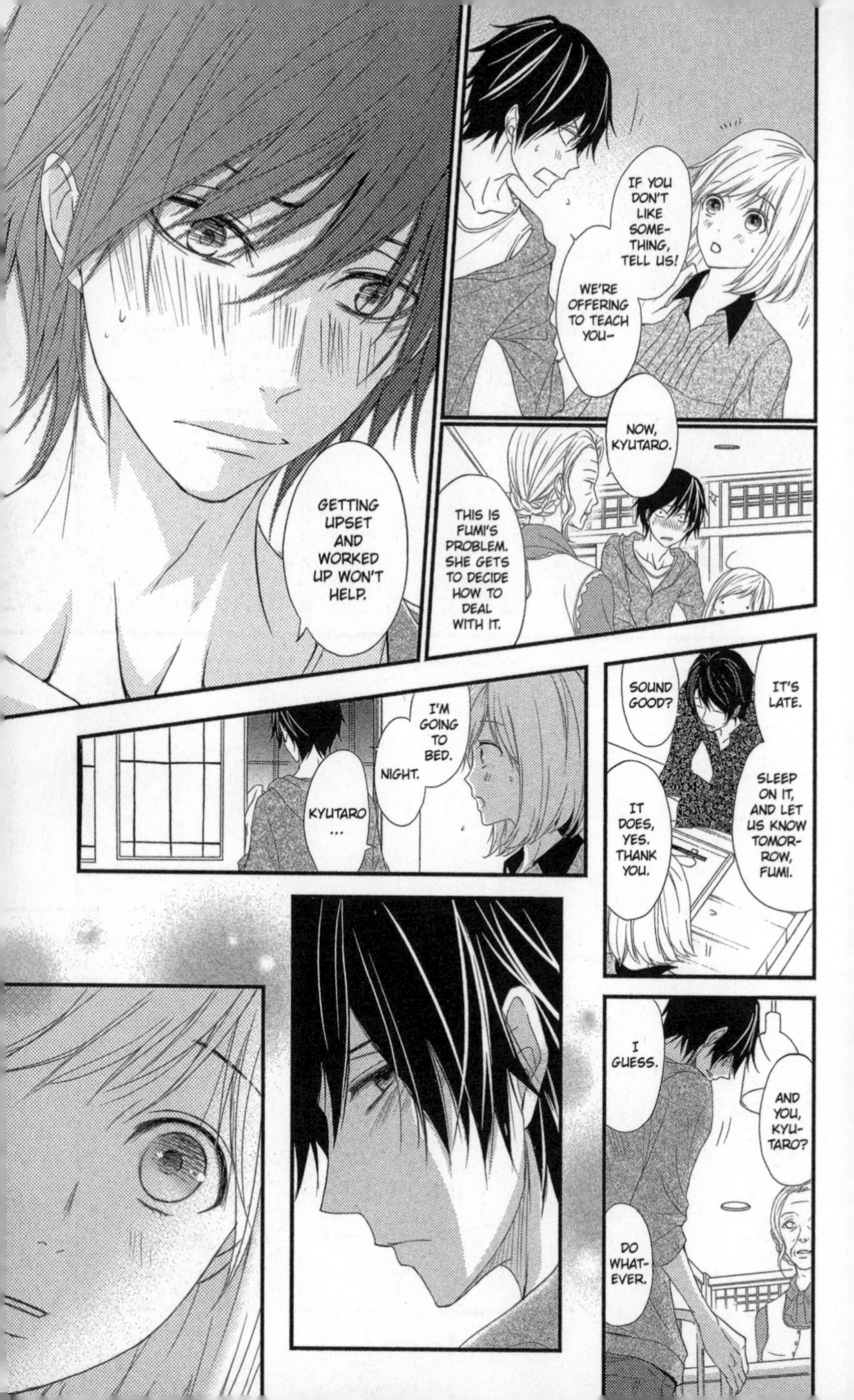
IF YOU DON'T LIKE SOME-THING, TELL US!
WE'RE OFFERING TO TEACH YOU-
NOW, KYUTARO.
THIS IS FUMI'S PROBLEM. SHE GETS TO DECIDE HOW TO DEAL WITH IT.
GETTING UPSET AND WORKED UP WON'T HELP.
IT'S LATE.
SLEEP ON IT, AND LET US KNOW TOMOR-ROW, FUMI.
SOUND GOOD?
IT DOES, YES. THANK YOU.
I'M GOING TO BED.
NIGHT.
KYUTARO...
AND YOU, KYU-TARO?
I GUESS.
DO WHAT-EVER.

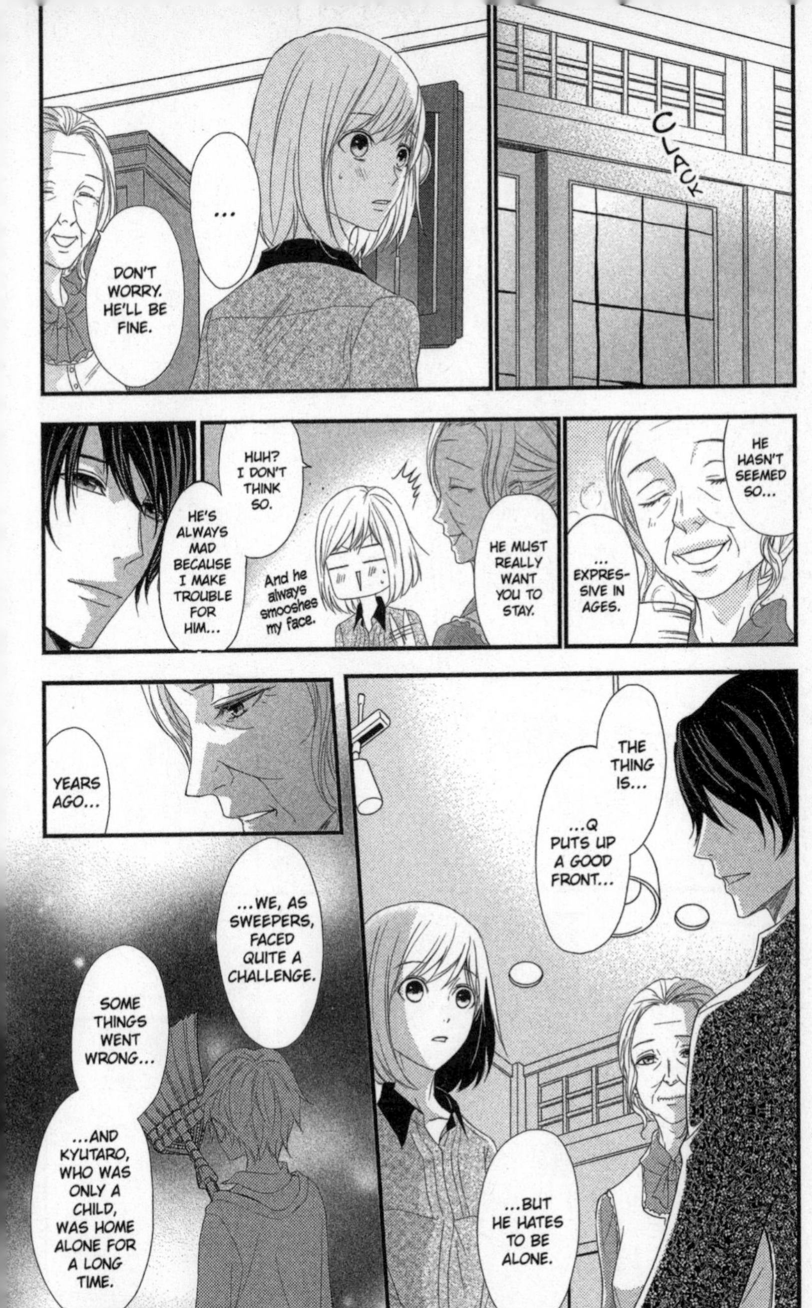
CLACK
...
DON'T WORRY. HE'LL BE FINE.
HE HASN'T SEEMED SO...
...EXPRESSIVE IN AGES.
HE MUST REALLY WANT YOU TO STAY.
HUH? I DON'T THINK SO.
HE'S ALWAYS MAD BECAUSE I MAKE TROUBLE FOR HIM...
And he always smooshes my face.
THE THING IS...
...Q PUTS UP A GOOD FRONT...
...BUT HE HATES TO BE ALONE.
YEARS AGO...
...WE, AS SWEEPERS, FACED QUITE A CHALLENGE.
SOME THINGS WENT WRONG...
...AND KYUTARO, WHO WAS ONLY A CHILD, WAS HOME ALONE FOR A LONG TIME.

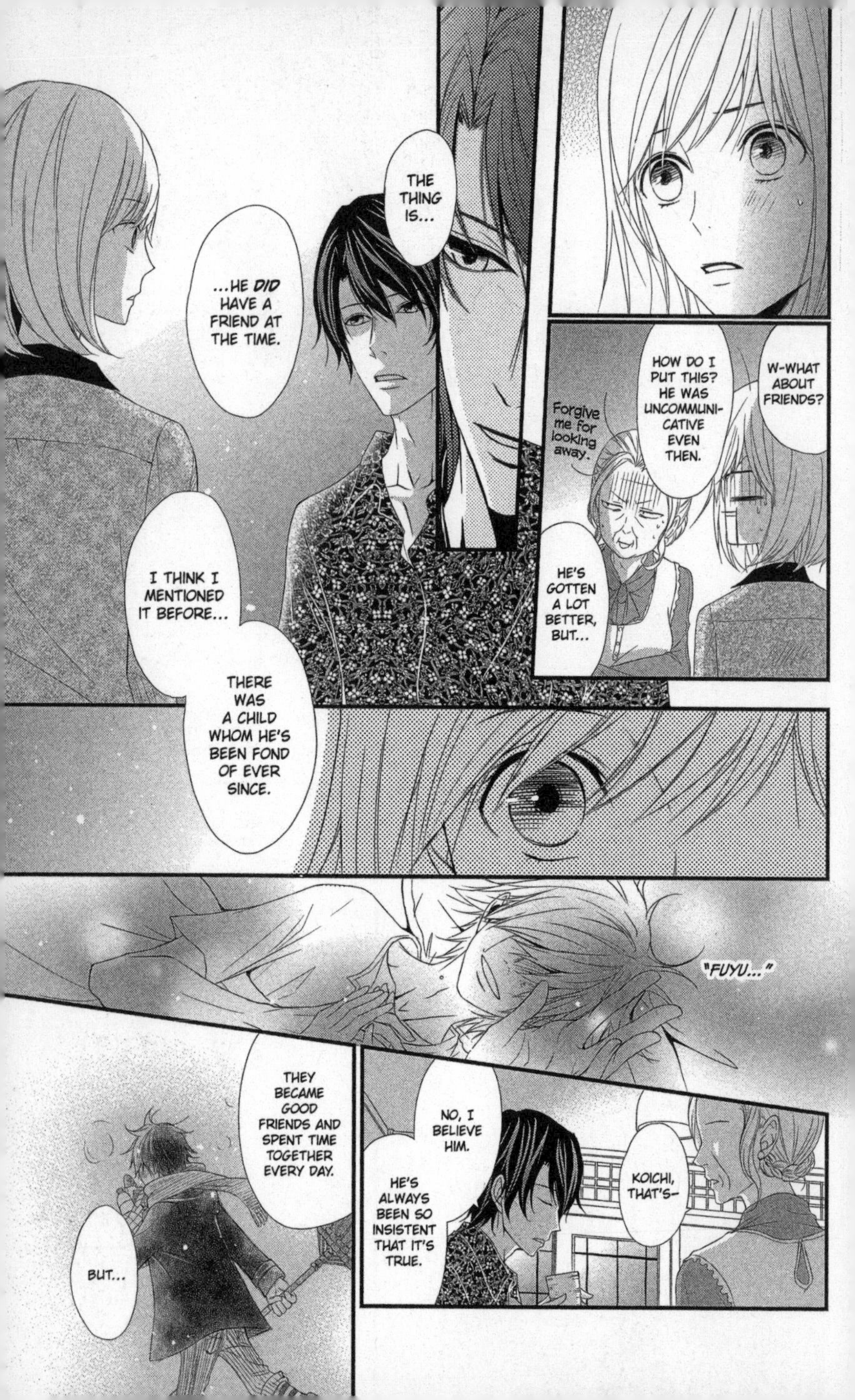
W-WHAT ABOUT FRIENDS?
HOW DO I PUT THIS? HE WAS UNCOMMUNICATIVE EVEN THEN.
Forgive me for looking away.
HE'S GOTTEN A LOT BETTER, BUT...
THE THING IS...
...HE *DID* HAVE A FRIEND AT THE TIME.
I THINK I MENTIONED IT BEFORE...
THERE WAS A CHILD WHOM HE'S BEEN FOND OF EVER SINCE.
"FUYU..."
KOICHI, THAT'S-
NO, I BELIEVE HIM.
HE'S ALWAYS BEEN SO INSISTENT THAT IT'S TRUE.
THEY BECAME GOOD FRIENDS AND SPENT TIME TOGETHER EVERY DAY.
BUT...

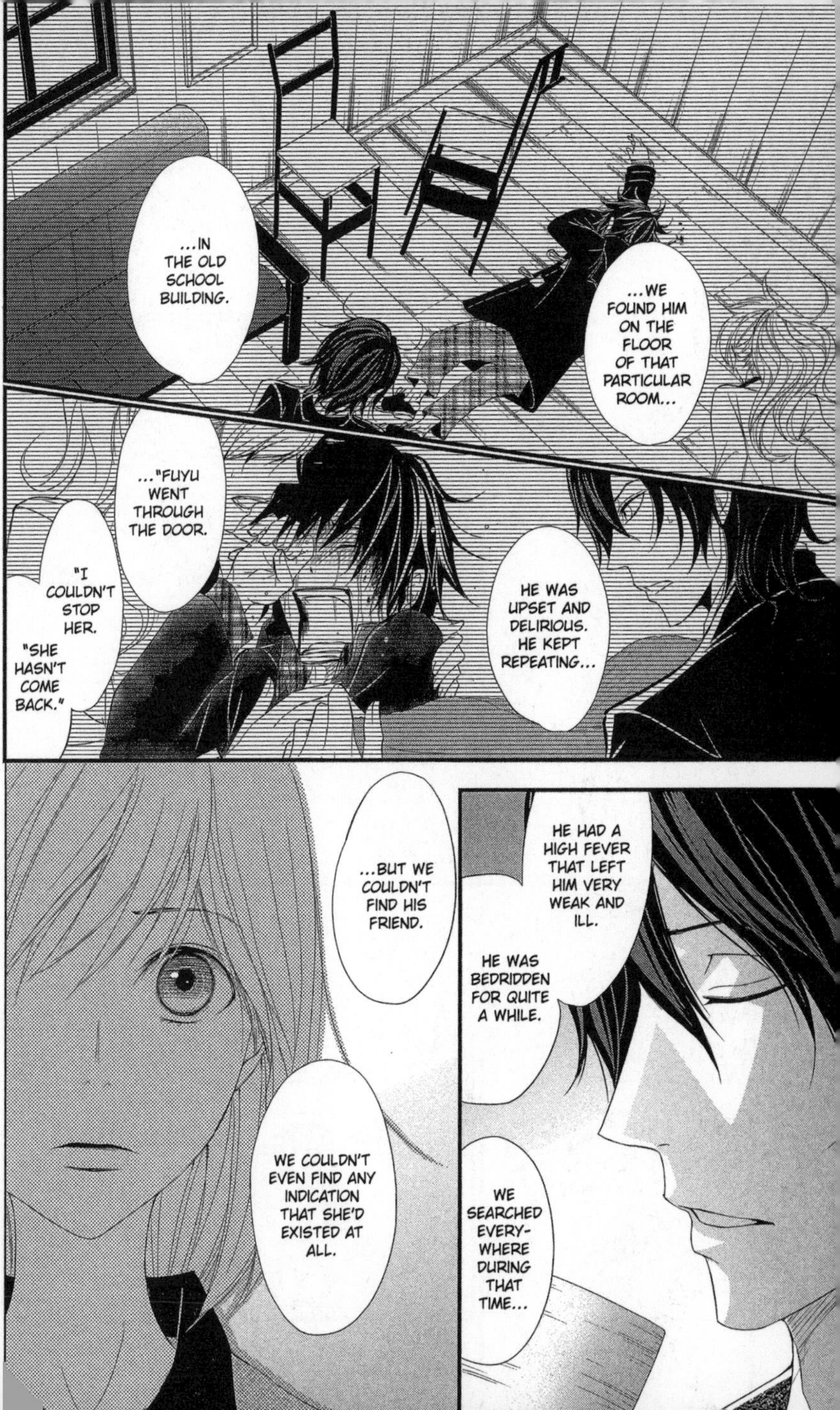
...WE FOUND HIM ON THE FLOOR OF THAT PARTICULAR ROOM...
...IN THE OLD SCHOOL BUILDING.
HE WAS UPSET AND DELIRIOUS. HE KEPT REPEATING...
..."FUYU WENT THROUGH THE DOOR.
"I COULDN'T STOP HER.
"SHE HASN'T COME BACK."
HE HAD A HIGH FEVER THAT LEFT HIM VERY WEAK AND ILL.
HE WAS BEDRIDDEN FOR QUITE A WHILE.
WE SEARCHED EVERY-WHERE DURING THAT TIME...
...BUT WE COULDN'T FIND HIS FRIEND.
WE COULDN'T EVEN FIND ANY INDICATION THAT SHE'D EXISTED AT ALL.

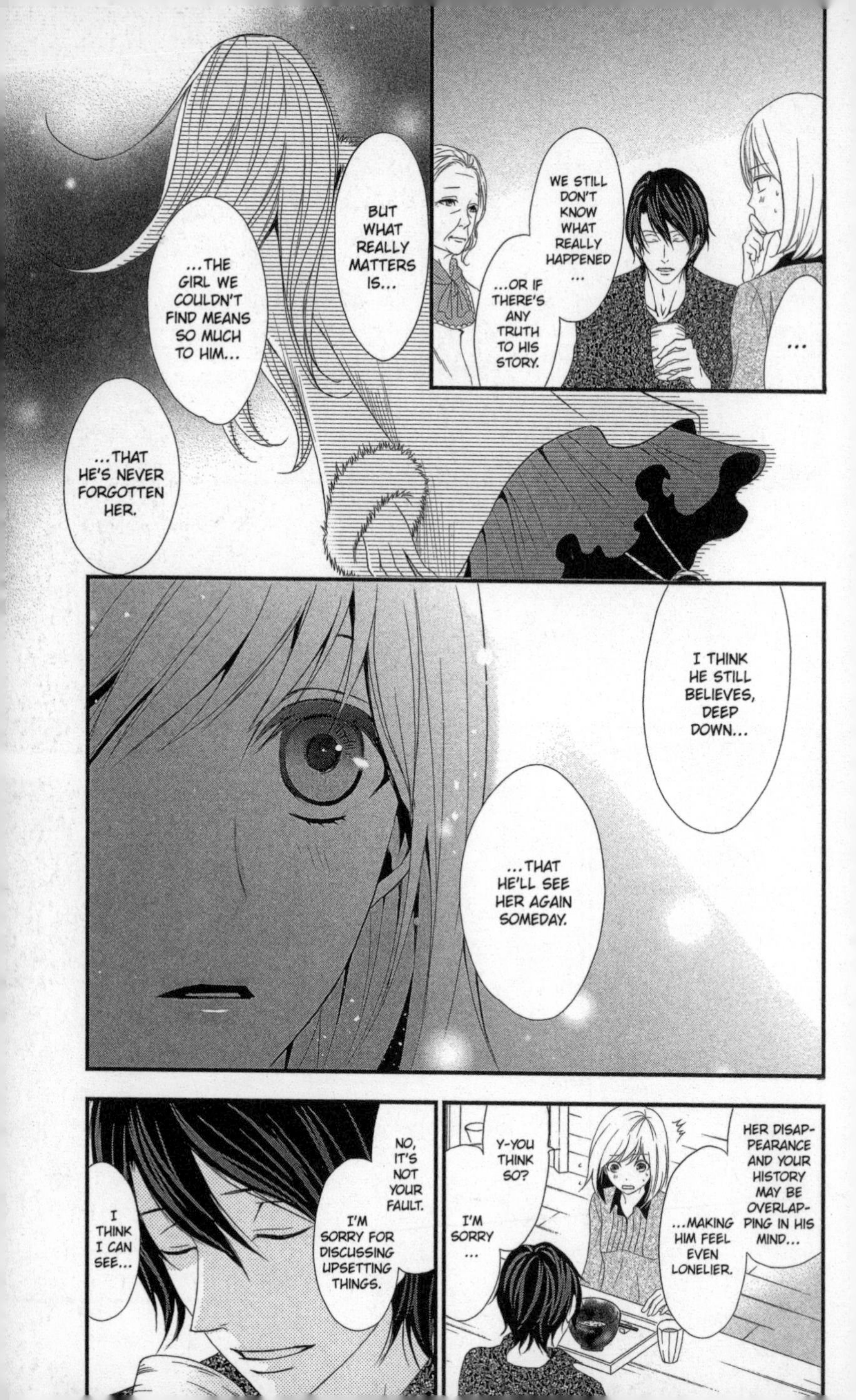
WE STILL DON'T KNOW WHAT REALLY HAPPENED...
...OR IF THERE'S ANY TRUTH TO HIS STORY.
...
BUT WHAT REALLY MATTERS IS...
...THE GIRL WE COULDN'T FIND MEANS SO MUCH TO HIM...
...THAT HE'S NEVER FORGOTTEN HER.
I THINK HE STILL BELIEVES, DEEP DOWN...
...THAT HE'LL SEE HER AGAIN SOMEDAY.
HER DISAPPEARANCE AND YOUR HISTORY MAY BE OVERLAPPING IN HIS MIND...
...MAKING HIM FEEL EVEN LONELIER.
Y-YOU THINK SO?
I'M SORRY...
NO, IT'S NOT YOUR FAULT.
I'M SORRY FOR DISCUSSING UPSETTING THINGS.
I THINK I CAN SEE...

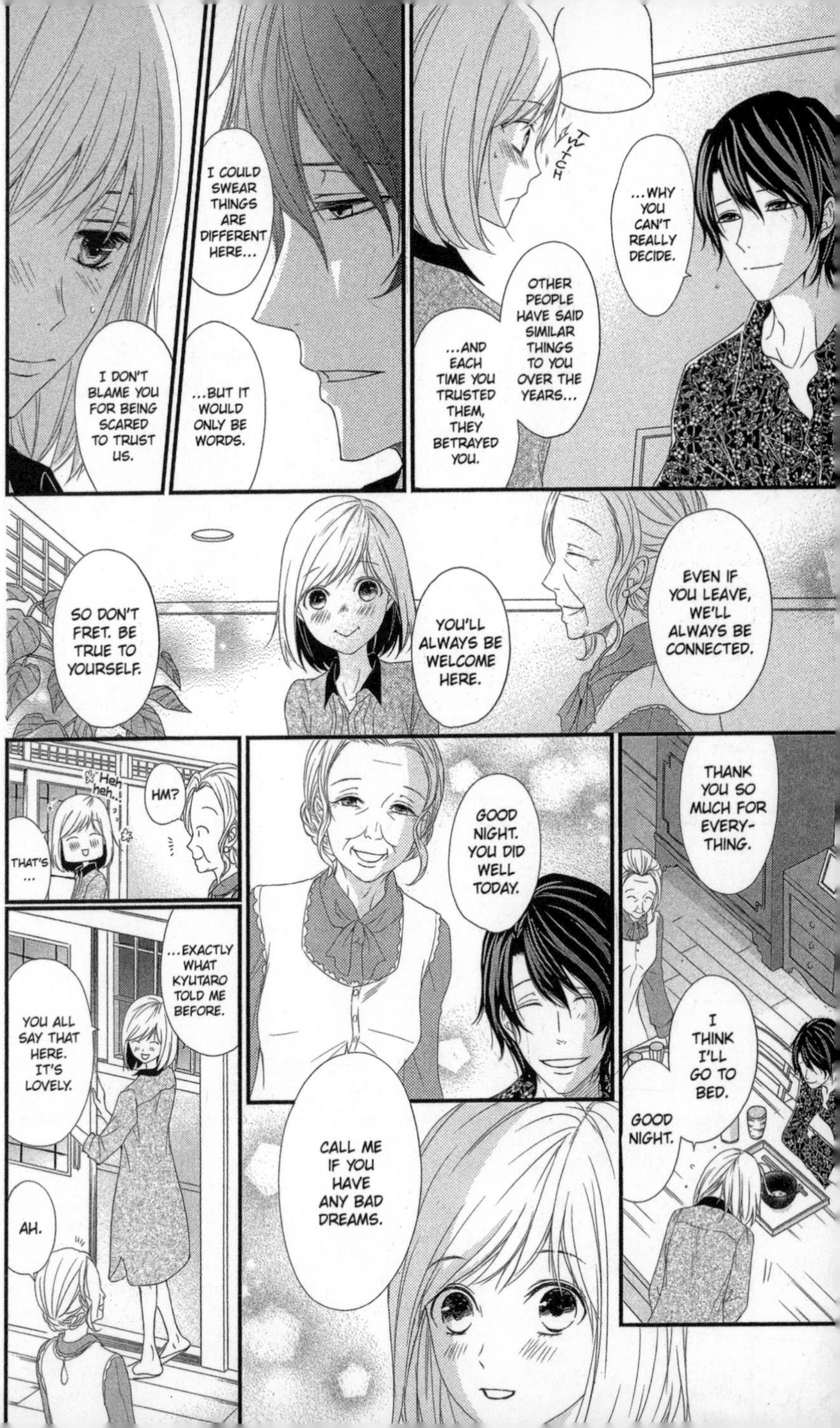
...WHY YOU CAN'T REALLY DECIDE.
TWITCH
OTHER PEOPLE HAVE SAID SIMILAR THINGS TO YOU OVER THE YEARS...
...AND EACH TIME YOU TRUSTED THEM, THEY BETRAYED YOU.
I COULD SWEAR THINGS ARE DIFFERENT HERE...
...BUT IT WOULD ONLY BE WORDS.
I DON'T BLAME YOU FOR BEING SCARED TO TRUST US.
EVEN IF YOU LEAVE, WE'LL ALWAYS BE CONNECTED.
YOU'LL ALWAYS BE WELCOME HERE.
SO DON'T FRET. BE TRUE TO YOURSELF.
THANK YOU SO MUCH FOR EVERY-THING.
I THINK I'LL GO TO BED.
GOOD NIGHT.
GOOD NIGHT. YOU DID WELL TODAY.
CALL ME IF YOU HAVE ANY BAD DREAMS.
HM?
Heh heh...
THAT'S...
...EXACTLY WHAT KYUTARO TOLD ME BEFORE.
YOU ALL SAY THAT HERE. IT'S LOVELY.
AH.

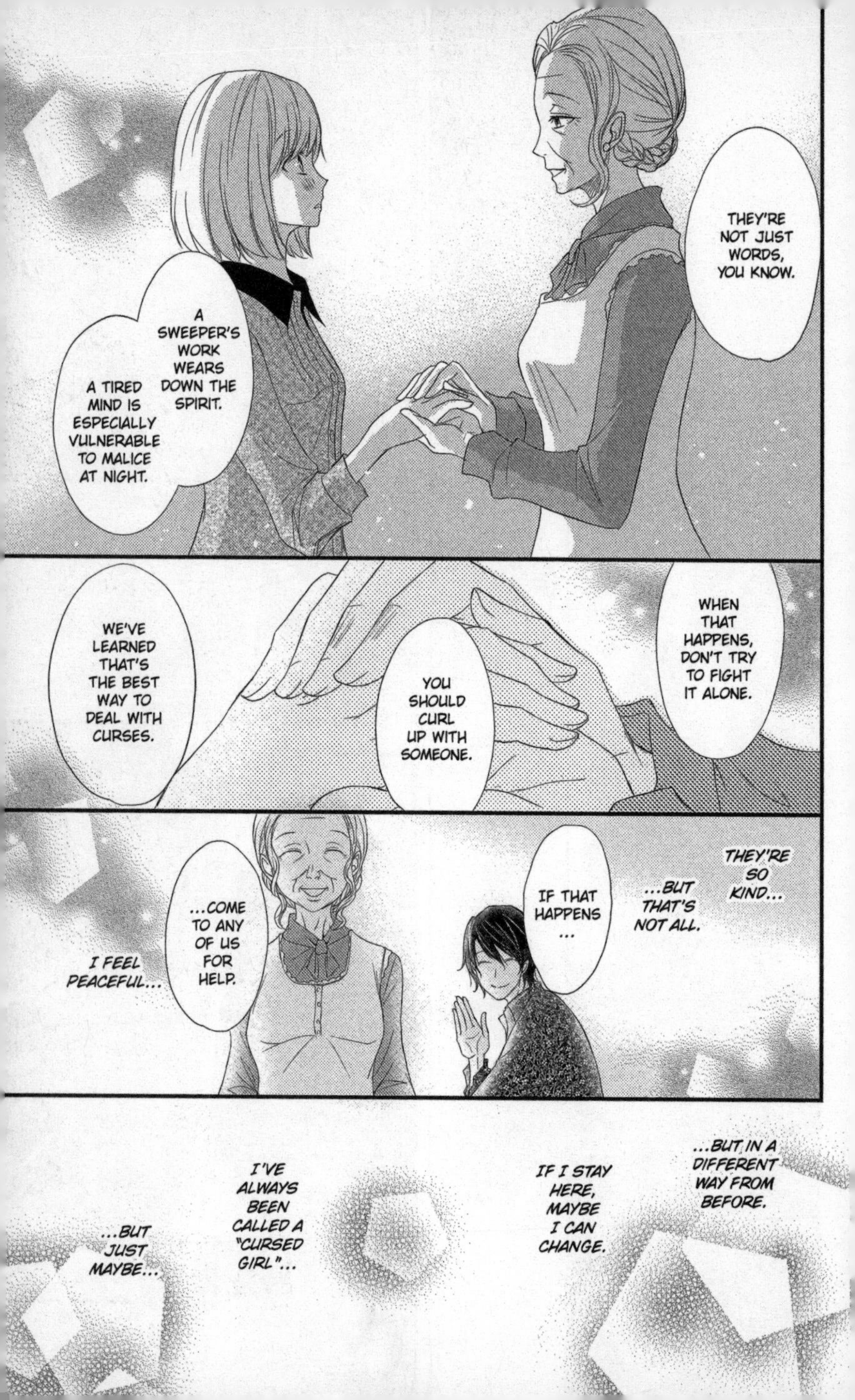
THEY'RE NOT JUST WORDS, YOU KNOW.
A SWEEPER'S WORK WEARS DOWN THE SPIRIT.
A TIRED MIND IS ESPECIALLY VULNERABLE TO MALICE AT NIGHT.
WHEN THAT HAPPENS, DON'T TRY TO FIGHT IT ALONE.
YOU SHOULD CURL UP WITH SOMEONE.
WE'VE LEARNED THAT'S THE BEST WAY TO DEAL WITH CURSES.
THEY'RE SO KIND...
...BUT THAT'S NOT ALL.
IF THAT HAPPENS ...
...COME TO ANY OF US FOR HELP.
I FEEL PEACEFUL...
...BUT IN A DIFFERENT WAY FROM BEFORE.
IF I STAY HERE, MAYBE I CAN CHANGE.
I'VE ALWAYS BEEN CALLED A "CURSED GIRL"...
...BUT JUST MAYBE...

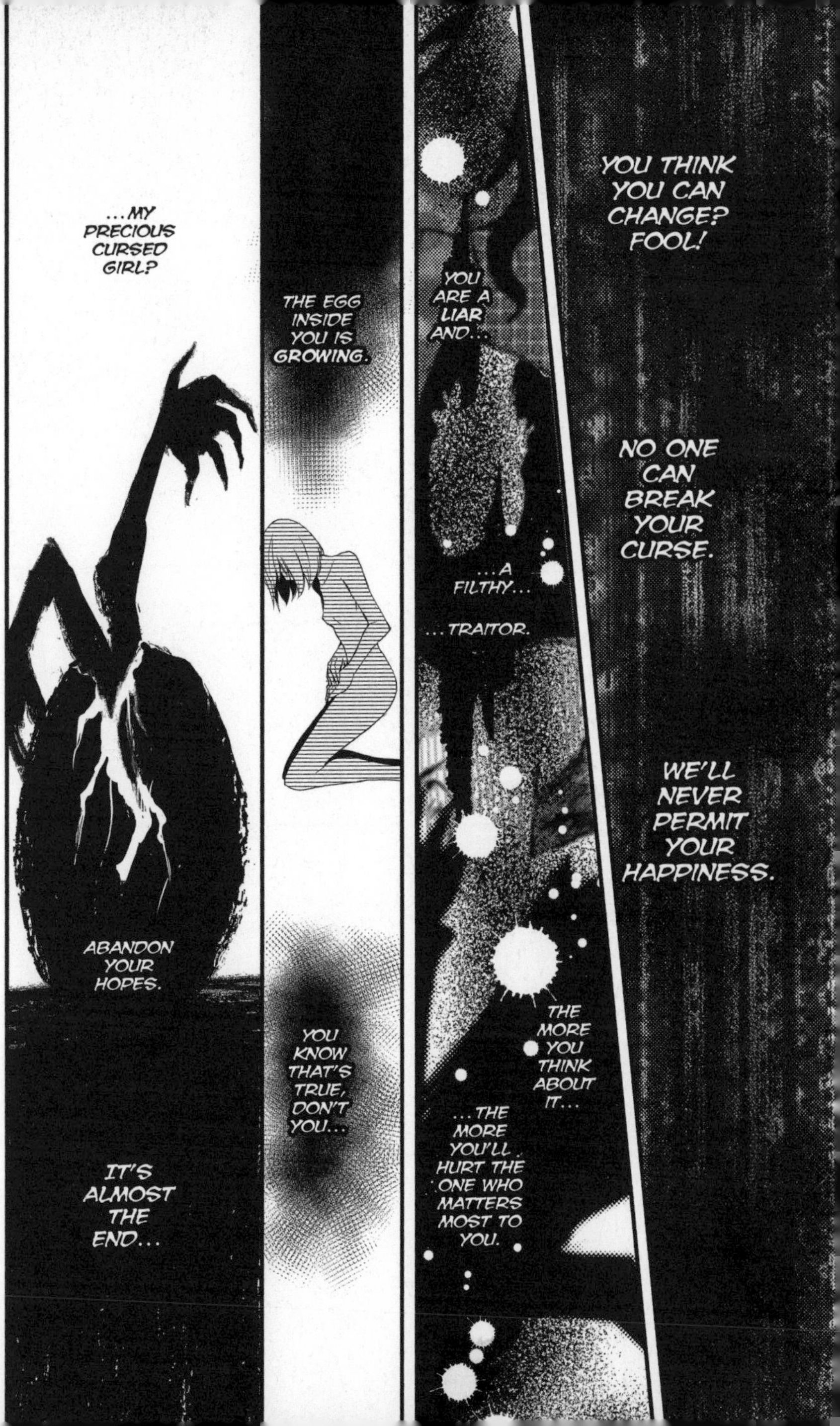
YOU THINK YOU CAN CHANGE? FOOL!
NO ONE CAN BREAK YOUR CURSE.
WE'LL NEVER PERMIT YOUR HAPPINESS.
YOU ARE A LIAR AND...
...A FILTHY...
...TRAITOR.
THE MORE YOU THINK ABOUT IT...
...THE MORE YOU'LL HURT THE ONE WHO MATTERS MOST TO YOU.
THE EGG INSIDE YOU IS GROWING.
YOU KNOW THAT'S TRUE, DON'T YOU...
...MY PRECIOUS CURSED GIRL?
ABANDON YOUR HOPES.
IT'S ALMOST THE END...

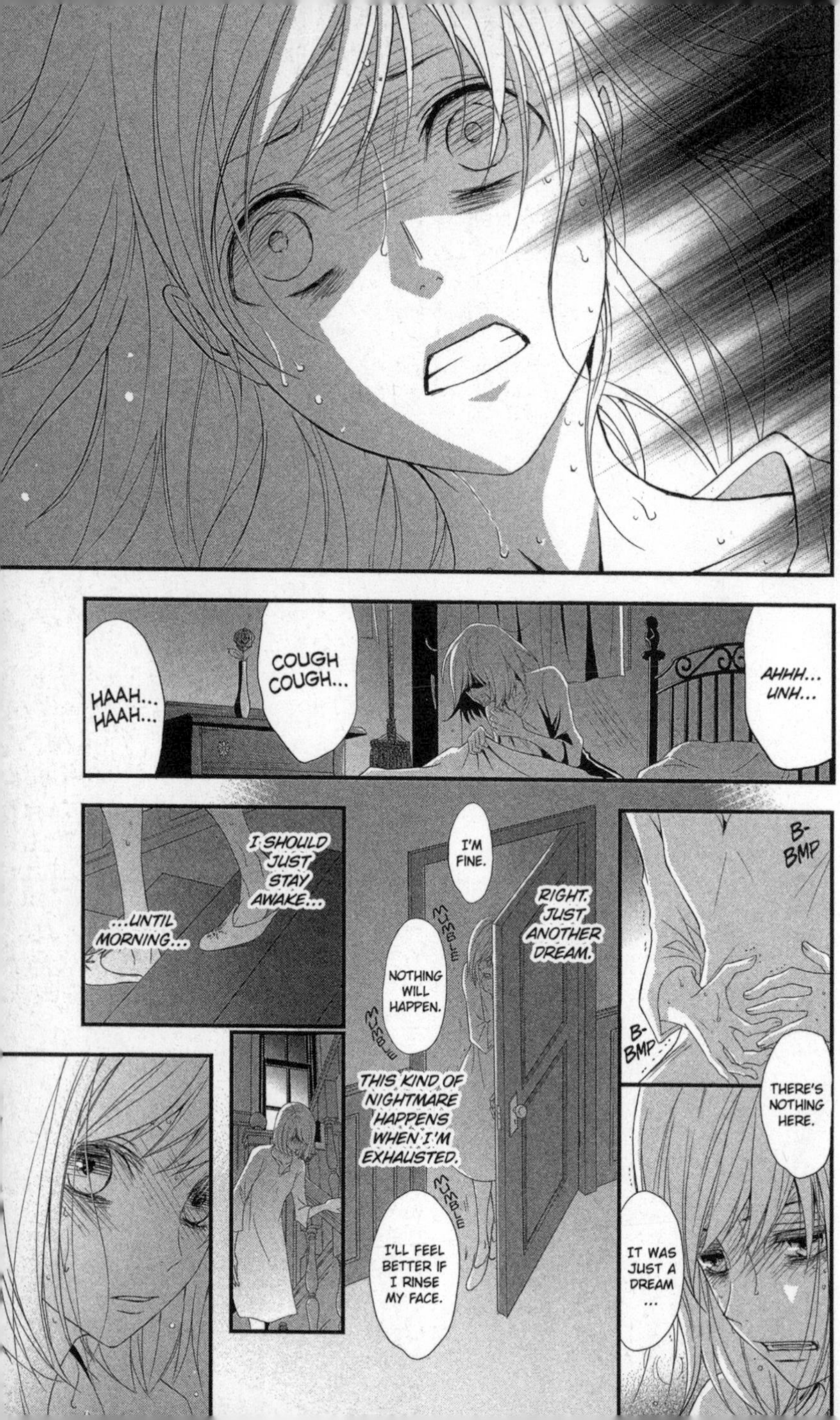
AHHH... UNH...
COUGH COUGH...
HAAH... HAAH...
B-BMP
B-BMP
THERE'S NOTHING HERE.
IT WAS JUST A DREAM ...
I'M FINE.
RIGHT. JUST ANOTHER DREAM.
MUMBLE
NOTHING WILL HAPPEN.
MUMBLE
THIS KIND OF NIGHTMARE HAPPENS WHEN I'M EXHAUSTED.
MUMBLE
I'LL FEEL BETTER IF I RINSE MY FACE.
I SHOULD JUST STAY AWAKE...
...UNTIL MORNING...

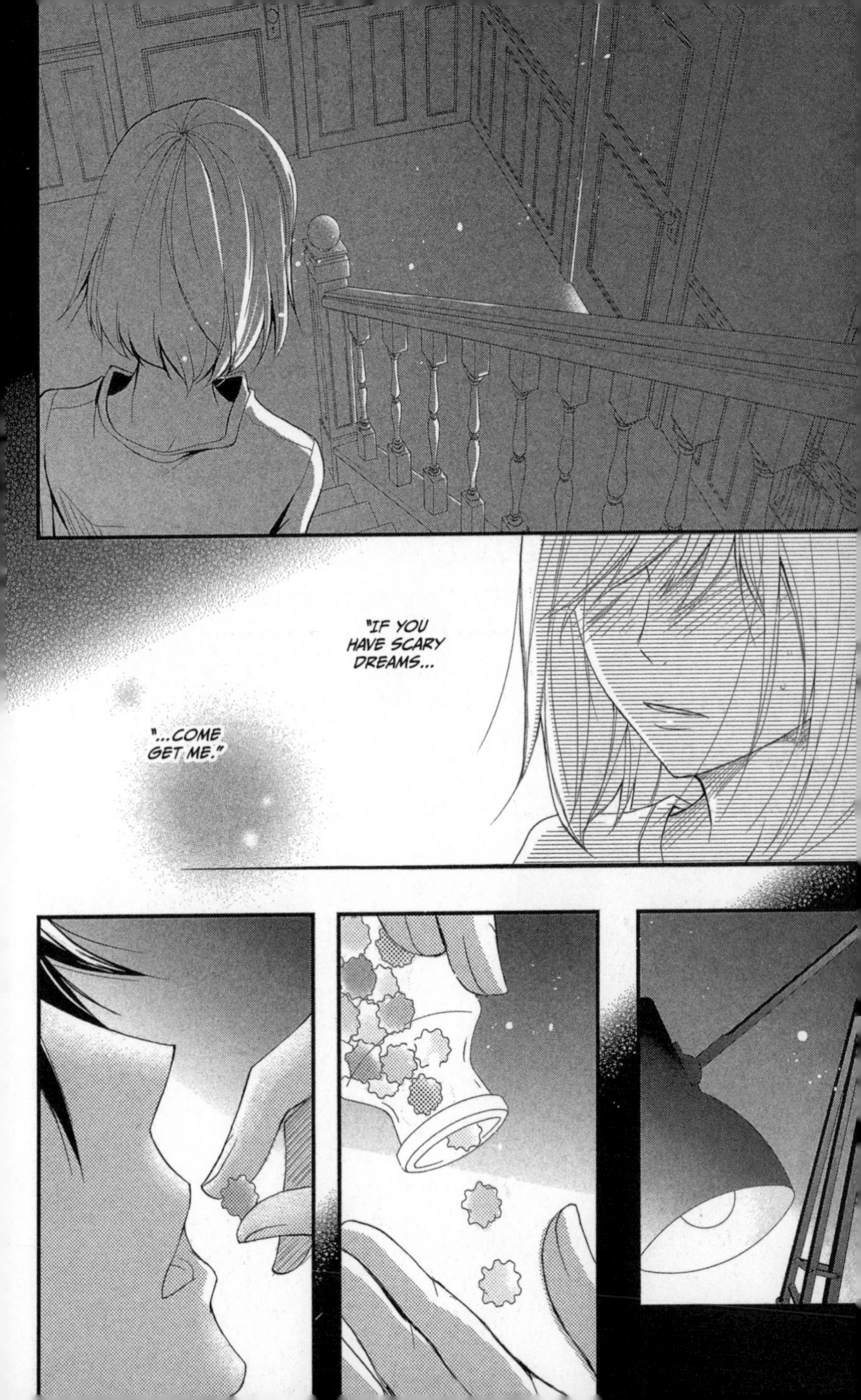
"IF YOU HAVE SCARY DREAMS...
"...COME GET ME."

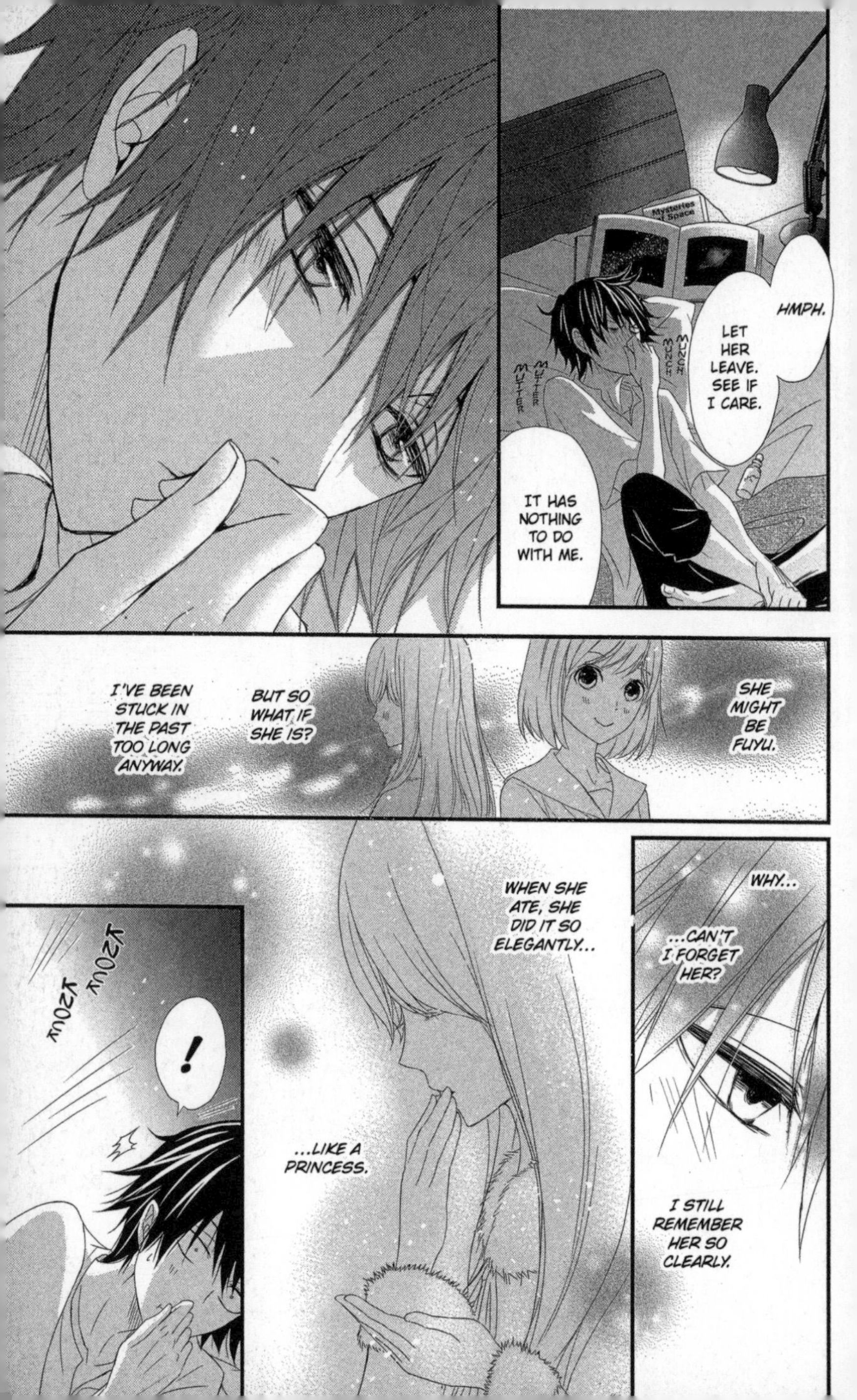
HMPH.
LET HER LEAVE. SEE IF I CARE.
MUNCH MUNCH
MUTTER MUTTER
IT HAS NOTHING TO DO WITH ME.
SHE MIGHT BE FUYU.
BUT SO WHAT IF SHE IS?
I'VE BEEN STUCK IN THE PAST TOO LONG ANYWAY.
WHY...
...CAN'T I FORGET HER?
I STILL REMEMBER HER SO CLEARLY.
WHEN SHE ATE, SHE DID IT SO ELEGANTLY...
...LIKE A PRINCESS.
!

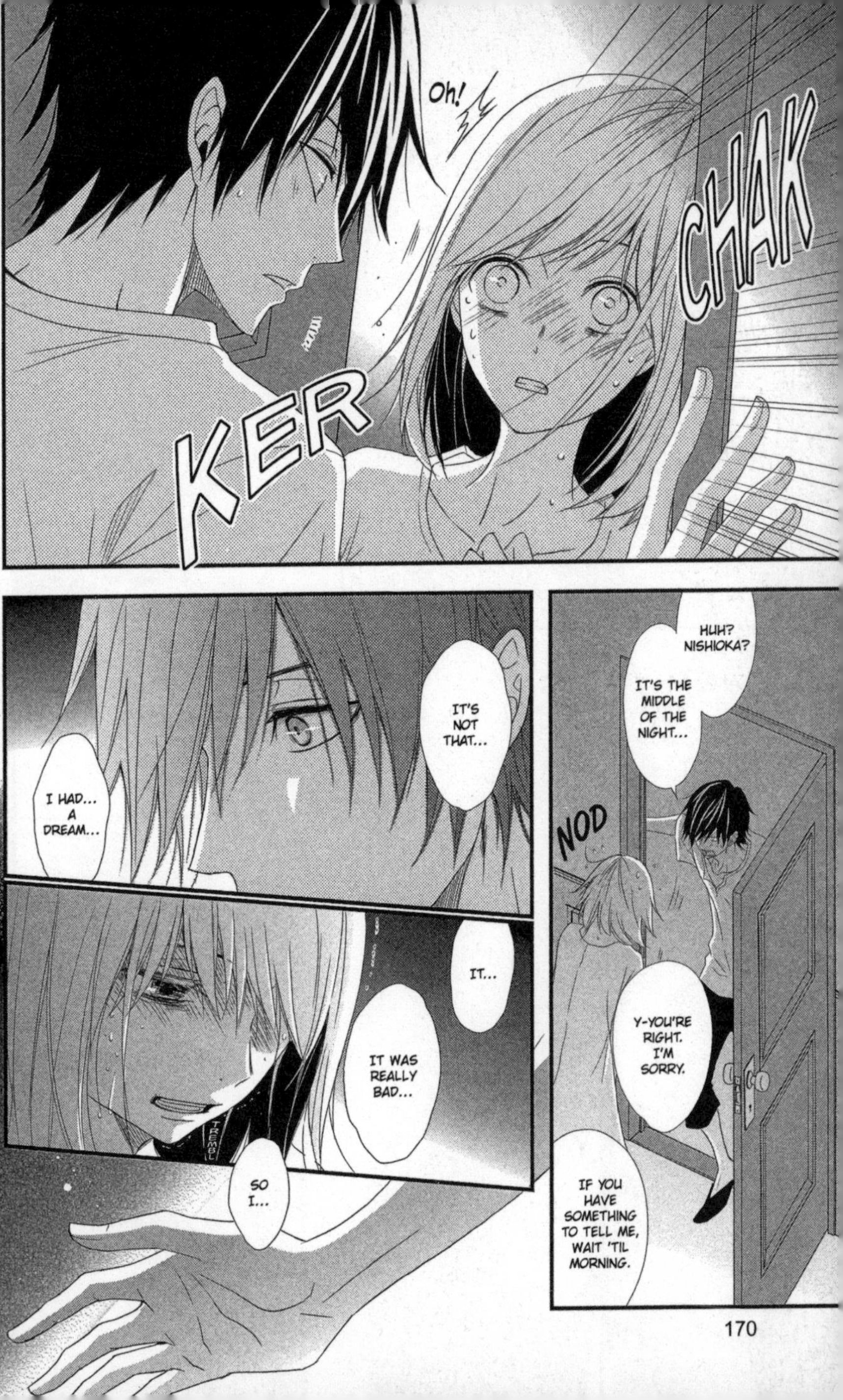
CHAK
Oh!
KER
HUH? NISHIOKA?
IT'S THE MIDDLE OF THE NIGHT...
NOD
Y-YOU'RE RIGHT. I'M SORRY.
IF YOU HAVE SOMETHING TO TELL ME, WAIT 'TIL MORNING.
IT'S NOT THAT...
I HAD... A DREAM...
IT...
IT WAS REALLY BAD...
TREMBL
SO I...

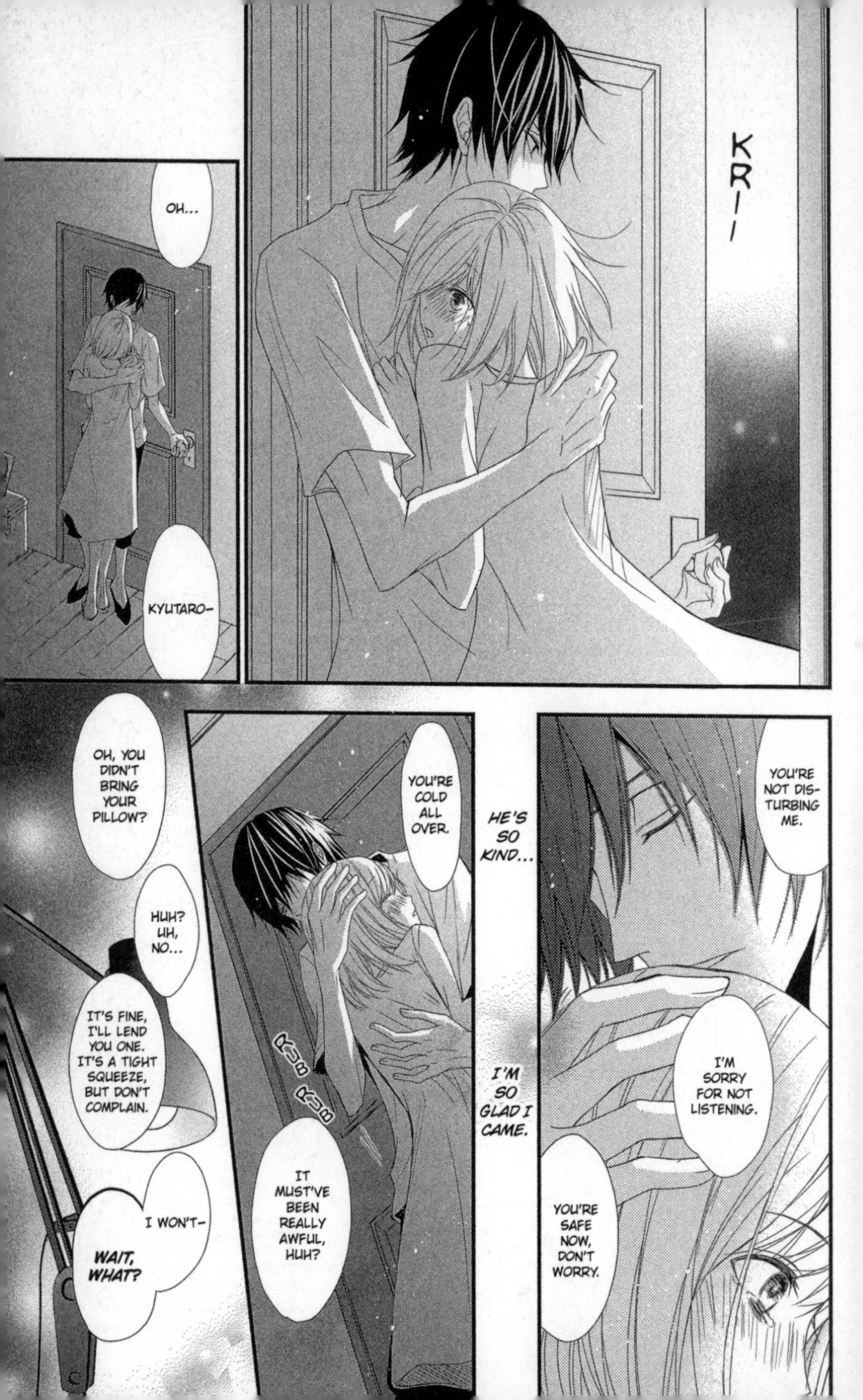
KRI-I
OH...
KYUTARO–
YOU'RE NOT DISTURBING ME.
I'M SORRY FOR NOT LISTENING.
YOU'RE SAFE NOW, DON'T WORRY.
YOU'RE COLD ALL OVER.
HE'S SO KIND...
I'M SO GLAD I CAME.
IT MUST'VE BEEN REALLY AWFUL, HUH?
OH, YOU DIDN'T BRING YOUR PILLOW?
HUH? UH, NO...
IT'S FINE, I'LL LEND YOU ONE. IT'S A TIGHT SQUEEZE, BUT DON'T COMPLAIN.
I WON'T–
WAIT, WHAT?

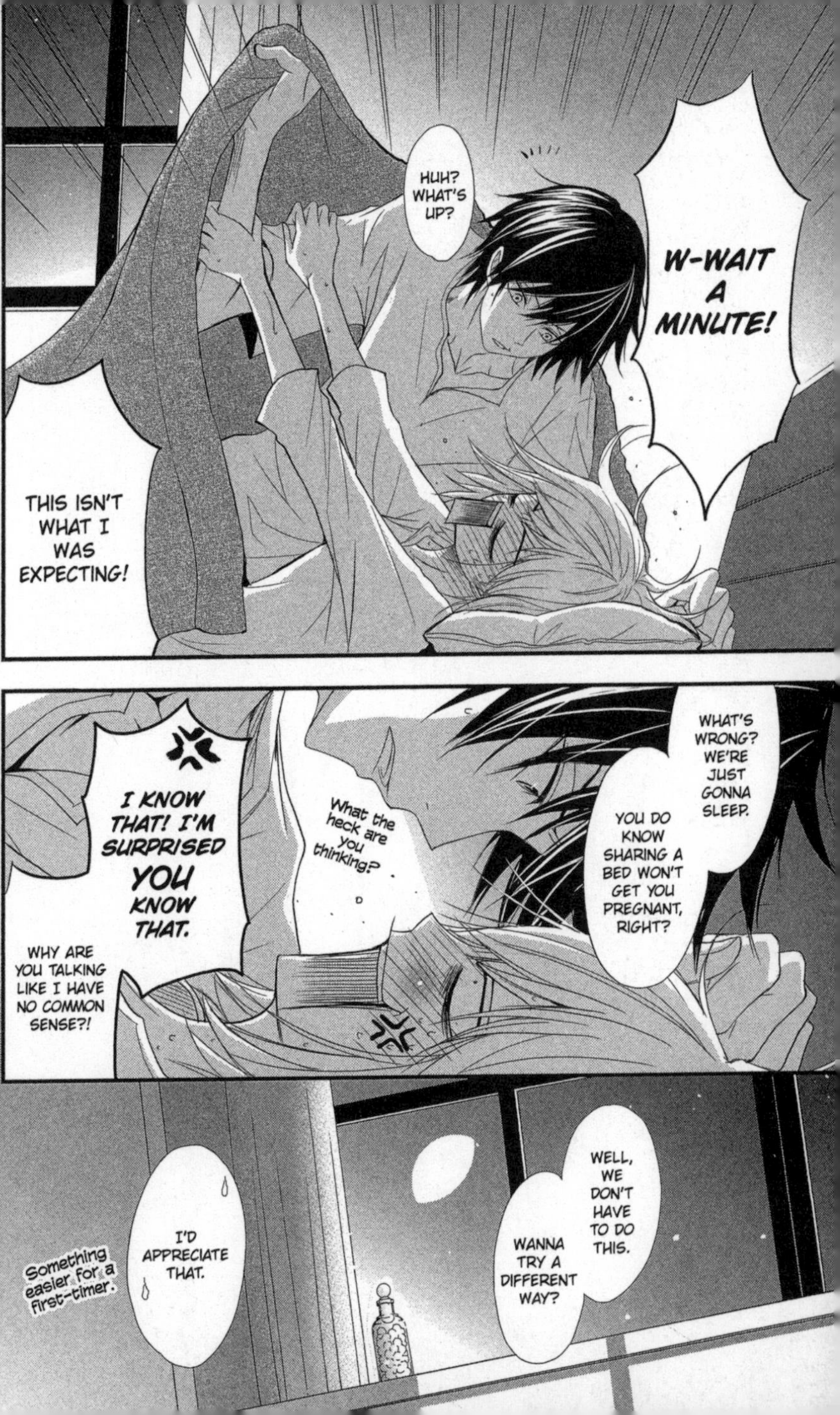
W-WAIT A MINUTE!
HUH? WHAT'S UP?
THIS ISN'T WHAT I WAS EXPECTING!
WHAT'S WRONG? WE'RE JUST GONNA SLEEP.
YOU DO KNOW SHARING A BED WON'T GET YOU PREGNANT, RIGHT?
What the heck are you thinking?
I KNOW THAT! I'M SURPRISED YOU KNOW THAT.
WHY ARE YOU TALKING LIKE I HAVE NO COMMON SENSE?!
WELL, WE DON'T HAVE TO DO THIS.
WANNA TRY A DIFFERENT WAY?
I'D APPRECIATE THAT.
Something easier for a first-timer.

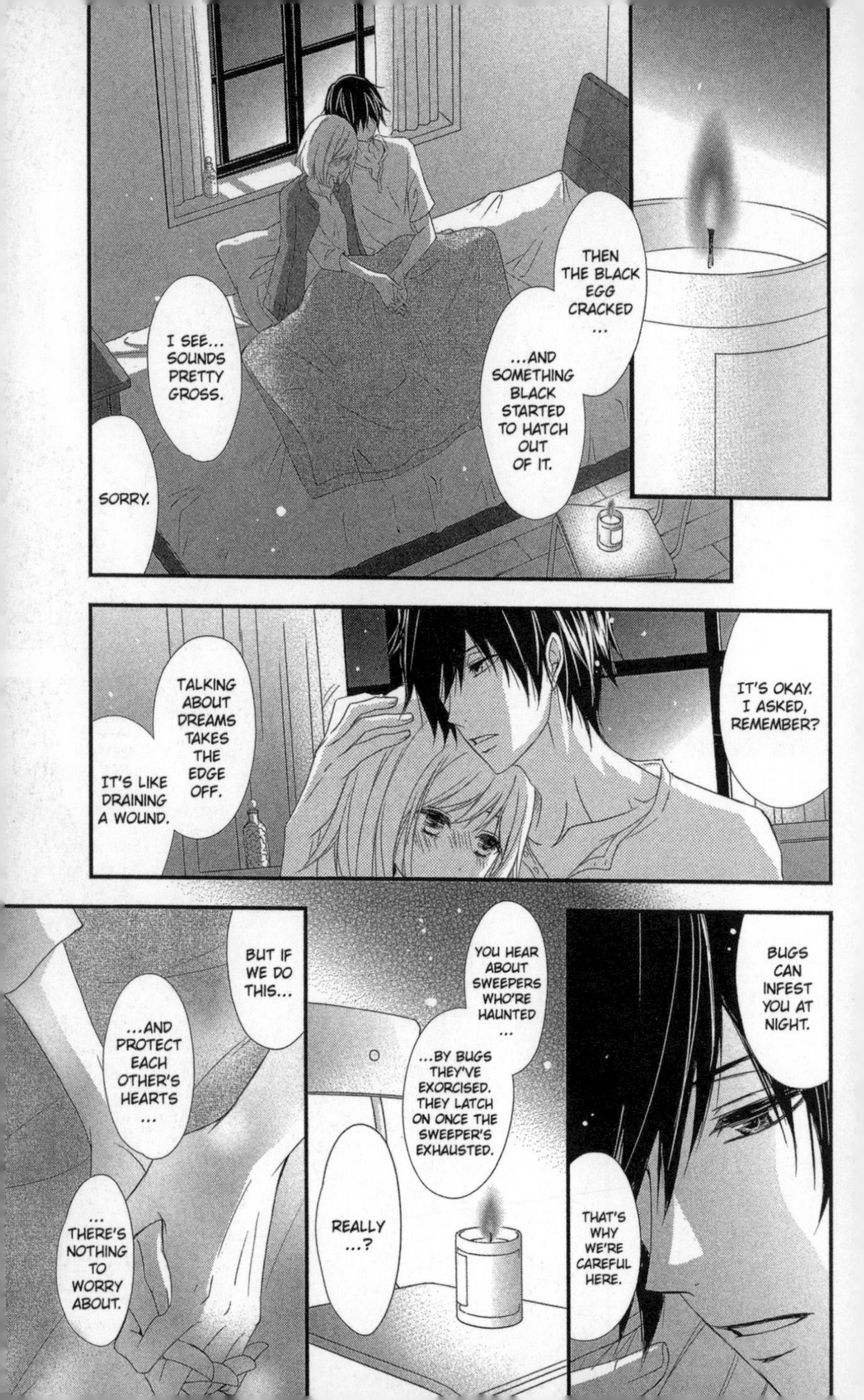
THEN THE BLACK EGG CRACKED ...
...AND SOMETHING BLACK STARTED TO HATCH OUT OF IT.
I SEE... SOUNDS PRETTY GROSS.
SORRY.
IT'S OKAY. I ASKED, REMEMBER?
TALKING ABOUT DREAMS TAKES THE EDGE OFF.
IT'S LIKE DRAINING A WOUND.
BUGS CAN INFEST YOU AT NIGHT.
THAT'S WHY WE'RE CAREFUL HERE.
YOU HEAR ABOUT SWEEPERS WHO'RE HAUNTED ...
...BY BUGS THEY'VE EXORCISED. THEY LATCH ON ONCE THE SWEEPER'S EXHAUSTED.
REALLY ...?
BUT IF WE DO THIS...
...AND PROTECT EACH OTHER'S HEARTS ...
... THERE'S NOTHING TO WORRY ABOUT.

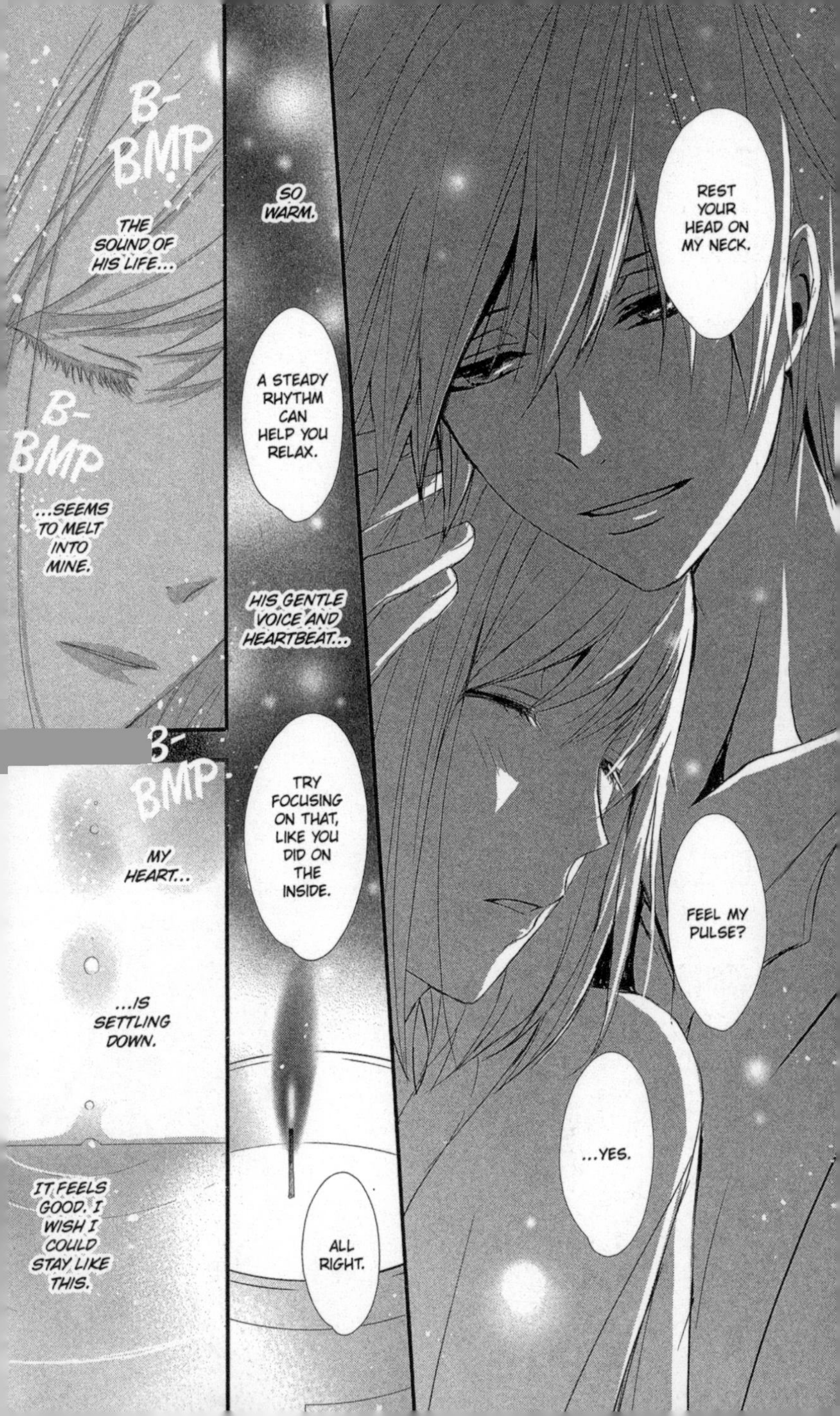
REST YOUR HEAD ON MY NECK.
FEEL MY PULSE?
...YES.
SO WARM.
A STEADY RHYTHM CAN HELP YOU RELAX.
HIS GENTLE VOICE AND HEARTBEAT...
TRY FOCUSING ON THAT, LIKE YOU DID ON THE INSIDE.
ALL RIGHT.
B-BMP
THE SOUND OF HIS LIFE...
B-BMP
...SEEMS TO MELT INTO MINE.
B-BMP
MY HEART...
...IS SETTLING DOWN.
IT FEELS GOOD. I WISH I COULD STAY LIKE THIS.

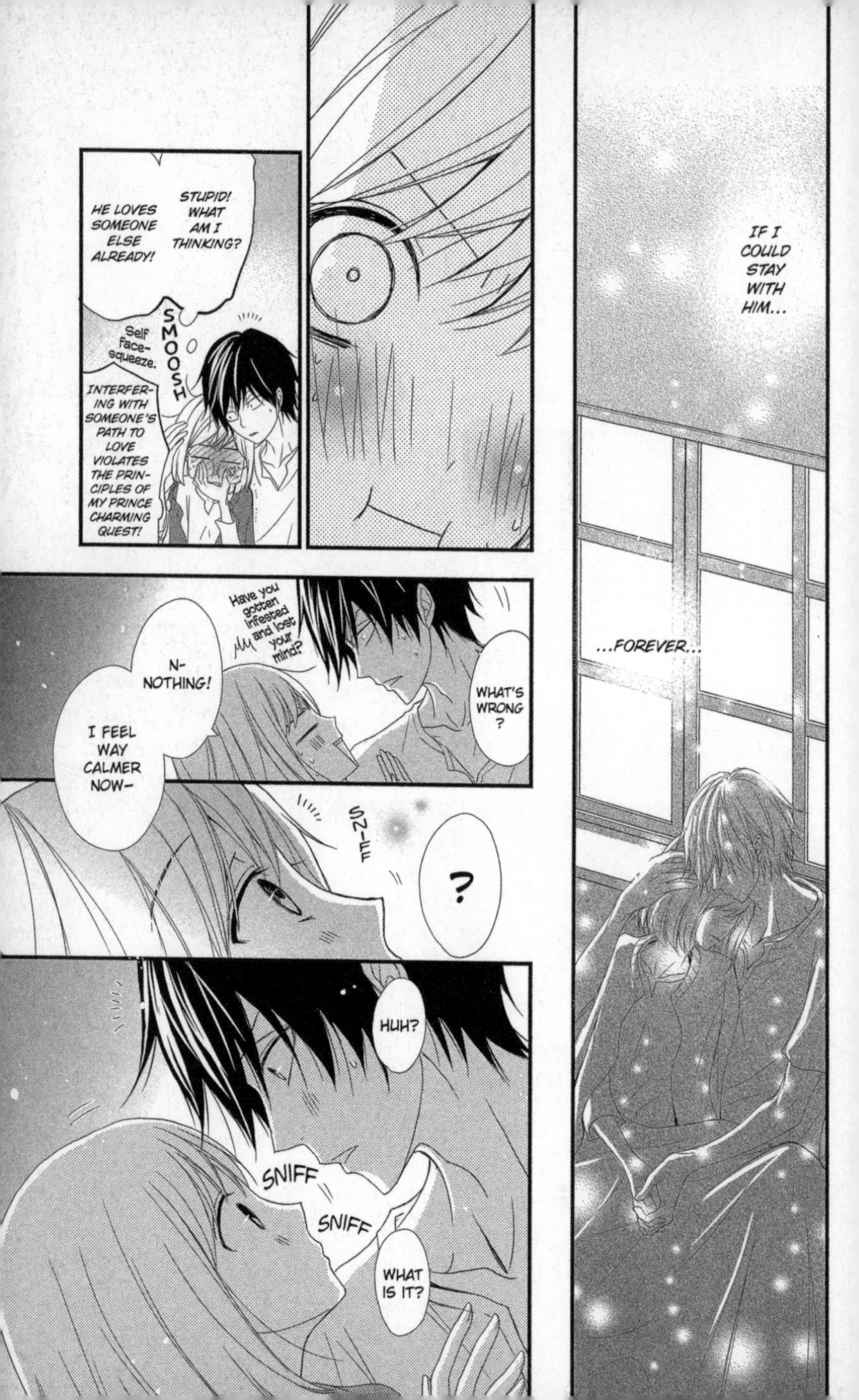
IF I COULD STAY WITH HIM...
...FOREVER...
STUPID! WHAT AM I THINKING?
HE LOVES SOMEONE ELSE ALREADY!
SMOOSH
Self face-squeeze.
INTERFERING WITH SOMEONE'S PATH TO LOVE VIOLATES THE PRINCIPLES OF MY PRINCE CHARMING QUEST!
WHAT'S WRONG?
Have you gotten infested and lost your mind?
N-NOTHING!
I FEEL WAY CALMER NOW-
SNIFF
?
HUH?
SNIFF
SNIFF
WHAT IS IT?

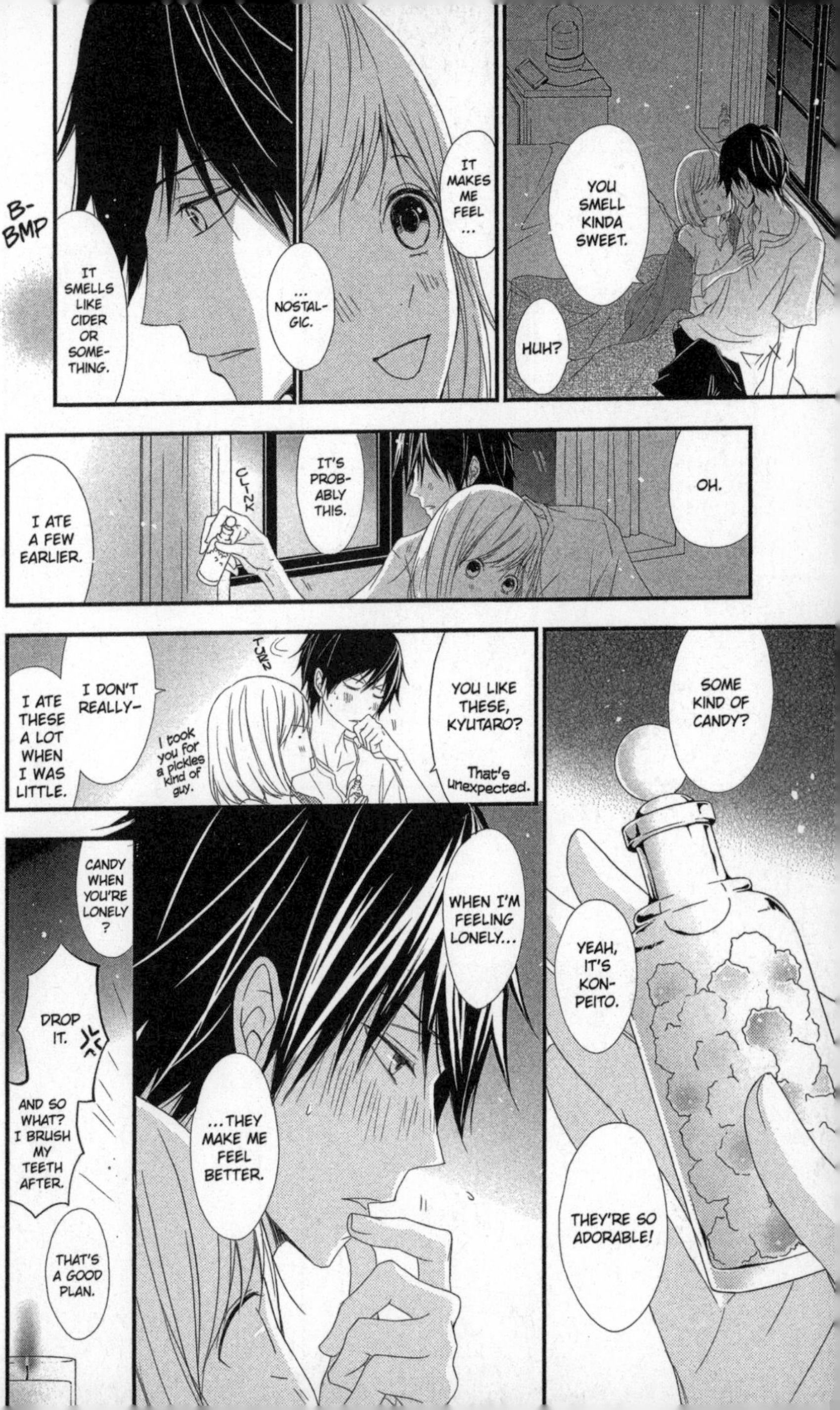
YOU SMELL KINDA SWEET.
HUH?
IT MAKES ME FEEL ...
... NOSTALGIC.
B-BMP
IT SMELLS LIKE CIDER OR SOMETHING.
OH.
IT'S PROBABLY THIS.
CLINK
I ATE A FEW EARLIER.
SOME KIND OF CANDY?
YEAH, IT'S KONPEITO.
THEY'RE SO ADORABLE!
YOU LIKE THESE, KYUTARO?
That's unexpected.
TURN
I took you for a pickles kind of guy.
I DON'T REALLY–
I ATE THESE A LOT WHEN I WAS LITTLE.
WHEN I'M FEELING LONELY...
...THEY MAKE ME FEEL BETTER.
CANDY WHEN YOU'RE LONELY?
DROP IT.
AND SO WHAT? I BRUSH MY TEETH AFTER.
THAT'S A GOOD PLAN.

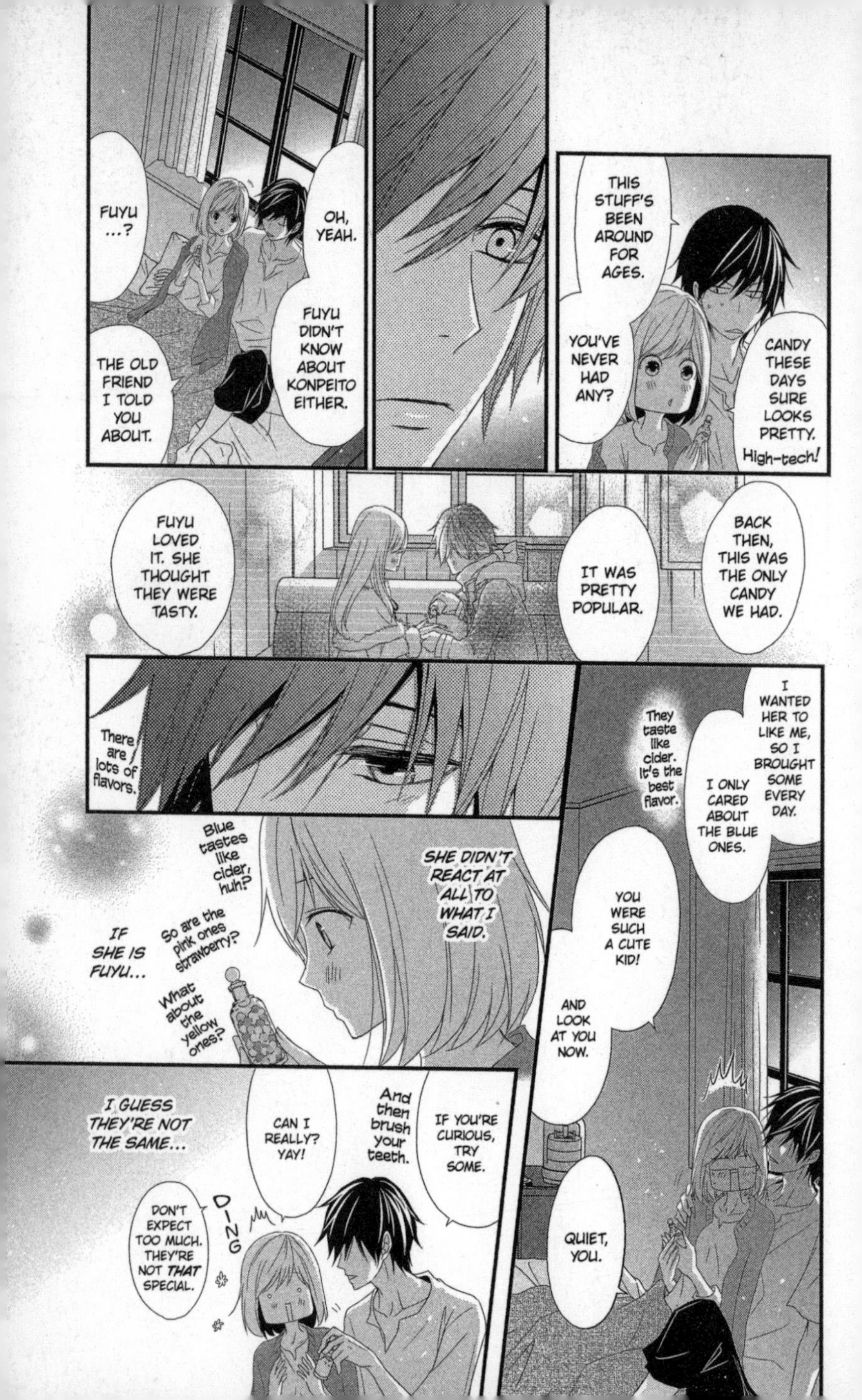
THIS STUFF'S BEEN AROUND FOR AGES.
CANDY THESE DAYS SURE LOOKS PRETTY.
High-tech!
YOU'VE NEVER HAD ANY?
OH, YEAH.
FUYU DIDN'T KNOW ABOUT KONPEITO EITHER.
FUYU ...?
THE OLD FRIEND I TOLD YOU ABOUT.
BACK THEN, THIS WAS THE ONLY CANDY WE HAD.
IT WAS PRETTY POPULAR.
FUYU LOVED IT. SHE THOUGHT THEY WERE TASTY.
I WANTED HER TO LIKE ME, SO I BROUGHT SOME EVERY DAY.
I ONLY CARED ABOUT THE BLUE ONES.
They taste like cider. It's the best flavor.
YOU WERE SUCH A CUTE KID!
AND LOOK AT YOU NOW.
QUIET, YOU.
There are lots of flavors.
Blue tastes like cider, huh?
SHE DIDN'T REACT AT ALL TO WHAT I SAID.
So are the pink ones strawberry?
What about the yellow ones?
IF SHE IS FUYU...
IF YOU'RE CURIOUS, TRY SOME.
And then brush your teeth.
CAN I REALLY? YAY!
I GUESS THEY'RE NOT THE SAME...
DON'T EXPECT TOO MUCH. THEY'RE NOT *THAT* SPECIAL.
DING

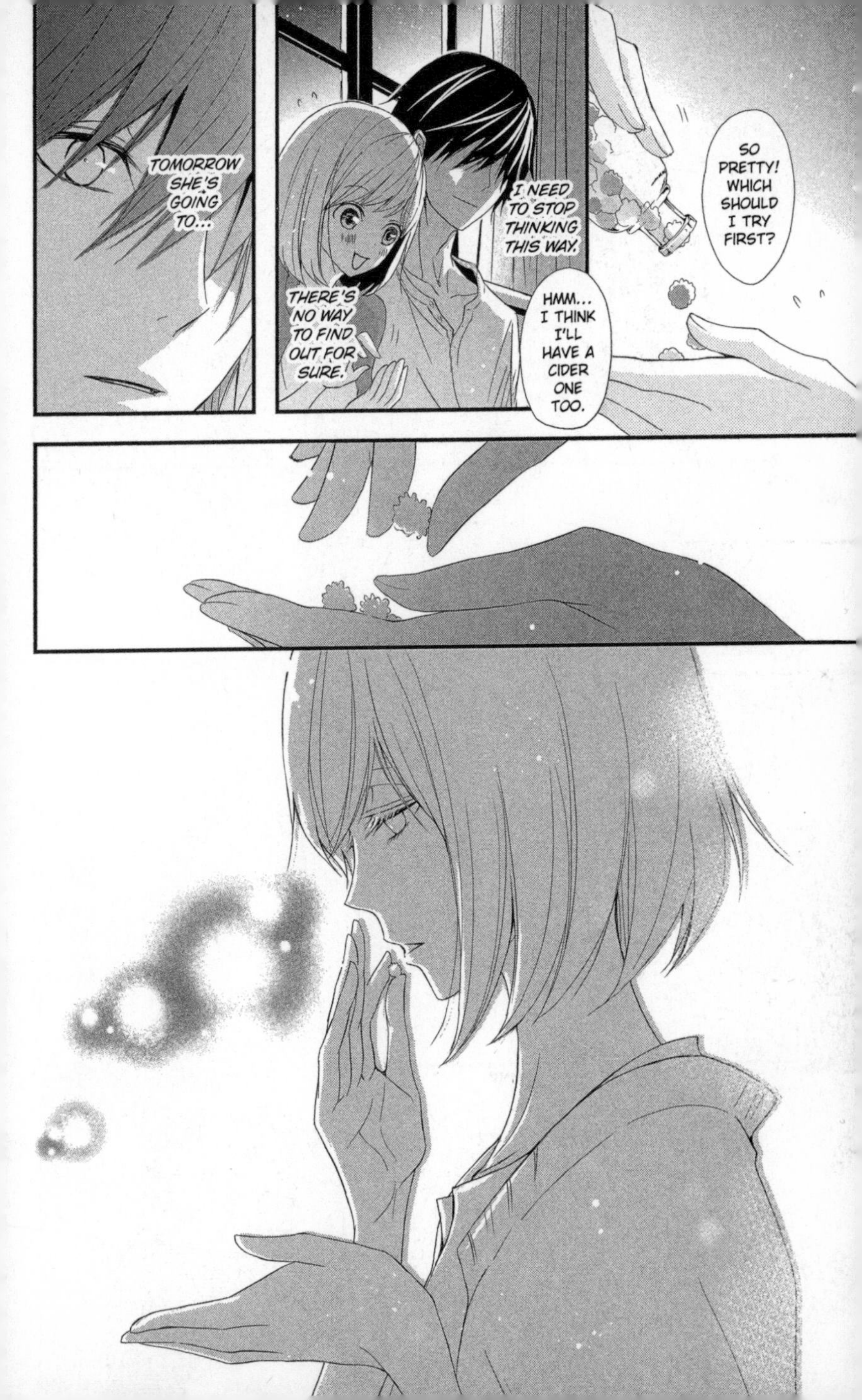
SO PRETTY! WHICH SHOULD I TRY FIRST?
HMM... I THINK I'LL HAVE A CIDER ONE TOO.
I NEED TO STOP THINKING THIS WAY.
THERE'S NO WAY TO FIND OUT FOR SURE.
TOMORROW SHE'S GOING TO...

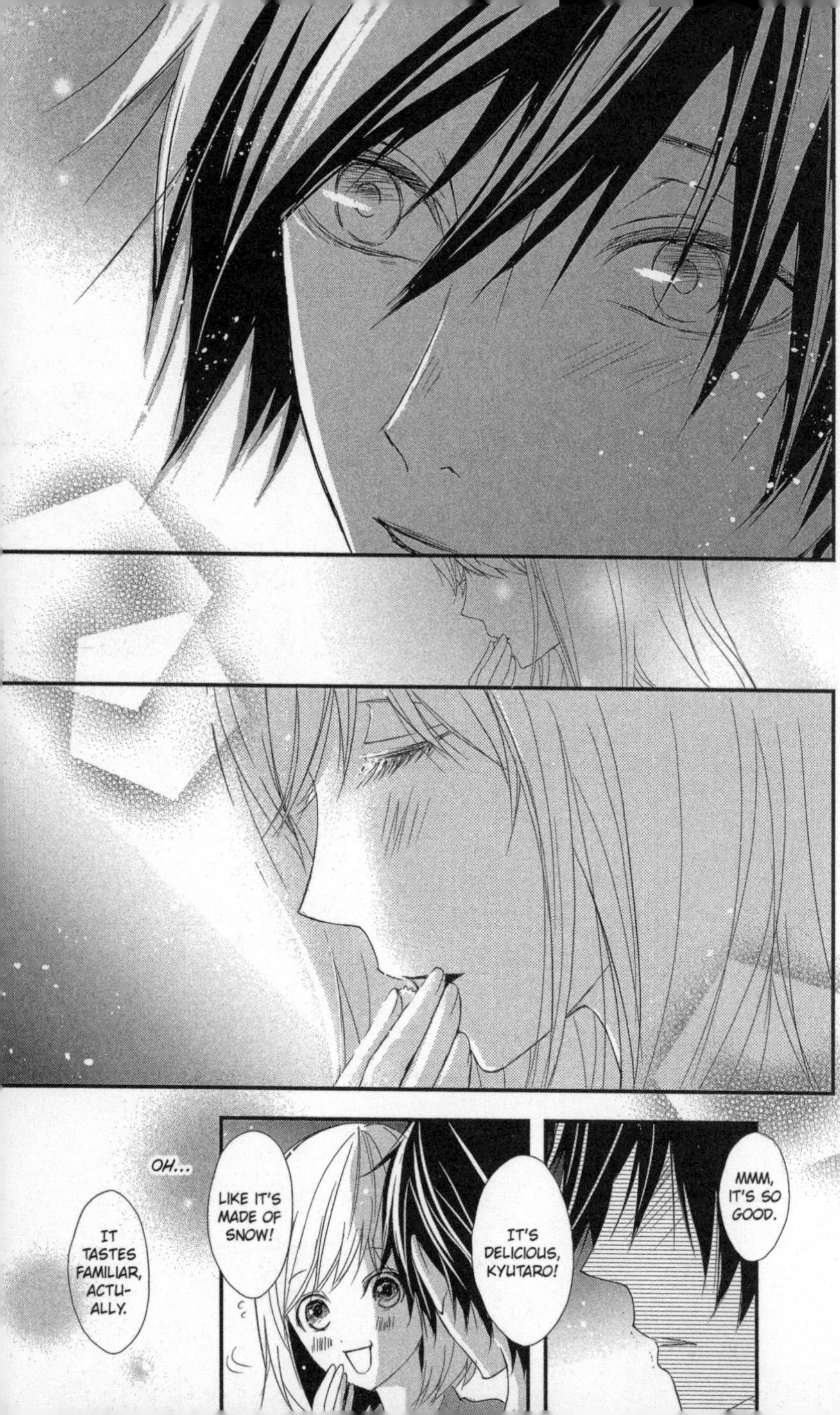
MMM, IT'S SO GOOD.
IT'S DELICIOUS, KYUTARO!
LIKE IT'S MADE OF SNOW!
OH...
IT TASTES FAMILIAR, ACTUALLY.

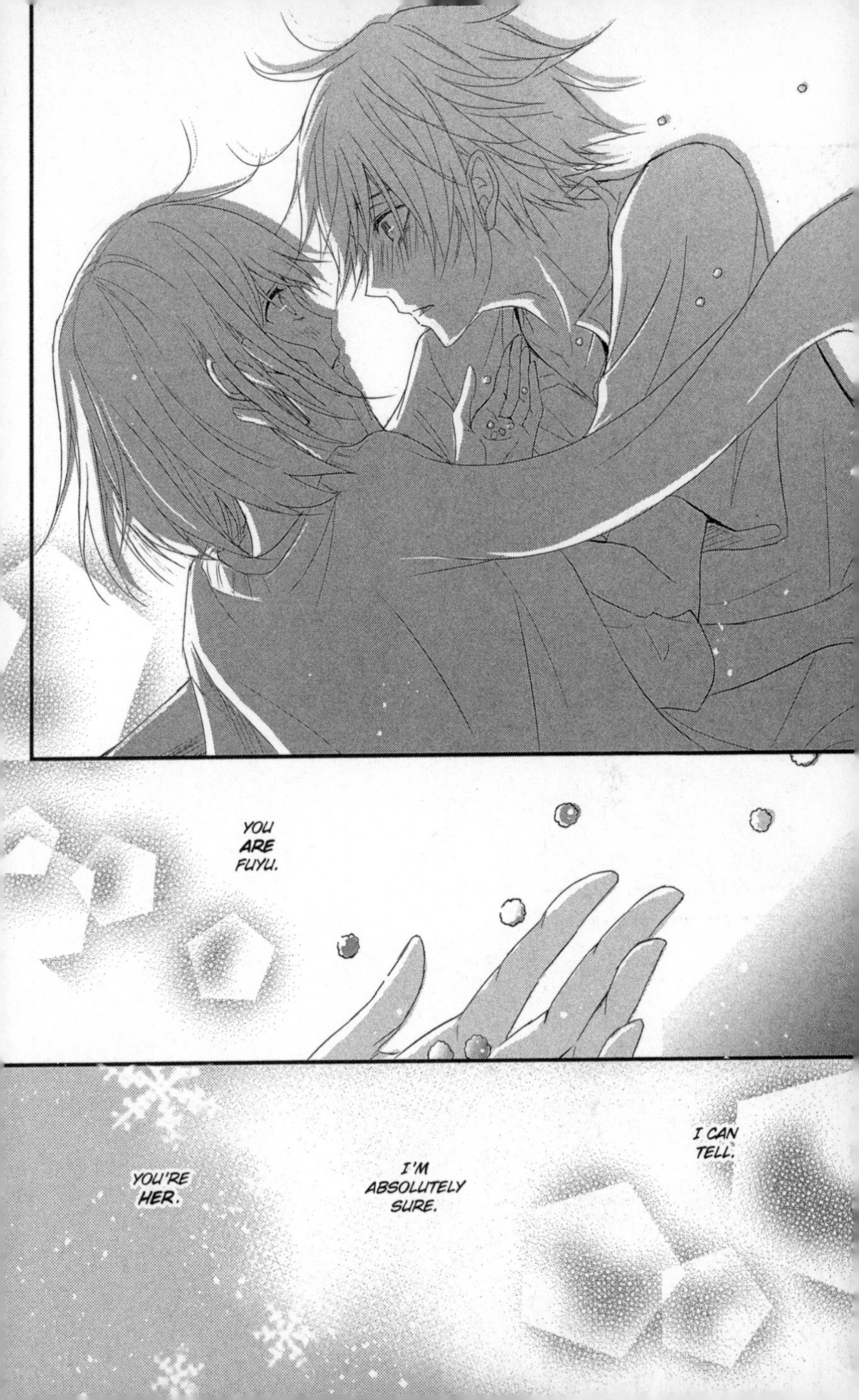
YOU ARE FUYU.
I CAN TELL.
I'M ABSOLUTELY SURE.
YOU'RE HER.

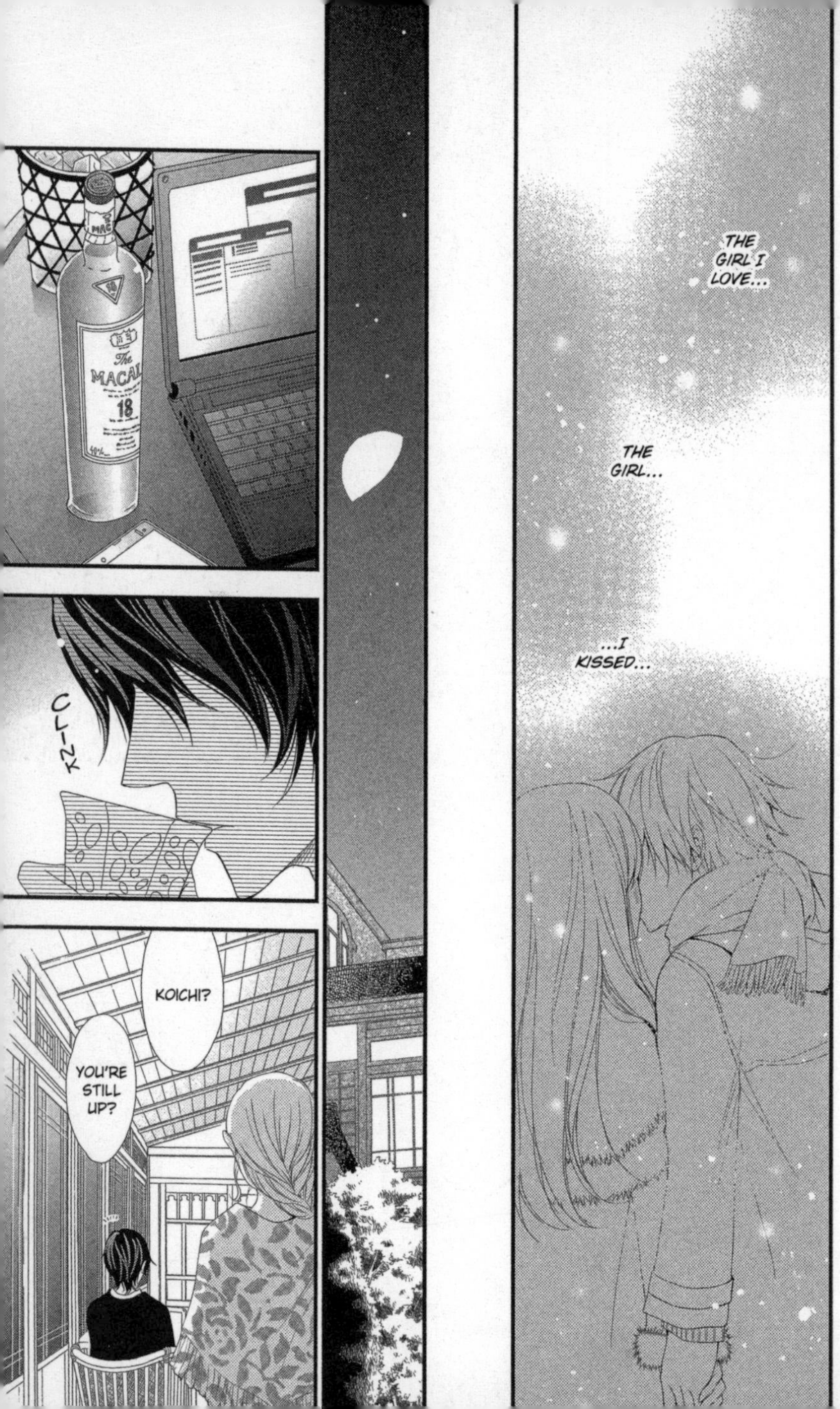
THE GIRL I LOVE...
THE GIRL...
...I KISSED...
The MACAL
18
CLINK
KOICHI?
YOU'RE STILL UP?

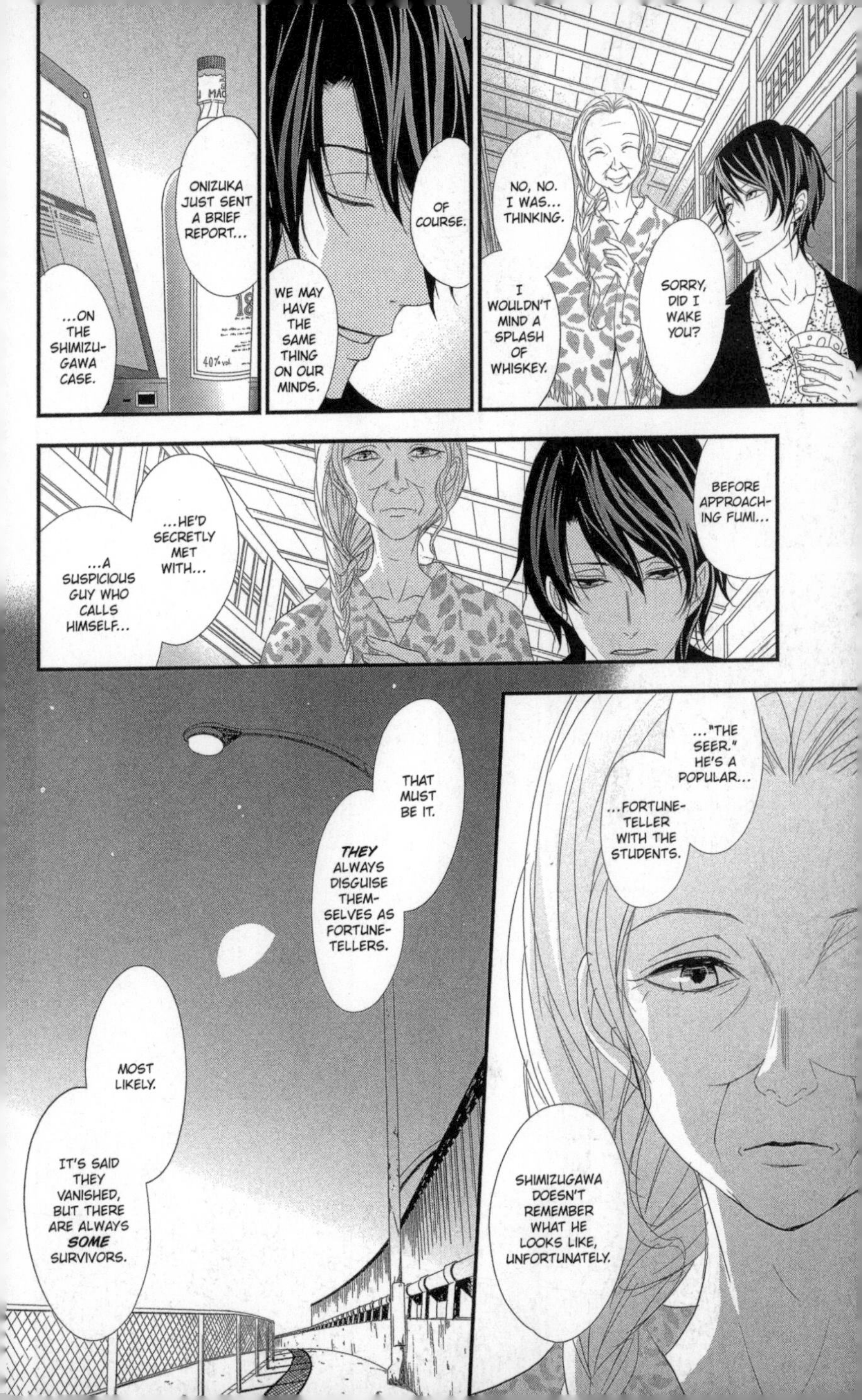
SORRY, DID I WAKE YOU?
NO, NO. I WAS... THINKING.
I WOULDN'T MIND A SPLASH OF WHISKEY.
OF COURSE.
WE MAY HAVE THE SAME THING ON OUR MINDS.
ONIZUKA JUST SENT A BRIEF REPORT...
...ON THE SHIMIZUGAWA CASE.
BEFORE APPROACHING FUMI...
...HE'D SECRETLY MET WITH...
...A SUSPICIOUS GUY WHO CALLS HIMSELF...
..."THE SEER." HE'S A POPULAR...
...FORTUNE-TELLER WITH THE STUDENTS.
THAT MUST BE IT.
THEY ALWAYS DISGUISE THEMSELVES AS FORTUNE-TELLERS.
SHIMIZUGAWA DOESN'T REMEMBER WHAT HE LOOKS LIKE, UNFORTUNATELY.
MOST LIKELY.
IT'S SAID THEY VANISHED, BUT THERE ARE ALWAYS *SOME* SURVIVORS.

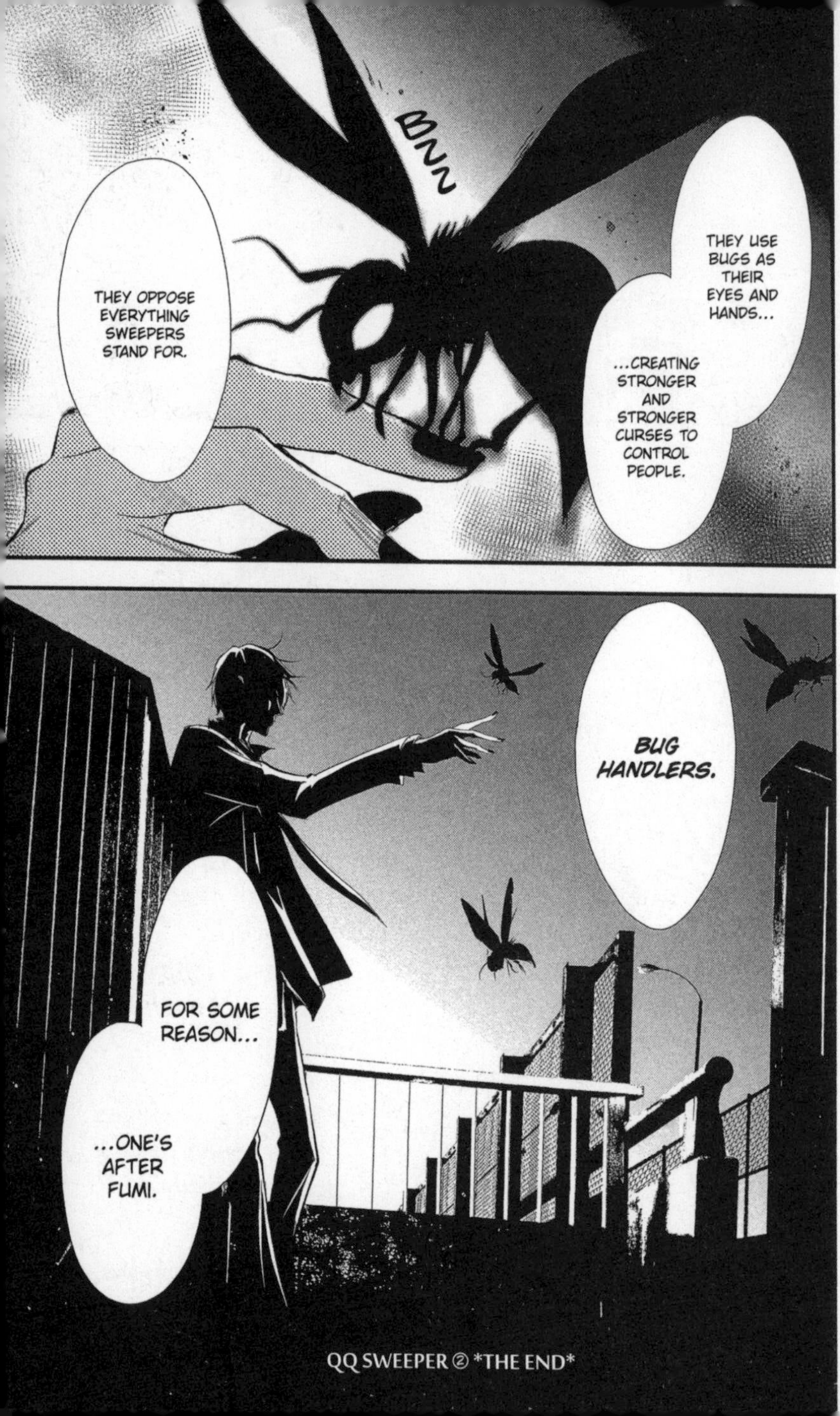
THEY USE BUGS AS THEIR EYES AND HANDS...
...CREATING STRONGER AND STRONGER CURSES TO CONTROL PEOPLE.
BZZ
THEY OPPOSE EVERYTHING SWEEPERS STAND FOR.
BUG HANDLERS.
FOR SOME REASON...
...ONE'S AFTER FUMI.

QQ SWEEPER ② *THE END*

Hey, Tasuku. Teru sounded really sleepy this morning. What's going on?

Eye pack

Onizuka, Part-time Counselor

She may seem like a suspicious person, but she really isn't. She gets called in to work pretty often.

• 165 cm, D-cup, blood type B
• Young and single (but well over 20 years old)
• Loves drinking
• She lives with a gal who's like a younger sister.
• The guy who lives in the condo next door has his hair dyed blond.

*For more details, see Dengeki Daisy (16 volumes)!

Afterword

Okay, okay. Here...
I'll give you one. Stop drooling.
Your stomach's so loud.
I... I wouldn't eat your family's midnight snack...
PANT PANT
GRRWL

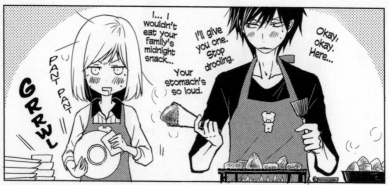

This is the end of *QQ Sweeper* volume 2.

Thanks so much for reading the whole thing!

For all that this is a story about cleaning, there weren't many cleaning scenes. Actually, there's another theme too, and I want to devote some time to it so you can enjoy reading about it.

Like their author, Fumi and Kyutaro still aren't full-fledged, but I hope you'll watch us grow together. And I hope to see you again in my next volume. Bye for now!

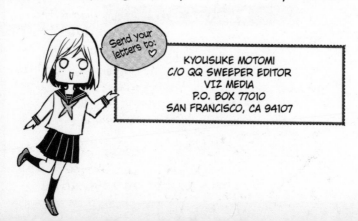

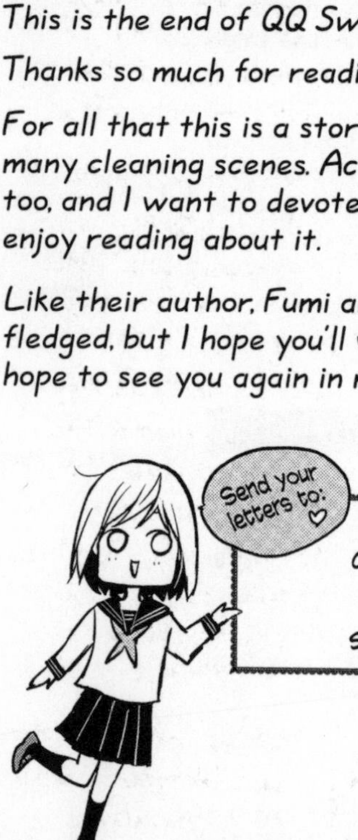

Send your letters to: ♡

KYOUSUKE MOTOMI
C/O QQ SWEEPER EDITOR
VIZ MEDIA
P.O. BOX 77010
SAN FRANCISCO, CA 94107

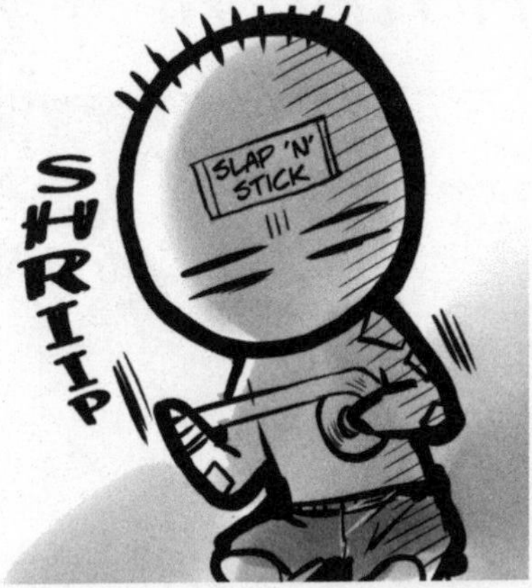
SHRIIP
SLAP 'N' STICK

The cover art is the full-color version of a popular black-and-white title page picture! I don't get suggestions like that very often, so I was glad to do it. I'm a lot more nervous working on color pictures than I am with black-and-white ones, so I wound up using a lot of correction tape. I think that's pretty common among manga artists...

—Kyousuke Motomi

Author Bio

Born on August 1, Kyousuke Motomi debuted in *Deluxe Betsucomi* with *Hetakuso Kyupiddo* (No Good Cupid) in 2002. She is the creator of *Dengeki Daisy* and *Beast Master*, both available in North America from Viz Media. Motomi enjoys sleeping, tea ceremonies and reading Haruki Murakami.

QQ SWEEPER

VOL. 2
Shojo Beat Edition

STORY AND ART BY
KYOUSUKE MOTOMI

QQ SWEEPER Vol. 2
by Kyousuke MOTOMI
© 2014 Kyousuke MOTOMI
All rights reserved.
Original Japanese edition published by SHOGAKUKAN.
English translation rights in the United States of America, Canada, United Kingdom and Ireland, arranged with SHOGAKUKAN.

English Adaptation/Ysabet Reinhardt MacFarlane
Translation/JN Productions
Touch-Up Art & Lettering/Eric Erbes
Design/Izumi Evers
Editor/Amy Yu

Printed in the U.S.A.

Published by VIZ Media, LLC
P.O. Box 77010
San Francisco, CA 94107

10 9 8 7 6 5 4 3 2 1
First printing, February 2016

www.viz.com   www.shojobeat.com

Honey Blood

Story & Art by Miko Mitsuki

Hinata can't help but be drawn to Junya, but could it be that he's actually a vampire?

When a girl at her school is attacked by what seems to be a vampire, high school student Hinata Sorazono refuses to believe that vampires even exist. But then she meets her new neighbor, Junya Tokinaga, the author of an incredibly popular vampire romance novel… Could it be that Junya's actually a vampire—and worse yet, the culprit?!

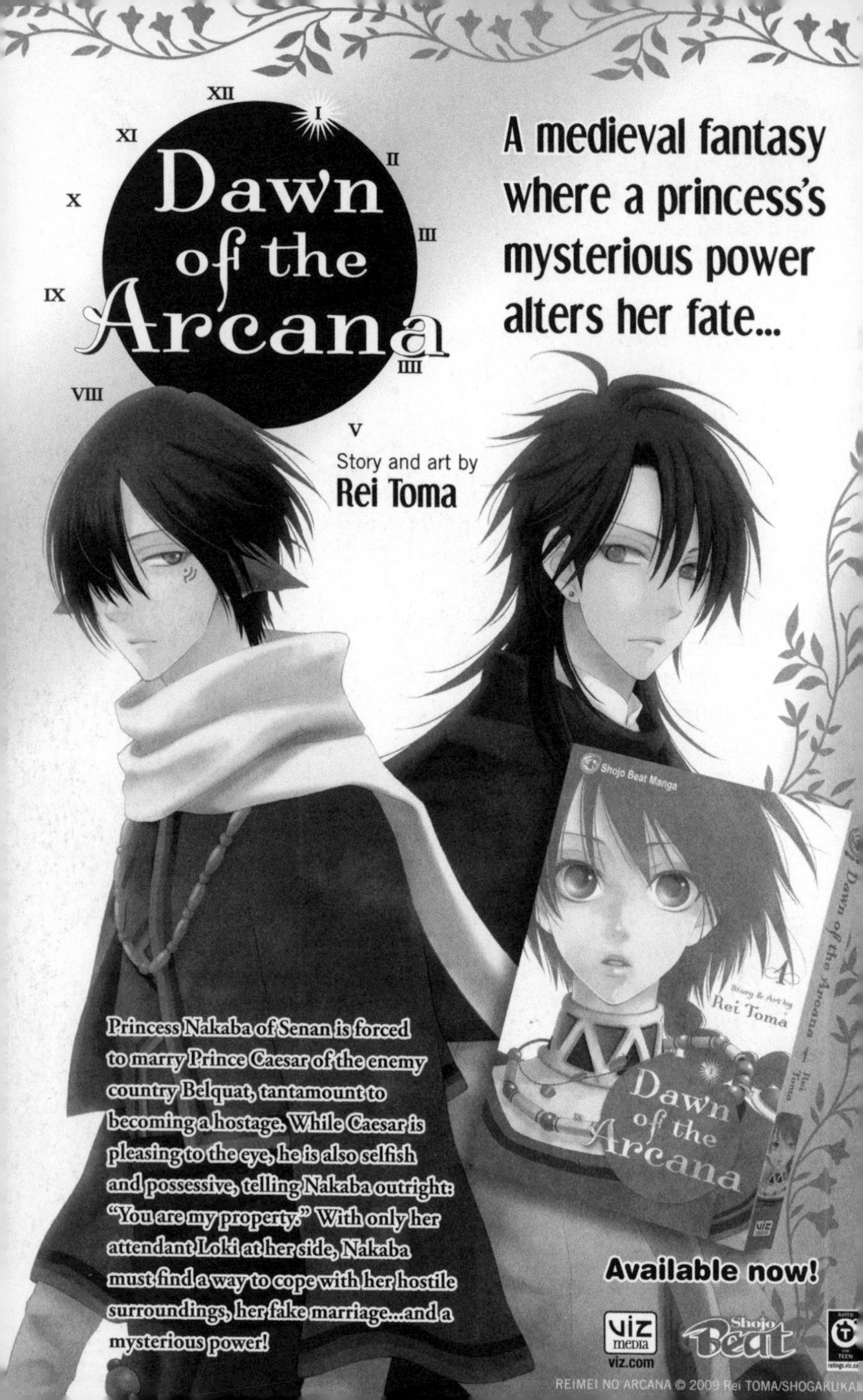
XII
I
XI
II
X
III
IX
IIII
VIII
V
Dawn of the Arcana
A medieval fantasy where a princess's mysterious power alters her fate...
Story and art by
Rei Toma
Princess Nakaba of Senan is forced to marry Prince Caesar of the enemy country Belquat, tantamount to becoming a hostage. While Caesar is pleasing to the eye, he is also selfish and possessive, telling Nakaba outright: "You are my property." With only her attendant Loki at her side, Nakaba must find a way to cope with her hostile surroundings, her fake marriage...and a mysterious power!
Shojo Beat Manga
Story & Art by Rei Toma
Dawn of the Arcana
Available now!
VIZ media
viz.com
Shojo Beat
RATED T TEEN
REIMEI NO ARCANA © 2009 Rei TOMA/SHOGAKUKAN

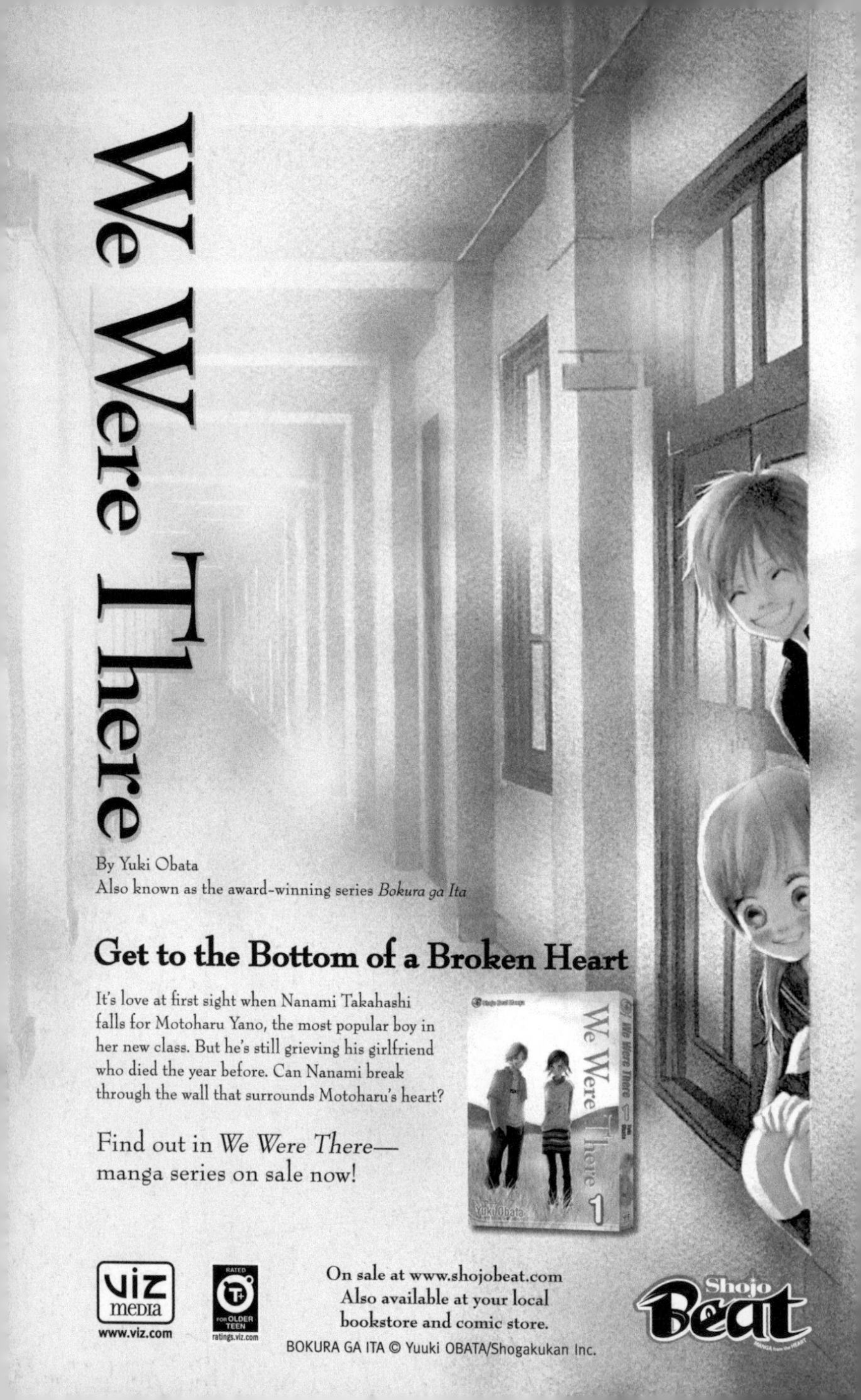
We Were There
By Yuki Obata
Also known as the award-winning series Bokura ga Ita
Get to the Bottom of a Broken Heart
It's love at first sight when Nanami Takahashi falls for Motoharu Yano, the most popular boy in her new class. But he's still grieving his girlfriend who died the year before. Can Nanami break through the wall that surrounds Motoharu's heart?
Find out in We Were There—manga series on sale now!
We Were There
Yuki Obata
1
viz media
www.viz.com
RATED
T+
FOR OLDER TEEN
ratings.viz.com
On sale at www.shojobeat.com
Also available at your local bookstore and comic store.
BOKURA GA ITA © Yuuki OBATA/Shogakukan Inc.
Shojo Beat

This is the last page.

In keeping with the original Japanese comic format, this book reads from right to left—so action, sound effects and word balloons are completely reversed. This preserves the orientation of the original artwork—plus, it's fun! Check out the diagram shown here to get the hang of things, and then turn to the other side of the book to get started!

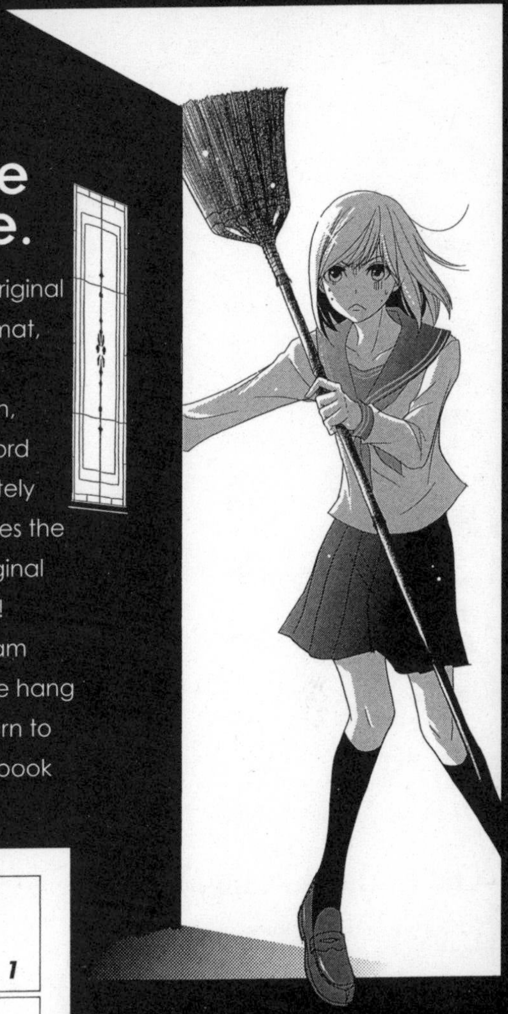

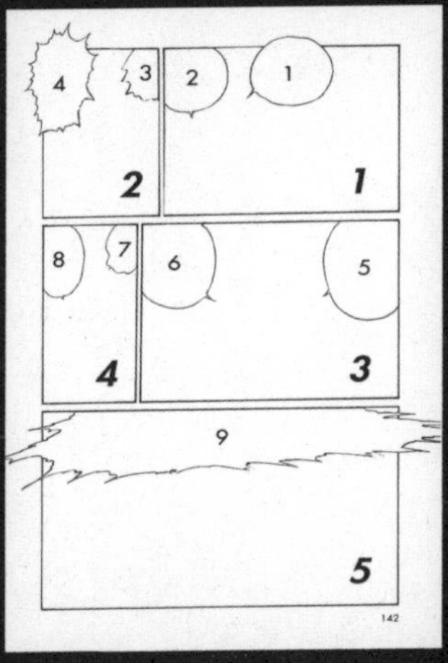
1
2
1
3
4
2
5
6
3
7
8
4
9
5
142